WITHDRAWN FROM

Educating the Young Child

Advances in Theory and Research, Implications for Practice

Volume 10

Series Editors
Mary Renck Jalongo
Indiana, PA, USA

Joan Packer Isenberg
Fairfax, VA, USA

Kin Wai Michael Siu
Hunghom Kowloon, Hong Kong SAR

This academic and scholarly book series will focus on the education and development of young children from infancy through eight years of age. The series will provide a synthesis of current theory and research on trends, issues, controversies, and challenges in the early childhood field and examine implications for practice. One hallmark of the series will be comprehensive reviews of research on a variety of topics with particular relevance for early childhood educators worldwide. The mission of the series is to enrich and enlarge early childhood educators' knowledge, enhance their professional development, and reassert the importance of early childhood education to the international community. The audience for the series includes college students, teachers of young children, college and university faculty, and professionals from fields other than education who are unified by their commitment to the care and education of young children. In many ways, the proposed series is an outgrowth of the success of *Early Childhood Education Journal* which has grown from a quarterly magazine to a respected and international professional journal that is published six times a year.

Book proposals for the series can be submitted to the Springer Publishing Editor (ms.) Yoka Janssen at Yoka.Janssen@springer.com

More information about this series at http://www.springer.com/series/7205

Kelly L. Heider • Mary Renck Jalongo
Editors

Young Children and Families in the Information Age

Applications of Technology
in Early Childhood

Editors
Kelly L. Heider
Indiana University of Pennsylvania
Indiana
Pennsylvania
USA

Mary Renck Jalongo
Indiana University of Pennsylvania
Indiana
Pennsylvania
USA

ISBN 978-94-017-9183-0   ISBN 978-94-017-9184-7 (eBook)
DOI 10.1007/978-94-017-9184-7
Springer Dordrecht Heidelberg New York London

Library of Congress Control Number: 2014954749

© Springer Science+Business Media Dordrecht 2015
This work is subject to copyright. All rights are reserved by the Publisher, whether the whole or part of the material is concerned, specifically the rights of translation, reprinting, reuse of illustrations, recitation, broadcasting, reproduction on microfilms or in any other physical way, and transmission or information storage and retrieval, electronic adaptation, computer software, or by similar or dissimilar methodology now known or hereafter developed. Exempted from this legal reservation are brief excerpts in connection with reviews or scholarly analysis or material supplied specifically for the purpose of being entered and executed on a computer system, for exclusive use by the purchaser of the work. Duplication of this publication or parts thereof is permitted only under the provisions of the Copyright Law of the Publisher's location, in its current version, and permission for use must always be obtained from Springer. Permissions for use may be obtained through RightsLink at the Copyright Clearance Center. Violations are liable to prosecution under the respective Copyright Law.
The use of general descriptive names, registered names, trademarks, service marks, etc. in this publication does not imply, even in the absence of a specific statement, that such names are exempt from the relevant protective laws and regulations and therefore free for general use.
While the advice and information in this book are believed to be true and accurate at the date of publication, neither the authors nor the editors nor the publisher can accept any legal responsibility for any errors or omissions that may be made. The publisher makes no warranty, express or implied, with respect to the material contained herein.

Printed on acid-free paper

Springer is part of Springer Science+Business Media (www.springer.com)

Foreword

Information Literacy in Early Childhood: What, Why, How, and Where to Next?

Children become adept at using advanced technology at an early age.

Abstract This introduction to the volume on young children in the information age begins by defining information literacy within the context of early childhood education. Next, it discusses the importance of information literacy for the field and its place in the curriculum. The introduction concludes with a description of new roles for early childhood professionals—teachers and teacher educators—as they strive to make pedagogy and programs more engaging for and responsive to diverse groups of young children.

Keywords Information literacy · Technology · The new literacies

While shopping at a discount store, I heard—well before I saw—a preschool child and his frazzled grandfather. As the elderly man pushed the cart, the boy continued to sob and beg, "Grandpap, get met iPad" to which the grandfather replied, "But you're not even three yet. You don't know what an iPad is or how to use it...come to think of it, neither do I." In response, the child's pleading grew even louder, "BUT GET IT. BUY IT. GET ME iPAD!"

There is little question that today's young children are immersed in new technologies in unprecedented ways and, as always, want to participate in what they see adults, older children, and peers doing with electronic devices (Berson and Berson 2010). As media expert Innis (1951) argued long ago, with each new tool that is embraced, the communication environment is irrevocably altered. From printing press to tablet computer, we change—and are changed by—the things we invent.

What Is Information Literacy?

An ERIC Digest published over two decades ago foreshadowed the direction of those changes: "Education systems and institutions must take seriously the challenges of the Information Age. This includes restructuring the learning process to reflect the use of information in the real world, changing the role of the teacher from presenter of prefabricated facts to facilitator of active learning, and including the library/media specialist as a collaborator in curriculum planning for effective use of information resources" (Hancock 1993, p. 1). Stated in more contemporary terms, education systems need to emphasize information literacy, defined by The United States National Forum on Information Literacy (2012) as "… the ability to know when there is a need for information, to be able to identify, locate, evaluate, and effectively use that information for the issue or problem at hand."

Taking a somewhat different perspective, information literacy can be conceptualized as a set of competencies that an informed citizen of an information society ought to possess in order to participate intelligently and actively in that society. This includes "skepticism, judgment, free thinking, questioning, and understanding" (Gillmor 2012, p. 1). Thus, information literacy initiatives require a fundamental shift in what Paulo Freire (2000) called the "banking model" of education in which teachers "deposit" information in the minds of learners.

When students are involved in activities to promote information literacy, we would see them:

- seeking a rich range of information sources;
- communicating an understanding of content;
- posing questions about the content being learned;
- using the environment, people, and tools for learning;
- reflecting on their own learning;
- assessing their own learning; and
- taking responsibility for their own learning (Hancock 1993).

How Has the Communication Environment Changed?

Throughout the world, many, if not most, young children today are in very different communication contexts from those of their grandparents or even their parents. In the days before popular electronic media, it was the adults who "knew" and who shared that knowledge in what they believed to be appropriate ways (Postman 1982). Today, technology has turned the tables to some extent because young children often are adept at using new technologies in ways that outstrip those of their elders. Yet thoughtful examination of these tools—both the advantages that they represent and their drawbacks—is necessary if they are to be more than the latest gadget or heavily-advertised purchase. At the very time when the American Academy of Pediatrics (2012) discourages any screen time for children under two years of age, apps are being heavily marketed to this group with promises of accelerating the learning of the very young. These actions are not without controversy.

The Campaign for Commercial-Free Childhood (2013) invoked the Federal Trade Commission to pursue allegations against the "Baby Einstein" videos, arguing that they did not make children smarter as the advertising claimed. Ultimately, the Boston-based advocacy group's efforts led to successful, nationwide consumer refunds. The Campaign for Commercial-Free Childhood is now pursuing similar charges against mobile app companies, contending that two toy companies—Open Solutions ("Baby Hear and Read", "Baby's First Puzzle") and Fisher-Price ("Laugh & Learn" mobile apps)—are attempting to dupe parents into believing that apps alone can advance their child's learning and language (Boog 2013). Susan Linn, the group's director said, "What babies need for healthy brain development is active play, hands-on creative play and face-to-face interactions." In a statement issued by Kathleen Alfano, senior director of child research for Fisher-Price, she stated that the new apps reflect the company's 80-year mission; namely "to create appropriate toys for the ways children play, discover, and grow" and that the company is now extending "these well-researched play patterns into the digital space" (Boog 2013, para. 6).

Evidently, we are entering an era in which "bells and whistles" and entertainment are insufficient; consumers are beginning to demand evidence that technology is cost effective. This important book on information literacy in early childhood calls upon all of us to confront the contradictory times in which we live for, at the very moment when teachers are being pressured to emphasize memorization of bits of information as a way to improve test performance of students, the virtual tsunami of information demands something very different. It calls for information literacy, the focus of this volume.

Why Is Information Literacy Important in Early Childhood?

Much of the writing to date on information literacy has focused on secondary and postsecondary students or adults yet, as is the case with so many fundamental concepts, it is clear that information literacy needs to begin much earlier. Perhaps the most compelling support for this statement comes from survey research documenting that young children are using technology and the popular media more often and begin this use much younger. Consider, for example, the following recent statistics:

- Contemporary children spend, on average, 7 h a day on entertainment media, including televisions, computers, phones and other electronic devices (American Academy of Pediatrics 2012).
- Children 8–18 are exposed to the media for 10 h and 45 min a day because, with the use of mobile media, they are "always connected" and usually are multitasking (Kaiser Family Foundation 2010).
- During the summer months, children's television viewing increases by 150 % (Smart Television Alliance 2009).
- Although television watching is not considered to be a suitable past time for children under the age of 2 years, 59 % of children have started watching TV by the age of 6 months (Ofcom 2008).

In response, definitions of literacy have expanded well beyond the traditional subjects of reading, writing, and arithmetic to include a constellation of information processing skills that rely upon critical thinking processes. As David Weinberger (2012) argues, the realities of networked knowledge and the need to assess the quality of information–rather than just locate it—have made this an opportune time to become a seeker of knowledge, but only if a person has learned how. Part of "knowing how," involves the "Big 6" of information literacy, a framework shaped by Michael Eisenberg. In early childhood, the "Big 6" of information literacy are: (1) task definition (finding a focus), (2) information seeking strategies (selecting suitable resources), (3) location and access (obtaining resources), (4) use of information (choosing material), (5) synthesis/sharing (presenting information to others effectively), and (6) evaluation (determining if the task was performed well). The Utah Education Network (2013) has combined the "Big 6" framework with the well-known early childhood High/Scope Curriculum's Plan/Do/Review phases.

Where to Next?

As early childhood educators, we cannot allow adult enthusiasm to overshadow important questions such as:

- What is the true cost of keeping current with these tools, not only in terms of cash outlay but also with respect to how children spend their time?

- What are the effects on children's well-being—cognitively, physically, socio-emotionally?
- Is the children's learning deeper and wider than it would be without this expensive tool? How can we make pedagogically defensible decisions about Instructional and Communication Technologies during the early years?
- How do we address the perennial issue of the "haves" and "have nots" on either side of the technology gap throughout the world? (Parette and Blum 2013; Simon and Nemeth 2012; Neuman and Celano 2012)
- What are effective ways to introduce the very young to media literacy instruction, defined as the application of principles of information literacy to popular media?

As the esteemed authors of this volume will so amply demonstrate, the capacity to adapt to the perpetually new and challenging landscapes for learning well may be the survival skill of the future. Although early childhood educators cannot afford to be uncritically accepting of innovation, technological advances, and information, they also cannot afford to ignore it and cling to ineffective pedagogies.

What sets this book apart from many others is the clear sense that the authors have truly lived these experiences in information literacy with the very young, their families, and their teachers. Tech-savvy readers will see the familiar tools used in highly effective ways while those who are less familiar with technology will explore new terrain.

Clearly, the call for information literacy in early childhood extends to teacher preparation as well. "The information Age is part of the new reality of working with students in colleges of education. Students turn to the Web as their first (and often their only) information resource—they want their information full text, online, right now" (Repman and Carson 2002, p. 22). Effective approaches to infusing technology and information literacy into teacher education rely on a socio-cultural perspective. As described by Lankshear et al. (2000) it joins together the operational, critical, and cultural dimensions as depicted in Fig. 1.

Thus, early childhood educators at all levels need not only technology skills but also information literacy skills "to inform their teaching practice and to facilitate their ongoing professional development" (Berthelsen et al. 2000, unpaged).

To that end, the *Information Literacy Competency Standards for Higher Education* identify five standards for college students:

1. The information literate student determines the nature and extent of the information needed.
2. The information literate student accesses needed information effectively and efficiently.
3. The information literate student evaluates information and its sources critically and incorporates selected information into his or her knowledge base and value system.
4. The information literate student, individually or as a member of a group, uses information effectively to accomplish a specific purpose.
5. The information literate student understands many of the economic, legal, and social issues surrounding the use of information and accesses and uses information ethically and legally (Association of College and Research Libraries 2000).

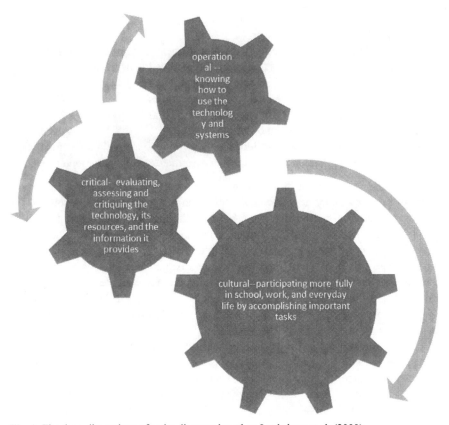

Fig. 1 The three dimensions of technoliteracy, based on Lankshear et al. (2000)

Many years ago, there was a conference with the provocative title, "If Technology Is the Answer, What Was the Question?" Part of being information literate ourselves is refusing to give over to consumerism, rejecting glib solutions, and reflecting deeply on the consequences of our decisions for young children.

Mary Renck Jalongo

References

Association of College and Research Libraries. (2000). *Information literacy competency standards for higher education.* Retrieved from http://www.ala.org/acrl/sites/ala.org.acrl/files/content/standards/standards.pdf.

American Academy of Pediatrics. (2012). *Media and children* (21 May). http://www.aap.org/en-us/search/pages/results.aspx?k=children%20and%20television.

Berson, I. R., & Berson, M. J. (Eds.). (2010). *High-tech tots: Childhood in a digital world.* Charlotte, NC: Information Age Publishing.

Berthelsen, D., Halliwell, G., Peacock, J., Burke, J., & Ryan, I. (2000). *Information literacy—Implications for early childhood teaching.* http://publications.aare.edu.au/00pap/ber00006.htm.

Boog, J. (2013). Campaign for a Commercial-Free Childhood files FTC complaint over baby apps (8 August). http://www.mediabistro.com/appnewser/campaign-for-a-commercial-free-childhood-files-ftc-complaint-over-baby-apps_b39447.

Campaign for Commercial-Free Childhood. (2013). http://www.commercialfreechildhood.org/.

Gillmor, D. (2012). 2.0 Chapter 2: Becoming an active user: Principles. [*Mediactive Website*]. http://mediactive.com/2-0-chapter-2-becoming-an-active-user-principles.

Freire, P. (2000). *Pedagogy of the oppressed* (30th anniversary edition). New York, NY: Bloomsbury Academic.

Hancock, V. E. (1993). Information literacy for lifelong learning. [*ERIC Digest*]. http://ericae.net/edo/ED358870.htm.

Innis, H. (1951). *The bias of communication*. Toronto, Canada: University of Toronto Press.

Kaiser Family Foundation. (2010). *Daily media use among children and teens up dramatically from five years ago: Big increase in mobile media helps drive increased consumption*. http://www.kff.org/entmedia/entmedia012010nr.cfm.

Lankshear, C., Snyder, I., & Green, G. (2000). *Teachers and technoliteracy: Managing literacy, technology and learning in schools*. Sydney, Australia: Allen & Unwin.

National Forum on Information Literacy. (2012). *What is the NFIL?* http://infolit.org/about-the-nfil/what-is-the-nfil/. Accessed 25 Oct 2012.

Neuman, S. B., & Celano, D. C. (2012). *Giving our children a fighting chance: Poverty, literacy, and the development of information capital*. New York: Teachers College Press.

Ofcom. (2008). *Media literacy audit: Report on UK children's media literacy*. www.ofcom.org.uk.

Parette, H., & Blum, C. (2013). *Instructional technology in early childhood: Teaching in the digital age*. Baltimore, MD: Paul H. Brookes.

Postman, N. (1982). *The disappearance of childhood*. New York, NY: Dell.

Repman, J., & Carson, R. (2002). Building blocks for information literacy. *Education Libraries, 25*(2), 22–25. http://rci.rutgers.edu/~estec/webpagesample/TSG.pdf.

Simon, F., & Nemeth, K. (2012). *Digital decisions: Choosing the right technology tools for early childhood education*. Lewisville, NC: Gryphon House.

Smart Television Alliance. (2009). *TV gone wrong*. www.smarttelevisionalliance.org.

Utah Education Network. (2013). *Format #2—The Big 6 Information Literacy*. http://www.uen.org/k-2educator/integrated/big6.shtml.

Weinberger, D. (2012). *Too big to know: Rethinking knowledge now that the facts aren't the facts, experts are everywhere, and the smartest person in the room is the room*. New York, NY: Basic Books.

Photo Credit: Huachuan Wen

Acknowledgements

The editors would like to thank family members, friends, and Chi-Chen Jennifer Tsai for their assistance in obtaining the children's photographs that appear in this book.

Contents

Foreword
Information Literacy in Early Childhood: What, Why, How, and Where to Next? v
Mary Renck Jalongo

Part I Tools and Strategies

1 **Virtual Worlds: Young Children Using the Internet** 3
   Ithel Jones and Young Park

2 **Supporting Young Children's Visual Literacy through the Use of E-books**.. 15
   Natalie Conrad Barnyak and Tracy A. McNelly

3 **Technology-based Literacies for Young Children: Digital Literacy through Learning to Code** 43
   Elizabeth R. Kazakoff

4 **Teaching with Technology and Interactive Media to Promote Creativity and Arts-based Learning in Young Children** 61
   DeAnna M. Laverick

5 **Opening Young Minds and Hearts: Employing Technology-infused Critical Pedagogy in Hybrid Border Spaces** 77
   Crystal Machado

6 **Using Multimedia Technologies to Support Culturally and Linguistically Diverse Learners and Young Children with Disabilities**... 101
   Kavita Rao and James Skouge

Part I (continued)

7 Using Mobile Media Devices and Apps to Promote Young Children's Learning 117
Sharon Judge, Kimberly Floyd and Tara Jeffs

8 Planning, Designing, and Implementing Effective Interactive Portfolios in the Primary Grades: Suggestions for Forming Partnerships among Teachers, Students, and Parents 133
Esther Ntuli and Lydia Kyei-Blankson

Part II Issues and Trends

9 Young Children as Multimodal Learners in the Information Age 151
Nicola Yelland

10 Universal Design for Learning and Technology in the Early Childhood Classroom 165
Craig Blum and Howard P. Parette

11 Developmentally-appropriate Technology and Interactive Media in Early Childhood Education 183
Olivia N. Saracho

12 Could Computer Games-based Problem Solving Positively Affect the Development of Creativity in Young Children? A Mixed Method Case Study 207
Georgios Fessakis, Dimitrios Lappas and Elisavet Mavroudi

13 The Impact of Popular Media on Infant/Toddler Language Development: Research-based Recommendations for Working with Families 227
Melissa Calderon

14 Participatory Youth Culture: Young Children as Media and MOC Makers in a Post-millennial Mode 245
Marissa McClure and Robert W. Sweeny

15 Young Children at Risk of Digital Disadvantage 255
Genevieve Marie Johnson

16 Cybersafety in Early Childhood: What Parents and Educators Need to Know 277
Kelly L. Heider

Contributors

Natalie Conrad Barnyak University of Pittsburgh at Johnstown, Johnstown, PA, USA

Craig Blum Illinois State University, Normal, USA

Melissa Calderon Community College of Allegheny County, Pittsburgh, PA, USA

Georgios Fessakis Learning Technology and Education Engineering Lab, School of Humanities, University of the Aegean, Rhodes, Greece

Kimberly Floyd West Virginia University, Morgantown, USA

Kelly L. Heider Indiana University of Pennsylvania, Indiana, USA

Mary Renck Jalongo Indiana University of Pennsylvania, Indiana, USA

Tara Jeffs Loundon County Public Schools, Ashburn, USA

Genevieve Marie Johnson Curtin University, Perth, Australia

Ithel Jones Florida State University, Tallahassee, USA

Sharon Judge Old Dominion University, Norfolk, USA

Elizabeth R. Kazakoff Tufts University, Medford, MA, USA

Lydia Kyei-Blankson Illinois State University, Normal, USA

Dimitrios Lappas Learning Technology and Education Engineering Lab, School of Humanities, University of the Aegean, Rhodes, Greece

DeAnna M. Laverick Indiana University of Pennsylvania, Indiana, PA, USA

Crystal Machado Indiana University of Pennsylvania, Indiana, USA

Elisavet Mavroudi Learning Technology and Education Engineering Lab, School of Humanities, University of the Aegean, Rhodes, Greece

Marissa McClure The Pennsylvania State University, University Park, USA

Tracy A. McNelly Norwin School District, North Huntingdon, PA, USA

Esther Ntuli Idaho State University, Pocatello, USA

Howard P. Parette Illinois State University, Normal, USA

Young Park Pusan National University, Pusan, South Korea

Kavita Rao University of Hawai'i at Mānoa, Honolulu, USA

Olivia N. Saracho University of Maryland, College Park, USA

James Skouge University of Hawai'i at Mānoa, Honolulu, USA

Robert W. Sweeny Indiana University of Pennsylvania, Indiana, USA

Nicola Yelland Victoria University, Melbourne, Australia

About the Editors

Kelly L. Heider D.Ed. is a professor at Indiana University of Pennsylvania (IUP) where she serves as an embedded librarian in the College of Education and Educational Technology. In 2012, she received the Lloyd W. Briscoe Award for outstanding service to students in IUP's Department of Professional Studies in Education. Before joining the faculty at IUP, Kelly was a public school teacher for the Burrell School District where she taught middle and high school English, worked as a library media specialist, and served as chair of the library department. Her research interests include embedded librarianship, information literacy, the integration of technology and curricula, and service-learning programs. She currently coordinates a service-learning program for students enrolled in IUP's Early Childhood—Special Education Program. Kelly has published several journal articles in Springer's *Early Childhood Education Journal* and has presented at numerous international conferences sponsored by organizations such as the Association for Childhood Education International and the Society for Information Technology and Teacher Education.

Stabley Library, Indiana University of Pennsylvania Libraries, Indiana, PA, USA

Mary Renck Jalongo Ph.D. is a professor at Indiana University of Pennsylvania where she earned the university-wide outstanding professor award and coordinates the Doctoral Program in Curriculum and Instruction. As a classroom teacher, she worked with children of migrant farm workers in a federally funded bilingual preschool program. She has written, co-authored, or edited more than 25 books, including *Early Childhood Language Arts*, 6th edition, *Creative Thinking and Arts-Based Learning*, 6th edition, *Exploring Your Role: An Introduction to Early Childhood Education*, 3rd edition, and *Major Trends and Issues in Early Childhood Education: Challenges, Controversies, and Insights*, 2nd edition. In addition, she has written two books for NAEYC (*Learning to Listen, Listening to Learn and Young Children and Picture Books*, 2nd edition) and two for ACEI. Her writing has earned seven national awards for excellence that include two EDPRESS awards for Position Papers published by the Association for Childhood Education International. Since 1995, she has served as editor-in-chief of the Springer international publication, *Early Childhood Education Journal* and, since 2006, as series editor for Springer's edited book series, *Educating the Young Child: Advances in Theory and Research, Implications for Practice*. She has made presentations throughout the world on various aspects of early childhood education.

Department of Professional Studies in Education, Indiana University of Pennsylvania, Indiana, PA, USA

About the Contributors

Natalie Conrad Barnyak D.Ed. is an Associate Professor in the Division of Education at the University of Pittsburgh at Johnstown. She taught preschool, kindergarten, and elementary grades before completing her doctorate at Indiana University of Pennsylvania. Her research and writing focuses on literacy, early childhood, and parent/family engagement.

University of Pittsburgh at Johnstown, Johnstown, PA, USA

Craig Blum Ph.D. is an associate professor of Special Education, Illinois State University. He has co-authored two books, publishes in peer-reviewed journals, and presents nationally on technology integration and early childhood settings. His work focuses on practical technology integration models for early childhood educators, readily-available technology, response to intervention, and positive behavior support.

Special Education Department, Illinois State University, Normal, IL, USA

Melissa Calderon is an adjunct faculty member at the Community College of Allegheny County located in Pittsburgh, Pennsylvania. She currently teaches undergraduate students in the Early Education and Child Development Department. Melissa is interested in the developmental outcomes of young children while exposed to media technology. The research she conducts has the potential to inform early educators and families about the appropriate use of media with young children.

Department of Early Education and Child Development, Community College of Allegheny County, West Mifflin, PA, USA

Georgios Fessakis Ph.D. holds a B.Sc. in Informatics, a M.Sc. in Advanced Informatics Systems from National and Kapodistrian University of Athens, and a Ph.D. in Informatics Didactics form the University of the Aegean. He had been teaching undergraduate and postgraduate ICT-related courses since 2004 at the University of the Aegean where he currently serves as an assistant professor. His main research interests include ICT design and development for learning, ICT and Mathematics Didactics, and Computer Supported Collaborative Learning (CSCL).

Learning Technologies and Educational Engineering (LTEE) Lab, University of the Aegean, Rhodes, Greece

Kim K. Floyd Ph.D. is an Assistant Professor in the Department of Special Education. She also serves as Coordinator for the Collaborative Assistive Technology Education Lab housed in the College of Education and Human Services. Her research interests include the infusion of assistive technology devices into natural and inclusive settings, inclusion of technology in teacher preparation programs, and postsecondary technology accommodations for students with learning disabilities.

Department of Special Education, West Virginia University, Morgantown, WV, USA

Tara Jeffs Ph.D. is an assistive technology specialist for Loudoun County Public Schools, Loudoun County, VA. Her primary research areas include implementing assistive and emerging technologies in general and special education classrooms and facilitating universal design for learning. She is particularly interested in exploring, learning, and integrating both common and cutting-edge assistive technologies in the home, school, community, and workplace.

Loundon County Public Schools, Loundon County, VA, USA

Genevieve Marie Johnson Ph.D. received a doctoral degree from the University of Alberta (Canada) in 1990 and a Graduate Diploma in Distance Education Technology from Athabasca University (Canada) in 2007. Having been actively involved in university teaching for more than 20 years, she is currently a senior lecturer in the School of Education at Curtin University in Western Australia. Dr. Johnson has conducted many studies and published and presented widely on the impact of technology on child learning and development (a complete list of publications is available at http://www.members.shaw.ca/gen.johnson/).

School of Education, Curtin University, Perth, Australia

Ithel Jones Ed.D. is a Professor in the School of Teacher Education at the Florida State University. He teaches graduate and undergraduate courses in Early Childhood Education. He conducts research in the areas of science and technology in early childhood, service learning, and early childhood teacher education.

School of Teacher Education, Florida State University, Tallahassee, FL, USA

Sharon Judge Ph.D. is a Professor in the Department of Communication Disorders and Special Education. She has published numerous articles, chapters, and a book in the areas of assistive technology, professional development, and children with special needs. She has been a partner in many district-university collaborations and evaluations as well as community-based efforts to provide effective services to children with disabilities and their families.

Department of Communication Disorders and Special Education, Old Dominion University, Norfolk, VA, USA

Elizabeth R. Kazakoff is a doctoral candidate in the Developmental Technologies (DevTech) Research Group at the Eliot-Pearson Department of Child Development at Tufts University. She has published papers and presented at national and international conferences on topics related to young children and new technologies. Her dissertation research focuses on the interaction between self-regulation and learning to code in early childhood.

Eliot-Pearson Department of Child Development, Tufts University, Medford, MA, USA

Lydia Kyei-Blankson Ph.D. is an Associate Professor in the Educational Administration and Foundations Department at Illinois State University. Her expertise and training is in research methods, applied statistics, and psychometrics. Her assignment at ISU includes teaching research methods and statistics graduate courses in the College of Education. Dr. Kyei-Blankson's research agenda focuses on the scholarship of teaching and learning and the implications of effective technology integration in teaching and learning.

Department of Educational Administration and Foundations, Illinois State University, Normal, IL, USA

Dimitrios Lappas graduated from the Hellenic Military Academy, Evelpidon, in 2005. He also has a Bachelor's Degree from the Preschool Education and Educational Design Department of the University of the Aegean. He is currently a postgraduate student in Models of Designing and Planning Educational Units, a Master's and Ph.D. Degree program at the University of the Aegean. He is a scientific associate of the Learning Technology and Educational Engineering Laboratory at the University of the Aegean. His research interests concern the area of fostering and developing creativity competences using ICT.

Learning Technologies and Educational Engineering (LTEE) Lab, University of the Aegean, Rhodes, Greece

DeAnna M. Laverick D.Ed. is an associate professor in the Department of Professional Studies in Education at Indiana University of Pennsylvania (IUP). Prior to teaching at the university level, Dr. Laverick was an elementary school teacher and reading specialist. She taught kindergarten for the majority of her career as an early childhood educator. At IUP, Dr. Laverick teaches undergraduate and graduate courses related to literacy and creative experiences and play. Dr. Laverick has made numerous conference presentations related to technology and literacy and has published articles and book chapters on these topics.

Department of Professional Studies in Education, Indiana University of Pennsylvania, Indiana, PA, USA

Crystal Machado Ed.D. is an Assistant Professor in the Professional Studies in Education Department at Indiana University of Pennsylvania where she teaches education courses at the doctoral, master's, and undergraduate levels. Prior to her work in the U.S., Crystal worked as a K-12 teacher and administrator for

6 years in Pakistan. She also provided training to pre-service and in-service teachers through the Notre Dame Institute of Education, affiliated with Australian Catholic University. Her research interests include multicultural and global education, critical thinking and reflective practice, innovative web-based technology, and school reform and renewal; she has presented on these topics at international, national, and regional conferences.

Department of Professional Studies in Education, Indiana University of Pennsylvania, Indiana, PA, USA

Elisavet Mavroudi holds a B.Sc. in Informatics from the Department of Informatics and Telecommunications, N.K.U. of Athens and a degree in Pedagogical Training from the Pedagogical Technical School (PATES) of the Technical and Vocational Teacher Training Institute (SELETE) in Salonica. She has been working as a secondary school teacher of informatics since 1997. She also participates, as a researcher, in research projects and studies conducted by the Learning Technology and Educational Engineering Laboratory, University of the Aegean. Her research interests primarily lie in the areas of didactics of informatics and ICT applications in education.

Learning Technologies and Educational Engineering (LTEE) Lab, University of the Aegean, Rhodes, Greece

Marissa McClure Ph.D. is visiting assistant professor of art education at Pennsylvania State University. Marissa is interested in contemporary theories of child art, children and visual and media culture, community-based art education, Feminist theory, and curriculum inquiry and design. Her articles have appeared in *Studies in Art Education*, the *Journal of Social Theory in Art Education*, *Visual Arts Research*, and *Visual Culture and Gender*. Marissa is associate editor of the *International Journal of Education and the Arts* and a member of several editorial review boards. Marissa was president of the Early Childhood Art Educators from 2010–2012. NAEA Press will publish her co-authored book *Curriculum Inquiry and Design for Schools and Community* in 2014.

School of Visual Art, Pennsylvania State University, University Park, PA, USA

Tracy A. McNelly D.Ed. is the Assistant Superintendent of the Norwin School District and an adjunct professor in the Department of Education at St. Vincent College. She has also held positions as Director of Secondary Education, Director of Pupil Personnel and Special Services, Junior/Senior High School Principal, High School Assistant Principal, English/Journalism teacher, and Reading Specialist.

Norwin School District, North Huntingdon, PA, USA

Esther Ntuli Ed.D. is an Assistant Professor in the Department of Educational Foundations at Idaho State University (ISU). Her expertise is in curriculum and instruction, early childhood education, instructional technology, and children's literature and writing. Dr. Ntuli teaches undergraduate instructional technology courses and blended early childhood undergraduate and graduate courses at ISU.

Her research interests focus on technology use and practice in early childhood instruction, teacher education, and assessment.

Department of Educational Foundations, Idaho State University, Pocatello, ID, USA

Young-Hee Park Ph.D. completed her Ph.D. at Florida State University. She is currently a researcher at Pusan National University in Korea. Her scholarly work focuses on parenting influences on children's early learning and development.

Department of Education, Busan, Korea

Howard P. Parette Ed.D. is a professor in the Department of Special Education, Illinois State University and former Kara Peters Endowed Chair in Assistive Technology and Director of the Special Education Assistive Technology (SEAT) Center. He has published extensively on assistive technology service delivery issues for more than two decades, and his research interests in recent years have focused on readily-available technology integration in early childhood education settings.

Special Education Department, Illinois State University, Normal, IL, USA

Kavita Rao Ph.D. is an assistant professor in the Department of Special Education of the College of Education at the University of Hawai'i at Mānoa. Her research focuses on technology for students with disabilities, universal design for learning, and technology-based instructional strategies for culturally and linguistically diverse learners. Kavita has worked with teachers in Hawaii, Guam, American Samoa, Commonwealth of the Marianas Islands, Palau, Republic of the Marshall Islands, and the Federated States of Micronesia developing curriculum resources, multimedia materials, and online programs for Pacific educators.

Department of Special Education, University of Hawai'i at Mānoa, Honolulu, HI, USA

Olivia N. Saracho Ph.D. is professor of education in the Department of Teaching, Learning, Policy and Leadership at the University of Maryland. Her areas of scholarship include family literacy, cognitive style, play, and teaching and teacher education in early childhood education. She has published widely in the field of early childhood education. Olivia is coeditor, with Bernard Spodek, of the *Handbook of Research on the Education of Young Children*, 3/ed. (2012, Taylor & Francis). They also co-edited *Contemporary Perspectives in Science and Technology* (2008), a volume that is part of the series on *Contemporary Perspectives in Early Childhood Education* (Information Age).

Department of Teaching and Learning, Policy and Leadership, University of Maryland, College Park, MD, USA

James Skouge Ed.D. is an associate professor in the Department of Special Education of the College of Education at the University of Hawai'i at Mānoa. He specializes in assistive technology, media, and distance education. He has worked throughout the Hawaiian islands, American Samoa, and Micronesia supporting persons with disabilities and their families in exploring assistive technologies for independence. He focuses on use of media for "voice and inclusion," especially in relation to indigenous peoples of the Pacific.

Department of Special Education, University of Hawai'i at Mānoa, Honolulu, HI, USA

Robert W. Sweeny Ph.D. Professor of Art and Art Education at Indiana University of Pennsylvania (USA), is the author of *Dysfunction and Decentralization in New Media Art Education* (forthcoming), published by Intellect Press. He is the editor of *Inter/Actions/ Inter/Sections: Art Education in a Digital Visual Culture* (2011), published by NAEA Press as well as the editor of *The Journal of the National Art Education Association*. Bob publishes and presents widely on the topic of digital visual culture, including the relationship between art educational practices and complexity theory, videogames, social and locative media, and surveillance technologies.

Department of Art, Indiana University of Pennsylvania, Indiana, PA, USA

Nicola J. Yelland Ph.D. is a Research Professor in the School of Education at Victoria University in Melbourne Australia. Over the last decade, her teaching and research has been related to the use of new technologies in school and community contexts. This has involved projects that have investigated the innovative learning of children as well as a broader consideration of the ways in which new technologies can impact on the pedagogies that teachers use and the curriculum in schools. Her multidisciplinary research focus has enabled her to work with early childhood, primary, and middle school teachers to enhance the ways in which new technologies can be incorporated into learning contexts to make them more interesting and motivating for students so that educational outcomes are improved. Professor Yelland is the founding editor of two journals *Contemporary Issues in Early Childhood* and *Global Studies of Childhood*.

College of Education, Victoria University, Footscray, Victoria, Australia

Part I
Tools and Strategies

Chapter 1
Virtual Worlds: Young Children Using the Internet

Ithel Jones and Young Park

Abstract There has been a dramatic increase in the number of young children using digital media. Children are regularly using the internet to play, communicate, and explore. Educators and researchers are beginning to examine the social and cognitive implications of children's use of interactive media and the internet. Socio-cultural and ecological systems theories offer a perspective that can support our understanding of internet use and young children's cognitive development. This chapter examines three popular internet applications: virtual worlds, virtual field trips, and tele-collaborative projects. Drawing on the ecological systems and socio-cultural theories, implications for children's development are considered.

Keywords Cognitive development · Digital media · Early childhood · Internet · Socio-cultural theories · Technology · Tele-collaboration · Virtual worlds · Virtual field trip

An Online World

Megan is a bright 8-year-old girl from a middle-class family. She lives in a media-rich house with her parents and younger brother. She is an avid reader, and she loves writing stories. She also loves her pet cat, as well as her collection of soft toys and dolls. One of her favorite activities is playing on the computer in her parents' home office. Her daily engagement with technology usually includes going on the internet to visit sites such as Webkins, Club Penguin, and Nickelodeon's Petpet Park.

From the moment Megan was born, images of her have been posted online. Her digital life began when her proud parents uploaded prenatal sonogram scans to the internet followed by regular photos and other information. As Megan's digital profile, or footprint, increased, so did her experiences with interactive technologies. As an

I. Jones (✉)
Florida State University, Tallahassee, USA
e-mail: ijones@admin.fsu.edu

Y. Park
Pusan National University, Pusan, South Korea

active 2-year-old, Megan often begged her mother to take her to the playground. But, instead of heading to the local community park, her mother would settle with Megan in a cozy chair and visit the virtual world of Elmo's Playground on their iPad. Scrolling through family photos on her mother's handheld device would often relieve Megan from the boredom of long car journeys. Then, after a long and busy day, the favorite part of her bedtime routine was to share and talk about a picture book on an e-reader.

As a preschooler, Megan enjoyed the challenges of the interactive programs at the computer station. During center time, she and her friend would chat and giggle as they worked together using the SMART Table drawing application. Then, by the time she was in kindergarten, Megan was a frequent visitor to the virtual world of Club Penguin. Having shaped her online presence through the creation and modification of an avatar, Megan played games, communicated, and interacted with other online faces. In this virtual world, she could dress up, purchase virtual goods, and even care for a virtual pet.

Changing Childhood

Children like Megan have more access to all kinds of electronic media and online activities than ever before. Changes in media use, and widespread internet use, have drastically altered childhood experiences. For young children, electronic media are part of the landscape and contexts of their lives. The ubiquity of the internet and new online technologies, in particular, permeates all aspects of children's lives. The internet encompasses a diverse, interactive space that blurs the boundaries between the real and imaginary, or virtual world, in ways that we never could have envisioned. One of the most compelling aspects of the internet, however, is its interactivity. Using the internet, children can practice their skills, test their knowledge, or contribute their work using one of the many interactive sites available on the Web.

This chapter examines the ways young children can use the internet to support their learning and enhance their problem-solving skills. First, we explore the nature and extent of young children's use of digital media in the U.S. Next, we discuss children's online access and internet use. In doing so, we consider the social impact of the internet as well as critical dimensions of media technology and the internet that influence young children's learning. Specifically, we examine how using the internet can enrich children's experiences and consider theoretical perspectives concerning how the internet might influence children's cognitive development. Then, finally, we examine three popular online applications including virtual worlds, virtual field trips, and tele-collaborative projects.

Young Children Using the Internet

According to recent research findings, young children are spending more time using digital media than ever before (Common Sense Media 2011; Gutnick et al. 2011). The various digital media used by children include computers, handheld and console video game players, cell phones, iPods, and iPad-style tablet devices. In a recent study, the Common Sense Media group (2011) reported that more than half of all children have home access to mobile devices such as smartphones, video iPods, or tablet devices such as an iPad. In addition, more than two-thirds of families with young children have computers, typically with an internet connection (Gutnick et al. 2011). While children's exposure to digital media has significantly increased, so have the capabilities of the various electronic devices. Thus, activities are not restricted to any one type of media. Television, for example, can be streamed via the internet on a desktop computer, iPad, or a smartphone. How and when young children use various digital media, however, is largely determined by their parents or caregivers.

It seems that most parents support and encourage children's use of digital devices. In the United Kingdom, for example, households with young children are more likely to be connected to the internet (Ofcom 2007), and ever-younger children are regularly going online. It was recently reported that almost a third (29%) of all parents in the United States have downloaded "apps" to their mobile devices for their children to use. Thus, increasing numbers of children are using such apps on mobile devices, including 10% of 0–1-year-olds, 39% of 2–4-year-olds, and 53% of 5–8-year-olds (Common Sense Media Group 2011).

Such use of mobile digital devices is matched by extensive use of computers by children under 8 years of age. More than half of 2–4-year-old children have used a computer and 90% of 5–8-year-olds (Common Sense Media 2011). It is further reported that young children are regularly using computers, most on a weekly basis and many on a daily basis. A recent trend in computer use is the popularity of portable devices. Since 2005, for example, ownership of desktop computers in the United States has declined by 18%, while ownership of laptops has increased to 60% of families (Gutnick et al. 2011). It seems, therefore, that families and children like to use portable electronic media.

Given that children's access to an ever-increasing inventory of electronic devices has increased significantly, it is hardly surprising that they are spending more and more time with media. Indeed, use of all types of media has increased in the last decade and, by the time children are 8 years old, they are spending more than 5 hours a day using media (Gutnick et al. 2011). While television continues to dominate children's media use (Common Sense Media 2011), young children also regularly consume other media, particularly as they mature. Contemporary children from affluent families living in economically-developed countries seem to have an increasing appetite for smartphones, tablet devices, and video consoles, and most are using these technologies to access the internet. Moreover, those children who do go online are doing so several times a week, with usage increasing with age (Gutnick et al. 2011). In short, the internet is rapidly becoming embedded in children's everyday lives.

From 2000 to 2002, internet use among American 6–8-year-old children doubled. In 2003, it was reported that 91% of children from 3 years old to 12th grade use computers, and 59% use the internet (De Bell and Chapman 2006). Approximately 23% of children in nursery school use the internet and 50% by third grade (De Bell and Chapman 2006). Such widespread internet use by young children raises many questions concerning access, as well as the nature and quality of use. In addition, practitioners and parents have voiced concern about the appropriateness of technology use by young children. According to Simon and Memeth (2012), these include concerns that:

- children spend too much time with technology and that it will dominate their activities
- infants and toddlers are being forced to use technology
- children will be exposed to inappropriate content and inappropriate marketing

Similarly, early childhood educators fear that using technology will lead to negative effects on children's imagination and creativity and their socio-emotional development (Cordes and Miller 1999). In addition, there is some concern that children are less active when they use digital media and that this could contribute to childhood obesity and other health problems (Strasburger et al. 2011).

Despite these concerns, young children are going online; and they are doing so at younger and younger ages. Professional organizations such as the National Association for the Education of Young Children (NAEYC), however, recognize that "technology and interactive media are here to stay" (NAEYC 2012, p. 2). In their most recent position statement concerning the use of digital media in early childhood programs, the NAEYC paved the way for early childhood educators to embrace digital media, albeit with some degree of caution. Although they voiced concern about conflicting evidence on the value of technology in children's development, they adopted the position that "technology and interactive media are tools that can promote effective learning and development when they are used intentionally by early childhood educators" (NAEYC 2012, p. 5). What, then, are the benefits of the internet and digital media for young children? In the following paragraphs we discuss the internet and analyze components that may be pertinent to children's learning and development.

Essentially, the internet is a system of interconnected computer networks. The internet encompasses communication from one-to-many, one-to-one, and many-to-many. Since its widespread use beginning in the 1990s, the internet had a significant cultural impact including increases in communication using email and interactive video calls, the world wide web with forums and blogs, as well as social networking and online commerce. In fact, there is hardly any aspect of the lives of individuals living in developed countries that has not been transformed by the power of the internet including entertainment (e.g., video and audio), education (e.g., online courses), electronic business, telecommuting, crowd sourcing, politics, and philanthropy.

In considering internet use by young children, perhaps what is more important is, not so much the range of computer connections, but its social and cognitive affordances. That is, the social and cognitive actions that are made possible and enhanced through the use of computer technologies. These affordances include communication, connectivity, access to information and, most importantly perhaps, interactivity. Simply put, the internet can be viewed as a cognitive tool. The internet allows information to be instantly available to everyone. At the same time, it allows for input and response from the user. It is this interactive aspect that potentially leads to social and cognitive outcomes for young children. Indeed, there is increasing evidence that use of the internet is associated with positive social and cognitive benefits for children (Greenfield and Yan 2006; Johnson 2006; Young 2007).

There is a small, yet growing, body of research concerning the social and cognitive effects of internet use with young children. In a study of children in a Head Start program, Fish et al. (2008) found that children who had home computer access scored significantly higher on a standardized cognitive development test. Similarly, Jackson et al. (2006) reported that children who had used the internet had higher scores on reading tests and higher grades in comparison to students who had limited internet access. There is also some evidence that internet use during the preschool years may be associated with school readiness (Li and Atkins 2004).

In other studies, researchers reported that internet use could lead to positive outcomes in the area of literacy development (Hisrich and Blanchard 2009; Jackson et al. 2006). This is because much of the internet is text based and, in using the internet, children are exposed to a print-rich environment. Moreover, when using the internet, children are engaging with information in a variety of ways (Burnett and Wilkinson 2005). The digital texts of the internet are considered distinct from traditional print texts (Leu et al. 2004; Snyder 2002), thereby requiring different skills. It is hardly surprising, therefore, that there is increasing emphasis in the literature on multimodal texts and exploration of children's reading of digital texts (Primary National Strategy 2004).

The limited research concerning the cognitive and social effects of internet use on young children is matched by an emerging focus on a theoretical description of internet use and cognitive development. As a new field of inquiry, developing a theoretical framework is important in order to understand how "children and adolescents live in a new, massive, and complex virtual universe, even as they carry on their lives in the real world" (Greenfield and Yan 2006, p. 391).

Toward a Theory of Internet Use and Cognitive Development

Young children and the internet is a relatively new field of inquiry in developmental psychology (Greenfield and Yan 2006). It is also an area of study that is of considerable interest to educators as well as policy makers. Much has been written about the internet's potential to shape children's learning at home as well as in school (Livingstone 2009). While many experts claim that digital media and using the internet can have a positive effect on children's cognitive development (Johnson 2012; Kirkorian and Anderson 2009), research in this area is sparse. There is, therefore, a need to develop theoretical models or frameworks to guide our understanding of the potential effects of the internet on children's learning and their cognitive development. Given the complex nature of the internet, developing theoretical models is particularly challenging.

Typically, in examining children's cognitive development, researchers consider the influence of social contexts, activities, or concrete artifacts. The internet, however, is a complex virtual universe with immense capabilities. Yan (2006) noted that the internet is essentially a hybrid of artifacts and social and mental systems.

In other words, the internet includes objects, such as tablets and screens, opportunities to communicate with others, and a complex virtual world (Yan 2006). Yet, for the most part, the internet lacks concrete artifacts, and while the social interactions can be real-time and face-to-face, it is often in a virtual space. At the same time, the internet is an interactive space that requires input and response from the user. For the purposes of considering a theoretical model, it is useful to consider the internet as a cultural tool that children use in their daily lives.

Contemporary theories of child development assume that individual attributes of the child, biological factors, and environmental experiences, individually and collectively, shape children's cognitive growth. Bronfenbrenner's (1979) ecological systems succeeds in capturing environmental influences on cognitive development by situating children at the center of multiple levels of the environment, labeled as systems theory (e.g., microsystem, mesosystem). These systems are organized as five nested layers, each influencing the other, thereby producing direct and indirect influences on development. Bronfenbrenner (1979) primarily focuses on the social contexts in which children live and the people who influence their development. Viewed this way, development occurs in increasingly-complex reciprocal interactions between the individual and the environment. Understanding cognitive development, therefore, requires considering all factors (e.g., environmental, family, political, social, etc.) and how they interact. Recently, researchers (Johnson and Puplampu 2008; Johnson 2010) proposed that children's internet use is a component of Bronfenbrenner's microsystem, or the child's immediate environment. Described as the "ecological techno sub-system" (Johnson 2010, p. 178), it includes interaction with "non living elements of communication, information, and recreation technologies" (Johnson 2010, p. 178). This view seems to be consistent with Bronfenbrenner's (1979) position that the child is not a passive recipient of experiences in the various settings, or contexts, but someone who reciprocally interacts with others and helps to construct the settings. Clearly, this type of interaction occurs when young children use the internet for various tasks.

While embedding children's internet use within the microsystem is appealing, it fails to capture the role of culture and community in learning. Vygotsky's (1978) sociocultural perspective on cognitive development is based on the simple, yet powerful, idea that development is a product of culture. His theory presents the radical idea that thought and intelligence are the product of history and culture. Culture creates mental tools that transform cognitive processes. Then, the internalizing of these processes leads to the development of higher-order psychological processes. In other words, the internalized processes shape our thinking. According to Vygotsky, acquisition of mental tools occurs through meaningful participation in authentic, social activities, and the Zone of Proximal Development (ZPD) describes how we learn from others as we participate in social activity. "Human learning presupposes a specific social nature and a process by which children grow into the intellectual life of those around them" (Vygotsky 1978, p. 88).

The internet can be considered a particularly powerful and sophisticated cultural tool that can influence cognitive development. Yet, arguably, using the internet takes children away from the social activity that plays such a pivotal role in Vygotsky's sociocultural theory. Since interactivity is a hallmark of the internet, a reasonable assumption is that it can succeed in creating and maintaining social activity in a unique way.

In the following section, we consider the application of Bronfenbrenner's (1979) ecological systems theory and Vygotsky's (1978) sociocultural theory in the context of three increasingly-popular internet activities: virtual worlds, virtual field trips, and tele-collaborative projects.

Virtual Worlds

The popularity of virtual world web sites such as *Club Penguin* (http://www.clubpenguin.com), *Webkins* (http://www.webkins.com), *Whyville* (http://www.whyville.net), and *SqwishLand* (http://www.sqwishland.com) is staggering, to say the least. It is reported that *Club Penguin,* a game-themed world for children from 6 to 14 years old, has more than 150 million registered members. One of the newer virtual worlds, called *SqwishLand,* was launched in 2010, and it had 9000 registered users in just 10 days. As one of the more popular virtual spaces, the world of *Webkins* receives upward of 40 million logins every month.

Virtual worlds are three-dimensional environments that allow children to engage in various activities such as playing games, communicating with others, dressing up, or purchasing virtual goods. Players assume the persona of an avatar by shaping its appearance, such as hair and skin color, furnishing their online home, and caring for virtual pets. Users can easily navigate their avatar through various spaces (e.g., rooms, islands, neighborhoods) using text or following signs and icons. Most of the virtual worlds have their own currency that players can earn by participating in various activities and then use to purchase virtual goods. Social interaction is a key part of virtual worlds whereby users can use preselected words or phrases or enter their own words. Beyond interacting and communicating with other avatars, users can play games and attend parties or social events, often based on holiday themes. User motivation and interest is maintained by way of regular updates using blogs, or virtual newspapers.

These digital virtual worlds have been compared to children's school playgrounds (Meyers 2009) in that they include "play, group norms, reward structures, and socialization opportunities" (p. 51). It is claimed that such online environments create opportunities for education, socialization, and creativity (Hew and Cheung 2010). Much of children's activity in a virtual world is similar to their play (Marsh 2010) in that they are allowed to engage in pretend play, fantasy, and creating narratives. Beyond play, virtual worlds allow children to engage in new literacies (Meyers 2009) through participation in a discourse community. Users also engage in problem solving by making observations and decisions and drawing appropriate conclusions (Meyers 2009).

From a theoretical perspective, children's engagement in virtual worlds is clearly situated in Bronfenbrenner's (1979) microsystem. At the same time, the virtual world seems to create a conduit into the larger social network of the exosystem in which the child does not directly participate. This seems to function much like the "techno sub-system" described by Johnson and Pumplampu (2008). Then, from a Vygotskian perspective, the virtual worlds described here are the newest cultural tools and, as such, they influence children's thinking and learning. Potentially, these tools also elicit and develop new and different cognitive skills. Despite the "virtual" nature of the experience, from a cognitive developmental perspective, the child's participation constitutes an authentic social experience. This is because both the real and virtual contexts share similar interactive and cognitive elements.

Virtual Field Trips

Much like the virtual worlds of *Club Penguin* and *Webkinz,* the virtual field trip (VFT) takes children on an educational excursion from the safe confines of their classrooms. Teachers use the VFT to provide learning experiences beyond what children would typically be provided (Cox and Su 2004). Typically, the VFT consists of multimedia presentations created by teachers, themselves, or accessed through web sites such as S*cholastic* or *PBS Kids*. Organizing traditional field trips can be challenging for teachers because they have to deal with issues such as expense, safety, liability, transportation, and time constraints. The VFT, on the other hand, allows teachers to focus on the educational content. VFTs are particularly appealing to preschool or kindergarten teachers because of the difficulties of arranging field trips for younger children.

Using digital media, the VFT offers children rich educational experiences within the classroom. For example, children can experience other communities, they can interact with experts and other individuals, and even observe real-time events that may pose significant risks in the real world (e.g., observing wild animals up close). Unlike the virtual worlds where children are individual participants, the VFT offers classroom-based experiences. The VFT is embedded in the curriculum and might include use of online texts and images, streamed video, audio clips, and video conferences. In short, the VFT immerses children in an environment they would not otherwise have access to.

For younger children, the VFT provides a suitable alternative to first-hand experiences and a fun and engaging way for children to learn new concepts. Like the virtual worlds, the VFT positively shapes the child's microsystem by allowing the child to engage in new and different experiences. Since the experiences of the VFT shape the socio-cultural environment, Vygotsky's theory is also relevant here. Vygotsky's sociocultural perspective emphasizes the situatedness of thinking and speaking in the context of activity (Wertsch et al. 1995). For teachers, the VFT brings rich experiences into the supportive, interactive space of the classroom. For children, the VFT provides real-world experiences because most of the interactions, though spatially and temporally separated, are real-time and face-to-face. In turn, such experiences allow children, as social learners, to actively construct meaning about how the world works. Furthermore, engagement with more experienced others and direct observation of real-time events encourages children to reflect on the meaning of their interactions. This reflection potentially involves careful consideration, analysis of information, and in turn, critical thinking.

Tele-collaborative Projects

Many early childhood teachers are also extending the classroom boundaries by utilizing tele-collaborative projects. Using the internet, teachers and students are connecting with others around the world using email, listservs, discussion boards, and other platforms. According to Harris (1998), there are three categories of tele-collaborative activities: interpersonal exchanges, information collection and analysis, and problem solving. Each of these categories includes five to seven activities that can support children's learning. For example, interpersonal exchanges include electronic communication with individuals and with groups, keypals, and electronic appearances. Information collection and analysis includes creating databases, publishing, and data analysis. Problem-solving activities include information searches, simulations, or social action projects; all of which can potentially promote critical thinking.

For young children who are immersed in the interactive digital age of television, interactive computers, and video games, the tele-collaborative project is simply an extension of what they are experiencing at home. Such projects can provide direct social encounters that enrich and support children's learning. Moreover, such use is supported by Vygotskian theory (1978), which suggests that children can achieve much more when they are engaged in collective activities. As social learners, children actively construct meaning (Rushton and Larkin 2001), and their learning is embedded within social contexts (Tudge and Rogoff 1989). Tele-collaboration can potentially create and enhance such social contexts, whereby the dialectic relationship of interaction and context leads to the social construction of shared understanding. Also, as with the VFT, tele-collaborative activites can alter and shape the child's micro- and meso-system (Bronfenbrenner 1979). This is because the activities modify and shape the child's immediate environment in positive ways.

Summary and Conclusions

In conclusion, increasing numbers of young children in the United States are becoming regular consumers of digital media. They are accessing the internet at home and becoming regular players in virtual worlds such as *Club Penguin* or *Petpet*. Similarly, at school, the internet is being harnessed to enhance children's educational experiences using multi-media applications and approaches such as virtual field trips or tele-collaborative projects. While the virtual world of *Club Penguin* is an imaginary world with some resemblance of real-life events and activities, the school-based virtual field trips are real-life events accessed virtually.

The multiple uses and applications available through and via the internet can have positive consequences for children's learning and development. Educators, researchers, and policymakers are in agreement that there are social and cognitive effects of internet use by young children. Yet, to date, the research concerning the effects of internet use on cognitive development is sparse. Furthermore, the development of theoretical frameworks for understanding the effect of digital media on children's development is still in its infancy. Clearly, there is a pressing need for research examining the psychological and educational consequences of children's widespread and extensive use of internet activities.

Most theories of cognitive development were developed prior to the widespread use of digital media. As such, they fail to take into account the significant influence of children's extensive exposure to a wide range of internet-based activities such as virtual worlds and online communication. Two theoretical perspectives, Bronfenbrenner's ecological systems theory and Vygotsky's sociocultural theory, seem applicable and relevant in considering the internet's effect on children's cognitive development. By drawing on such theories, we can begin to understand how children's engagement in online worlds can shape their learning and development. We can also further our understanding of how children's experiences with digital media and the internet can be built upon and enhanced in early childhood settings.

References

Bronfenbrenner, U. (1979). *The ecology of human behavior: Experiments by nature and design*. Cambridge, MA: Harvard University Press.
Burnett, C., & Wilkinson, J. (2005). Holy lemons! Learning from children' uses of the internet in out-of-school contexts. *Literacy, 39*, 158–165.
Common Sense Media. (2011). *Zero to eight: Children's media use in America*. New York, NY: Common Sense Media.
Cordes, C., & Miller, E. (1999). *Fool's gold: A critical look at computers in childhood*. New York: Alliance for Childhood.
Cox, E. S., & Su, T. (2004). Integrating student learning with practitioner experience via virtual field trips. *Journal of Educational Media, 29*, 113–123.
DeBell, M., & Chapman, C. (2006). *Computer and internet use by students in 2003 (NCES 2006–065). U.S. Department of Education*. Washington, DC: National Center for Education Statistics.
Fish, A. M., Li, X., McCarrick, K., Butler, S. T., Stanton, B., & Brumitt, G. A. (2008). Early childhood computer experience and cognitive development among urban low-income preschoolers. *Journal of Educational Computing Research, 38*, 97–113.
Greenfield, P., & Yan, Z. (2006). Children, adolescents, and the internet: A new field of inquiry in developmental psychology. *Developmental Psychology, 42*, 291–394.
Gutnick, A. L., Robb, M., Takeuchi, L., & Kotler, J. (2011). *Always connected: The new digital media habits of young children*. New York, NY: The Joan Ganz Cooney Center at Sesame Workshop.
Harris, J. (1998). *Virtual architecture: Designing and directing curriculum-based telecollaboration*. Eugene, OR: International Society for Technology in Education.
Hew, K. F., & Cheung, W. S. (2010). Use of three-dimensional (3-D) immersive virtual worlds in K-12 and higher education settings: A review of the research. *British Journal of Educational Technology, 41*, 33–55.

Hisrich, K., & Blanchard, J. (2009). Digital media and emergent literacy. *Computers in the Schools, 26,* 240.

Jackson, L. A., Von Eye, A., Biocca, F. A., Barbatsis, G., Zhao, Y., & Fitzgerald, H. E. (2006). Does home internet use influence the academic performance of low income children? *Developmental Psychology, 42,* 429–435.

Johnson, G. M. (2006). Internet use and cognitive development: A theoretical framework. *E-learning, 4,* 433–441.

Johnson, G. M. (2010). Internet use and child development: Validation of the ecological techno-subsystem. *Educational Technology and Society, 13,* 176–185.

Johnson, G. (2012). The ecology of internet use during middle childhood: Physical, social, emotional and cognitive development. In T. Amiel & B. Wilson (Eds.), *Proceedings of world conference on educational multimedia, hypermedia and telecommunications* (pp. 1311–1316). Chesapeake, VA: AACE.

Johnson, G. M., & Puplampu, P. (2008). A conceptual framework for understanding the effects of the internet on child development: The ecological techno-subsystem. *Canadian Journal of Learning and Technology, 34,* 19–28.

Kirkorian, H. L., & Anderson, D. R. (2009) Learning from educational media. In S. L. Calvert & B. J. Wilson (Eds.), The handbook of children, media, and development (pp. 188–213). Oxford, UK: Blackwell. doi:10.1002/9781444302752.ch9.

Leu, D. J., Kinzer, C. K., Coiro, J., & McCammock, D. W. (2004). *Toward a theory of new literacies emerging from the internet and other information and communication technologies.* Paper presented at the International Reading Conference, Reno, NV.

Li, X., & Atkins, M. S. (2004). Early childhood computer experience and cognitive and motor development. *Pediatrics, 113,* 1715–1722.

Livingstone, S. (2009). *Children and the internet.* Malden, MA: Polity Press.

Marsh, J. (2010). Young children's play in online virtual worlds. *Journal of Early Childhood Research, 8,* 23–39.

Meyers, E. M. (2009). Virtual worlds, real learning. *School Library Monthly, 3,* 50–52.

NAEYC. (2012). *Joint position statement of the National Association for the Education of Young Children and the Fred Rogers Center for Early Learning and Children's Media at Saint Vincent College: Technology as tools in early childhood programs serving children from birth through age 8.* Washington, DC: NAEYC.

Ofcom. (2007). *Ofcom's submission to the Byron Review. Annex 5: The evidence base. The views of children, young people, and parents.* London, UK: Office of Communications.

Primary National Strategy. (2004). *Learning and teaching using ICT.* London, UK: DfES Publications.

Rushton, S., & Larkin, E. (2001). Shaping the learning environment: Connecting developmentally appropriate practices to brain research. *Early Childhood Education Journal, 29,* 25–33.

Simon, F. S., & Memeth, K. (2012). *Digital decisions: Choosing technology tools for early childhood.* Lewisville, NC: Gryphon.

Snyder, I. (2002). Communication, imagination, critique-literacy communication for the electronic age. In I. Snyder (Ed.), *Silicon literacies: Communication innovation and education in the electronic age* (pp. 173–183). London, UK: Routledge (Falmer Press).

Strasburger, V. C., Jordan, A. B., & Donnerstein, E. (2011). Health effects of media and television on children and adolescents. *Pediatrics, 125,* 756–767.

Tudge, J., & Rogoff, B. (1989). Peer influences on cognitive development: Piagetian and Vygotskian perspectives. In M. H. Bornstein & J. S. Bruner (Eds.), *Interaction in human development: Crosscurrents in contemporary psychology* (pp. 17–40). Hillsdale, NJ: Erlbaum.

Vygotsky, L. (1978). *Mind in society. The development of higher mental processes.* Cambridge, MA: Harvard University Press.

Wertsch, J., Hagstrom, F., & Kikas, E. (1995). Voices of thinking and speaking. In L. Martin, K. Nelson, & E. Tobach (Eds.), *Sociocultural psychology: Theory and practice of doing and knowing* (pp. 276–290). New York: Cambridge University Press.

Yan, Z. (2006). What influences children's and adolescents' understanding of the complexity of the internet? *Developmental Psychology, 42*(3), 418–428. doi:10.1037/0012–1649.42.3.418.

Young, K. (2007). Toward a model for the study of children's internet use. *Computers in Human Behavior, 24,* 173–184.

Chapter 2
Supporting Young Children's Visual Literacy through the Use of E-books

Natalie Conrad Barnyak and Tracy A. McNelly

E-books are one form of visual literacy technology that "digital natives" have experiences with even prior to beginning school.

Abstract This chapter begins by defining the various categories of e-books and the role of scaffolding in early literacy. Next, the chapter discusses the advances in the creation of e-books for children and a review of pertinent research on the use of e-books to support young children's acquisition of literacy. Selecting and evaluating e-books in connection with the joint position statement, *Technology in Early Childhood Programs*, made by the National Association for the Education of Young Children and the Fred Rogers Center for Early Learning and Children's Media at Saint Vincent College (2012) are included. Then, the chapter provides guidelines for selecting quality e-books and using them to meet the diverse needs of young

N. C. Barnyak (✉)
University of Pittsburgh at Johnstown, Johnstown, PA, USA
e-mail: nconrad@pitt.edu

T. A. McNelly
Norwin School District, North Huntingdon, PA, USA

children. It concludes with implications for using e-books in the field of early childhood education and an appendix of various developmentally-appropriate e-books.

Keywords E-books · Visual literacy · Emergent literacy

Scenario

Sofia is seated on the living room couch with her children–Justin, who is 6 years old and in first grade, and Vanessa, who is 4 years old and in preschool. Sofia loves to read to her children and has been doing so since they were born. The children have access to children's literature in both print and electronic formats. "Let's read How Rocket Learned to Read (Hills 2010)*!" Justin exclaims. "I like that one too!" Vanessa agrees. Sofia smiles and tells the children to turn on their Nook and locate the e-book. The children eagerly grab the Nook and find it with ease. Sofia says, "It's Justin's turn to hold the Nook, and Vanessa can turn the pages." The children get excited as the book's title page is displayed and read; they then follow along as each word in the text is highlighted in synchrony with the words that they hear. As the story continues, both children chime in with the recorded text of this award-winning e-book. After they read the word "marveled," Vanessa pauses and does not "turn" the page immediately. Sophia asks the children, "Do you remember what 'marveled' means? We looked it up in the dictionary feature yesterday when we read this book." Vanessa responds, "I know Mommy! It means the yellow bird thought, 'Wow! What a great alphabet banner!' She was amazed." Justin adds, "Yes, I think she's right. Let's check the dictionary to make sure." By touching the word on the screen, they locate the definition and confirm their understanding. Sofia says, "I'm so proud of both of you for remembering the definition and using the dictionary!" Justin mentions that they are always learning new vocabulary words at school too. As they continue the read-aloud, the children intently watch the graphics, which directly correlate to the text. Upon completion of the e-book, Sofia asks the children, "What do you remember about the story that we just read?" Justin and Vanessa give an accurate retelling and conclude with, "Read it again!"*

Introduction

Children are exposed to a variety of media in their everyday lives and have been described as "digital natives" because they have been surrounded by technology since birth (Houston 2011; Prensky 2001). In an effort to develop literate children, it is imperative that educators and parents/families understand the influence such media plays on early literacy development. E-books, or electronic books, are one form of visual literacy technology that "digital natives" have experiences with even prior to beginning school. E-books also may be described as living books, CD-ROM storybooks, talking books, interactive books, computer books, disc books, or digital books (de Jong and Bus 2003). The books include oral dialogue and typically encourage interactions between reader and computer—known as interactive legibility—through pictures, words, and multimedia additions (de Jong and Bus 2003, 2004; Medwell 1996; Shiratuddin and Landoni 2002) which can help develop children's emergent literacy skills (Shamir and Korat 2006, 2009). Emergent literacy, defined as children's continuous literacy acquisition throughout early childhood (Justice and Kaderavek 2002; Whitehurst and Lonigan 1998), can be fostered through teachers' and parents'/families' selection and interactive use of e-books. Scaffolding includes a more capable other (e.g., parent or teacher) providing children with support (e.g., giving verbal cues or prompts to assist learning) so that they may grasp concepts and/ or perform tasks that they are unable to on their own. Scaffolding was originally proposed by Vygotsky (1978) and elaborated on by Bruner (1978) in regard to children's early language learning. Bruner (1978) states that it is necessary to provide children with social interactional frameworks in familiar contexts (e.g., parent reading bedtime stories each night to his/her child) in order to assist their language development.

E-books provide scaffolding because they afford children with immediate feedback on word meanings (Grant 2004; Medwell 1998), picture cues, and audio features (Doty et al. 2001). Nonetheless, we caution teachers and parents/families to carefully consider the features of e-books and select quality e-books for children. Korat and Shamir (2007) claim that "new technologies have the potential to support cognitive development and learning" (p. 258). However, e-books must be educational and developmentally appropriate in order to build children's emergent literacy skills (Shamir and Korat 2009) and meet their diverse needs and interests.

This chapter will begin with a discussion of scaffolding (Vygotsky 1978) and its importance while sharing e-books with young children. Next, a brief historical overview of the advances in e-books and a review of pertinent literature on e-books will be highlighted. Then, the chapter will address selecting and evaluating quality e-books for young children. The chapter concludes with a discussion of how to meet children's diverse needs pertaining to the use of e-books and implications for using e-books in the field of early childhood.

The Role of Scaffolding in Early Literacy

Smith (2004) states that, while learning to read, children need good books and adults who are supportive while sharing the books. Vygotsky's (1978) work suggests that children learn through their interactions and learn best through scaffolded experiences delivered within the Zone of Proximal Development (ZPD) (i.e., the range between children's current abilities and their potential abilities). Scaffolding occurs when a more competent other provides support to a learner. The most effective forms of scaffolding occur when children's individual needs are considered and a flexible approach using a variety of strategies is implemented (Berk and Winsler 1999). Many theories of reading development include scaffolding for literacy promotion (Moody 2010). E-books are interactive, and the research provides evidence that scaffolding occurs as young children interact with e-books. For example, the text is read aloud and highlighted; children can read and reread e-books independently; animations and graphics complement the text; dictionary features promote vocabulary development and comprehension; and children can read at an individualized pace (Karemaker et al. 2008; Moody 2010). Teachers and parents/families should interact with young children and engage them in shared reading experiences with e-books while scaffolding their experiences. In addition, adults can enhance children's reading motivation through scaffolding while orally sharing e-books together (Lutz et al. 2006). Thus, the selection of appropriate e-books for children, coupled with e-book features and adult support that provides scaffolding during reading, help to promote young children's literacy acquisition.

Advances in E-books for Children

The e-book evolution began in 1971 when Project Gutenberg began digitizing books. In 1985, the Voyager Company developed and began producing CD-ROM books. Then in 1998, NuvoMedia, Inc. released the first e-book readers, Rocket E-book and SoftBook (Falconer 2011). From there, many other companies began creating handheld reading devices for digital content (Shiratuddin and Landoni 2002). Digitized versions of books became popular around 2002 when Random House and HarperCollins began digitizing their publications. In 2007, the e-book revolution took off with Amazon's launch of the Kindle and the Kindle Store, followed in 2009 by the release of the Nook by Barnes and Noble. Then, in 2010, Apple released the iPad and iBooks (Falconer 2011).

Today's e-books are quite different from the e-books of 1971. E-books today come in many different forms, which make defining e-books difficult. Jeremy Brueck, a pioneer in children's digital reading research, feels the term "e-book" is too broad (Guernsey 2011). E-books fall on a spectrum. At one end, they can be as simple as PDF files of books and, at the other end, as complex as resources with animation, quizzes, games and other multimedia features (Guernsey 2011). By definition, an e-book is a computer file which contains the text of a printed book read on a personal computer, a personal digital assistant, a laptop computer, or an electronic device designed specifically for reading e-books (Yoon 2003).

E-books have many features similar to a traditional book. They contain printed text, page numbers, pictures, and parts of a book, such as the table of contents, chapter headings, and index. However, their features are also remarkably different (Roskos et al. 2009). At the most basic level, e-books contain digitized speech that provides word pronunciation and definitions. At a more advanced level, electronic books provide readers complete narration, highlighting of text, and page turning capacity. E-books also provide interactive digital narrative that includes a variety of multimedia such as written text, oral reading, music, sound, and animation. They may also include buttons activated by the reader (Shamir and Korat 2006). Newer electronic books are multimodal and provide a storyline with diversions that the reader controls. Diversions are features that change the traditional path of the reader. Diversions include cued animations, touch screen activation, and speech recognition (Baird and Henninger 2011). For example, *Wild About Books* (Sierra 2004), an e-book app published by Random House Digital Inc., is an example of a high-quality e-book that contains many interactive and multimedia features, such as animated and interactive screens whereby children can tilt their mobile device for a 3-D experience. Throughout the book, children can tap and swipe animals and illustrations for animation and sound effects. A navigation wheel provides options to move through the book to visit different pages. Children can select the "read to me" option and have the book read aloud with highlighted text.

The ways in which children interact with e-books is considerably different from their interaction with traditional books. Children negotiate e-books in different ways than they do traditional books. Page turning using an electronic text requires children to use different motor skills, such as pressing a key or activation button, in contrast to reading traditional books when children use the pincer grasp to hold pages while turning them. Additionally, e-books require children to process reading differently because they provide printed text enhanced by multimedia features. Finally, e-books require less adult mediation than traditional books and provide additional opportunities for independent exploration and practice (Roskos et al. 2009).

Research on the Effects of E-books for Children

E-books are a medium that can support the "opportunity for the promotion of emergent literacy among young children, including those at risk for learning disabilities, before they have reached school age" (Shamir et al. 2013, p. 173). Although traditional literature and e-books both contain text, pages that turn, and illustrations, the enhancements (e.g., animations, read-to-me option, games, music, and sound) of e-books distinguish them from traditional text (Zucker et al. 2009). E-books may provide different reading mode options (e.g., read-to-me, read and play, play only); however, adults must ensure that children do not heavily rely on the read-to-me option and use it as a "crutch" (Schugar et al. 2013, p. 619).

Research suggests the use of high-quality e-books enhances young children's emergent literacy. Shamir and Korat (2007) conducted a study by using a self-designed, developmentally-appropriate e-book for children in kindergarten to measure their emergent literacy development. Phonological awareness (i.e., syllabication), writing skills, and word recognition improved for all children after reading the e-book. They concluded that both individual learning and paired-learning of kindergarten students while reading e-books is beneficial to their general emergent literacy levels.

Media effects, closely matched with the text, foster children's comprehension while reading e-books (Labbo and Kuhn 2000). E-books that include high-quality picture cues and text that is read aloud support comprehension (Doty et al. 2001). However, scaffolding is important, and adults should model for children how to predict, retell, and monitor comprehension while reading e-books (Schugar et al. 2013). Matthew (1996, 1997) found that when children read e-books as compared to traditional literature, they produced better retellings. Verhallen et al. (2006) state that there was increased comprehension for children who are second language learners after reading e-books. In a study by Grimshaw et al. (2007), children who read an electronic storybook with narration scored significantly higher on comprehension tests than children who read a regular print copy of the text.

Vocabulary development is essential for children to become proficient readers (Scott et al. 2008). While reading e-books, children become familiar with book language (Bus et al. 2009), and the multimedia features support word recognition skills (de Jong and Bus 2002; Karemaker et al. 2008). When e-books supply instant information pertaining to text, such as dictionary features, children's vocabulary development is supported (Grant 2004; Medwell 1998; Shamir and Korat 2009). In addition, e-books that include text in a rebus format appear to promote children's word recognition skills (de Jong and Bus 2002). As with print books, Higgins and Hess (1999) found that linking children's new and prior knowledge while reading electronic books increased their vocabulary. Grant (2004) suggests that children's word recognition in-context is supported through the use of electronic books, while Medwell (1996) posits that the greatest gains in children's word recognition out-of-context was made when they read an electronic book with support from a teacher. Within a study by Medwell (1996), both boys and girls who read electronic text, gained greater word accuracy than the children in the teacher-led group who read the same text in a traditional format. However, the boys, as compared to the girls, had higher word accuracy after reading the e-books in relation to reading the printed text with the teacher. Overall, the children who read the e-book and received teacher support made the greatest gains in word accuracy. The research clearly documents that parents/families support children's understanding of traditional literature through discussions of print, illustrations, and content (Hammett et al. 2003). However, Roskos and Brueck (2009) state that adults are often minimally involved while children read e-books.

Although it is necessary for adults to scaffold young children's experiences with e-books, they often spend less time interacting during e-book readings than they do with traditional literature. Kim and Anderson (2008) conducted a study and compared mother-child interactions during shared reading sessions in three different contexts (i.e., reading a traditional book, reading a CD-ROM storybook, and reading a video clip formatted e-book). The session during which the print book was read was the longest, but the results indicated that overall talk was more complex with more non-immediate talk (i.e., talk that is more abstract) during the shared reading of e-books as compared to the shared reading of the print book. A study by Korat and Or (2010) compared mother-child interactions during different types of shared reading sessions. The dyads, comprised of 48 kindergarten children and their mothers, were randomly assigned to one of four groups, which included reading of two different types of e-books (i.e., educational and commercial) and two different printed books. While reading the printed books, there were more initiations and responses made by the mothers. Overall, expanded talk was higher while reading the printed text as compared to the readings of the e-books. The authors suggest the expanding support (e.g., animation, sound, and highlighted text) is already built into e-books and, therefore, may result in less expanded talk between the dyads.

Motivation for reading e-books is an additional factor to consider when selecting text for young children (Ciampa 2012). Glasglow (1996) found the use of interactive texts enhanced children's reading motivation. In a study by Larson (2010), children enjoyed reading e-books, which allowed for personal digital note-taking and control regarding their reading engagement. Within a study by Maynard (2010), a reluctant young reader gained enthusiasm for reading using e-books and was excited to download and choose books. Therefore, consideration of children's reading preferences and interests are necessary when selecting high-quality children's e-books.

Selection of Quality E-books for Young Children

In order to support children's literacy acquisition, educators must foster their comprehension development and scaffold children's literacy experiences (Block and Duffy 2008; Block and Pressley 2007; Pearson and Duke 2002; Stahl 2006). E-books are useful for scaffolding because they provide children with immediate feedback on word meanings to promote comprehension (Grant 2004; Medwell 1998) and provide picture cues and audio features to support comprehension as well (Doty et al. 2001). Labbo and Kuhn (2000) assert that, in order to foster comprehension, the media effects within e-books must be consistent with the text.

While there is evidence that the use of high-quality e-books advances children's early literacy skills, there is also evidence that the interactive elements that support literacy may also be distractions (de Jong and Bus 2003; Moody 2010; Shamir and Korat 2006). Some researchers are concerned that electronic books might put early readers at a disadvantage. While the electronic features may provide scaffolding during the reading process by giving cues to students, they may be undermining a reader's capacity to develop competency in important text indictors that lead to comprehension (Birkerts 1995; Labbo et al. 2003; Lewin 1996). According to de Jong and Bus (2003), e-books that include games can be distracting to children's reading comprehension. Trushell et al. (2003) found that graphics and sound effects that did not help to further the storyline or reinforce the text negatively affected students' ability to retell story events. Lewis and Ashton (1999) found that, while reading electronic books, students spent 65 % of their reading time on non-reading activities that included activating graphics and playing games.

Young children are faced with numerous decisions when they are provided with new literacies. The National Association for the Education of Young Children (NAEYC) and the Fred Rogers Center for Early Learning and Children's Media (FRC) (2012) state that teachers should not abandon traditional literacy practices, but should use technology within a high-quality pedagogical framework. With young children, Pearman and Chang (2010) found the interactive text features offer

Table 2.1 Web-based e-book resources for young children

A Story Before Bed	http://www.astorybeforebed.com/
Between the Lions	http://www.pbskids.org/lions
Big Universe	http://www.biguniverse.com
iStoryBooks	https://www.istorybooks.co/
MagicBlox digital library	http://magicblox.com
Memetales	http://www.memetales.com
Makin VIA	http://www.mackin.com/ESERVICES/MACKIN-VIA.aspx
Oxford Owl	http://www.oxfordowl.co.uk/teacher
Raz-Kids	http://www.raz-kids.com/
RIF Reading Planet	http://www.rif.org/readingpslanet
Scholastic BookFLIX	http://teacher.scholastic.com/products/bookflixfreetrial/
Starfall	http://www.starfall.com
Storyline Online	http://www.storylineonline.net
Storyplace: The Children's Digital Library	http://www.storyplace.org
TumbleBooks	http://www.tumblebooks.com/library/asp/home_tumblebooks.asp
Wizz-e	http://www.wizz-e.com

support for literacy acquisition but recommend teacher supervision and support with all digital activities. Teacher support for literacy begins at the planning stage during the selection of text. With the countless numbers of e-books available today, it is important that educators and parents/families understand the design elements and features of e-books that will support young children's emergent literacy development. According to NAEYC and FRC (2012) "the adult's role is critical in making certain that thoughtful planning, careful implementation, reflection, and evaluation guide decision making about how to introduce and integrate any form of technology into the classroom experience" (p. 5). Table 2.1 includes web-based e-books designed for young children.

Karchmer-Klein and Shinas (2012) argue that students must be taught a new set of skills in order to participate in the electronic environment. As described in Table 2.2, they recommend four principles teachers should consider as they think about how to use technology to support literacy.

In their position paper *Technology in Early Childhood Programs Serving Children from Birth through Age 8*, NAEYC and FRC (2012) stress the importance of professional judgment needed to determine technology that is developmentally appropriate for young children. They suggest the following three dimensions of appropriateness that adults should consider when selecting technology for use with young children: age, individual needs, and cultural and linguistic background. As with the selection of any learning materials, "teachers must constantly make reflective, responsive, and intentional judgments to promote positive outcomes for each child" (NAEYC and FRC 2012, p. 6).

Educators and parents/families also need to consider how to choose technology to ensure it is not harmful to children. NAEYC and FRC (2012) encourage educators and parents/families to regularly monitor the research related to technology's

Table 2.2 Principles of technology for educators to consider. (Karchmer-Klein and Shinas 2012, pp. 289–291)

Principles	Definition
Principle 1: Keep your eye on the moving target	Technology is changing at a rapid pace and so will new literacies. New literacies allow a transactional relationship between author and reader. Readers are encouraged to be active participants.
Principle 2: Recognize the complexity of new literacies	The author dictates the traditional text format and it is typically linear in nature. Internet-based texts are non-linear and include graphics, videos and images. In this inquiry-based environment, readers have more decisions to make as they read.
Principle 3: Digital natives still have a lot to learn	Digital natives are those born since 1980 that have been immersed in a technology-filled world. However, immersion in a technology-filled world does not equate to a use and understanding of new literacies. Students need instruction in how to develop critical literacy skills.
Principle 4: Reconsider assessment methods	Teachers need to assess students' knowledge and understanding of technology before they expect them to use it effectively.

influence on children's health and developmental issues. The use of technology should not hinder the development of the whole child. Hence, the amount of screen time and the type of technology children are using needs to be closely monitored. Technology, in all forms, should be free of bias, violence, and exploitative material.

Within Table 2.3, we grouped e-book features into the following categories that encapsulate all of the relevant design features mentioned in the research and literature: developmentally-appropriate digital features that support emergent literacy skills, instructional design features, technical features, and accessibility for children with special needs. After each category, we provide a series of questions to consider in the process of evaluating e-books. Educators and parents/families should consider the features in all of the categories as a whole when selecting appropriate e-books for young children. Roskos et al. (2009) posit, "high-performing analytic tools can provide insights into effective multimedia designs that support early literacy learning" (p. 234). They conclude by stating there is a need to use multiple analytic tools when examining e-book design elements.

Digital Features of Children's E-books that Support Literacy Development

Educators and parents/families should take deliberate care in choosing texts, including both traditional literature and e-books, which support the development of young children's literacy skills. Evaluations of many e-books reveal that they have limited potential in supporting literacy (de Jong and Bus 2003). Shamir and Korat (2009) recommend that e-book designers emphasize activities that support early development of literacy. The No Child Left Behind Act of 2001 identifies four areas

Table 2.3 Teacher and parent/family checklist for evaluating e-books for young children. (Adapted from: Clark and Mayer 2008; Moody 2010; Roskos et al. 2009; Shamir and Korat 2006; WCAG 2.0 Guidelines 2012)

Category	Does the e-book …	Yes/No	Comments/notes
I. Emergent Literacy Skills			
Alphabetic principle and phonological awareness	Give the pronunciation of letters and words?		
	Highlight letters and words?		
Print awareness	Read and highlight text?		
	Provide options for moving through the book (e.g., forward and back options, swipe page turning, arrow page turning, click page turning)?		
Use of language	Present questions about what was read?		
	Use different voices for characters' dialogue?		
Comprehension	Use animations to support understanding of the text?		
	Build comprehension through interactive multimedia?		
Vocabulary	Support the reader in making text-based inferences?		
	Offer word definition features?		
Reading engagement	Encourage interaction through animations, sounds, games and activities for read and play modes?		
Text features	Present the story/text effectively?		
	Repeat words to support young readers?		
	Use appropriate syntax/grammar?		
	Display text effectively (e.g., font size, print conventions, and text density on screen)?		
Clear instructions	Offer verbal, written and visual instructions?		
	Supply clear and precise instructions?		
Independence	Support independent use by young children?		
II. Instructional Design Features			
Multimedia	Use graphics to enhance the text?		
	Use illustrations to clarify facts and concepts within the text?		
	Include animations relevant to the text?		
Contiguous features	Place print near the graphic it describes?		
	Coordinate the narration to the graphics?		
Coherence	Include pages containing details essential to the text?		
	Include pages containing illustrations essential to the text?		
	Include pages containing adequate words and graphics to assist the reader in understanding the text?		

Table 2.3 (continued)

Category	Does the e-book ...	Yes/No	Comments/notes
Personalization	Supply narration matched to the tone of the text?		
III. Technical Features			
Multimedia	Include music or songs?		
	Include active illustrations?		
Controls	Give different reading mode options (e.g., read only, read and play, and play only)?		
	Allow the child to pause or restart?		
	Have an overview screen?		
	Spontaneously load the pages?		
Installation/Operation	Install easily?		
	Open easily?		
	Operate consistently?		
IV. Accessibility for Children with Special Needs			
Perceivability	Provide text alternatives for non-text content, such as text resizing, color, and contrast alteration?		
	Provide captions and other alternatives, such as audio descriptions for multimedia?		
Operability	Make all functions operable from a keyboard?		
	Give users *enough time* to read and use content?		
	Eliminate any content (blinking and/or moving) that may cause seizures?		
	Provide consistent navigation symbols and content that is easy to locate?		
Understandability	Make all text readable and understandable?		
	Include content that operates in predictable ways?		
Robustness	Provide compatibility with current and future assistive technology?		

of emergent literacy that must be developed prior to learning to read: oral language, phonological awareness, print awareness, and alphabet knowledge. The National Institute for Reading (2006) has identified five components of effective literacy instruction: (1) phonemic awareness, (2) phonics, (3) fluency, (4) vocabulary, and (5) text comprehension. These areas of literacy development should guide the selection of e-books.

E-books designed for young children should support the development of important literacy skills. To enhance development of alphabetic principle and phonemic awareness, educators and parents/families should look for e-books that provide opportunities for children to manipulate letters and sounds within the text. E-books should highlight and pronounce individual letters and words when children select them. To support print, e-books should read and highlight text in a fluent manner (Shamir and Shlafer 2011), provide children with options for page turning, and include all relevant parts of a book.

E-books can help to develop children's vocabulary and comprehension of text, and educators and parents/families should look for features that provide embedded dictionaries, animations and/or interactive multimedia that support text, the use of effective narration throughout the text, and questions about the text. Shamir and Korat (2007) found that many e-books with multimedia games and options do not support text and can be distractors to text comprehension; they stress the importance of close examination to make sure these features support the text. Korat and Shamir (2004) urge designers of e-books to incorporate animated dictionaries while carefully considering children's age and verbal knowledge.

In the selection of e-books for children, it is also important to determine if the content is age appropriate. Educators and parents/families should examine the e-book's text structure. E-books designed for preschool children should consist of simple structures, while e-books for older children can contain structures that are more complex and include a series of problem-solution events (Shamir and Korat 2006). Other features to consider in determining age-appropriateness are font size, syntax, and the amount of text on each page.

Instructional Design Features of E-books

Many of the current e-books available for young children are loaded with in multimedia features, including text, graphics, colors, sound clips, video clips, simulations and games. Although these features may seem enticing to educators and parents/families, too many may be a distraction to learning. Garner et al. (1989) state that it is important to make children aware of text distractions, which they term as "seductive details," while reading so they do not interfere with comprehension. Within e-books, distractions may include unrelated "hot spots" or unconnected animations (Schugar et al. 2013). In the educational setting, Clark and Mayer (2003) suggest a more grounded approach to multimedia design and state, "What we have learned from all the media comparison research is that it's not the medium, but rather the instructional methods that cause learning" (p. 21). They have identified six principles of multimedia design to keep in mind for the development and selection of all types of resources for e-learning, including e-books: multimedia features, contiguity, modality, redundancy, coherence, and personalization.

Multimedia features, such as graphics and animations, should serve a purpose beyond decoration in the e-learning environment and should assist the learner in making sense of the content. Contiguity refers to the use of text and images in multimedia to promote learning. The text should appear near the correlating animations, and the spoken words should be aligned with corresponding graphics in order to create a connection for the learner. Modality refers to visual and auditory presentation of information. In the e-learning environment, the use of both modes can lower the effects of cognitive overload. Redundancy suggests that having more is not always better. Working memory has limitations when it comes to processing new information; thus, redundant information that is not necessary for skill reinforcement may interfere with learning. In the e-learning environment, the coherence principle recommends limiting information to what is necessary to help the learner make sense of the text and eliminating any non-essential multimedia. Personalization in e-books refers to the presence of a human voice verses a machine voice (Clark and Mayer 2003/2008). Educators and parents/families should consider these design elements when selecting e-books for young children.

These questions should not be the sole determinant of what makes an e-book effective. In a study conducted by Roskos et al. (2009), six instructional design principles were used to evaluate a series of mixed-genre e-books from five online e-book sources. The tool was useful in identifying multimedia learning that supports early literacy. It did not, however, provide enough information on interface design (i.e., usability/accessibility), a key element in print awareness. As stated earlier, it is important to use a variety of tools to evaluate the appropriateness of e-books for young children.

Technical Features of E-books

In addition to considering literacy skill development and instructional design features, the selection of e-books should also include an analysis of the technical features. These features, not found in a traditional text, are important to determine usability and reliability. No matter how engaging the text and features, e-books need to function correctly to be of benefit to children, and low-quality books can add distractions for readers (Moody 2010). One important technical aspect not to overlook when selecting e-books for young children is the control options. E-books provide a variety of read-and-play modes for children. Research recommends avoiding books that provide a read-and-play option in the same mode because it may be a distraction to comprehension (Shamir and Korat 2007). Educators and parents/families should look for books with games played separately from reading. Additionally, e-books should include options that allow a child to interrupt and restart the reading passage, a skill that good readers use with traditional text when they need to reread to get a better understanding of the text. Finally, the technical quality of e-books should allow children to enjoy the books without distractions due to operational difficulties, such as pages not loading quickly or words not highlighting properly.

E-Books that Address the Special Needs of Young Children

Children with disabilities can use assistive technology to make growth toward reading standards under the No Child Left Behind Act of 2001. Assistive technology is defined as an item or piece of equipment used to assist in maintaining or improving the functional capacities of children with disabilities. Electronic books are one piece of assistive technology that enhance book retellings of students with disabilities (Rhodes and Milby 2007).

Electronic books have several advantages over traditional audiotaped books. E-books expose children with physical and learning disabilities to audio, animation, and interactivity that help scaffold learning. Other features include the ability to change text format and text-to-speech readers (Rhodes and Milby 2007). Cavanaugh (2002) suggests that e-books can be a good way to provide reading accommodations or modifications for students with special needs. E-books provide scaffolding benefits, such as voice output, dictionaries, and note-taking features for students with special needs (Cavanaugh 2002).

Just as e-books provide support for children with disabilities, they too have benefits for English language learners. Tuget and Tuncer (2011) suggest that online dual literacy books, which present the text in two languages, help support language and literacy learning for English language learners. Additionally, reading e-books can improve vocabulary acquisition (Yoon 2013), reading attitudes, and confidence (Lin 2010; Yoon 2013). Both Yoon (2013) and Lin (2010) found that e-books positively influenced English language learners' desire and commitment to continue to read and study the English language.

To ensure that educational materials, such as e-books, are available to all and meet the needs of special learners, applications and software must follow accessibility guidelines. The Center for Applied Special Technology recommends materials that are flexible to meet all learning needs (Cavanaugh 2002). Web Content Accessibility Guidelines (WCAG) 2.0 (2008), initially developed for Web application, have recently been applied to the evaluation of mobile devices and applications, including e-books (Baird and Henninger 2011; WCAG 2012). These guidelines include four principles: perceivability, operability, understandability, and robustness. A document is considered accessible if it meets all four guidelines. Perceivability means that presented information can be easily accessed. Providing audio modes, text resizing, or the ability to alter the contrast and color would ensure access to a child who is visually impaired. A child who is deaf or who has difficulty hearing may receive captions or a description of the content for media embedded in the application to explain a picture within the text.

Operability means that everyone, despite disabilities, can use the tools required to run the application and that the tools are not a hindrance to the operation of the application. The tools must help users navigate the application with ease. The Web Content Accessibility Guidelines (2012) recommend that all devices enable keyboard functionality for users and that time constraints are removed or are adjustable within the applications to ensure that users with disabilities have enough time to complete all tasks. Additionally, applications should permit users to disable content that blinks or moves to remove distractions. This is especially important for children who suffer from seizures. Operable also means navigable. Devices should assist users in finding ways to locate content, such as easily-recognizable and consistently-located navigation bars that are voice-enabled. Understandability reinforces the importance of ensuring that the device can understand the information presented. WCAG (2012) recommends using HTML language. Additionally, understandability requires that features having the same functionality throughout the application are identified in the same manner. For example, arrows that advance pages would be identified in the same way throughout the book. The last principle, robustness, lends itself more to the web environment than to the e-book environment. Essentially, robustness requires applications be compatible with assistive technology. E-books located within web pages should follow these guidelines.

A study by Baird and Henninger (2011) used the WCAG 2.0 guidelines to examine the use of the VoiceOver tool with ten children's e-books on the iPad with focus on accessibility of the books for children with visual impairments. Findings indicate design inconsistencies that lead to a lack of accessibility. The e-books that were examined failed to include the capability to adjust brightness/contrast, enable VoiceOver buttons, enlarge text, or change font type. Moreover, the e-books had navigation and page turning errors and inconsistencies, which would make navigation difficult for a child with visual impairments. The authors recognize that multimodal e-books are new and propose a continued focus on creating technologies that support literacy for all.

Implications for Practice in the Field of Early Childhood Education

According to Roskos and Brueck (2009), e-books "offer a potentially rich material resource for literacy learning at an early age" (p. 80). However, it is often difficult for parents/families and educators to choose high quality e-books due to the great variation in multimedia features that are incorporated (de Jong and Bus 2003; Karemaker et al. 2008). Adults must carefully consider their choice of e-books for young children (NAEYC and FRC 2012) and critique the following features: literacy skill development features (Moody 2010; Shamir and Korat 2006), instructional design features (Clark and Mayer 2008; Roskos et al. 2009), and technical features (Sharmir and Korat 2009). Developmentally-appropriate e-books for young children should maintain technical quality and include the following: relevant content, highlighted text that is read aloud, dictionary features, well-defined instructions, and related activation hot spots that include audio and/or visual responses correlated to the text (Sharmir and Korat 2009). In addition, children's diverse needs and literacy goals must be at the forefront of the decision-making process when selecting e-books. "Digital readers show promise in supporting struggling readers through multiple tools and features, including manipulation of font size, text-to-speech options, expandable dictionary, and note capabilities" (Larson 2010, p. 21). Educators and parents/families should carefully consider the growing body of research in order to generate informed decisions.

Implementation of e-books in early childhood classrooms in various contexts, such as independent or paired reading during center time, shared reading, and literature circles, provide for active learning experiences. Children may work individually or in pairs reading e-books (Shamir and Korat 2007) throughout center time on already-taught literacy skills. E-books used during shared reading can be projected on a Promethean or SMARTboard. Educators can encourage children to interact with the text and illustrations while chorally reading or echo reading. During literature circles, students who are reading the same e-book can record electronic notes in their e-books based upon their roles. For example, when locating new vocabulary, children could highlight and define words throughout the e-book. Teachers and students can go to the "annotations page" and read the notes that were made throughout the book. Although e-books afford children the opportunity for interactive reading experiences by using multimedia features (e.g., sound, animation, narration), adults should not assume that all children can navigate and effectively read e-books (Schugar et al. 2013).

Adults should show children the functions of e-books prior to using the technology to read. Schugar et al. (2013) recommend four steps for familiarizing and modeling the use of e-books with children. The first step includes turning on the device (e.g., iPad, computer) and accessing the e-book (e.g., an app, website). Second, if the screen is moveable (i.e., iPad), model how to orient it in one position or, if possible, lock the screen so that it does not move while reading. The third step includes opening the e-book and showing children the interactive features. Finally, in order to avoid distractions, discuss with children if they should use the interactive features during reading, after reading, or while rereading the e-book. It is imperative to help children transfer their knowledge of strategy use from reading print to reading e-books (Schugar et al. 2013). Adults must scaffold and model strategies with e-books while comparing and contrasting how the strategies differ when using traditional literature and e-books (Schugar et al. 2013).

Conclusion

In conclusion, high-quality, developmentally-appropriate e-books can be used to scaffold young children's literacy experiences. The combined use of traditional picture books and e-books, with adult support, is the best way to address the needs of diverse groups of young children and individual children with varied interests, literacy levels, and special needs. "Traditional books won't go away; they'll just become part of a new mix of reading resources for a new breed of reader" (Lamb and Johnson 2011, p. 62). As advances in the creation of e-books for children are made, research on instructional strategies and best practices in the classroom are necessary. When selecting high-quality e-books for young children, it is important to consider emergent literacy skills, instructional design features, technical features, and accessibility for children with special needs. In addition, it is necessary to take into account children's interests in order to support their motivation and reading engagement. Through the incorporation of a variety of texts, today's digital natives can enhance their emergent literacy skills and promote their desire to read.

Appendix

Children's E-books and E-book Publishers

Web-based E-books on Scholastic BookFLIX

Title: *Click, Clack, Moo: Cows That Type*
Written by: Doreen Cronin
Illustrated by: Betsy Lewin
Publisher: Atheneum Books for Young Readers (2000)
E-book Publisher: Weston Woods Studios, Inc.
Age Range: 3 and up

The cows use an old typewriter to persuade Farmer Brown, through their writing, to provide them with electric blankets. The ducks on the farm soon learn the power of writing.

The beginning of the e-book displays the title and author in a "type-writer" style format with corresponding typewriter sound effects and "mooing" to correlate with the theme of the e-book. To turn the page, the reader must click on a button at the bottom of the page. A pause button is present as well. As the text is read aloud with appropriate expression, the animations clearly support the text (e.g., cows typing on the typewriter; Farmer Brown slamming the door when he is furious). In the "read along" option, each word is highlighted as it is read. When a note written by one of the characters is read aloud, the font of the print is in italics and again highlighted word-by-word. Background music accompanies the text. A Spanish edition of the e-book is also available.

Title: *Let's Visit a Dairy Farm*
Written by: Alyse Sweeney
Publisher: Scholastic (2006)
E-book Publisher: Weston Woods Studios, Inc.
Age Range: 6–7

This nonfiction text takes the reader through activities (e.g., milking the cows) that occur on a dairy farm.

In the "read along" option, each word is highlighted in red font as it is read expressively. A built-in dictionary feature is present and various vocabulary words are highlighted in yellow throughout the text. When the reader places the cursor over a highlighted word and clicks on the "listen" symbol, the definition displayed in a "bubble" is read aloud. The reader must click on a button at the bottom of the page to "turn" to the next page. A pause button is present as well. Photographs of a dairy farm that closely correlate with the text are displayed. A Spanish edition of the e-book is also available.

Title: *The Snowy Day*
Written by: Ezra Jack Keats

Illustrated by: Ezra Jack Keats
Publisher: Viking Press (1962)
E-book Publisher: Weston Woods Studios, Inc.
Age Range: 3 and up

This award-winning book depicts a young boy's snowy adventure. To his dismay, the snowball tucked inside his pocket melts after he comes indoors.

The Caldecott award, title, and author are displayed at the beginning of the e-book. The reader must click on a button at the bottom of the page to advance to the next page. A pause button is present as well. Guitar music accompanies the text as it is read aloud. In the "read along" option, each word is highlighted word-by-word as it is read. The animations accurately correlate to the text (e.g., the boy smacking the tree with a stick and snow falling; the boy making snow angels; as the boy dreams of the sun melting the snow, a sun is displayed). A Spanish edition of the e-book is also available.

The following are interactive book apps of children's e-books.
The e-book app reviews are adapted from *Kirkus Reviews* at https://www.kirkusreviews.com/book-reviews/childrens-books/

Title: *Piccadilly's Circus*
Author: Ink Robin
Illustrated by: Adam Larkum
E-book Publisher: Ink Robin (2012)
Age Range: 2–8

This story's setting is the circus where characters learn the importance of appreciating others' talents after the ringmaster becomes ill and cannot perform his duties.

The illustrations operate like a virtual flannel board and include characters positioned in one place on the screen while performing a movement (e.g., balancing, swaying). The reader is able to dress characters in the ringmaster's clothes. Animations and sound correlate to the text (e.g., chirping crickets when bear has stage fright). Expression is used during the narration of the e-book. It includes "read it to me" and "read it myself" options.

Title: *Franklin Frog*
Written by: Emma Tranter
Illustrated by: Barry Tranter
E-book Publisher: Nosy Crow (2012)
Age Range: 2–5

This app is a mix of fiction and non-fiction regarding a frog's lifecycle.

Franklin the frog, who is able to speak in the story, travels through the land and pond. If the reader taps Franklin, he will state facts such as, "Frogs like to live in damp places." The reader can make Franklin jump, swim, capture food, and hibernate. When eggs are laid, the reader can help keep predators away. The story will repeat twice and includes two descendants of Franklin. Music, sound effects, and expressive narration are included. The illustrations are simplistic and include portions of circles or circles.

Title: *A Day in the Market*
Written by: Tobias Papa
Illustrated by: Isabel Roxas
E-book Publisher: Adarna House, Inc. (2013)
Age Range: 3–6

This bilingual e-book app tells the story of a little girl's first trip to the market with her grandmother where she experiences an authentic Filipino market.

Option controls at the beginning of the e-book allow children to select between English or Filipino languages in a "read to me" or "read alone" mode. Narration is provided by a young female; however, words are not highlighted during narration. Each page offers moving illustrations and interactive elements. For example, on one page, the reader helps the little girl get dressed. Each page provides arrow buttons for navigation. The arrows only appear after the text is read. Readers cannot navigate to prior pages.

Title: *Arthur's Birthday*
Written by: Marc Brown
Illustrated by: Marc Brown
Publisher: Little, Brown Books for Young Readers (1991)
E-book Publisher: Wanderful, Inc. (2013)
Age Range: 4–8

This bilingual e-book app, available in English and Spanish, tells the story of Arthur and Muffy who have planned their birthday parties on the same day. Arthur comes up with an idea to make both birthdays special.

Options at the beginning of the e-book provide "read to me" and "let me play" options as well as other options that adults can select. In the "read to me" mode, groups of words are highlighted as they are read aloud. There is a different narrator voice for each character in the story. The e-book plays by itself. There is no need for children to navigate through the pages. Each page provides animations. In the "let me play" mode, the story is narrated in the same manner as the "read to me" mode, but the "let me play" option allows children to tap on illustrations to make them interactive. This mode also provides arrows for navigation through the pages and permits children to tap individual words to hear them narrated.

Title: *You are Stardust*
Written by: Elin Kelsey
Illustrated by: Soyeon Kim
E-book Publisher: Owlkids Books (2012)
Age Range: 5–12

You are Stardust provides information on how everything in the world is connected. This e-book app has two reading options, "read to me" or "I'll read the story." Children can also select the "make your own diorama" button. The "read to me" mode provides text narrated by a female voice. The words are not highlighted as they are read. Each page contains moving animations and children swipe each page to navigate.

Title: *How Rocket Learned to Read*
Written by: Tad Hills
Illustrated by: Tad Hills
Publisher: Schwartz & Wade Books (2010)
E-book Publisher: Random House Digital Inc.
Age Range: 3–6

The little dog, Rocket, loves exploring the world. One day, a little bird shows up and announces that Rocket is her student. Rocket has no interest in going to school, but the little bird is determined to teach Rocket to read. Eventually, the bird's persistence pays off when Rocket learns to love reading.

The title page of the book provides three options: "read to me," "read it myself," and "games." Additionally, from this page, children can learn more about the author/illustrator or "More from Random House Children's Books." Throughout the e-book, each page displays a home, question, and an arrow button for easy navigation. The question button provides page hints. For example, children can select, "Tap Words," a function that allows them to tap individual words on the page that are narrated for them. The arrow button allows children to navigate forward and backward in the book. During the "read to me" option, each word is highlighted as it is read aloud by a soft, friendly, female voice. Each page also features animation. For example, Rocket is running on one page and napping and snoring on another page. Additionally, throughout the book, children can interact with many of the illustrations (e.g., children can touch a sign that says, "Class Starts Today," and it will read the words to them). The "read it myself" mode provides the same features as the "read to me" mode except there is no narration. Children still have the option to tap on words and have them narrated. In the "games" mode, children have an option to play "Bird's Words" or "Alphabet Drop." "Bird's Words" provides practice in learning sight words and "Alphabet Drop" provides practice with letter recognition and alphabetical order. The e-book does not contain a dictionary feature. At the end of the e-book, children have options to read the story again or to return to the main menu.

Title: *Wild about Books*
Written by: Judy Sierra
Illustrated by: Marc Brown
Publisher: Knopf, Borzoi Books (2004)
E-book Publisher: Random House Digital Inc.
Age Range: 4–7

Springfield librarian, Molly McGrew, mistakenly drives her bookmobile into the zoo where she introduces the animals to reading. During the adventure, she finds the perfect book for each animal. The animals go wild for their books.

The *Wild about Books* e-book provides sixteen different animated and interactive screens. Children can tilt the iPad for a 3-D experience. Throughout the book, children can tap and swipe animals and illustrations for animation effects. A navigation wheel provides options to move through the book to visit different pages. Children can select the "read to me" option and have the book read aloud or can turn this feature off. There is also an option to turn background sounds off or on. Each page provides arrow and navigation buttons. In the "read to me" mode, individual words are highlighted as they are read aloud by a perky, female voice. There is not an option to tap on individual words to have them read aloud. At the end of the e-book, children have options to learn about the illustrator or author or to read the book again.

Title: *The Poky Little Puppy*
Written by: Janette Sebring Lowrey
Illustrated by: Gustaf Tenggren
Publisher: Simon and Shuster, Little Golden Books (1942)
E-book Publisher: Random House Digital Inc.
Age Range: 4 and up

Instead of playing with his siblings when they sneak out to play, the Poky Little Puppy decides to find his own adventures. He avoids punishment from his mother when his siblings go out without permission. Throughout the book, the Poky Little Puppy finds ways to avoid getting into trouble. At the end of the book, the Poky Little Puppy's siblings get rewarded for doing a good deed, but the Poky Little Puppy arrives too late and is the only puppy that does not get a treat.

The Poky Little Puppy e-book provides three different reading options. Children can have the book read aloud to them, they can read on their own, or adults and/or children can record their own voice to read the story. In the "read to me" mode, individual words are highlighted and narrated by a cheerful female voice. All modes allow children to tap and hear individual words within the story. Each page also contains animation where illustrations move and/or can be manipulated by children. For example, on one page, children have the option of touching a caterpillar to make it move. On another page, when children touch one of the puppies, a barking sound occurs. Each page also contains a magnifying glass. Once tapped, it displays and narrates a question (e.g., "Can you tap the Poky Little Puppy's tail?"). To navigate through the pages, children must use their finger to swipe the page. At the end of the story, children have the option to read the story again or to go to the stickers tab.

Title: *Go Clifford Go!*
Written by: Norman Bridwell
Illustrated by: Norman Bridwell
Publisher: Scholastic, Cartwheel Books (2010)
E-book Publisher: Scholastic Inc.
Age Range: 2 and up

Throughout the story, Clifford encounters many different vehicles, such as a boat, helicopter, skateboard, and bicycle that are in motion. At the end of the story, Clifford finds a way to put himself in motion. The story contains repetition of words on each page.

At the beginning of the e-book, children can select a setting function (i.e., off or on) and listen to the book with music and/or narration. In the narration mode, individual words are highlighted as they are read aloud. When the narration is turned off, children can still tap on the words to hear the text on the page. The e-book contains touch and tilt animation. Children can touch the pictures and words to hear the story and see characters move, and they can tilt their devices to watch illustrations move (e.g., swaying trees and rolling waves). Children use their fingers to swipe the pages to navigate forward and backward. At the end of the story, children can play an interactive game.

Title: *Pop Out! The Tale of Peter Rabbit*
Written by: Beatrix Potter
Illustrated by: Beatrix Potter
Publisher: Frederick Warne and Co. (1902)
E-book Publisher: Loud Crow Interactive
Age Range: 3 and up

This classic tale tells the story of a mischievous rabbit who does not heed his mother's orders to stay out of the Mr. McGregor's garden. While in the garden, Peter gets into all sorts of trouble and almost gets captured by the farmer.

Pop Out! The Tale of Peter Rabbit offers interactive features including pull tabs on each page. From the beginning screen, children can select from "read to me" or "read to myself" features. In the "read to me" feature, individual words are highlighted as a British female voice reads the text. Children can tap their finger and select single words that are pronounced. The pull-tabs on each page, as well as the touch and drag objects, make the illustrations come to life. Children can use their finger to swipe the screen to navigate from page to page.

Title: *I Love You Through and Through*
Written by: Bernadette Rossetti-Shustak
Illustrated by: Caroline Jayne Church
Publisher: Scholastic (2005)
E-book Publisher: Scholastic Inc.
Age Range: Birth-3

This e-book features a young boy and his teddy bear and is told in rhyme. The simple text that describes various emotions and moods is suitable for the very young.

Music, sound effects, and narration are incorporated into this interactive e-book. In the "read to me" option, each word is individually highlighted as it is read aloud and a pause option is included. Narration and music may be turned off in order to read on your own. Animated interactions include "touch and tilt" to engage young readers. When objects or characters are touched or the device is tilted, lively animations occur.

Title: *Goodnight Moon*
Written by: Margret Wise Brown
Illustrated by: Clement Hurd
Publisher: HaperCollins (1947)
E-book Publisher: Loud Crow Interactive
Age Range: 1 and up

This classic story has been re-imagined to create an interactive e-book for young children. The bunny's bedtime routine comes to life in the "great green room" while saying goodnight.

This e-book includes "read-to-me," "auto-play," and "read myself" options. Each word is highlighted as it is read aloud. The music and narration are soothing, which fit with the night-time routine outlined in the text. The "tilt and touch" features offer a variety of animations correlated directly with the text to foster comprehension (e.g., the cow jumps over the moon; the red balloon floats; the quiet old lady whispers "hush" while rocking on the chair). At the end of the story, all characters and objects are calm as the bunny goes to sleep.

E-book Publishers

Adarna House
Adarna House is a producer of educational products and multilingual books, specializing in the promotion of the Filipino language. Information about their services can be found at http://adarnahouse.com.ph/

Loud Crow Interactive
Loud Crow Interactive has developed interactive digital children's books available in a variety of mobile platforms. More information about their books can be found at their website http://www.loudcrow.com

Nosy Crow
Nosy Crow is an independent company that publishes interactive apps and children's literature for ages 0–14. Information may be obtained at http://nosycrow.com/about

Owlkids Books
Owlkids Books is a publisher of children's books. They offer a few interactive e-book apps. Additional information about Owlkids Books can be found at http://www.owlkidsbooks.com

Random House Digital, Inc. iPad Apps
Random House Digital, Inc. has created several animated e-books available for purchase on iTunes. To view the e-books, you can visit the Random House Digital Apps website at http://www.rhkidsapps.com/

Scholastic Inc.
Scholastic BookFLIX

Scholastic BookFLIX is an online resource for children's e-books geared to pre-K through 3rd grade. Scholastic and Weston Woods provide both fiction and nonfiction e-books categorized in themed pairs based upon the following categories: "Animals and Nature," "Earth and Sky," "People and Places," "A, B, C's and 1, 2, 3's," "Family and Community," and "Music and Rhythm." For each pair of books, various resources are provided: corresponding games (e.g., Fact or Fiction), meet the author for the fiction text, additional websites related to the theme, and lesson plans for educators. A free 30-day trial is available upon request at http://teacher.scholastic.com/products/bookflixfreetrial/

Scholastic: Mobile Apps for iPad, iPhone, iPod Touch, Android, and Windows Phone
Apps of e-books for young children may be purchased at the following website http://www.scholastic.com/apps

Wanderful Interactive Storybooks
Wanderful, Inc. provides interactive e-books apps for stories from Marc Brown, Stan and Jan Berenstain, and a few other authors. Information about the apps can be found at http://www.wanderfulstorybooks.com

Weston Woods Studios, Inc.
Weston Woods Studios Inc. began partnering with Scholastic Inc. in 1996. Their mission is to provide high-quality learning tools to promote children's love of literature and reading. Visit http://westonwoods.scholastic.com/products/westonwoods/mission.asp for more information.

References

Baird, C., & Henninger, M. (2011). Serious play, serious problems: Issues with eBook applications. *Cosmopolitan Civil Societies Journal, 3*(2), 1–17.
Berk, L. E., & Winsler, A. (1999). *Scaffolding children's learning: Vygotsky and early childhood education*. Washington, DC: National Association for the Education of Young Children.
Birkerts, S. (1995). *The Gutenberg elegies*. New York, NY: Fawcett Columbine.
Block, C. C., & Duffy, G. (2008). Research on teaching comprehension. In C. C. Block & S. R. Parris (Eds.), *Comprehension instruction: Research-based best practices* (pp. 19–37). New York, NY: Guilford Press.
Block, C. C., & Pressley, M. (2007). Best practices in teaching comprehension. In L. B. Gambrell, L. M. Morrow, & M. Pressley (Eds.), *Best practices in literacy instruction* (3rd ed., pp. 220–242). New York, NY: Guilford Press.
Bruner, J. S. (1978). The role of dialogue in language acquisition. In A. Sinclair, R. J. Jarvella, & W. J. M. Levelt (Eds.), *The child's conception of language* (pp. 241–256). New York, NY: Springer-Verlag.
Bus, A. G., Verhallen, M. J. A. J., & de Jong, M. T. (2009). How onscreen storybooks contribute to early literacy. In A. G. Bus & S. B. Neuman (Eds.), *Multimedia and literacy development: Improving achievement for young learners* (pp. 153–167). New York, NY: Routledge.
Cavanaugh, T. (2002). Ebooks and accommodations: Is this the future of print accommodations? *Council for Exceptional Children, 35*(2), 56–61.

Ciampa, K. (2012). Improving grade one students' reading motivation with online electronic storybooks. *Journal of Educational Media and Hypermedia, 21*(1), 5–28.

Clark, R., & Mayer, R. (2003/2008). *E-learning and the science of instruction*. San Francisco, CA: Pfieffer.

de Jong, M. T., & Bus, A. G. (2002). Quality of book-reading matters for emergent readers: An experiment with the same book in a regular or electronic format. *Journal of Educational Psychology, 94*, 145–155.

de Jong, M. T., & Bus, A. G. (2003). How well suited are electronic books to supporting literacy? *Journal of Early Childhood Literacy, 3*(2), 147–164.

de Jong, M. T., & Bus, A. G. (2004). The efficacy of electronic books in fostering kindergarten children's emergent story understanding. *Reading Research Quarterly, 39*(4), 378–393.

Doty, D. E., Popplewell, S. R., & Byers, G. O. (2001). Interactive CD ROM storybooks and young readers' reading comprehension. *Journal of Research on Computing in Education, 33*, 374–384.

Falconer, J. (2011). The 40-year history of e-books. *The Next Web*. http://thenextweb.com/shareables/2011/03/17/the-40-year-history-of-ebooks-illustrated/?fromcat=all.

Garner, R., Gillingham, M. G., & White, C. S. (1989). Effects of "seductive details" on macroprocessing and microprocessing in adults and children. *Cognition and Instruction, 6*(1), 41–57.

Glasgow, J. N. (1996). It's my turn! Part II: Motivating young readers using CD-ROM storybooks. *Learning and Leading with Technology, 24*(4), 18–22.

Grant, J. M. A. (2004). Are electronic books effective in teaching young children reading and comprehension? *International Journal of Instructional Media, 31*(3), 303–308.

Grimshaw, S., Dungworth, N., McKnight, C., & Morris, A. (2007). Electronic books: Children's reading and comprehension. *British Journal of Educational Technology, 38*(4), 583–599.

Guernsey, L. (2011). Are ebooks any good? *School Library Journal, 57*(6), 28–32.

Hammett, L. A., van Kleeck, A., & Huberty, C. J. (2003). Patterns of parents' extratextual interactions during book sharing with preschool children: A cluster analysis study. *Reading Research Quarterly, 38*(4), 442–468.

Higgins, N., & Hess, L. (1999). Using electronic books to promote vocabulary development. *Journal of Research on Computing in Education, 31*, 425–430.

Houston, C. (2011). Digital books for digital natives: A tour of open access children's digital literature collections. *Children and Libraries: The Journal of the Association for Library Service to Children, 9*(3), 39–42.

Justice, L. M., & Kaderavek, J. (2002). Using shared storybook reading to promote emergent literacy. *Teaching Exceptional Children, 34*(4), 8–13.

Karchmer-Klein, R., & Shinas, V. H. (2012). Guiding principles for supporting new literacies in your classroom. *The Reading Teacher, 65*(5), 288–293.

Karemaker, A., Pitchford, N. J., & O'Malley, C. (2008). Using wholeword multimedia software to support literacy acquisition: A comparison with traditional books. *Educational & Child Psychology, 25*(3), 97–118.

Kim, J. E., & Anderson, J. (2008). Mother-child shared reading with print and digital texts. *Journal of Early Childhood Literacy, 8*(2), 213–245.

Korat, O., & Or, T. (2010). How new technology influences parent-child interaction: The case of e-book reading. *First Language, 30*(2), 139–154.

Korat, O., & Shamir, A. (2004). Do Hebrew electronic books differ from Dutch electronic books? A replication of a Dutch content analysis. *Journal of Computer Assisted Learning, 20*, 257–268.

Korat, O., & Shamir, A. (2007). Electronic books versus adult readers: Effects on children's emergent literacy as a function of social class. *Journal of Computer Assisted Learning, 23*(3), 248–259.

Labbo, L. D., & Kuhn, M. R. (2000). Weaving chains of affect and cognition: A young child's understanding of CD-ROM talking books. *Journal of Literacy Research, 32*, 187–210.

Labbo, L. D., Leu, D. J., Kinzer, C., Teale, W. H., Cammack, D., & Soteriou, J. K. (2003). Teacher wisdom stories: Cautions and recommendations for using computer-related technologies for literacy instruction. *The Reading Teacher, 57*(3), 300–304.

Lamb, A., & Johnson, L. (2011). Nurturing a new breed of reader: Five real-world issues. *Teacher Librarian, 39*(1), 56–63.

Larson, L. C. (2010). Digital readers: The next chapter in e-book reading and response. *The Reading Teacher, 64*(1), 15–22.

Lewin, C. (1996). *Improving talking book software design: Evaluating the supportive tutor.* Bradford, England: Center for Information Technology in Education, The Open University.

Lewis, R. B., & Ashton, T. M. (1999). Interactive books on CD-ROM and reading instruction for students with learning disabilities: What are your views? *Conference proceedings on-line: 1999 "Technology and Persons with Disabilities" Conference.* http://www.dinf.org/csun_99/session0027.html.

Lin, C. (2010). E-book flood for changing EFL learners' reading attitudes. *US-China Education Review, 11*(72), 36–43.

Lutz, S. L., Guthrie, J. T., & Davis, M. H. (2006). Scaffolding for engagement in elementary school reading instruction. *The Journal of Education Research, 100*(1), 3–20.

Matthew, K. (1996). What do children think of CD-ROM storybooks? *Texas Reading Report, 18,* 6.

Matthew, K. (1997). A comparison of the influence of interactive CD ROM storybooks and traditional print storybooks on reading comprehension. *Journal of Research on Computing in Education, 29,* 263–275.

Maynard, S. (2010). The impact of e-books on young children's reading habits. *Publishing Research Quarterly, 26*(4), 236–248.

Medwell, J. (1996). Talking books and reading. *Reading, 30*(1), 41–46.

Medwell, J. (1998). The talking books projects: Some further insights into the use of talking books to develop reading. *Reading, 32*(1), 3–8.

Moody, A. K. (2010). Using electronic books in the classroom to enhance emergent literacy skills in young children. *Journal of Literacy and Technology, 11*(4), 22–52.

National Association of Young Children, & Fred Rogers Center for Early Learning and Children's Media. (2012). Technology and interactive media as tools in early childhood programs serving children from birth through age 8. http://www.naeyc.org/files/naeyc/file/positions/PS_technology_WEB2.pdf. Accessed 7 Jan 2013.

National Institute for Reading. (2006). *Put reading first* (3rd ed.). Washington, DC: The National Institute for Reading.

No Child Left Behind Act of 2001. PL107-110, 115 Stat. 1425, 20 U.S.C. § 630 *et seq.*

Pearman, C., & Chang, C. (2010). Scaffolding or distracting: CD-ROM storybooks and young readers. *TechTrends, 54*(4), 52–57.

Pearson, P. D., & Duke, N. K. (2002). Comprehension instruction in the primary grades. In C. C. Block & M. Pressley (Eds.), *Comprehension instruction: Research-based best practices* (pp. 247–258). New York, NY: Guilford Press.

Prensky, M. (2001). Digital natives: Digital immigrants. *On the Horizon, 9*(5), 1–9.

Rhodes, J. A., & Milby, T. M. (2007). Teacher-created electronic books: Integrating technology to support readers with disabilities. *The Reading Teacher, 61*(3), 255–259.

Roskos, K., & Brueck, J. (2009). The ebook as a learning object in an online world. In A. G. Bus & S. B. Neuman (Eds.), *Multimedia and literacy development: Improving achievement for young learners* (pp. 77–88). New York, NY: Routledge.

Roskos, K., Brueck, J., & Widman, S. (2009). Investigating analytic tools for e-book design in early literacy learning. *Journal of Interactive Online Learning, 8*(3), 1541–4914.

Schugar, H. R., Smith, C. A., & Schugar, J. T. (2013). Teaching with interactive picture e-books in grades k-6. *The Reading Teacher, 66*(8), 615–624.

Scott, J., Skobel, B., & Wells, J. (2008). *The word conscious classroom: Building the vocabulary readers and writers need.* New York, NY: Scholastic Theory into Practice Series.

Shamir, A., & Korat, O. (2006). How to select CD-ROM storybooks for young children: The teacher's role. *The Reading Teacher, 59,* 532–544.

Shamir, A., & Korat, O. (2007). Developing an educational e-book for fostering kindergarten children's emergent literacy. *Computers in Schools, 24*(1/2), 125–143.

Shamir, A., & Korat, O. (2009). The educational electronic book as a tool to support children's emergent literacy. In A. G. Bus & S. B. Neuman (Eds.), *Multimedia and literacy development: Improving achievement for young learners* (pp. 168–181). New York, NY: Routledge.

Shamir, A., & Shlafer, I. (2011). E-books effectiveness in promoting phonological awareness and concept about print: A comparison between children at risk for learning disabilities and typically developing kindergarteners. *Computers & Education, 57*(3), 1989–1997.

Shamir, A., Korat, O., & Fellah, R. (2013). Promoting emergent literacy of children at risk for learning disabilities: Do e-books make a difference? In A. Shamir & O. Korat (Eds.), *Technology as a support for literacy achievements for children at risk* (pp. 173–186). New York, NY: Springer.

Shiratuddin, N., & Landoni, M. (2002). E-Books, e-publishers and e-book builders for children. *The New Review of Children's Literature and Librarianship, 8*(1), 71–88.

Smith, F. (2004). *Understanding reading: A psycholinguistic analysis of reading and learning to read*. Florence, Kentucky: Routledge.

Stahl, S. A. (2006). Understanding shifts in reading and its instruction. In K. A. D. Shahl & M. C. McKenna (Eds.), *Reading research at work: Foundations of effective practice* (pp. 45–75). New York, NY: Guilford Press.

Trushell, J., Maitland, A., & Burrell, C. (2003). Pupils' recall of an interactive storybook on CD-ROM. *Journal of Assisted Learning, 19*(1), 80–89.

Tuget, Y., & Tuncer, U. (2011). Literacy development in multicultural settings with digital dual-language books. *The Journal of Language and Linguistic Studies, 7*(2), 117–143.

Verhallen, M., Bus, A. G., & de Jong, M. T. (2006). The promise of multimedia stories for kindergarten children at risk. *Journal of Educational Psychology, 98,* 410–419.

Vygotsky, L. (1978). *Mind in society*. Cambridge, MA: Harvard University Press.

Web Content Accessibility Guidelines (WCAG) 2.0. (2008). W3C 2008, Web ContentAccessibility Guidelines (WCAG) 2.0. http://www.w3.org/TR/2008/REC-WCAG20-20081211/. Accessed 13 April 2013.

Web Content Accessibility Guidelines (WCAG) 2.0. (2012). Web Content Accessibility Guidelines Overview. http://www.w3.org/WAI/intro/wcag. Accessed 13 April 2013.

Whitehurst, G. J., & Lonigan, C. J. (1998). Child development and emergent literacy. *Child Development, 69*(3), 848–872.

Yoon, T. (2013). Beyond the traditional reading class: The application of an e-book in EFL English classroom. *International Journal of Research Studies in Language Learning, 2*(1), 17–26.

Zucker, T. A., Moody, A. K., & McKenna, M. C. (2009). The effects of electronic books on pre-kindergarten-to-grade 5 students' literacy and language outcomes: A research synthesis. *Journal of Educational Computing Research, 40*(1), 47–87.

Children's Literature

Hills, T. (2010). *How Rocket learned to read: Read and listen edition [NOOK Book]*. New York, NY: Random House Children's Books.

Sierra, J. (2004). *Wild about books*. New York: Random House Digital, Inc., Knopf, Borzio Books.

Photo Credit: Ka-msiyara Corbett

Chapter 3
Technology-based Literacies for Young Children: Digital Literacy through Learning to Code

Elizabeth R. Kazakoff

Abstract Most research on literacies afforded by new technologies focuses primarily on older children and adolescents. However, developmentally-appropriate technologies exist for young children, and some technologies designed for older children may be used with a younger age group through adapted learning expectations and curricular supports. This chapter focuses on an area of technology education traditionally seen as academically advanced—learning to code—and describes how learning to code in early childhood can provide a pathway for young children to express themselves creatively as well as gain problem-solving and critical thinking skills through using technological tools added to existing classroom curricula. Innovative technologies used with age-appropriate curricula can teach children about the digital elements of our world along with skills that are beneficial beyond the computer screen.

Keywords Early childhood · Computer programming · Digital literacy · Literacy · Storytelling · Technology · Learning to code

Programming in Kindergarten

Amanda moves her cursor around the screen to click on the paintbrush icon next to the orange cat. A window opens with a selection of colors. She smiles as she spots pink (her favorite), clicks on the color, then the paint bucket icon, and again on her cat. She giggles as her cat turns pink and then returns to the main programming screen. Amanda browses the menu of programming blocks and selects a "green flag" for her cat followed by a "hide" icon and a "show" icon. She clicks the "green flag" and watches what happens. Her cat disappears from view then reappears. She smiles, excitedly claps her hands together, and asks classmates to come see her program. Amanda then systematically adds alternating "hide" and "show" icon blocks until she has a program almost as long as the screen. Every time she

---

E. R. Kazakoff (✉)
Tufts University, Medford, MA, USA
e-mail: elizabeth.kazakoff@tufts.edu

adds two more blocks, she plays the program by clicking the "green flag" and mouths quietly "invisible, visible, invisible, visible" in time with the cat's performed actions.

When the teacher walks by, Amanda asks, "Do you want to see my movie?" The teacher responds, "Sure, I would love to see your program," attempting to reinforce the correct language. "What does the character in your program do?"

Amanda responds enthusiastically, "I made a blinking pink cat!"

This was the first time Amanda, age five, programmed a computer, and this was accomplished during her first three months of kindergarten.

Reading, writing, arithmetic … and algorithms? Technology in general, and learning to code, in particular, are not typically covered by kindergarten through grade two curricula. This chapter explores the changing role of technology in the early childhood curriculum by discussing digital literacy and learning to code in the early childhood classroom. First, this chapter will begin with an overview of early childhood technology policies and standards. Then, this chapter will focus on digital literacy, in particular (1) the lack of cohesive definitions of digital literacy and related terms when talking about young children and (2) the use of computer programming/learning to code as a way to teach digital literacy in the early childhood classroom. Finally, a new programming language for young children, ScratchJr, will be used as an illustrative example of digital literacy through learning to code.

Early Childhood Technology Policies and Standards

Both from an economic and a developmental standpoint, educational interventions that begin in early childhood are associated with lower costs and longer-lasting effects than interventions that begin later in childhood (Cuhna and Heckman 2007; Reynolds et al. 2011). Preliminary research suggests that children who are exposed to STEM (Science, Technology, Engineering, and Math) curricula, including programming languages, at an early age demonstrate fewer gender-based stereotypes regarding STEM careers (Metz 2007; Steele 1997) and fewer obstacles entering these fields (Madill et al. 2007; Markert 1996). However, the limited research on new technologies for young children has hampered widespread introduction of developmentally-appropriate, new technologies into the classroom in the United States, although, there is a NAEYC/Fred Rogers policy statement on technology for young children as a reference point (see NAEYC & Fred Rogers 2012). However, internationally, more attention has been paid to integrating computing education in the curriculum starting in the early grades. In particular, the United Kingdom announced inclusion of technology design and computing components in their curriculum starting August 2014 (Coughlan 2013; Department of Education 2013a, b). Estonia has also implemented a coding curriculum, beginning in the first grade (O'Dell 2012).

Consulting classic developmental theory, from a constructivist perspective, children learn by doing, by being engaged with and manipulating their environments (Piaget 1928). Inspired by Jean Piaget's work, Seymour Papert created one of the first computer programming languages for children, Logo, and built on Piaget's theory of constructivism by changing the "V" to an "N" yielding the term construc*tion*ism (Papert 1991) to consider what constructivism meant in the digital age.

Lev Vygotsky's theory of development stressed the social-cultural influences on children—in particular, the impact adults have on enhancing and directing children's learning and on cultural artifacts as teaching tools (1978). Vygotsky's ideas are relevant today when considering children under 8 years old are not purchasing their own technology and, therefore, teachers and parents play a key role in introducing children to technological tools (Gutnick et al. 2010). For young children who are in the developmental process of learning how to work with others, the design features of certain types of technological tools can promote social and prosocial development (Bers 2012).

Early work with technology and young children has shown that computers may serve as catalysts for social interaction in early childhood education classrooms (Clements 1999) and that children have twice as many interactions in front of the computer than when they are doing other classroom activities (Svensson 2000). Children are also more likely to go to their peers for help when using the computer, even when an adult is present, thus increasing the amount of peer collaboration in the classroom (Wartella and Jennings 2000). Research specifically on computer programming environments supports the argument that children's computer programming with age-appropriate materials allows them to learn and apply concepts such as abstraction, automation, analysis, decomposition, and iterative design (Lee et al. 2011; Mioduser and Levy 2010; Mioduser et al. 2009; Resnick 2006; Resnick et al. 2009).

The current American Academy of Pediatrics (AAP) position statement, however, still defines "screen time" as television viewing, as it did a decade earlier, despite massive changes in technology such as tablet computers and mobile devices (AAP 1999, 2011). With this limited definition still in place, the AAP continues their recommendation of no screens before the age of two and limited screen time for young children. One of the key reasons for this recommendation is lack of peer-reviewed research on interactive media to demonstrate its educational or developmental effectiveness (AAP 2011).

The field of technology tools for young children is constantly changing, and there is very little research or agreement among parents, educators, and researchers as to the best recommendations for this kind of media use (AAP 2011; Gutnick et al. 2010). However, the screens on new digital technologies for children are now far more interactive than conventional TV screens ranging from iPad and Android apps to programming languages (Scratch, http://scratch.mit.edu), to robotics (Mindstorms and WeDo, http://www.legoeducation.com). With these and other technological tools, children are not just consuming media; they are capable of interacting with digital devices and producing digital content as well (Bers 2010). The International Reading Association states that literacy in today's world requires proficiency in new literacies, and literacy educators have a responsibility to integrate these new technologies into their curricula (IRA 2009). But what do terms like *technology literacy*, *digital literacy*, and *new literacy* mean in early childhood?

Definitions of Literacy in the Digital Age

There are many terms to describe the changing face of literacy (e.g., new literacy, new literacies, technology literacy, digital literacy, ICT literacy) with overlapping and conflicting definitions. However, despite increasing technology use by young children, definitions of digital literacy and these related terms tend to be defined primarily with older children and adults in mind. The definitions do not take into consideration the specific needs of the under-eight demographic (Barron et al. 2011). For example, *A New Literacies Sampler* points out "typical" examples of new literacies as "video gaming, fan fiction writing, weblogging, using websites, social practices involved in mobile computing" (Knobel and Lankshear 2007, p. 1). Almost none of these tasks are applicable to early childhood. In terms of U.S. government policy on digital literacy, Sect. 9.3 of the National Broadband Plan states that there is no universal definition of digital literacy, and the definition is always evolving. The statement notes someone in fourth grade does not need the same skills as an adult, but does not mention younger children. The National Broadband Plan summarizes digital literacy as skills to find, evaluate, create, and communicate information (FCC 2010).

The term "new literacy studies" has been used to describe the discipline of studying new types of literacy beyond reading and writing in the context of popular culture (Gee 2010a). New literacies, however, are defined in different ways for different people (Leu 2010), and new literacies lack concise and consistent definitions, which are holding researchers back in their discussions and studies of new literacies: what they are, what they mean, their impact, and the tools children need for success (Leu 2010). Knobel and Lankshear state that new literacies are not just about new technologies; they must also contain "ethos." For example, Knobel and Lankshear argue that just taking a classic task, such as writing with a pen and turning it into typing online, is not a "new literacy" because new literacies are collaborative, participatory, constructive, and user-centered (Knobel and Lankshear 2007).

In the current literature, the term "digital literacy" tends be discussed in conjunction with, or under the umbrella of, "new literacies." The term "digital literacy" was, by many accounts, originally defined by Paul Gilster (1997) as "the ability to understand and use information in multiple formats from a wide range of sources when it is presented via computers" (p. 1). Of course, the technological world has changed dramatically since 1997, and we are no longer referring exclusively to computer-based presentations of information. Digital literacy has also been defined as "a set of habits through which children use computer technology for learning, work, socializing, and fun" (Ba et al. 2002, p. 1). Again, this definition focuses on computer use, not the breadth of digital tools available, but moves towards integrating more child-oriented motivations for use. More recently, James Paul Gee (2010b) described digital literacy as "different ways of using digital tools within different sorts of sociocultural practices" (p. 172). This definition encompasses more than just the computer as a tool and gives a social-cultural context to the behaviors in which children engage when using digital technologies.

Digital Literacy for Early Childhood

Digital literacy is a term used by many researchers, but it does not have a concrete definition. According to Aviram and Eshet-Alkalai (2006) "the discourse on this important subject has been practice-oriented, and lacks a sound integrative framework and theoretical foundation" (Abstract, para. 1). For the purpose of this chapter, a framework of digital literacy specifically for early childhood should be considered. A model of digital literacy in early childhood must take into consideration the cognitive level of children, preschool to second grade, and stress the need to examine and understand a child's level of executive function skills; in particular, a child's ability to self-regulate his or her interaction with and reaction to digital media use, as children of different ages manifest a great deal of variability in levels of self-regulation throughout early childhood (Blair and Diamond 2008; Bodrova et al. 2011; McClelland et. al. 2007).

With digital literacy for young children in mind, Table 3.1 draws from the ideas of Yoram Eshet-Alkali & colleague's conceptual model of digital literacy (Aviram and Eshet-Alkalai 2006, Eshet-Alkalai 2004, Eshet-Alkalai and Chajut 2009) combined with Marina Bers's Positive Technological Development Framework (Bers 2007, 2010, 2012), to create an outline of digital literacy specifically for children in preschool to second grade.

Yoram Eshet-Alkalai and colleagues (Aviram and Eshet-Alkalai 2006; Eshet 2005; Eshet-Alkalai 2004) have created an extensive model of digital literacy that encompasses cognitive skills, rather than just functional skills. This model is based on six skills, in sum (Aviram and Eshet-Alkalai 2006):

1. Photo-visual Literacy—ability to understand graphically-presented information such as symbols, icons, and graphical user interfaces;
2. Reproduction Literacy—the combination of existing media to create new media;
3. Branching Literacy—ability to navigate hypermedia; (navigation of digital media is non-linear, branching requires good spatial skills to navigate information across many different pathways and not get "lost" in cyberspace);
4. Information Literacy—the use of critical thinking skills to decipher false, biased, and/or irrelevant information;
5. Socio-emotional Literacy—communication and collaboration skills in an online environment; and
6. Real-time Thinking Skills—ability to process and evaluate information in real-time (Eshet-Alkalai and Chajut 2009).

Research conducted around the framework was pilot tested on adolescents and adults (Eshet-Alkalai and Chajut 2010), and studies did not include anyone younger than high school. In addition, most of the components of this framework are targeted towards adolescents and adults who have the ability to read and write. However, one may use the simplified definitions outlined above (which intentionally disregard the adolescent and adult-oriented examples from the literature), combined with theories of early childhood development, to work towards a definition of digital literacy

Table 3.1 Digital literacy in early childhood. (Aviram and Eshet-Alkalai 2006; Bers 2007, 2010, 2012; Eshet-Alkalai 2004; Eshet-Alkalai and Chajut 2009)

Components of digital literacy in early Childhood	Targeted developmental areas	Influencing perspectives
Understanding & utilizing digital interfaces	Symbol understanding	Bers's *content creation*—engage in use of applications that work with text, video, audio, graphics, and animations
	Fine motor skills Hand-eye coordination Linguistic Social-emotional Social-cultural	Eshet-Alkali's *photo-visual literacy*—ability to work effectively with digital environments, such as user interfaces, that employ graphical communication
Non-linear navigation	Cognitive Symbol Understanding Linguistic	Eshet-Alkali's *Branching Literacy*—ability to construct knowledge by nonlinear navigation of the Internet and other hypermedia
Critical-thinking and problem-solving Skills in digital Domains	Cognitive Social-emotional	Eshet-Alkali's *Information Literacy*—ability to consume information critically and sort out false and biased information
Cooperative learning and play afforded by digital tools in early childhood	Social-emotional	Bers's *Collaboration*—working with others and willing to cooperate toward a shared task
	Social-cultural	Bers's *Community Building*—using technology to enhance the community and the quality of relationships among the people of that community; contribute to society by using and inventing new digital tools to solve social problems
		Bers's *Communication*—exchanging thoughts, opinions, or information by using technologies
		Eshet-Alkali's—*Social-Emotional Literacy*—ability to communicate effectively in online communication platforms
Creative design afforded by digital tools in early childhood	Social-emotional	Eshet-Alkali's *Reproductive Literacy*—ability to create new artwork by reproducing and manipulating preexisting digital text, visual, or audio pieces
	Social-cultural	Bers's *Content Creation*—engage users in applications that work with text, video, audio, graphics, and animation
	Fine-motor Skills	Bers's *Creativity*—ability to create and imagine original new ideas, forms, and methods for using new technologies
Digitally-enhanced communications in early childhood	Social-emotional	Bers's *Collaboration*—working with others and willing to cooperate toward a shared task
	Social-cultural	Bers's *Community Building*—using technology to enhance the community and the quality of relationships among the people of that community; contribute to society by using and inventing new digital tools to solve social problems
		Bers's *Communication*—exchanging thoughts, opinions, or information by using technologies
		Eshet-Alkali's *Social-Emotional Literacy*—ability to communicate effectively in online communication platforms

specifically for early childhood. Referring back to Table 3.1, this task is accomplished by combining Eshet-Alkalai, et al.'s work (Aviram and Eshet-Alkalai 2006; Eshet 2005; Eshet-Alkalai 2004; Eshet-Alkalai and Chajut 2009) with Marina Bers's Positive Technological Development Framework (PTD) (Bers 2007, 2010, 2012).

The core questions of PTD ask, "How can children use technology in positive ways to help themselves and the world?" and "How can educators and researchers develop programs that help children use technology to learn new things, to express themselves in creative ways, to communicate effectively, to take care of themselves and each other, and to contribute in positive ways to the self and the world?" (Bers 2007, 2012). The Positive Technological Development framework (PTD) is derived from the Positive Youth Development (PYD) framework combined with Papert's (1980) constructionism (Bers 2007). PTD emphasizes the developmental aspects of the Positive Youth Development six "C's" framework: caring, connection, contribution, competence, confidence, and character (Bers 2012; Lerner et al. 2005) and connects those "C's" to corresponding action-oriented "C's" that can be conducted within the realm of new technologies: communication, collaboration, community-building, content-creation, creativity, and conduct (Bers 2007, 2012).

Although the Positive Technological Development framework has been applied across age groups, early childhood is not the specific focus of the framework. Both PTD and Eshet-Alkalai, et al.'s Conceptual Model of Digital Literacy explore, discuss, and define experiences of older children and adolescents. When combined, the two perspectives address themes that are relevant to early childhood (i.e., understanding symbols, creativity, collaboration, building a sense of community, social-emotional development etc.). Furthermore, the two perspectives can be analyzed with early childhood development theory in mind, considering young children as producers, not only consumers, of digital content. These ideas are summarized in Table 3.1 above.

Why Digital Literacy in Schools?

Digital literacy is prone to the "Matthew Effect"—the rich get richer, the poor get poorer. The more one uses digital tools, the more adept one becomes with the tools. The less one uses the tools, the worse one gets or one stops using digital tools all together (Gee 2012). This point is particularly important for two reasons: (1) the notion of digital natives and (2) the digital divide.

The so-called digital natives (Prensky 2001) are children growing up in a world surrounded by new digital technologies. They will never know what life was like before technological tools like the Internet and iPads, the ability to pause television, or GPS navigation that prevents their parents from getting lost (Oblinger 2003; Prensky 2001; Tapscott 1998).

Though the term "digital native" (Prenksy 2001) is widely used, it is not universally applicable. Children from lower-income households are historically at a greater disadvantage compared to their peers in terms of accessing new technological tools. In addition to more limited access to expensive digital devices, children of lower-income households typically have less parental influence when choosing which digital media to access and, therefore, may be less likely to choose educational websites or apps (Gutnick et al. 2010).

North America has the highest Internet penetration in the world with 78.6% of the population having access (Internet World Stats 2012). However, Asia, has the largest percentage of Internet users in the world, with 44.8% of all Internet users globally; although, that only represents 27.5% of Asia's total population (Internet World Stats 2012). Africa has the lowest percentage of Internet users with 15.6% of their population with Internet access (Internet World Stats 2012). These numbers are important for perspective when considering the following USA-based information on young children's access to technology, as the global digital divide between developed and developing nations is much different than the digital divide within developed countries (Chen and Wellman 2004).

Although some studies estimate between 70 and 80% of households in the United States with children under 8 years old have computers (Common Sense Media 2011), the range actually varies by income, with around 48% of families who make less than $30,000 a year owning a computer to 91% of families who make over $75,000 per year owning a computer (Common Sense Media 2011). In addition, 10% of lower-income parents surveyed have a smart device (e.g., iPhone) versus 34% of upper-income parents. Only 2% of lower-income families have a tablet computer versus 17% of upper-income families, and 38% of lower-income parents are unfamiliar with the meaning of the term "app," compared with 3% of higher-income parents—47% of whom have downloaded apps for their children, compared to only 14% of the lower-income parents (Common Sense Media 2011).

Even though children in North America grow up in a world full of digital devices, this fact does not necessarily mean children understand their digital worlds. Research indicates that simply providing access to technology is not enough to encapsulate an understanding of technology. It is also important to understand the social context of the use of technology (Palfrey and Gasser 2008; Zillien and Hargittai 2009). Policies are in place to try to educate children about the technology around them, to decrease the discrepancies between higher- and lower-income households in technology use, and to teach skills that will help students be productive for the twenty-first century workforce (which will likely be filled with technology and engineering-focused careers).

The digital divide is a phenomenon that impacts digital literacy. Children who have more exposure to digital devices are likely to have more time to develop fluency. In the US, schools are a place where children who may not receive technology experiences at home may be able to gain more exposure and expertise with technological tools. However, even if schools are places where children have more opportunities to use digital tools or access the Internet, thus narrowing the digital divide to an extent, a new discrepancy develops called the participation gap (Jenkins 2008). The participation gap refers to what youth can accomplish with near constant access to the Internet versus youth with only school and library access (Jenkins 2008). New educational policies and initiatives, described in the first section, aim to stress the importance of teaching technology in schools, beginning in early childhood. The next section describes the development of tools for use in teaching digital literacy skills in the classroom.

Exploring Digital Literacy in Early Childhood with ScratchJr

ScratchJr is a graphical programming tool currently in development for kindergarten through second grade students. ScratchJr builds on the graphical programming language Scratch (Resnick 2007) which uses interconnecting on-screen blocks to program character animations. ScratchJr is uniquely focused on the developmental needs of 5- to 7-year-olds, such as emerging fine motor skills, reading ability, and self-regulation. The software could stand alone as a technology tool; however, the ScratchJr team has also created fun, engaging, curricular activities which complement and scaffold the software (Flannery et al. 2013). These activities encourage children to use the tool in ways they find personally relevant and motivating.

With ScratchJr, students can program their own interactive stories, games, animations, and simulations. By snapping together graphical programming blocks, children can create a story with characters that dance, play sounds, and interact with one another. In the process, children learn early math and literacy concepts and develop valuable problem-solving skills. At a high level, ScratchJr ultimately will have:

1. A developmentally-appropriate interface for children ages 5–7, with both touch screen and mouse options
2. Curriculum modules that meet federal and state standards for early childhood education
3. An online community for early childhood educators and parents to share resources and ideas

ScratchJr grows out of a constructivist tradition in which children learn by constructing knowledge, building on prior knowledge (Bruner 1961). Technology use is a way to put children in a child-centered, active-learning role, rather than a passive role (Ferguson 2001). Since computers were first introduced to schools, researchers have noted that they can be powerful tools for education, given their flexibility and adaptability. Computers have a way of being anything to anyone and are interactive rather than passive (Papert 1980). Constructivism speaks to engaging children in interactive, meaningful experiences rather than classroom experiences that are meant to directly impart the knowledge of the teacher into the child. With a constructivist tool, the child is allowed to play the role of problem-solver (Ferguson 2001).

At the core of constructivist theory is the idea that knowledge is constructed actively by the learner, not passively absorbed (Taber 2006). The ScratchJr curriculum provides children with an opportunity to construct their own programs and make connections between concepts they are already familiar with in their early childhood classroom (e.g., books, painting, and themes such as family and community) and programming an object's actions. The ScratchJr programming language is designed to have a low floor, with easily-accessible features for young children. With little-to-no instruction, children can find ways to paint their characters and program movement. The ScratchJr programming language also has a high ceiling. Projects can be made with up to four interconnected pages in order to create complex stories, plays, games, or animations, and programs can be made with repeats (similar to a loop) and broadcast messages (similar to a function call) in order to allow older children or experienced programmers to experiment with more advanced programming concepts. Projects can be as basic as one page with one character or as complex as four pages that automatically advance with dozens of characters that interact with each other.

Connecting Digital Literacy and Traditional Literacy Practices

Gee (2012) argues the pathway to digital literacy is the same as with traditional literacy–that interaction with adults is critical for foundational development of digital literacy skills. Adults demonstrate for children how digital tools are to be used actively, not passively, and connect these tools to content knowledge, problem solving, and creative thinking. The next section describes how ScratchJr was used to connect digital literacy and traditional literacy practices in the classroom, with teachers and researchers as guides. Building on one of the key aspects of the ScratchJr project—the ability to integrate ScratchJr into an existing curriculum—this section highlights how ScratchJr was used for teaching traditional literacy practices and digital literacy skills within the standard classroom curriculum.

ScratchJr was piloted in four kindergarten and one combined first/second grade classroom. This section explores the three classrooms (two kindergarten and the combined 1st/2nd grade classroom) that chose to use an author study lesson as their "final project." The two kindergarten classrooms were in a public school, and the combined first/second grade classroom was part of a university's laboratory school.

The children in each classroom (18–20 per class) were led through instructions of the ScratchJr interface for up to 1 h per day, up to 2 days per week, for eight lessons before their "final project" sessions. This took up to 2 months. For the final projects, children had sessions of 45–60 min with their ScratchJr laptops to create their project. One kindergarten classroom used Jonathan London's Froggy books, another kindergarten classroom used Dr. Seuss's library, and the combined first/second grade classroom chose Mo Willem's catalogue of books.

A ScratchJr researcher and 1–3 assistants taught all sessions. For the regular ScratchJr class sessions, the children were instructed on a component of the ScratchJr interface and how to use the component in a story scenario. For example, an intermediate lesson would proceed as follows: "A caterpillar, pig, and chicken want to race each other. What blocks do we need to make the characters race?" [The

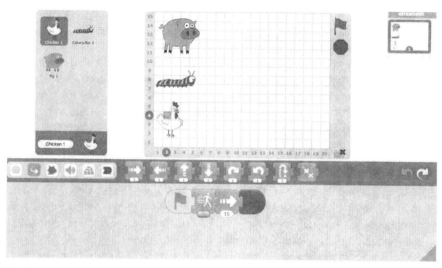

Fig. 3.1 ScratchJr "Race" program. The "chicken" program is displayed. Speed for each character is changed by using the *orange* "change speed" block.

correct response would be: start block, speed control block, move right block, end block]. After a whole class discussion and demonstration of the necessary programming blocks, the children each went to their own computers to build the program themselves. In the case of this race example, after building the program, children experimented with changing the speed of their characters to determine their own race winner (Fig. 3.1).

During the time ScratchJr researchers were not in the classrooms, teachers continued their planned curriculum, including studying books of interest to their students. The ScratchJr researchers discussed with the teachers which books may lend themselves well to ScratchJr projects, and the teachers and researchers had the students create their own plans for how to create a story in ScratchJr based on the books the class was studying. ScratchJr researchers provided teachers and children with paper copies of the ScratchJr characters and programming blocks for use in brainstorming programming ideas when children were not at the computer. In addition, classroom #3, the Dr. Seuss classroom, approached the storytelling with ScratchJr task after the ScratchJr developers had integrated an image-importing tool into the ScratchJr system. This allowed the teacher to provide students with actual pictures of the Cat in the Hat, Thing 1, and Thing 2 rather than the children having to draw their own or use a representation from ScratchJr's existing character library. In addition to characters and backgrounds, ScratchJr lends itself well to storytelling due to specific design considerations:

- Pages—In each ScratchJr project, up to four pages can be included.
- Linked Pages End Block—After a page is added, a "go to page #" block appears in the menu of ending blocks. This allows for navigation between pages in any order specified by using the end blocks.

- Text (add/change size/change color/program)—Text can be added to any page and manipulated by the programming blocks just like any other character. The size and color of text can also be changed.
- Characters/Background—Characters and backgrounds can be selected from a menu, easily color-filled to make them more personally relevant to students (changing skin tone, hair color, clothing color), or drawn on a blank canvas. In later versions of ScratchJr, characters and backgrounds can also be imported from outside sources.

In using ScratchJr, young children can work on digital literacy skills, tailored to their developmental level, as outlined in Table 3.1. A few examples are as follows:

- "Understanding & Utilizing Digital Interfaces"—When using ScratchJr, children are engaged in learning about and through a new digital interface. ScratchJr is designed to be a developmentally-appropriate interface, into consideration the fine and gross motor needs and cognitive levels of children ages 5–7.
- "Non-linear Navigation"—ScratchJr allows for children to create and navigate between four separate storytelling pages per program. Children may also code as many characters per page as they wish with unlimited programs per character.
- "Critical-thinking and Problem-solving Skills in Digital Domains"—When a child learns to program with ScratchJr, he or she is using problem-solving skills to "debug" unexpected results in the playback of his or her code. A child is also working towards iteratively solving the challenge of a given or self-directed goal.
- "Cooperative Learning and Play Afforded by Digital Tools in Early Childhood"—Children spontaneously, from the very first day, ask each other for guidance in how to use the ScratchJr tool and are eager to show off what areas of the ScratchJr interface they find. The ScratchJr version used in this study had a "gallery" setting where all (or just selected) projects from a classroom could be displayed for easy sharing.
- "Creative Design Afforded by Digital Tools in Early Childhood"—Children are engaged in creative problem solving when using ScratchJr. For example, children demonstrate flexibility if a character or background they want does not exist. A child can choose a different character or background to stand in for a desired element, customize an existing element, or draw something entirely new.
- "Digitally-enhanced Communications in Early Childhood"—Children use the ScratchJr platform to express their own ideas about storybooks (and in other lessons, about their own lives) to their peers, teachers, and parents. They were able to bring their imaginations and understanding of the curriculum to life through programmed animations of graphics and text.

When children create their stories in ScratchJr, they transfer their flat, drawn story to the screen, creating animations to convey their thoughts. The use of computers and a graphical programming language like ScratchJr to create storybooks does not necessarily take any additional time out of the traditional curriculum (the ScratchJr interface lessons in this study were delivered during "choice" time—when children are traditionally given 4–6 options of which activity in the classroom they would like to engage in, such as Lego®, computer games, reading nook, blocks, board

Fig. 3.2 "Froggy" ScratchJr story. This ScratchJr project builds on Jonathan London's Froggy books. Children drew or selected their characters. This child chose the frog character, which is highlighted on the *left* side of the screen, in the character select library. The highlighted character's program is the one on display *below* the animation area. This program tells the character to move side to side, say "hi," make a clapping sound, and then wait (six-tenths of a second). This child colored her frog a *bright green* and drew her own sailboat when she found there was only a tugboat character. On the *right*, there are four different pages created for her frog's day using ScratchJr's page feature.

games, sand table, and the pretend play kitchen) and provides a source of digital literacy lessons within the confines of the traditional curriculum. Classroom teachers have commented that children not only learn computational thinking, problem solving, and literacy skills, they also build flexibility (when they need to choose a character that is not an exact match for their thoughts) and sequencing skills (when they need to put the action blocks in order to fit their story). This parallels earlier studies that quantified changes in sequencing skills when using developmentally-appropriate programming languages in early childhood classrooms (Kazakoff and Bers 2012; Kazakoff et al. 2013).

Bearing in mind the connections between digital literacy and literacy described above, the next section presents and discusses two examples of the specific ScratchJr projects created by 5 to 7-year-old students.

Examples of ScratchJr Literacy Projects (Figs. 3.2 and 3.3)

In addition to the Froggy and Dinosaur stories depicted in Figs. 3.2 and 3.3, a third classroom was able to use a late-added feature to import photos. As noted, the teacher with this option chose to import photos from the Cat in the Hat books, and

Fig. 3.3 Edwina the Dinosaur ScratchJr story. This example reinterprets Mo Willems' story about Edwina the Dinosaur into a ScratchJr project. This child uses the *pink* dialogue boxes to have a conversation between Edwina the Dinosaur and the child characters about Edwina's delicious, chocolate chip cookies. This child drew her own Dinosaur character and used standard ScratchJr characters for children.

the children built ScratchJr programs where the boy and girl characters from the ScratchJr library interacted with the Cat in the Hat book characters.

Through re-creating stories in ScratchJr, kindergarten, first, and second grade students integrated traditional and digital literacy skills in unique and powerful ways. Children experimented with the concepts of narrative structure, sequencing actions, scene selection, dialogue between characters, and using text for describing the actions on the page. In addition to these traditional literacy areas, children engaged in artistic self-expression by creating their own characters, recoloring and redesigning existing characters, using flexible thinking to reimagine limited characters and backgrounds into their desired props, and drawing entirely new characters and backgrounds from a blank page.

Working on these traditional literacy and artistic self-expression skills are not unique to the ScratchJr software and curriculum. What is unique is that children were able to integrate complex ideas of computer programming into their stories to make them more vibrant, expressive, engaging, and interactive. In turn, the children were engaged in complex problem-solving exercises by breaking down their larger ideas and vision into pieces of code and using interconnecting programming blocks to bring their stories to life. Through integrating programming concepts into the creation of stories, the students learned key digital literacy skills, in developmentally-appropriate ways, within the context of traditional early childhood curricular themes.

Conclusion

This chapter discussed the idea of digital literacy in early childhood and the relative lack of definitions specifically designed for this age group. The graphical programming language, ScratchJr, was introduced as one possible tool for teaching digital literacy in the classroom, using a traditional literacy lesson as an example for integrating the technology tool into the general early childhood curriculum while also addressing digital literacy skills. Ways in which technology education is relevant to young children, especially in the unexpected area of learning to code, were introduced. When computers and other technological devices are used as tools in the classroom or at home—just like paintbrushes and blocks—they can be powerful devices for children to learn both traditional literacy and digital literacy concepts while simultaneously helping children further understand their digital worlds.

References

American Academy of Pediatrics. (1999). Media education. *Pediatrics, 104,* 341–342.
American Academy of Pediatrics. (2011). Media use by children younger than 2 years. *Pediatrics, 128*(5), 1–6.
Aviram, A., & Eshet-Alkalai, Y. (2006). Towards a theory of digital literacy: Three scenarios for the next steps. European Journal of Open, Distance and E-Learning. http://www.eurodl.org/materials/contrib/2006/Aharon_Aviram.htm. Accessed 16 July 2014.
Ba, H., Tally, W., & Tsikalas, K. (2002). Investigating children's emerging digital literacy. *Journal of Technology, Learning, and Assessment, 1*(4), 1–49.
Barron, B., Cayton-Hodges, G., Bofferding, L., Copple, C., Darling-Hammond, L., & Levine, M. (2011). *Take a giant step: A blueprint for teaching children in a digital age.* New York: The Joan Ganz Cooney Center at Sesame Workshop.
Bers, M. (2007). Positive technological development: Working with computers, children, and the Internet. *MassPsych, 51*(1), 5–7, 18–19.
Bers, M. (2010). Beyond computer literacy: Supporting youth's positive development through technology. *New Directions for Youth Development, 128,* 13–23.
Bers, M. (2012). *Designing digital experiences for positive youth development: From playpen to playground.* New York, NY: Oxford University Press.
Blair, C., & Diamond, A. (2008). Biological processes in prevention and intervention: The promotion of self-regulation as a means of preventing school failure. *Development and Psychopathology, 20,* 899–911.

Bodrova, E., Leong, D. J., & Akhutina, T. V. (2011). When everything new is well-forgotten old: Vygotsky/Luria insights in the development of executive functions. *New Directions for Child and Adolescent Development, 133*, 11–28.

Bruner, J. (1961). The act of discovery. *Harvard Educational Review, 31*(1), 21–32.

Chen, W., & Wellman, B. (2004). The global digital divide: Within and between countries. *It & Society, 1*(7), 39–45.

Clements, D. H. (1999). The future of educational computing research: The case of computer programming. *Information Technology in Childhood Education Annual, 1999*(1), 147–179. Norfolk, VA: Association for the Advancement of Computing in Education.

Common Sense Media. (2011). Zero to eight: Children's media use in America. http://www.commonsensemedia.org/ research/zero-eight-children's-media-use-america.

Coughlan, S. (2013). Curriculum changes 'to catch up with world's best.' BBC News. http://www.bbc.co.uk/news/education-23222068. Accessed 16 July 2014.

Cunha, F., & Heckman, J. (2007). The technology of skill formation. *American Economic Review, 97*(2), 31–47.

Department of Education. (2013a). Computing programmes of study: Key stages 1 and 2. http://www.computingatschool.org.uk/data/uploads/primary_national_curriculum_-_computing.pdf. Accessed 16 July 2014.

Department of Education. (2013b). The national curriculum in England. https://www.gov.uk/government/uploads/system/uploads/attachment_data/file/210969/NC_framework_document_-_FINAL.pdf. Accessed 16 July 2014.

Eshet, Y. (2005). Computers and Cognition: Cognitive Skills Employed in Digital Work. *IADIS Virtual Multi Conference on Computer Science and Information Systems*, 51–56.

Eshet-Alkalai, Y. (2004). Digital literacy: A conceptual framework for survival skills in the digital era. *Journal of Educational Multimedia and Hypermedia, 13*(1), 93–106.

Eshet-Alkalai, Y., & Chajut, E. (2009). Changes over time in digital literacy. *Cyberpsychology & Behavior, 12*(6), 713–715.

Eshet-Alkalai, Y., & Chajut, E. (2010). You can teach old dogs new tricks: The factors that affect changes over time in digital literacy. *Journal of Information Technology Education, 9*, 173–181.

FCC. (2010). National broadband plan. http://www.broadband.gov/download-plan/. Accessed 16 July 2014.

Ferguson, D. (2001). Technology in a constructivist classroom. *Information Technology in Childhood Education Annual, 2001*(1), 45–55. Norfolk, VA: Association for the Advancement of Computing in Education.

Flannery, L. P., Kazakoff, E. R., Bontá, P., Silverman, B., Bers, M. U., & Resnick, M. (2013). Designing ScratchJr: Support for early childhood learning through computer programming. In Proceedings of the 12th International Conference on Interaction Design and Children (IDC '13). ACM, New York, NY, USA, 1–10.

Gee, J. P. (2010a). *New digital media and learning as an emerging area and 'worked examples' as one way forward.* Cambridge, MA: MIT Press.

Gee, J. P. (2010b). A situated-sociocultural approach to literacy and technology. In E. A. Baker (Ed.), *The new literacies: Multiple perspectives on research and practice* (pp. 165–189). New York, NY: The Guilford Press.

Gee, J. P. (2012). The old and the new in the new digital literacies. *The Educational Forum, 76*(4), 418–420.

Gilster, P. (1997). *Digital literacy.* New York, NY: Wiley.

Gutnick, A. L., Robb, M., Takeuchi, L., & Kotler, J. (2010). *Always connected: The new digital media habits of young children.* New York, NY: The Joan Ganz Cooney Center at Sesame Workshop.

International Reading Association (IRA). (2009). *New Literacies and 21st century technologies: A position statement of the international reading association.* Newark, DE: IRA.

Internet World Stats. (2012). Internet users in the world distributed by world regions—2012 Q2. http://www.internetworldstats.com. Accessed 16 July 2014.

Jenkins, H. (March 2008). The participation gap: A conversation with media expert and MIT Professor Henry Jenkins. *NEA Today Magazine.* http://www.nea.org/home/15468.htm. Accessed 16 July 2014.

Kazakoff, E., & Bers, M. (2012). Programming in a robotics context in the kindergarten classroom: The impact on sequencing skills. *Journal of Educational Multimedia and Hypermedia, 21*(4), 371–391.

Kazakoff, E., Sullivan, A., & Bers, M. U. (2013). The effect of a classroom-based intensive robotics and programming workshop on sequencing ability in early childhood. *Early Childhood Education Journal, 41*(4), 245–255.

Knobel, M., & Lankshear, M. (2007). *A new literacies sampler.* New York, NY: Peter Lang.

Lee, I., Martin, F., Denner, J., Coulter, B., Allan, W., Erickson, J., Malyn-Smith, J., & Werner, L. (2011). Computational thinking for youth in practice. *ACM Inroads, 2*(1), 32–37.

Lerner, R. M., Lerner, J. V., Almerigi, J., Theokas, C., Phelps, E., Gestsdottir, S., Naudeau, S., Jelicic, H., Alberts, A. E., Ma, L., Smith, L. M., Bobek, D. L., Richman-Raphael, D., Simpson, I., Christiansen, E. D., & von Eye, A. (2005). Positive youth development, participation in community youth development programs, and community contributions of fifth grade adolescents: Findings from the first wave of the 4-H Study of Positive Youth Development. *Journal of Early Adolescence, 25*(1), 17–71.

Leu, D. J. (2010). Forward. In E. A. Baker (Ed.), *The new literacies: Multiple perspectives on research and practice* (pp. vii–xi). New York, NY: The Guilford Press.

Madill, H. M., Campbell, R. G., Cullen, D. M., Armour, M. A., Einsiedel, A. A., Ciccocioppo, A. L., & Coffin, W. L. (2007). Developing career commitment in STEM-related fields: Myth versus reality. In R. J. Burke, M. C. Mattis, & E. Elgar (Eds.), *Women and minorities in science, technology, engineering and mathematics: Upping the numbers* (pp. 210–244). Northampton, MA: Edward Elgar Publishing.

Markert, L. R. (1996). Gender related to success in science and technology. *The Journal of Technology Studies, 22*(2), 21–29.

McClelland, M. M., Cameron, C. E., Connor, C. M., Farris, C. L., Jewkes, A. M., & Morrison, F. J. (2007). Links between behavioral regulation and pre-schoolers' literacy, vocabulary and math skills. *Developmental Psychology, 43*, 947–959.

Metz, S. S. (2007). Attracting the engineering of 2020 today. In R. Burke & M. Mattis (Eds.), *Women and minorities in science, technology, engineering and mathematics: Upping the numbers* (pp 184–209). Northampton, MA: Edward Elgar Publishing.

Mioduser, D., & Levy, S. (2010). Making sense by building sense: Kindergarten children's construction and understanding of adaptive robot behaviors. *International Journal of Computers for Mathematical Learning, 15*(2), 99–127.

Mioduser, D., Levy, S., & Talis, V. (2009). Episodes to scripts to rules: concrete-abstractions in kindergarten children's explanations of a robot's behaviors. *International Journal of Technology and Design Education, 19*(1), 15–36.

National Association for the Education of Young Children & Fred Rogers Center. (2012). Technology and interactive media as tools in early childhood programs serving children from birth through age 8. http://www.naeyc.org/files/naeyc/file/positions/PS_technology_WEB2.pdf. Accessed 16 July 2014.

O'Dell, J. (2012). Guess who's winning the brains race, with 100% of first graders learning to code? VentureBeat. http://venturebeat.com/2012/09/04/estonia-code-academy/. Accessed 16 July 2014.

Oblinger, D. (2003). Boomers, Gen Xers, Millennials: Understanding the new students. *Educause Review, 38*, 37–47.

Palfrey, J., & Gasser, U. (2008). *Born digital: Understanding the first generation of digital natives.* New York, NY: Basic Books.

Papert, S. (1980). *Mindstorms: Children, computers, and powerful ideas.* New York: Basic Books.

Papert, S. (1991). Situating constructionism. In I. Harel & S. Papert (Eds.), *Constructionism* (pp. 161–191). Norwood, NJ: Ablex.

Piaget, J. (1928). *Judgment and reasoning in the child.* London: Routledge & Kegan Paul.

Prensky, M. (2001). Digital natives, digital immigrants part 1. *On the Horizon, 9*(5), 1–6.
Resnick, M. (2006). Computer as paintbrush: Technology, play, and the creative society. In D. Singer, R. Golikoff, & K. Hirsh-Pasek (Eds.), Play = learning: How play motivates and enhances children's cognitive and social-emotional growth. New York, NY: Oxford University Press.
Resnick, M. (2007). Scratch [software]. http://scratch.mit.edu. Accessed 16 July 2014.
Resnick, M., Maloney, J., Monroy-Hernandez, A., Rusk, N., Eastmond, E., Brennan, K., Kafai, Y. (2009). Scratch: Programming for All. *Communications of the ACM, 52*(11), 60–67.
Reynolds, A. J., Temple, J. A., Ou, S. R., Arteaga, I. A., & White, B. A. B. (2011). School-based early childhood education and age-28 well-being: Effects by timing, dosage, and subgroups. *Science, 333*(6040), 360–364.
Steele, C. M. (1997). A threat in the air: How stereotypes shape intellectual identity and performance. *American Psychologist, 52,* 613–629.
Svensson, A. (2000). Computers in school: Socially isolating or a tool to promote collaboration? *Journal of Educational Computing Research, 22*(4), 437–453.
Taber, K. S. (2006). Beyond constructivism: The progressive research programme into learning science. *Studies in Science Education, 42*(1), 125–184.
Tapscott, D. (1998). *Growing up digital: The rise of the net generation.* New York: McGraw-Hill.
Vygotsky, L. S. (1978). *Mind in society: The development of higher psychological processes.* Cambridge, MA: Harvard University Press.
Wartella, E., & Jennings, N. (2000). Children and computers: New technology—old concerns. *Children and Computer Technology, 10*(2), 31–43.
Zillien, N., & Hargittai, E. (2009). Digital distinction: Status-specific internet uses. *Social Science Quarterly, 90*(2), 274–291.

Chapter 4
Teaching with Technology and Interactive Media to Promote Creativity and Arts-based Learning in Young Children

DeAnna M. Laverick

Abstract Providing many and varied opportunities for young children to engage in creative experiences is a vital role of early childhood teachers. This chapter describes how technology and interactive media may be used as a vehicle for nurturing children's creativity and as a means for arts-based teaching and learning. Key ideas from early childhood theories are shared, as they align with recommendations for developmentally-appropriate practice. Technology-based teaching strategies for the creative arts are described, along with technology tools and materials that are needed to plan developmentally-appropriate and effective creative activities. Additionally, interdisciplinary creative experiences through technology and the arts are offered.

Keywords Technology · Interactive media · Creativity · Arts · Young children

Braden is 6 years old and is beginning to read and spell sight words and simple words with the consonant/vowel/consonant pattern. He is sitting at his desk, concentrating intently on an iPad as he uses the Paint Sparkles (Kids Games Club 2012) app to "write" by touching the screen to form letters. The effect of his touch is a sparkly and colorful display of letters strung together to form words. Braden's teacher, Mrs. Smith, is sitting next to him and prompting him to manipulate onsets to create words in the –at word family. Braden quickly discovers that he can read and write many words that rhyme with "hat." Braden's excitement is contagious as he reacts enthusiastically and asks, "Can I draw it, too?" Mrs. Smith encourages Braden to draw the hat and then prompts him to change the /h/ in hat to /k/. "It's cat!" Braden writes "cat" and draws a picture of one. Then, he quickly "erases" his cat and redraws it. "Look! It's a fat cat!" This process continues as Braden writes words and draws pictures to accompany other words in this word family: "sat" (a person sitting on a chair), "bat," "mat" (a rectangle shape), "pat." Braden tells Mrs. Smith, "I know another word that rhymes, but I don't know how to spell it." "What word is that, Braden?" asks Mrs. Smith. "It's chat. My mom had a chat with me." Mrs. Smith asked, "What other words do you know that sound like /ch/ at the beginning?" Braden looked around the classroom and noticed the poster with a

---

D. M. Laverick (✉)
Indiana University of Pennsylvania, Indiana, PA, USA
e-mail: laverick@iup.edu

K. L. Heider, M. Renck Jalongo (eds.), *Young Children and Families in the Information Age*, Educating the Young Child 10, DOI 10.1007/978-94-017-9184-7_4,
© Springer Science+Business Media Dordrecht 2015

chick on it. The students had recently visited the fourth-grade classroom to observe the chicks that hatched and created a class story about the experience. Excitedly, he said, "Chick!" Mrs. Smith encouraged Braden to say the beginning sound of "chick" and add this onset to the "–at" rime. With Mrs. Smith's assistance, along with his prior knowledge, Braden quickly discovered that manipulating the /h/ in "hat" to a /ch/ would create a new word, "chat."

Nurturing children's creativity is vital in early childhood education. By integrating technology and interactive media into the early childhood curriculum, early childhood educators provide opportunities for creative experiences that support a range of higher-level learning goals and promote arts-oriented learning. As illustrated in the scenario above, the interactive effect of using an iPad to promote Braden's understanding of a phonogram was motivating and enjoyable. The development of new technologies, such as interactive white boards (IWBs) and tablets, have changed the way children engage with technology (McManis and Gunnewig 2012). According to McManis and Gunnewig, "Educational technology plays an important role in children's learning when it is based on research, child development theory, and developmentally appropriate practices, and when it aligns with curriculum goals" (p. 15). The use of technology and interactive media allows children to accomplish these goals.

The joint position statement of the National Association for the Education of Young Children (NAEYC) and the Fred Rogers Center for Early Learning and Children's Media at Saint Vincent College (2012) defines interactive media as:

> digital and analog materials, including software programs, applications (apps), broadcast and streaming media, some children's television programming, e-books, the Internet, and other forms of content designed to facilitate active and creative use by young children and to encourage social engagement with other children and adults. (p. 1)

Throughout this chapter, the terms "technology and interactive media" are used in ways consistent with the joint position statement of NAEYC and the Fred Rogers Center. This chapter begins with a description of the theoretical basis of early childhood education, which creates a foundation upon which developmentally-effective uses of technology and interactive media and creative, arts-based educational experiences in early childhood education are built. A rationale for this approach to teaching and learning is provided, followed by specific interdisciplinary strategies for educating young children in the creative arts through technology and interactive media. Descriptions and examples of the technology tools and materials that are needed to plan developmentally-appropriate and effective creative activities are offered throughout this section.

Theoretical Orientation

The theoretical orientation of this chapter is based upon the works of John Dewey, Maria Montessori, Erik Erikson, Jean Piaget, and Lev Vygotsky. Mooney (2000) summarized the key ideas of these theorists as applied to early childhood education.

Her book, *Theories of Childhood: An Introduction to Dewey, Montessori, Erikson, Piaget, and Vygotsky*, provides a valuable resource for educators as they seek to implement educational practices that are rooted in theory. The ideas shared by Mooney are presented in Table 4.1 and are aligned with the guidelines provided in *Technology and Interactive Media as Tools in Early Childhood Programs Serving Children from Birth through Age 8*—a joint position statement of the National Association for the Education of Young Children (NAEYC) and the Fred Rogers Center for Early Learning and Children's Needs (2012). According to the position statement:

> When the integration of technology and interactive media in early childhood programs is built upon solid developmental foundations, and early childhood professionals are aware of both the challenges and the opportunities, educators are positioned to improve program quality by intentionally leveraging the potential of technology and media for the benefit of every child. (NAEYC and the Fred Rogers Center 2012, p. 1)

The theoretical underpinnings and guidelines presented in Table 4.1 are important for early childhood teachers to follow as they use technology to promote arts-based learning.

As shown in Table 4.1, many connections between theories of early childhood education and recommended practices for using technology and interactive media may be drawn. The theories are also evident in the principles and guidelines for developmentally-appropriate practice, which are shared next.

Developmentally-Appropriate Practice

In this section, the use of technology and interactive media to promote arts-based learning in young children is used as a lens through which the principles and guidelines of developmentally-appropriate practice put forth in the Position Statement of the National Association for the Education of Young Children (NAEYC) (2009) are viewed. A key point in NAEYC's position statement on developmentally-appropriate practice reveals that a concern exists in which "schools are curtailing valuable experiences such as problem solving, rich play, collaboration with peers… and the arts" as a result of the standards and accountability movement (p. 4). Principle #9 of the *Principles of Child Development and Learning that Inform Practice* contained in the position statement maintains that, "always mentally active in seeking to understand the world around them, children learn in a variety of ways; a wide range of teaching strategies and interactions are effective in supporting all these kinds of learning" (NAEYC 2009, p. 14). This principle further explains that, "young children construct their knowledge and understanding of the world in the course of their own experiences, as well as from teachers, family members, peers and older children, and from books and other media" (p. 14). Given this explanation, the use of media and the opportunities that technology affords children to engage in social learning experiences offers valuable support in their construction of knowledge.

NAEYC (2009) provides guidelines for developmentally-appropriate practice in early childhood education that are described according to the following areas

Table 4.1 Recommendations for technology use and interactive media: Alignment with theories of early childhood education. (Note: Adapted from NAEYC and the Fred Rogers Center for Early Learning and Children's Media (2012) and Mooney (2000))

Recommendations for early childhood educators for the use of technology and interactive media (NAEYC and Fred Rogers Center 2012)	Theorist and key ideas for early childhood education (Mooney 2000)
1. "Select, use, integrate, and evaluate technology and interactive media tools in intentional and developmentally appropriate ways, giving careful attention to the appropriateness and the quality of the content, the child's experience, and the opportunities for co-engagement" (p. 11).	*John Dewey*: "It is the teacher's job to determine the curriculum based on knowledge of the children and their abilities" (p. 6). Education should be child-centered and based on their experience. "Children's interests should form the basis for curriculum planning" (p. 5). "An activity is not a learning activity if it lacks purpose and organization" (p. 14). *Piaget*: Plan open-ended activities; also, organize small group work while others are engaged in large blocks of free play (pp. 74–76). *Vygotsky*: "Interaction contributes to children's construction of knowledge" (p. 83). "Personal and social experience cannot be separated" (p. 84).
2. Recognize that "technology and interactive media can be valuable tools when used intentionally with children to extend and support active, hands-on, creative, and authentic engagement with those around them and with their world" (p. 11).	*John Dewey*: Education should be active, and teachers should help children make sense of their world. "Teachers do not teach just subject matter, but also how to live in society" (p. 5). *Montessori*: "Children needed real tools if they were to do the real work that interested them so" (p. 25). *Jean Piaget*: "The child's interactions with his environment are what create learning" (p. 61). *Vygotsky*: In order to scaffold well… teachers need to use observations to determine where children are in the learning process and where they are capable of going, given their individual needs and the social context that surrounds them" (p. 84).
3. Prohibit passive use of "non-interactive technologies and media in early childhood programs for children younger than 2, and discourage passive and non-interactive uses with children ages 2 through 5" (p. 11).	*Dewey*: Education should be interactive *Montessori*: Keep supplies available and well organized "so that choices and opportunities continually invite the children to be creative" (p. 26). *Erikson*: The developmental task for children in the stage of "initiative versus guilt" is to "acquire a sense of purpose" and "so they act less for the sake of individual control and more to get things done" (p. 50). *Piaget*: "How important it is for children to experience whatever we want them to learn about" (p. 75). *Vygotsky*: With regard to the Zone of Proximal Development a "child on the edge of learning a new concept can benefit from the interaction with a teacher or a classmate" (p. 83).
4. "Limit any use of technology and interactive media in programs for children younger than 2 to those that appropriately support responsive interactions between caregivers and children and that strengthen adult-child relationships" (p. 11).	*Montessori*: "Children who are not allowed to do something for themselves, do not learn how to do it" (p. 28). *Erikson*: Stressed "how important it is for babies to have significant relationships with a few key adults in order to accomplish the task of developing basic trust" (p. 44). *Piaget*: "Keep children curious, make them wonder, and offer them real problem-solving challenges, rather than giving them information" (p. 62). The teacher "nurtures inquiry and supports the child's own search for answers" (p. 62).

Table 4.1 (continued)

Recommendations for early childhood educators for the use of technology and interactive media (NAEYC and Fred Rogers Center 2012)	Theorist and key ideas for early childhood education (Mooney 2000)
5. "Carefully consider the screen time recommendations… when determining appropriate limits on technology and media use in early childhood settings" (p. 11).	*Erikson*: Children need to "experience the independence of being able to make some choices for themselves" (p. 48). Teachers may offer children the control they need by phrasing "necessary changes in a way that offers a choice of *how* (not *whether*) the task will be accomplished" (p. 49).
6. "Provide leadership in ensuring equitable access to technology and interactive media experiences for the children in their care and for parents and families" (p. 11).	*John Dewey*: "Teachers must be sensitive to the values and needs of families" (p. 5).

of practice: (1) creating a caring community of learners; (2) teaching to enhance development and learning; (3) planning curriculum to achieve important goals; (4) assessing children's development and learning; and (5) establishing reciprocal relationships with families (p. 16). With regard to using technology to promote creativity and arts-based learning in young children, the following guidelines set forth by NAEYC are especially relevant:

- "Teachers plan for learning in experiences that effectively implement a comprehensive curriculum" (p. 18) and "teachers plan curriculum experiences that integrate children's learning within and across domains… and the disciplines" (p. 21). These disciplines include art and music.
- Teachers should plan "meaningful experiences that are intellectually and creatively stimulating" (p. 18), as well as challenging.
- Teachers should provide opportunities for children to make meaningful choices.
- Teachers should organize the schedule to provide extended blocks of time for investigation, exploration, and interaction.
- Teachers know how and when to scaffold. Scaffolding can take a variety of forms and can be provided in a variety of contexts.
- Teachers incorporate a wide variety of experiences, materials, and equipment to accommodate the range of individual differences, including needs and interests.
- "Teachers are familiar with the understandings and skills key for that age group in each domain" (p. 21).
- Teachers "carefully shape and adapt the experiences they provide children to enable each child to reach the goals outlined in the curriculum" (p. 21).
- "Teachers make meaningful connections a priority in the learning experiences they provide children" (p. 21).
- "Teachers are familiar with the understandings and skills key for that age group in each domain" (p. 21).

- "In their planning and follow-through, teachers use the curriculum framework along with what they know (from their observation and other assessment) about the children's interests, progress, language proficiency, and learning needs" (p. 21).
- "In determining the sequence and pace of learning experiences, teachers consider the developmental paths that children typically follow and the typical sequences in which skills and concepts develop" (p. 21).
- "Teachers plan curriculum experiences to draw on children's own interests and introduce children to things likely to interest them" (p. 21).

These guidelines, established by NAEYC (2009), provide a measure by which the instructional strategies and technology-based tools may be used to promote arts-based learning in young children. Technology and interactive media support cognitive development if the teacher is knowledgeable about young children's development and chooses developmentally-appropriate programs (Mohammad and Mohammad 2012). Mohammad and Mohammad advised that it is not a matter of whether computers should be used in early childhood classrooms but rather how they can be integrated effectively into the curriculum; the interests, needs, and abilities of the children must be considered.

The Relationship Between Technology/Interactive Media and Creativity/Arts-Based Learning

Given the previous discussion of appropriate practices for technology and interactive media use, the focus will now turn to how these concepts relate to creativity and arts-based education. Fisher (2004) writes that many definitions of creativity have been developed but "the concept is ethereal and elusive" (p. 7). He explains, "To create is to generate something. At the simplest level, creativity is making, forming, or bringing something into being. To create is to be productive in thought, word or deed" (p. 8). Fisher further explains that, in addition to generation, variation and originality are also processes of creative evolution. According to Fisher, creativity requires risk taking, and it can also "be thought of as embodied imagination. Imaginative activity is the process by which we generate something that is original" (p. 9).

Leach (2001) advises, "Information and Communication Technology (ICT) has a significant role in developing and extending the creative process" (p. 177). Examples of ICTs used in early childhood education are computers, digital cameras, video cameras, DVD players, Internet, and interactive white boards (IWBs) (Terreni 2010). For the purpose of this chapter, the term ICT is synonymous with technology and interactive media. The work of Loveless and Wegerif (2004) is informative in linking creativity with technology and interactive media. Loveless and Wegerif list distinctive features of ICT and the ways in which these features support creativity: (1) provisionality (allows changes to be made and alternatives to be tried); (2) interactivity (engages users); (3) capacity and range (affords access to information);

(4) speed and automation (allows information to be stored, transformed, and used in different ways); (5) quality (allows work to be published); (6) multimodality (allows for interactions of various modes, such as text, images, sounds, etc.); and (7) neutrality and social credibility (opens debate about the impact of ICT on our lives). Loveless and Wegerif (2004) elaborate:

> Creative processes in the use of ICT can support the development of imagination, problem-solving, risk-taking, and divergent thinking. These processes, which describe pupils' creative thinking and behaviour can be summarized as: questioning and challenging; making connections and seeing relationships; envisaging what might be; playing with ideas; representing ideas; and evaluating the effects of ideas. (p. 96)

The role of the teacher is crucial in planning and implementing educational experiences for young children that hold true to the principles and guidelines that were previously discussed. There is enormous potential for technology and interactive media to promote creativity and arts-based learning in young children. The discussion will now turn to the use of instructional strategies and materials to accomplish this goal.

Technology and Interactive Media as a Means for Promoting Creativity and Arts-based Learning

Research on the use of technology and interactive media in arts-based learning supports its vast potential for fostering creativity. According to Mohammad and Mohammad (2012), "The use of computers by young children facilitates cognitive development by improving creative thinking and problem-solving skills and by improving their social interaction and language skills" (p. 98). Similarly, Loveless (2003) notes, "Creative activities with new technologies can include developing ideas, making connections, creating and making, collaboration, communication, and evaluation" (p. 12).

In general, the creative arts refer to visual arts, music, movement, dance, and drama (Bredekamp 2011). Joubert (2001) cautioned against referring to the arts as "creative arts," calling this reference "a serious misnomer, since the arts can sometimes be taught or practiced in very uncreative ways" (p. 23). This chapter considers Joubert's advice as it provides examples of how technology and interactive media are used to promote creativity in the arts. Terreni (2009) states, "ICTs can be powerful and useful tools for teaching and learning in the creative subjects, such as visual art" (p. 93).

Visual Arts

Technology and interactive media, through the use of Interactive White Boards (IWBs) was found by Terreni (2009, 2010) to be beneficial in teaching and learning visual arts with young children. Terreni's (2009, 2010) research review and study of the use of an IWB for teaching and learning visual arts with children ages two through four revealed: (1) collaboration and social interaction occurred when children shared their drawings and taught each other how to use the IWB; (2) IWBs provided opportunities for children to use large motor skills and also manipulate objects on the screen directly with their hands or other objects; (3) learning is supported through a tactile approach as children become involved in their artwork while using their fingers as drawing tools; (4) the IWB provides an effective means for storing and reviewing children's work; (5) children with special learning needs are engaged, as the IWB motivates them and helps them gain confidence and competence; (6) the IWB attracted learners who were shy and reluctant to participate in activities; (7) the IWB provided opportunities for children to work either individually or in small groups; (8) IWBs provide an opportunity for teachers to model and scaffold instruction, which in turn enables children to master increasingly complex skills; and (9) the use of IWBs provided opportunities for children to scaffold their peers' learning, which empowered their own learning.

A study conducted by Pavlou (2009) explored 5- and 6-year-olds' understandings of visual and design concepts of three-dimensional art. In this study, the children visited an ostrich farm and then created three-dimensional ostriches. Pavlou concluded that young children's level of representation exceeds most teachers' expectations and recommended that teachers allow for full development of creativity by avoiding giving children a fixed and ready-made end product to which they must adhere as they create their art.

To build on this example and show how technology may be used to create and manipulate three-dimensional art, the free iPad app *123 Catch* (AutoDesk 2012) is explained by Byrne (2012). Byrne shares that, by using this app, students can create 3D models from photographs taken with an iPad. He notes that the app can also be used to create 3D models of landmarks that would normally only be seen in 2D pictures. Thus, using this app to take pictures during a field trip would give children the potential to create 3D figures of landmarks visited. Additionally, this idea could be extended to apply to curriculum topics, such as landmarks in the community for social studies, "all about me" topics in which children share 3D models related to themselves, or 3D self-portraits. The possibilities are endless. Byrne noted that this app may be used with children of all ages, given that there are several public 3D models available that may be manipulated. He also suggested that the 3D models could be created for use as math manipulatives or to be used in science lessons.

To summarize, the work of Loveless (2003) emphasizes the value of using technology and interactive media for creative purposes:

> The weaving of imagination, fashioning, pursuing purposes and being original needs to move beyond the use of tools and techniques for their own sake in the creation, drafting, editing and refining processes. Creating tangible outcomes, such as an image, a poem, a drama, a 3D construction or a movie involves not only the physical act of making, but also an ongoing 'dialogue' where 'the maker produces and the work responds.' (p. 13)

An example of a resource that serves this creative purpose is found in Terreni's (2009) recommended use of *Tate Create* (http://kids.tate.org.uk/), which is an interactive website that allows children to "create their own digital painting which can also be animated, framed, sent to a friend via e-mail, and submitted to be hung in the Tate digital art gallery" (p. 104).

Music

Digital cameras and music go hand-in-hand to create musical stories. In a study of 4-year-olds' use of digital cameras, Blagojevic and Thomes (2008) found that the digital stories young children created provided opportunities for choice, personal expression, data collection, and scaffolding by the teacher to promote meaningful and effective learning. In addition, importing music into the digital stories allows for increased opportunities for choice and appreciation of the aesthetic qualities offered by the images and sounds. For example, digital stories that use bold colors, sharp lines, and deep contrast, similar to the works of Piet Mondrian, may likely be paired with a musical selection that creates a similar effect through sound. An example of a classical musical piece that would pair well with these types of images is Saint-Saëns' *Carnival of the Animals, Royal March of the Lion*. As other examples, pictures with patriotic themes may be paired with a march, or muted watercolor paintings created by children may be matched with waltzes or lullabies. In social studies, musical pieces that are specific to cultures, places, and historical time periods may be integrated into digital stories that depict related visual images.

It is important that young children are given the opportunity to create their own music through the use of traditional instruments and online tools. For example, the New York Philharmonic KidZone website (http://www.nyphilkids.org/main.phtml), gives children many opportunities to explore, listen to, and "play" instruments; compose musical compositions; meet musicians; and more. This resource allows children to engage in a variety of creative experiences through an interactive multimedia format.

Movement

In a study conducted by Laverick (2013, 2014) on the ways in which reading specialist candidates used technology and interactive media to promote the literacy learning of children who struggle with reading, reading specialist candidates incorporated the use of movement by having the children take a walking field trip. A digital video recorder was used to record the experience, and the images were used as a springboard for a descriptive writing experience. The participants explained that, by viewing the recording of the field trip, students were able to recall details that they would have otherwise forgotten. These details, in turn, were incorporated into the students' writing. The children's writing skills reflected details and vivid descriptions sparked by the recorded experiences. Another way that writing was enhanced was by having the children tell stories that were audio recorded. One participant explained that she told her student, "If you can 'tell' stories, then you can 'write' stories," and her student did just that. She elaborated that, as a teacher, "it helped me think outside the box." The audio-recorded stories acted as a scaffold to support the children as they wrote their stories. Also, by giving the children the option to write stories on the computer, rather than on paper, motivation was increased.

Dance

Websites such as http://www.dance-kids.org/ allow children to explore many genres of dance. This site allows children to create different effects on dance scenes by giving them choices for altering pictures that show different forms of dance. The "Lucky Dip" link presents children with a surprise, such as the "ABCs of Dance." This link promotes vocabulary and concept development with a dictionary of terms related to ethnic dances, such as Irish dancing, rumba, salsa, and paso doble. "Dance Stories" is another link on this site where children may read the stories that are posted and also write and submit their own stories to be shared with others. The "Dancing Globe" link presents information about dances and cultures around the world. After researching the different dances shared on this site, children may create their own dances to share with others. This site also provides a forum in which children are able to draw and post dance-related pictures for other users to view.

Mayesky (2012) offers suggestions for connecting music, dance, and art. She recommends having children listen to musical selections and then act them out. To add technology and interactive media to this approach, children may view dance-related paintings online and dance in the style that is projected, and to music of the time period.

Drama

Technology and interactive media may be used to support drama in numerous ways and have been found to impact the literacy development of children who struggle with reading. Reading specialist candidates reported the use of digital recording devices to capture, self-evaluate, and share performances with an audience (Laverick 2013, 2014). The children in this study read from scripts as their performances were recorded for self-evaluation. The reading specialist candidates reported that reading fluency improved as a result of the children self-evaluating their performance, continually practicing reading their scripts, and then polishing their performances to share with an audience. In preparation for the performances, the children created simple costumes, selected and used props, and used a computer to select and project backdrops for the scenery.

In a similar project, students in Australia created two Star Wars movies, one of which was a sequel (Hesterman 2011). The students in this case study created props and costumes and experimented with lighting and backdrops. Their parents joined them to view the sequel and celebrate their creation. Hesterman reported that, as a result of this project, the students' creativity was enhanced and their problem-solving skills were developed.

Another approach that supports the process of creative expression is *tableau* which, according to Isenberg and Jalongo (2014) is:

> … a drama technique in which actors do not speak or move. Sometimes tableau is calling living picture, frozen picture, or living statue because characters literally 'freeze' in expressive poses, gestures, and movements that represent a significant event, subject scene, picture, or character to create a 'human statue.' (p. 222)

This approach was described by Johnson (2004) as a method for having children use drama to think creatively. An extension of the use of still images is improvisation. Both of these methods can be successful in promoting critical thinking while requiring children to use their imagination. The use of a digital camera to record the still images presents a unique opportunity for children to "create a wordless story." The still pictures may be placed in sequence, digitally altered in creative ways, and then shared with an audience. According to Howard Gardner (1983), "In all forms of performance, but particularly in acting, one's ability to observe carefully and then to re-create scenes in detail is at a premium. Such mimetic ability begins very early…" (p. 226).

Arts-Based Literacy

Several of the examples previously presented are infused with literacy, which should be integrated across the curriculum. While the examples were presented individually with regard to distinct creative arts, integration of the arts around a common experience or theme lends itself more effectively to a unified approach. For example, a study by Toren et al. (2008) described how kindergarten children listened to a story read aloud, played music to express different parts of the story, drew images from the story using a computer program, and then transformed the story into a theatrical performance. Literacy is a natural vehicle for integrating the arts and teaching interdisciplinary concepts. According to Cornett (2006), teachers who practice arts-based literacy "believe drama, dance, music, and visual art should be integral to literacy instruction because they are essential means of constructing meaning" (p. 235). Cornett asserts that arts-based literacy instruction promotes creativity and uniqueness when art is incorporated in meaningful ways. Building on this concept, research has shown that digital media enhances narrative skills, writing skills, and emergent literacy skills (McMunn-Dooley et al. 2011).

Digital storytelling provides multiple means of expression through the use of digital cameras, story-making software, recording software, etc. (Nilsson 2010). In a study conducted in Bhutan, digital storytelling was found to be an engaging learning experience that helped students develop a sense of voice (Gyabak and Godina 2011). By using a variety of modes to create stories, such as images, music, sound, speech, writing, and technology, teachers are more likely to tap into children's interests, skills, and creativity (Nilsson 2010). To elaborate on this technique, children may take on the role of actor as they dramatize the stories being told digitally, either through still shots that are shown in frames or in recorded movies, such as the iMovie that participants in Laverick's (2013, 2014) study created. In this study, the children used the iMovie to "show" their audience the different reading strategies and experiences they encountered while enrolled in a summer reading program. The children shared their digital story with an audience comprised of family members and friends and were also able to keep a digital copy of the story to serve as a keepsake and instructional resource for families to use at home.

Curriculum integration was stressed in an arts-based early childhood program for 3- to 5-year-old children (Armisted 2007). The children in Armisted's study traveled among different studios for music, dance, and visual arts, participating in activities that surrounded a theme, such as a rainy day. The activities that took place in each individual studio converged to support one overall theme.

Role of the Family

The discussion will now turn to the important role that the family plays in the development of creativity in children. The family's role in nurturing creativity was examined in a study of the recollections of creative adults (Gute et al. 2008). Gute and colleagues described the familial influences on creativity as being:

- "Supporting children's existing aptitudes and interests;
- spending time together;
- teaching core values and behavioral boundaries.
- demonstrating tolerance for failure;
- coping with difficult circumstances;
- stimulating new interests and challenges;
- modeling habits of creativity; and
- building a demographically and psychologically diverse family unit" (p. 345).

Given the impact that the family has on the development of creativity (Gute et al. 2008), it is important that teachers communicate with parents about the types of experiences they may provide in the home to nurture creativity. Further, teachers may capitalize on the role of the family through the use of in-school activities, as was done in a study by Armisted (2007). Armisted affirmed the importance of family members as active participants in an interdisciplinary arts-based curriculum, particularly for assessment purposes and as a welcome audience for the recognition of children's achievements. With regard to using technology and interactive media to promote creativity and arts-based learning, teachers should apply these recommendations to include the use of these tools at home to support creative learning experiences.

It is critical that families become educated in choosing the best tools, applications, and programs to foster creativity, rather than constrain it. Table 4.2 provides suggestions for tools, apps, and programs that families may use to promote creativity through technology and interactive media.

Table 4.2 Recommended resources for families. (*Note*: Apps were retrieved from iPhone's App Store)

Name	Source	Description
Pintrest	www.pintrest.com	Provides ideas for creative experiences
Crayola	www.crayola.com	Shares resources, videos, information, and ideas for creative experiences
Kid Pix 3D	www.mackiev.com	Multimedia program for children to create and share their ideas
Glogster EDU	edu.glogster.com	Online multimedia tool that promotes learning and creativity
SpinArt Free	7twenty7 LLC	App for creating colorful spinart
Let's Create! Pottery HD Lite	Infinite Dreams Inc.	App for creating pottery
Creative Kids Birthday Cakes	Wealthbase Creation Limited	App for making choices to create a birthday cake and recording songs
Storylines for Schools	Root-One, Inc.	This app begins with a storyline that allows users to collaborate to write and illustrate a complete story
Fancy Nancy Dress Up	Bean Creative	Based on the "Fancy Nancy" books, this app allows children to read, create pictures and outfits, and share their creations
PianoBall-Fun with Learning	4baam	Young children may explore music and colors with this app
My Little Suitcase by Moms with Apps	Moms with Apps	App that allows children to make choices as they pack a suitcase for a trip and then play
Tiny Tiger and Friends	The Curio Dept.	An app that allows children to play games with animal friends
Kids Giant Draw Pad Free	P Chu	An app for creating artwork

Conclusion

The technology tools and interactive media that early childhood educators use have the potential to support children's creativity in a plethora of ways, similar to Braden's experience that was described at the beginning of this chapter. This chapter provided information on the use of technology and interactive media to support children's creativity development and arts-based learning. The chapter focused on theories of early childhood education that influence developmentally-appropriate practices and how these concepts could be applied to the use of technology and interactive media. The relationship between technology and interactive media and creativity and arts-based learning was described. Specific examples for the promotion of creative arts were given, along with ideas for supporting literacy and other subjects across the curriculum. Early childhood educators should capitalize on the potential that families have to influence their children's creativity. They may do so by recommending resources and sharing information on how families may support learning through technology-based creative experiences. There is tremendous potential to unlock creativity in every child through the use of technology and interactive media.

Author Note The author would like to thank Ms. Nichol Murray, doctoral candidate, for her assistance in preparing this manuscript.

References

Armisted, M. E. (2007). Kaleidoscope: How a creative arts enrichment program prepares children for kindergarten. *Young Children, 62*(6), 86–93.

Autodesk. (2012). *123Catch*. San Rafael: Autodesk, Inc. https://itunes.apple.com/us/app/123d-catch/id513913018?mt=8.

Blagojevic, B., & Thomes, K. (2008). Young photographers: Can 4-year-olds use a digital camera as a tool for learning? An investigation in progress. *Young Children, 63*(5), 66–70.

Bredekamp, S. (2011). *Effective practices in early childhood education: Building a foundation*. Upper Saddle River, NJ: Pearson.

Byrne, R. (2012). iPad apps for school. http://ipadapps4school.com/2012/12/12/turn-pictures-into-3d-models-on-your-ipad/.

Cornett, C. (2006). Center-stage: Arts-based read-alouds. *The Reading Teacher, 60*(3), 234–240. doi:10.1598/RT.60.3.3.

Fisher, R. (2004). What is creativity? In R. Fisher & M. Williams (Eds.), *Unlocking creativity: Teaching across the curriculum* (pp. 6–20). London, UK: David Fulton.

Gardner, H. (1983). *Frames of mind: The theory of multiple intelligences*. New York, NY: Basic Books.

Gute, G., Gute, D. S., Nakamura, J., & Csikszentmihályi, M. (2008). The early lives of highly creative persons: The influence of the complex family. *Creativity Research Journal, 20*(4), 343–357.

Gyabak, K., & Godina, H. (2011). Digital storytelling in Bhutan: A qualitative examination of new media tools used to bridge the digital divide in a rural community school. *Computers & Education, 57*(4), 2236–2243.

Hesterman, S. (2011). Multiliterate Star Warians: The force of popular culture and ICT in early learning. *Australasian Journal of Early Childhood, 36*(4), 86–95.

Isenberg, J. P., & Jalongo, M. R. (2014). *Creative thinking and arts-based learning: Preschool through fourth grade* (6th ed.). Upper Saddle River: Pearson.

Johnson, C. (2004). Creative drama: Thinking from within. In R. Fisher & M. Williams (Eds.), *Unlocking creativity: Teaching across the curriculum* (pp. 55–67). London, UK: David Fulton.

Joubert, M. M. (2001). The art of creative teaching: NACCCE and beyond. In A. Craft, B. Jeffrey, & M. Leibling (Eds.), *Creativity in education* (pp. 17–34). London, England: Continuum.

Kids Games Club. (2012). https://itunes.apple.com/ca/app/paint-sparkles-draw-my-first/id435539858?mt=8.

Laverick, D. M. (2013). *Teacher work sample as evidence of the effectiveness of technology-based instruction to support striving readers*. Paper presented at the 24th Annual Conference of the Society for Information Technology and Teacher Education (SITE). New Orleans, LA.

Laverick, D. M. (2014). Supporting striving readers through technology-based instruction. *Reading Improvement, 51*(1), 11–19.

Leach, J. (2001). A hundred possibilities: Creativity, community, and ICT. In A. Craft, B. Jeffrey, & M. Leibling (Eds.), *Creativity in education* (pp. 175–194). London: Continuum.

Loveless, A. (2003). Creating spaces in the primary curriculum: ICT in creative subjects. *Curriculum Journal, 14*(1), 5–21.

Loveless, A., & Wegerif, R. (2004). Unlocking creativity with ICT. In R. Fisher & M. Williams (Eds.), *Unlocking creativity: Teaching across the curriculum* (pp. 92–102). London, UK: David Fulton.

Mayesky, M. (2012). *Creative activities for young children* (10th ed.). Belmont, CA: Wadsworth Cengage Learning.

McManis, L. D., & Gunnewig, S. B. (2012). Finding the education in educational technology with early learners. *Young Children, 67*(3), 14–24.

McMunn-Dooley, C., Seely-Fink, A., Holbrook, T., May, L., & Albers, P. (2011). The digital frontier in early childhood education. *Language Arts, 89*(2), 83–85.

Mohammad, M., & Mohammad, H. (2012). Computer integration into the early childhood curriculum. *Education, 133*(1), 97–116.

Mooney, C. G. (2000). *Theories of childhood: An introduction to Dewey, Montessori, Erikson, Piaget, & Vygotsky*. St. Paul, MN: Redleaf.

National Association for the Education of Young Children (NAEYC). (2009). *Developmentally appropriate practice in early childhood programs serving children from birth through age 8*. Washington, DC: NAEYC. http://www.naeyc.org/files/naeyc/file/positions/PSDAP.pdf.

NAEYC. (2012). *Technology and interactive media as tools in early childhood programs serving children from birth through age 8*. Washington, DC: NAEYC and the Fred Rogers Center for Early Learning and Children's Media at Saint Vincent College. http://www.naeyc.org/files/naeyc/PS_technology_WEB.pdf.

Nilsson, M. (2010). Developing voice in digital storytelling through creativity, narrative and multimodality. *Seminar.net—International Journal of Media, Technology and Lifelong Learning, 6*(2), 148–160.

Pavlou, V. (2009). Understanding young children's three-dimensional creative potential in art making. *International Journal of Art & Design Education, 28*(2), 139–150.

Terreni, L. (2009). *A case study: How young children and teachers use an interactive whiteboard in a New Zealand kindergarten setting for visual art learning experiences*. Unpublished Master's thesis, Victoria University of Wellington College of Education, Wellington, New Zealand. http://researcharchive.vuw.ac.nz/handle/10063/983?show=full.

Terreni, L. (2010). Adding new possibilities for visual art education in early childhood settings: The potential of interactive whiteboards and ICT. *Australasian Journal of Early Childhood, 35*(4), 90–94.

Toren, Z., Maiselman, D., & Inbar, S. (2008). Curriculum integration: Art, literature, and technology in pre-service kindergarten teacher training. *Early Childhood Education Journal, 35*(4), 347–333. doi:10.1007/s10643-007-0197-0.

Chapter 5
Opening Young Minds and Hearts: Employing Technology-infused Critical Pedagogy in Hybrid Border Spaces

Crystal Machado

One out of 10 people now living in the United States was born in another country.

Abstract The large influx of immigrant children in the American classroom is deepening the ethnic texture and the linguistic and cultural diversity of classrooms. Given that 70 % of the world's cultures have a more collaborative, interdependent orientation than is found in the dominant culture in some regions, early childhood educators worldwide need to create learning spaces that support acculturation in all rather than assimilation in those who identify with non-dominant groups. In this chapter, the author provides the reader with a minoritized perspective which is often absent from the mainstream discourse in teacher education. She describes ways in which educators and caregivers of young children can create technology-infused

C. Machado (✉)
Indiana University of Pennsylvania, Indiana, USA
e-mail: cmachado@iup.edu

hybrid border spaces where effective cross-cultural interaction and transformative learning can take place.

Keywords Technology · Web 2.0 technologies · Culture · Communication · Collaboration · Critical thinking · Creativity

What Color is a Friend?

I will always remember the elevator in Elkin Hall. It was there that I met a preschooler who left an indelible mark on me. It all happened on March 15, 2010. As I walked into the elevator with a spring in my step, I saw an elderly couple and a preschooler. When I smiled at the young child and said, "Hello!" a look of horror spread across her face, and she ducked behind her grandmother. "What is wrong?" her grandmother asked. She shuddered, looked at me suspiciously, and then, in a loud voice, said, "I don't like HER TYPE!" I was stunned. I looked at her grandparents expecting a reaction to her expression of distaste. They looked at me and laughed – not with embarrassment, but with genuine amusement. I felt like the rug had been pulled out from under me. I was visibly shaken. Silently I walked out of the elevator and into my office.

I sat in my office for a long time thinking about what happened in the elevator, struggling to make sense of the disconcerting experience. For some reason, this encounter was more painful than every other act of discrimination that I have experienced in my 9 years in the United States. Why did I feel so disheartened? I found myself wondering how this young child's distaste for people who did not look like her would influence her behavior in the classroom. Would she be able to interact with racially, ethnically, culturally, and linguistically diverse children? Would her disdain rub off on the other white children in her classroom? What impact could this behavior have on the self-esteem of non-white American children in the classroom? What changes should caregivers and teachers make to the immediate environment of young children to help them understand that friends come in all different shapes, sizes, and colors?

This young child's reaction to an adult with a different physical appearance is not uncommon, especially in communities where populations continue to be racially and ethnically homogeneous. The genuine angst that I felt following the encounter is one that many non-white Americans and legal aliens feel on a regular basis. "When groups with different religions, cultures, and languages interact within a society, ethnocentrism and religious bigotry as well as other forms of institutionalized rejection and hostility occur" (Banks 2009, p. 9). America is changing. In his book *The Next Hundred Million: America in 2050,* Kotkin (2010) explains that one out of ten people now living in the U.S. was born in another country. Currently in the U.S., 25% of children under age 5 are Hispanic. This number is expected to grow to 40% by 2050. Similarly, the U.S. minority population is expected to grow from the current 30–50% by 2050. The demographics of suburbia are also changing, with more minorities moving to the suburbs (Kotkin 2010). The largest numbers of people are coming from Mexico, Central and South America, and Asia (Klein and Chen 2001). As the ethnic texture and the linguistic and cultural diversity of classrooms in the U.S. changes, the need to create an environment that supports acculturation instead of assimilation has become the moral imperative. Some important questions that educators and caregivers of young children such as the one that introduced this chapter need to answer are: Is the curriculum that we offer, both within and beyond the classroom, preparing children for success in a multicultural society? What essential skills do young children need to develop so they are able to interact effectively in an interconnected global world? What changes do we need to bring about to existing learning spaces in the home and beyond to make it possible for children to develop these skills? In what ways can educators and caregivers of young children use Web 2.0 technology to promote transformative learning when faced with limited ethnic, racial, and linguistic diversity?

A Call to Reinvent the Curriculum: Founding Fathers' Shattered Dreams

Schools in the U.S. are frozen in time. Children spend a great deal of classroom time, much as their grandparents did, listening to lectures, scribbling notes, completing worksheets, and taking tests. The shortcomings of our post-No Child Left Behind curriculum become evident when we compare this reality with the dreams our founding fathers had for us. Berliner (2010) reminds us that Ben Franklin would have favored a curriculum that allowed youth to think about the nature of justice and injustice; George Washington would have supported a "multicultural" curriculum that unifies divergent social groups; Thomas Jefferson would recommend one that nurtures good citizenship; and John Adams would advocate for an arts-based curriculum that results in the fulfillment of the American dream of liberty. The curriculum is no longer the means to an end, the path to a virtuous life; it has become a script enacted by teachers and young children who have been programmed to believe that high test scores are the only evidence of academic success that counts in contemporary schools.

Acculturation for *All* Children: The Moral Imperative

Few would dispute that the curricula offered in schools, colleges, and universities should reflect ethnic, racial, cultural, linguistic, and religious diversity. Unfortunately, this continues to be an ideal, rather than a reality. For example, "most Americans are socialized within ethnic or cultural enclaves and have low levels of cultural and ethnic literacy. Within their communities, people learn primarily about their own cultures and assume that their lifestyles are the legitimate ones and that other cultures are invalid, strange, and different" (Banks 2009, p. 15). *Enculturation* is the conscious and unconscious process by which individuals acquire the knowledge, attitudes, values, and skills that enable them to become functioning members of their societies. When children of the dominant culture move from the home environment to the school environment, the process of enculturation continues. If the norms and values that prevail in the school reflect almost exclusively the "funds of knowledge" of the dominant culture (Roseberry et al. 2001), these children will experience fewer challenges than those of non-dominant cultures. It is, therefore, not surprising that anti-immigrant sentiments continue to be rampant in many countries. Can children be faulted for treating "the other" with disdain when they have so few opportunities to experience the "funds of knowledge" that children from non-dominant homes, communities, and economic backgrounds have but are unable to share in the classroom? Children of the twenty-first century, their educators, and caregivers would be better served in a multicultural environment where *all children* are given the opportunity to acculturate. *Acculturation* is the process whereby groups who come into contact with each other engage in an exchange of cultural patterns; both groups are altered, without losing the characteristics that make them unique (Culbertson 2002).

In the U.S., the informal curriculum in the home and classroom is supplemented with textbooks and curricula developed by a 40-billion-dollar industry led by three textbook/testing giants: Harcourt-Brace, Pearson, and McGraw Hill. Schools across the nation are adopting textbooks and curriculum materials that were developed specifically for three states, Texas, California, and Florida, upon which this industry's financial success depends (Ansary 2004). In Trinley's film, *Monumental Myths* (2009), Loewen, the film's content advisor, describes how public monuments and textbooks have perpetuated the myths that are the basis for much of U.S. history in schools. While teachers, caregivers, and children are told that school knowledge is based on diversity of cultural and global sources, careful analysis of curricular offerings confirms that school knowledge continues to reflect the values of the dominant culture, class, and gender group (Apple 2001). At first glance, textbooks seem to be more inclusive of diversity. Critical analysis of the content reveals, however, that there is more than meets the eye; we now have "a history of many colors but one idea, culturally diverse yet intellectually static" (Zimmerman 2002, p. 15). Sleeter and Grant (2007) found that Whites continue to be presented in a positive light, featured in a wide variety of roles, with long lists of accomplishments. Critical and non-dominant perspectives are missing (Nieto and Bode 2008). African Americans are represented, but to a smaller degree, with much less attention historically. Asian Americans and Latinos appear in the background, with virtually no historical or contemporary experience. "In general, texts suggest that the U.S. is not class-stratified, that almost everyone is middle-class, and that people have not struggled over distribution of wealth. Furthermore, texts often link poverty with people of color, particularly in illustrations" (Sleeter and Grant 2007, p. 19). An ethnocentric curriculum that presents only the values of the dominant group is harmful; it not only marginalizes non-dominant groups, but it also instills in the dominant group a false sense of superiority, perpetuates ignorance, and robs all children of the opportunity to think critically and contribute meaningfully to civic engagement.

Over the last decade or so, it has become more obvious that the focus on state assessments has had minimal impact on individual academic growth, especially when we view these assessments in isolation (Popham 2001). State tests are not specific enough to pinpoint the unique learning needs of individual children, and they do not help us keep track of individual children's gains from one assessment to the next (Ainsworth 2007). We can turn the dreams of our founding fathers into a reality if we spent less time administering statewide and school-based tests that do not really provide us with meaningful data and more time offering our children a technology-infused curriculum grounded in critical pedagogy. This will allow us to cultivate a community of twenty-first-century learners who can live, work, and thrive in what is quickly becoming a very flat, globally competitive world.

Critical Pedagogy + the 4 Cs + Web 2.0 Technology = Hybrid Border Spaces for Transformative Learning

Inexpensive technology tools, both hardware and software, allow us to transcend the limits of time, space, and resources. With just one tablet and a high-speed internet connection, education professionals and caregivers can transport young learners to different parts of the world where they can experience first-hand the cultures and traditions they read about in books. Additionally, technology tools make it easier for education professionals and caregivers to address some of the barriers that exist between the school and the home.

Transformative Learning in a Hybrid Border Space

Wink (2011) describes three perspectives of pedagogy: the transmission model, the generative model, and the transformative model. The transmission model, often referred to as traditional instruction or "the banking model," is teacher-centered; the teacher plans and presents information, and children listen and regurgitate the information. "Transmission too often for too long will create a world of children who cannot think deeply, nor solve problems" (Wink 2011, p. 189). Generative learning, which employs a child-centered approach, makes it possible for children to interact with material, thus allowing communication to flow in several directions. With the transformative model, "the learner gets out into the real world and participates in real activities; thus, he or she gains realistic pictures to visualize and experience. The communication flows freely from learner to learner, and the teacher becomes a partner in the learning process" (Wink 2011, p. 8). The transformative model allows children to shift from being passive learners to active members of the community—they change themselves and their community.

Fig. 5.1 Technology-infused critical pedagogy in hybrid border spaces for transformative learning

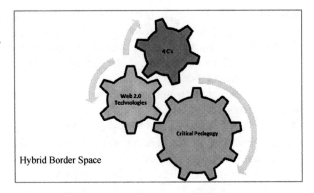

Wink goes on to explain the impact that transformative learning can have on individuals and society:

> The fundamental belief that drives these classroom behaviors is that we must act, we must relate our teaching and learning to real life. We must connect our teaching and learning with our communities, and we must always try to learn and teach so that we grow and so that our students' lives are improved, or so self- and social transformation occurs. (p. 29)

In the twenty-first century, with our access to a wide range of technology tools, transformative learning can take on a whole new meaning. Influenced by the work of Henry Giroux's "Border Pedagogy," Cronje (2010) recommends the creation of *hybrid border spaces*, metaphorical areas in the educational environment where children can share cultures and create identities. Educators and caregivers of young children can create, both in the home and the classroom, environments that support global awareness and transformative learning by consciously and explicitly creating spaces that are characterized by the elements highlighted in Fig. 5.1.

Critical Pedagogy: The Anchor and the Driving Force

Paolo Freire, a Brazilian educator who is widely regarded as a major influence on the concept of critical pedagogy (Kincheloe 2008), maintained that education has as much to do with a teachable heart as with the mind. Critical pedagogy is pedagogy that is grounded in equity and justice for all, and it places huge demands on practitioners in terms of critical thinking and attitudinal change. Even though the literature on critical pedagogy has been around for decades, it has been dismissed, ignored, and often excluded from the mainstream discourse in teacher education (Segall 2004). When included as part of pre-service teacher education, it is met with strong resistance by members of the dominant group (Cochran-Smith 2004).

Comprehensive reform of U.S public education will only be possible though critical examination of power relationship and structures of privilege (Gorski 2009; McLaren 1997). As a first step in this direction, educators and caregivers of young children need to recognize that "every dimension of schooling and every form of educational practice are politically contested spaces" (Kincheloe 2008, p. 2) that are "shaped by a plethora of often-invisible forces, and can operate even in the name of democracy and justice to be totalitarian and oppressive" (Kincheloe 2008, p. 2). Embracing critical pedagogy can be a challenge for members of the dominant group because it requires them to realize that the schools that were "good" for them could be perceived as hurtful for children who identify with non-dominant groups. Bell hooks (1994) urged teachers to "open... minds and hearts... so that [they can] celebrate teaching that enables transgressions—a movement against and beyond boundaries... [a] movement which makes education the practice of freedom" (p. 12). Recognizing the powerful role that teachers can play if they work together, Ayers (2004) invited teachers to "join one another to imagine and build a participatory movement for justice, a public space for the enactment of democratic dreams" (p. 96).

The transformation model is another name for critical pedagogy because "the teachers and the students are not only *doing* critical pedagogy, they are also *living* critical pedagogy" (Wink 2011, p. 29). Simply put, critical pedagogy is *to name, to reflect, and to act* (Wink 2011). Those interested in practicing critical pedagogy need to teach themselves how to use the curriculum, the standards, the textbook, and all the resources they can muster—including TV, radio, popular music, movies, the Internet, Web 2.0 technology, and others—to design learning experiences that will allow children to "see" the racism, gender bias, class bias, cultural bias, heterosexism, religious intolerance, and other forms of discrimination around them. The focus is placed not only subject matter but also the political structures of the home, the school, and society; thus, parents and caregivers play a pivotal role.

The 4 Cs: Essential Skills in an Interconnected World

Technology is not just a choice anymore; it is a necessity, primarily because it is impossible to teach children everything they need to know through the written word alone (Lewis 2009). The Partnership for 21st Century Skills (P21), formed by the U.S. Department of Education and eight companies, is the leading national advocacy organization focused on infusing twenty-first-century skills into education. Figure 5.2, represents both twenty-first-century skills and student outcomes (represented by the arches of the rainbow) and twenty-first-century skills support systems (represented by the pools at the bottom). The Learning and Innovation Skills, represented by yellow, include the 4 Cs—communication, collaboration, critical thinking, and creativity; the core subjects and twenty-first century themes, represented by the green, include the 3 Rs—reading, writing and arithmetic.

Educators and caregivers of young children can create a twenty-first-century learning environment that extends beyond the walls of the home or school. This space allows for the exploration of core projects, along with twenty-first-century interdisciplinary themes, which occur through face-to-face, virtual, and blended communications. The environment supports differentiated teaching and learning

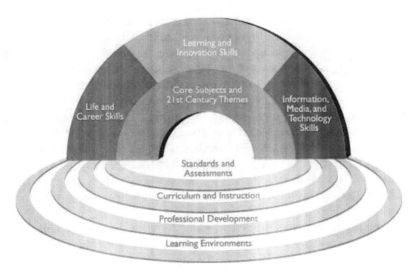

Fig. 5.2. The Partnership in 21st Century Skills framework for twenty-first century learning

based on children's learning styles, intelligence, strengths, and weaknesses. It is a place where educators and caregivers seamlessly integrate twenty-first-century skills, tools, and strategies into their instructional practices, using both direct instruction and project-oriented instructional methods, so that children can apply the skills across content areas within and beyond the space.

The 4 Cs reflected in the rainbow diagram have the potential to take on a whole new meaning in a school where technology-infused critical pedagogy is valued and practiced. With careful planning and scaffolding of young children's thinking during and following a cross-cultural interaction, educators and caregivers of young children can help them create a democratic consciousness and models of meaning-making that detect indoctrination and social regulation.

Communication and Collaboration Culture refers to cognitive, affective, and behavioral patterns that are shared by a group of people. Seventy percent of the world's cultures have a more collaborative, interdependent orientation than is found in the dominant U.S. culture. Triandis (1995) identifies Australia, Belgium, Germany, Switzerland, Canada, and the United States as prototypical individualistic cultures. In contrast, countries like China, Japan, South Korea, Ghana, Saudi Arabia, and Mexico have been prototyped as collectivistic cultures because "we" identities are favored over "I" identities, group obligations over personal rights, and group needs over personal interests. Hall (1959), Hofstede (1997), and Ting-Toomey (1999) found that individualism and collectivism have a direct effect on communication styles. Similarly, Li (2012) found that Western and East Asian people hold fundamentally different beliefs about learning that influence how they approach child-rearing and education. The purpose of learning reflected in the European-American model is cultivation of the mind/understanding the world, developing one's ability/skill, and reaching personal goals. On the other hand, the purpose of learning, as per the Chinese model, is perfection of oneself morally and socially, acquiring knowledge and skills for oneself, and contributing to society (Li 2012). As the world becomes smaller, and as people from collectivistic cultures like Asia, Africa, and Latin America move into the United States with its individualistic culture, educators of young children, especially in racially homogenous regions, have to reexamine the ways in which they prepare young children to communicate and collaborate.

Critical Thinking Scholars confirm that curiosity begins at an early age (Glimps and Ford 2008; Meadows and Murphy 2004; Moore-Hart 2004; O'Neill 2007). As early as infancy, children are testing their theories about how things work by "collecting data;" they tirelessly try out different actions on the world and watch to see what happens (Gopnik et al. 2000). Children's curiosity unfolds within a social context. They are curious about people, and the people around them influence their curiosity. When children encounter what Garner et al. (1992) call "seductive details," their interest is heightened, even when these vivid and intriguing details do not relate to that which they are exploring.

The developmental process of critical thinking begins as early as preschool, provided children are stimulated in this direction (Daniel and Gagnon 2011). In his seminal work, Paul (1993) describes, quite succinctly, why critical thinking has become the moral imperative.

> Only if we raise children to think critically, as a matter of course, about their use of language, the information they take in, the nature of propaganda which surrounds them, the multiple prejudices assumed to be self-evident truths; only if we educate children to probe the logical structures of thought, to test proposed knowledge against experience, to scrutinize experience from alternative perspectives; only if we reward those who think for themselves, who display intellectual courage, humility, and faith in reason; only then do we have a fighting chance that children will eventually become free and morally responsible adults and hence help eventually to create, through their example and commitments, genuinely free and moral societies. (p. xviii)

Reggio Emilia educators believe that children have "100 languages" at their disposal to communicate their ideas, knowledge, and experiences (Edwards et al. 1998). For example, through their use of play, children can demonstrate critical thinking. In a twenty-first-century learning environment "play" can be used to help children develop intercultural skills.

Creativity Robinson (2001) describes creativity as "the ability to make connections between ideas or experiences that were previously unconnected" (p. 11). He goes on to explain that "creative activity involves a combination of control and freedom, conscious and unconscious thought, intuition and rational analysis" (p. 135). One only has to study the artwork, dance, and language of young children to realize that children are at their creative best when they are very young. The challenge lies, not in cultivating creativity in them, but in preventing the *creativity loss* that unimaginative curricula could perpetuate. Educators and caregivers of young children should offer children a dynamic and interactive environment that spawns what Langer calls *generative ideas* and contributes to a consequent "ricochet of innovation" (Robinson 2001, p. 176).

Web 2.0 Technology: Powerful Tools that can be Used to Expand Global Awareness

Twenty-first century teaching and learning is not something new to be added to an already full curriculum. Instead, it is a new way of thinking about the curriculum. Strong leadership is needed to minimize the shortcomings of flawed textbooks, resist the different forms of teacher-proof curricula that are becoming so popular in the U.S., and support the "problem-posing" and "critical pedagogy" advocated by Freire and other advocates of inquiry-based learning, which has been an extremely effective way of teaching diverse children of all ages (Dyasi 1999). To successfully resist a culture of testing in favor of cultivating a twenty-first-century environment characterized by communication, collaboration, critical thinking, and creativity, school leaders need to have greater confidence in teachers and allow them to be the curriculum designers. Teachers should be taught how to engage in sophisticated, multilevel, critical, multicultural curriculum planning, which involves drawing "upon multiple sources, ranging from mandated curriculum guides and standards, to published teacher resource material, to the collection of alternative sources of multiculturally rich artifacts" (Oyler 2011, p. 157).

Tapscot and Williams (2006) compare the internet to a giant computer which everyone can program. Children who are raised in racially homogenous rural communities will benefit greatly from a curriculum that allows them to gain the cultural competency they need to function in a world that has gone global. It is not enough to integrate ethnic content into the curriculum; we need to transform it so that it can help children develop the "decision making, social action, and cross-cultural skills needed for the twenty-first century" (Banks 2009, p. 27). Web 2.0 technologies, in particular, provide us with the tools that allow us to enrich the curriculum, cultivate curious and creative minds, and establish an environment that supports cultural reciprocity, in which children of different cultures learn about each other, adapt to, and create an ever-changing society (Xu and Connelly 2010). Young children need opportunities to explore other worlds in order to understand "the other." With the help of technology tools, young children can be taught how to value diversity, develop a critical social consciousness, and learn to appreciate similarities and differences (Glimps and Ford 2008).

There is a growing body of literature that documents the ways in which technology tools are being used, over the last decade or so, to help upper elementary and middle school children learn about other cultures (Eristi 2009; Gowers 2009; Moore-Hart 2004). Through a study comprised of 12 American fifth-grade children and 33 Korean sixth-grade children over a period of 9 weeks, O'Neill (2007) found that the International Virtual Elementary Classroom can increase intercultural competence, develop social skills, enhance reading and writing abilities, and engage children with learning disabilities. International Virtual Elementary Classroom activities were used to show how children could develop meaningful interactions using asynchronous online communications through Blackboard. Data collected included observations, interviews, and student journals.

Eristi (2009) studied the influence of interactive art education applications using multiple technologies to promote cultural awareness in third- and fourth-graders in Turkey and Canada. Children in the Turkish and Canadian schools participated in lessons to discuss culture prior to beginning collaboration. The study used email, chat, video chat, photos, and drawings shared on the Internet. The researchers reported that children enjoyed learning about another culture and valued the experience.

Teachers can use the International Education and Resource Network (IEARN) to make it possible for children of all ages to collaborate with others in over 160 countries for a single lesson or for long-term projects. They can engage children in projects linked to subject areas and designated age groups to help them begin to understand a wide range of cultures and attitudes. The environment is secure and only open to members who are educators and children. Within the context of these cross-curricular projects, children are able to explore their own cultures and learn about the cultures and countries of other children of the same age/grade level. Gowers (2009) describes several similar projects, such as the Teddy Bear Exchange, the Folk Tale Project, Learning Circles, and the One World Project. Moore-Hart (2004) describes how teachers promoted a multicultural classroom using a hypermedia program called *Multicultural Links*. Children of different age groups were given access to interactive maps, pictures, and music from other countries that corresponded with the literature they were reading in class. Children also used the hypermedia environment to explore countries of choice. Other specific examples included Family Home pages, Web Kidz, KidPub, ePals, video conferencing, Hybrid Border Spaces, Global School Net, and Schools Online.

While children who live in cosmopolitan regions have the opportunity to interact with and learn from people who are different from them in terms of ethnicity, language, religion, race, social class, and political thought this might not happen, especially if intolerance is bred explicitly and implicitly. For such children, and those who live in places that lack diversity, Web 2.0 technology tools, like the ones listed in Table 5.1, can be used to connect with people in other parts of the world, and, in doing so, educators and caregivers of young children can demolish the metaphorical walls of the home and classroom to bring in diversity.

The use of Web 2.0 technologies in meaningful ways within and beyond the classroom will result in what Marshall et al. (2010) call *creative curiosity*. They describe this as "a symbiotic relationship between the two in order for either to positively impact a teacher's professional identity, pedagogy, and, ultimately, students' academic success" (p. 155). Teachers can use these tools to bring about what Banks calls *multiple acculturation*, a process which acknowledges that the world and the United States are developed by many groups. Web 2.0 tools, like the ones listed in Table 5.1, make it easier for teachers to engage young children in exploration of content from the perspectives of dominant and non-dominant groups. While the *creative curiosity* that is evoked has the potential to cause some discomfort and anxiety, it could lead to reform that builds on the transformative approach.

News media, like PBS Kids and National Geographic, and Web 2.0 technologies, like Kid Blog, Twitter, and Facebook, provide us with opportunities to make

Table 5.1 Technology tools that can be used to create hybrid border spaces

Links	Description of each technology tool	Twenty-first-century skills			
		Communication	Collaboration	Critical thinking	Creativity
Explore and share					
www.diigo.com	Diigo provides a browser add-on that improves childrens' ability to look for and bookmark sites. Children can use Diigo to highlight portions of web pages that are of particular interest to them. They can superimpose sticky notes to specific parts of web pages. They can search, access, sort, and share their collection of highlighted webpages from any PC or even their parents' iPhone.	*	*	*	
www.twitter.com	With adult supervision, children can connect to the latest stories, ideas, opinions, and news that they find interesting. They can use Twitter to find, follow, and share compelling pictures, video clips, and ideas with children from other parts of the world.	*	*		*
Virtual Field Trips (links vary as shown)	Children can discover new worlds by going on virtual field trips with friends and family. Utah Educational Network Field Trips: www.uen.org/utahlink/tour/volcano.und.nodak.edu/wocs/kids/vrtrips.html Virtual Field Trip Sites from AEA 267: www.aea2.k12ia.us/curriculum/virtualtrips.html Tramline: www.field-guides.com/trips.htm Surfaquarium: www.surfaquarium.com/virtual.htm Big Bend National Park Geology Field Trip: www.geoweb.tamu.edu/faculty/Herbert/bigbend The Mysterious Mayas: www.uen.org/utahlink/tours/tourFames.cgi?tour_id=14933			*	
Creation and presentation of content and ideas locally and globally					
www.wordle.net	Children can use this tool to convert their stories, rough notes, and/or web-based content to generate "word clouds" which give greater prominence to words that appear more frequently in the source text. They can tweak their clouds with different fonts, layouts, and color schemes; print out their clouds; share with peers and/or family; or share their clouds virtually in the Wordle gallery.	*		*	*

Table 5.1 (continued)

Links	Description of each technology tool	Twenty-first-century skills			
		Communication	Collaboration	Critical thinking	Creativity
www.common-craft.com/video/podcasting	With adult supervision, children can log onto a secure podcast host and gain access to the latest versions of podcasts to which they have subscribed. They can use programs like Audacity to create and share podcasts that they create with the help of an adult, like reader's theatres, story times, and/or poetry slams with friends and family.	*		*	*
www.glogster.com	Children can add video, audio, text, and images to visually and/or orally represent items like a book report, cultural representation, historical timeline, invention, cultural event, or a virtual poster.	*		*	*
www.flickr.com	Children can use this image-based social network site to upload and share photographs, videos, and animations. Folders can be shared with other children who can use the pictures to practice the language of opinion and speculation (I think it's… it must be… it can be…). Children can guess where the image is taken, select images to form a story, peer correct or make suggestions using the commentary function, and share all of this with other groups of children.	*	*	*	
www.animoto.com	Adults can apply for unlimited videos which they can share with children. Children can use this tool to create wonderful 30-s videos of the exciting things they do in the home or classroom with three simple steps.	*	*		*
www.skype.com	With adult supervision, children can share their world with other people in real time. They can use Skype to send friends instant messages, voice messages, text messages, photos, videos, and files of any size while they chat with them and see them in real time.	*	*		
www.voicethread.com	Children can use VoiceThread to create a collaborative, multimedia slideshow. They can invite children from all over the world to navigate slides and leave comments using voice (with a microphone or telephone), text, audio file, or video (via a Webcam). The commentary feature makes it possible to engage in a digital conversation asynchronously. Children have time to reflect and develop their responses—an important factor for mono-lingual children who need a translator and/or language learners.	*	*	*	*

Table 5.1 (continued)

Links	Description of each technology tool	Communication	Collaboration	Critical thinking	Creativity
Synchronous and asynchronous content development					
www.docs.google.com	Children can collaboratively work on a word-processed document, spreadsheet, presentation, drawing, or form through the Internet with multiple people in multiple connections in real time.	*	*	*	*
www.blogger.com www.wordpress.com www.edublogger.com	Children can create blogs for teachers, parents, peers, classes, or projects. Blogs are electronic journals where users can post their thoughts, opinions, insights, audio files (also known as podcasts), or other types of digital media on a regular basis. They can also add comments to others' posts.	*	*	*	*
www.wikimatrix.org www.wetpaint.com www.pbwiki.com www.wikispaces.com www.educationalwikis.wikispaces.com www.wiki.classroom20.com	Educators can use wikis to create online spaces for cross-cultural collaboration. They can teach children how to use these spaces to store and share resources and information, such as useful links, videos, and audio clips. They can use these wikis to brainstorm, draft, revise, edit, and publish, all of which can be done in real time. Because different versions of the text and edits are saved for ease of reference, wikis are an ideal tool for process writing.	*	*	*	*
Sharing digital media with friends and family					
www.music.google.com	Children can create an entertainment hub of all their favorite apps, music, movies, and books. They can store and stream these over the Internet.	*	*		
www.dropbox.com	Children can store multimedia projects using their teachers' and/or caregivers' Dropbox account. They can convert files to links and share these with friends and family.	*	*		

sense of events happening all over the world—Iraq, Afghanistan, Israel, and Darfur. Educators and caregivers of young children who make use of these events can raise social consciousness and incite civil action in children. New types of media make it possible for children to reach across continents to connect with children in another state or another country with ease. Global exchanges across cultures have the added benefit of increasing children's interest in subjects that might otherwise be deemed boring (O'Neill 2007). This allows children to learn content-specific information in the context of real-life situations; they will begin to value diversity, develop a critical social consciousness, and appreciate similarities and differences in cultures (Glimps and Ford 2008). Children will be better equipped to take advantage of authentic and meaningful experiences that take place beyond the classroom walls if they simultaneously receive direct and informal instruction relating to digital citizenship.

Technology-Infused Critical Pedagogy in Hybrid Border Spaces: Transformative Learning in Action

The vignettes below provide insight into how early childhood educators and parents around the world used advanced technology to create the hybrid border spaces advocated by Cronje (2010). In these technology-infused environments which support acculturation, children were given an opportunity to explore each other's cultures, create identities, and develop the twenty-first century skills they need to function in an interconnected world. Vignette 1 illustrates how Mrs. Mombatu in Ghana and her counterpart in Australia use Skype to create a hybrid border space where their kindergarten children can learn about each other's culture.

Vignette 1. Mrs. Mombatu's Kindergarten Class in Ghana Used Skype to Interact With Ms. Jennings' Kindergarten Class in Australia

Ms. Mombatu's class in Ghana and Ms. Jenning's class in Australia are exploring units on food and nutrition. Earlier this week, both classes read the book *The Sandwich Swap* written by Queen Rania of Jordan. With their respective teachers, they talked about the ways in which Lily and Salma expressed their distaste for each other's favorite sandwich and why such behavior is unacceptable. Following this, they used the ugly words and the food fight described in the book as a springboard for discussion about positive and negative impact of actions and words. They discussed the similarities and differences between peanut butter sandwiches and hummus sandwiches, their nutritional value, and the nutritional value of their favorite sandwiches.

Mrs. Mombatu and Ms. Jennings had coordinated a common meeting time to provide the children in their respective classes with an opportunity to interact with each other and learn, first hand, about meals they enjoyed. At 8:00 am in Accra, Ghana the children in Mrs. Mombatu's class logged on

> to Skype. A few minutes later, Ms. Jenning' class joined them via Skype. It was 4 pm in Sydney, Australia. Using an iPad, the teachers gave each other's class a tour of their respective classroom. They then placed the iPad near their respective tables so the children could see the assortment of snacks that they had each prepared, as well as some unfamilar ingredients they used.
>
> "Aussies love vegemite sandwiches," said Bill. He explained that vegemite is a brown paste made from yeast. Nurhaya explained that vegemite tastes best on toasted bread, and that she liked to add avocado and tomato to her sandwich.
>
> Kwaku happily explained that some children in Ghana enjoyed eating kokonte, made from dried cassava chips. He pointed to the cassava and cassava chips on the table and explained how he helped his mother to make kokonte on weekends. Yaw said he preferred to eat banku prepared from fermented corn or cassava dough. Olivia said her mother made her eat Tom Brown, a roasted maize porridge, because it is very nutritious.
>
> Before they signed off, Mrs. Mombatu and Ms. Jennings passed out the recipes that the children had helped their teachers write and email to each other the previous day. They encouraged the children to experience the cuisine of another culture by trying out one of the new recipes with an adult. They agreed to share their drawings and descriptions of the snack at their Skype meeting the following week.

With the help of well-thought-out follow-up activities and discussion, Mrs. Mombatu in Ghana and Ms. Jennings in Australia, can help their students appreciate not just food choices made by children from a different region, and the social and economic factors that influence these choices, but also the subtle ways in which the *power distance* between teachers and their young children might be evident. Simple questions like "How is their classroom different from our classroom?" can lead to discussions that can promote cultural awareness. The teachers can draw children's attention to how the teacher has arranged the furniture, the language children use to address their respective teachers, and the nature of the activities that children engage in at home and in school. They can also discuss the cross-cultural difference in terms of time orientation, where some cultures have more of a clock orientation and are driven by deadlines, while others see time as a fluid construct and have more of an event orientation.

Vignettes 2 and 3 show how teachers used a variety of technology tools and well-thought-out curricula to dissolve boundaries and provide children with opportunities to examine and appreciate each other's cultural traditions. While the focus of the activities are on the dominant culture tradition, technology allows the children of both classes to reflect on the ways in which some groups are privileged and to consider the impact that traditions and norms have on children who identify with non-dominant groups.

Vignette 2. Mr. Dixon's (USA) and Mrs. Chang's (China) 2nd-Graders Used VoiceThread to Discuss Cultural Traditions that they Celebrate at the Beginning of Each Calendar Year in Their Respective Countries

While Mr. Dixon's 2nd-graders in the U.S. were excited about Valentine's Day, Mrs. Chang's 2nd-graders were excited about Chinese New Year, which occurs around the same time. To learn more about each other's culture, they decided to create and exchange Voicethreads. The VoiceThread that the American children created included a video recording of a story they read, pictures of the valentines they made and exchanged, and an audio recording of the love song that they composed together as a class. On January 16, Mr. Dixon emailed a link of this VoiceThread to Mrs. Chang and asked her to send it back after her class had commented on the different slides.

A few days later they received the VoiceThread that Mrs. Chang's class had created. It was exciting to hear Mrs. Chang's class describe how families clean their homes to sweep away all traces of misfortune. They were surprised to hear that fireworks were used to frighten away monsters and evil spirits and to gain the attention of the gods. They enjoyed seeing pictures of the shops and homes that were decorated with lanterns, flowers, and bright banners.

"I wish Valentine's Day lasted 2 weeks, too," said Jim.

"Wouldn't it be nice if we got gifts of money in red?" said Bob.

"We don't get money, but we do get presents, candy and cards," said Beth.

"Can we celebrate Chinese New Year too, Mr. Dixon?"

"Do Chinese-American children in the U.S. get 2 weeks off to celebrate Chinese New year?" asked Susan.

"No, they do not; they get holidays for Christmas and Easter, just like you do."

"That's not fair. I think we should speak to the principal about *that*!" said Susan.

"If we have a meeting with the principal, we have to be well-prepared. What questions will he have for us? How do we prepare ourselves to answer these questions appropriately? We probably need to spend some time later today to come up with a plan before we request a meeting," said Mr. Dixon.

Mr. Dixon, through his response to Susan's concern about structural inequality, reflects his willingness to use critical pedagogy to empower his class to name, critically reflect, and act. Even though he can predict a negative outcome, he is willing to take the time to provide the children in his classroom with an opportunity to think critically and develop political consciousness.

By engaging children in photograph and conversation analysis, Mr. Dixon can help them understand why their Chinese counterparts have more of a collectivist orientation than they do. They can discuss why American children prefer to have their own set of crayons, as opposed to sharing bowls of crayons separated by color like their Chinese friends do. They can talk about the impact that a classroom where individualism is favored can have on an immigrant who favors a different orientation. Finally, they can discuss the changes that need to take place in the American classroom to embrace the *funds of knowledge* that other cultures bring to the U.S. At all times, he should emphasize that children need to learn how to adapt to different methods of communication, because one approach is not superior to another.

Vignette 3 shows how third-graders use three different Web 2.0 tools to *do* critical pedagogy. Mrs. Smith and Mrs. Patel, through their involvement with caregivers, have allowed the children in their class to become part of the hybrid border space. This ensures that cross-cultural conversations carry on long after children leave the school building at the end of the day.

> **Vignette 3. Mrs. Smith's (Canada) and Mrs. Patel's (India) 3rd-Graders Used Google Documents and Diigo to Learn About the Jobs People Do**
>
> Mrs. Smith's 3rd-grade in Canada and Mrs. Patel's class in India were learning about the work done by members of the community. Each class generated a list of occupations popular in their respective countries on a shared **Google Document**. The two classes worked together, asynchronously, to synthesize the list. Each class then used **Diigo** to bookmark websites that will provide them with more information about the different occupations on their list. Each class studied and discussed the different occupations on the list; they were then ready to share their thoughts on their shared class **blog**. Each child identified a job that is overpaid and one that is underpaid, and explained why they felt this is so. They made at least three comments on their classmates' posts. Each class discussed the similarities and differences that exist between the two countries. Finally, after reading all the posts, they worked in pairs and wrote letters of appreciation to the people in their community who do not get paid enough for the jobs that they do. Accompanied by their parents and/or guardians, they hand-delivered these letters to members of the community and personally expressed their gratitude.

Children as young as five or six can use Twitter. They might not have an account of their own but, with guidance, they can learn how to use their teacher's account to upload their pictures to the Web. The Twitter application makes it easy enough for children to teach each other how to tweet. Including parents and guardians in this process has multiple benefits. The activity will allow parents and guardians to overcome some of the fears associated with Twitter. Also, it will give them an opportunity to expand their own cultural knowledge, and could lead to stimulating conversations about the pictures and the ways in which traditions are upheld.

Vignette 4. Mrs. Sohail's 1st-Grade Class in Pakistan Used Twitter to Share Their Drawings with Mrs. Blake's Class in England

Mrs. Sohail's class had just finished coloring pictures that represented their favorite cultural celebration. "Mine is done, Mrs. Sohail; can we tweet it now?" asked Iqra.

"Raise your hand when you are ready, and I will bring the iPad to you. You can then pass it to the next person and show them how to tweet their picture to the Web."

"My picture shows friends dressing up the bride for her wedding. I wonder if brides in other countries wear red and gold like our brides do."

"The children in Mrs. Blake's class will be commenting on our pictures and sharing their own, too, so we will soon find out," said Mrs. Sohail.

"Tweet mine, Mrs. Sohail; I have drawn a picture of a masjid on Eid day," said Attaullah.

"Mine is an Eid picture, too; I have drawn animals being sacrificed on Eid morning."

"How long do we have to wait before we see their pictures, Mrs. Sohail?" Iqra inquired.

"Let us check the world clock app on the iPad, Iqra. That will help us to figure out what time it is in London right now."

After every child had tweeted his/her picture with a caption and the name of the artist, Mrs. Sohail said, "Your pictures are now on Twitter. Please show your family members how to find our picture gallery. Ask them to look for #PakUkpics. They can help you leave comments and respond to questions about your picture. If they do not have their own Twitter account, give them our "guest account." Please let your parents know that they are welcome to stop by and use the computer in our classroom to look at our gallery."

"My dad is going to Syria tomorrow. I asked him to upload pictures to our gallery. Is that ok?" asked Jamshed.

"Of course! Please ask him to describe each picture briefly so we understand what we are seeing," said Mrs. Sohail.

The children in Mrs. Blake's and Mrs. Sohail's classes might not agree on the most humane way to slaughter an animal, the most appropriate bridal attire, or the number of times a person should pray each day but, in conversing with each other, they will learn judgments should follow rather than precede careful analysis of context and circumstances.

Vignette 5. Second-Grade Children in Brazil and England Use Flickr to Exchange Videos, Digital Photos, and Other Media

"This is so fun, Mrs. Robinson," said Shane, with her eyes glued to the computer screen. "I did not know Spanish could be fun, even though it's hard." Shane's 2nd-grade class was visiting one of the school computer labs to look at the Flickr pictures 2nd-grade Brazilian children had shared with them. Their class was part of a project where English and Brazilian children exchanged ideas, cultural traditions, and class projects using Flickr as a platform. Children in both classrooms had created projects based around the theme "One Day in My Life." Children were sharing videos, digital photos, and other media that expressed what their lives were like on a given day. Shane then shared a photo of his family at breakfast in the morning. "See, you just click here, click browse, and there is my picture," Shane said excitedly. After he posted his own pictures, he looked at the pictures posted by his Brazilian friends and left comments in Spanish; they, in turn, left comments in English.

Final Thoughts

To make it possible for every young child to survive and thrive in an increasingly diverse interconnected world, educators and caregivers must provide young children with an environment where they think critically, communicate, collaborate, and create within and across physical and virtual spaces. Creative curiosity (Marshall et al. 2010), cultural reciprocity (Xu and Connelly 2010), multiple acculturation (Banks

2009), and global awareness are important not just for children of color who live in the inner-city, but also middle-class children of the dominant group, like the one described in the introductory vignette, who live in racially and ethnically homogenous areas. The technology tools to which we now have access can be used to create hybrid border spaces where children, guided by educators and caregivers, can explore different cultures, expand their cultural knowledge, and build a strong sense of who they are and the world in which they live. Technologically-infused critical pedagogy that requires naming, critical reflection, and action (Wink 2011) can be employed within these spaces to help young children gain the knowledge, attitudes, and skills needed to participate in cross-cultural interactions and in personal, social, and civic action, needed to create a more democratic and just society.

References

Ainsworth, L. (2007). Common formative assessments: The centerpiece of an integrated standards-based assessment system. In D. Reeves (Ed.), *Ahead of the curve: The power of assessment to transform teaching and learning*, (pp. 79–102). Bloomington, IN: Solution Tree.

Ansary, T. (2004). A textbook example of what's wrong with education. *Edutopia*. http://www.edutopia.org/textbook-publishing-controversy.

Apple, M. (2001). *Educating the "right" way: Markets, standards, God, and, inequality*. New York, NY: Routledge.

Ayers, W. C. (2004). Teaching towards freedom: Educational research in the public interest. In G. Ladson-Billings & W. F. Tate (Eds.), *Education research in the public interest: Social justice, action, and policy* (pp. 81–97). New York, NY: Teachers College Press.

Banks, J. A. (2009). *Teaching strategies for ethnic studies*. Boston, MA: Pearson.

Berliner, D. C. (2010). The incompatibility of high stakes testing and the development of skills for the twenty-first century. In R. Marzano (Ed.), *On excellence in teaching* (pp. 112–166). Bloomington, IN: Solution Tree.

Bonk, C. J. (2009). *World is open: How web technology is revolutionizing, education*. San Francisco, CA: Jossey-Bass.

Centers for Disease Control and Prevention. (2009). *Autism spectrum disorders (A.S.D.)*. http://www.cdc.gov/ncbddd/autism/facts.html.

Chak, A. (2007). Teachers' and parents' conceptions of children's curiosity and exploration. *International Journal of Early Years Education, 15*(2), 141–159.

Cochran-Smith, M. (2004). *Walking the road: Race, diversity, and social justice in teacher education*. New York, NY: Teachers College Press.

Cronje, F. (2010). Creating hybrid border spaces in the classroom through video production. *English Teaching: Practice and Critique, 9*, 36–47.

Daniel, M., & Gagnon, M. (2011). Developmental process of dialogical critical thinking in groups of pupils aged 4 to 12 years. *Creative Education, 2*(5), 418–428.

Dyasi, H. (1999). What children gain by learning through inquiry. In *Foundations: A monograph for professionals in science, mathematics, and technology education, vol. 2: Inquiry, thoughts, views, and strategies for the K-5 classroom* (pp. 9–13). Arlington, VA: Directorate of Education and Human Resources, National Science Foundation.

Edwards, C., Gandini, I., & Forman, C. (1998). *The hundred languages of children* (2nd ed.). Westport, CT: Ablex.

Eristi, S. (2009). Using an interactive art education application to promote cultural, awareness: A case study from Turkey. *International Journal of Education through Art, 5*(2/3), 241–256.

Garner, R., Brown, R., Sanders, S., & Menke, D. J. (1992). "Seductive details" and learning from text. In K. A. Renninger, S. Hidi, & A. Krapp (Eds.), *The role of interest in learning and development* (pp. 239–254). Hillsdale, NJ: Erlbaum.

Glimps, B. J., & Ford, T. (2008). Using Internet technology tools to teach about global diversity. *Clearing House, 82*, 91–95.

Gopnik, A., Meltzoff, A. N., & Kuhl, P. K. (2000). *The scientist in the crib: What early learning tells us about the mind.* New York, NY: Harper-Perennial.

Gorski, P. (2009). What we're teaching teachers: An analysis of multicultural teacher education coursework syllabi. *Teaching and Teacher, 25*, 309–318.

Gowers, M. (2009). Connecting youth–making a difference around the world. *Education Review, 21*, 41–46.

Hall, E. T. (1959). *The silent language.* New York, NY: Doubleday.

Hofstede, G. (1997). *Cultures and organizations: Software of the mind.* New York, NY: McGraw-Hill.

Hooks, B. (1994). *Teaching to transgress: Education as the practice of freedom.* New York, NY: Routledge.

Kincheloe, J. L. (2008). *Critical pedagogy primer.* New York, NY: Peter Lang.

Klein, M., & Chen, D. (2001). *Working with children from culturally diverse, backgrounds.* Clifton Park, NY: Delmar Thomson Learning.

Kotkin, J. (2010, August). The changing demographics of America. *Smithsonian Magazine.* http://www.smithsonian.com/specialsections/40th-anniversary/The-Changing-Demographics-of-America.html.

Lewis, G. (2009). *Bringing technology into the classroom.* New York, NY: Oxford University Press.

Li, J. (2012). *Cultural foundations of learning: East and West.* New York, NY: Cambridge University Press.

London, E., & Etzel, R. A. (2000). The environment as an etiologic factor in autism: A new direction for research. *Environmental Health Perspectives, 108*(3), 401–404.

Marshall, P. L., McCulloch, A. W., & DeCuir-Gunby, J. T. (2010). Nurturing a creative curiosity for K-12 mathematics teaching: Lessons from the dreamkeepers. In C. J. Craig & L. F. Deretchin (Eds.), *Cultivating curious and creative minds, the role of teachers and teacher educators, part 1: Teacher education yearbook XVII* (pp. 132–160). Lanham, MD: Rowan & Littlefield Education.

McLaren, P. (2007). *Revolutionary multiculturalism: Pedagogies of dissent for the new millennium.* Boulder, CO: Westview.

Meadows, M., & Murphy, F. (2004). Using technology in early childhood environments to strengthen cultural connections. *Information Technology in Childhood Education, 1*, 39–47.

Moore-Hart, P. (2004). Creating learning environments that invite all students to learn through multicultural literature and information technology. *Childhood Education, 81*, 87–91.

Nieto, S., & Bode, P. (2008). *Affirming diversity: The sociopolitical context of multicultural education* (5th ed.). Boston, MA: Pearson.

O'Neill, E. J. (2007). Implementing international virtual elementary classroom activities for public school students in the US and Korea. *Electronic Journal of E-Learning, 5*, 207–218.

Oyler, C. (2011). Preparing teachers of young children to be social justice-oriented educators. In B. Z. Fennimore & A. L. Goodwin (Eds.), *Promoting social justice for young children* (pp. 147–162). New York, NY: Springer.

Paul, R. W. (1993). *Critical thinking: What every person needs to survive in a changing world.* Tomales, CA: Foundation for Critical Thinking.

Popham, W. J. (2001). *The truth about testing: An educator's call to action.* Alexandria, VA: Association for Supervision and Curriculum Development.

Robinson, K. (2001). *Out of our minds: Learning to be creative.* Chichester, UK: Capstone Publishing Limited.

Rosebery, A., McIntyre, E., & Gonzalez, N. (2001). Connecting students' cultures to instruction. In E. McIntyre, A. Rosebery, & N. Gonzalez (Eds.), *Classroom diversity: Connecting curriculum to student lives* (pp. 1–13). Portsmouth, NH: Heinemann.

Segall, A. (2004). Revisiting pedagogical content knowledge: The pedagogy of content/the content of pedagogy. *Teaching and Teacher Education, 20,* 489–504.

Sleeter, C. E., & Grant, C. A. (2007). *Making choices for multicultural education: Five approaches to race, class, and gender.* Hoboken, NJ: Wiley.

Tapscott, D., & Williams, A. D. (2006). "The Perfect Storm." *Wikinomics: How mass collaboration changes everything.* New York: Portfolio (Penguin Group).

Ting-Toomey, S. (1999). *Communicating across cultures.* New York, NY: Guilford.

Triandis, H. C. (1995). *Individualism and collectivism.* Boulder, CO: Westview.

Trinley, T. (2009). *Monumental myths* [Motion picture]. United States: Films for Action. (Producer & Director). http://www.filmsforaction.org/watch/monumental_myths_2009/.

Wink, J. (2011). *Critical pedagogy: Notes from the real world.* Boston, MA: Pearson.

Xy, S., & Connelly, F. M. (2010). On the need for curious and creative minds in multicultural cross-cultural educational settings: Narrative possibilities. In C. J. Craig & L. F. Deretchin (Eds.), *Cultivating curious and creative minds, the role of teachers and teacher educators, part 1: Teacher education yearbook XVII* (pp. 252–266). Lanham, MD: Rowman & Littlefield Education.

Zimmerman, J. (2002). *Whose America? Culture wars in public schools.* Cambridge, MA: Harvard University Press.

Chapter 6
Using Multimedia Technologies to Support Culturally and Linguistically Diverse Learners and Young Children with Disabilities

Kavita Rao and James Skouge

Abstract Multimedia technologies can be used creatively to provide opportunities for children to practice skills and become producers of knowledge. In this chapter, we describe ways in which multimedia software can be used to support culturally and linguistically diverse students as well as young children with developmental delays or disabilities. The projects we describe are aligned with Universal Design for Learning (UDL) principles and best practices for culturally-responsive education. Using commonly-available productivity tools on computers and mobile devices, teachers and parents can create photo and video-based projects that give students the opportunity to practice communication, social, and behavior skills. We emphasize ways to honor the diverse cultural backgrounds of students and to foster first language literacy along with acquisition of language skills.

Keywords Multimedia technology · Culturally and linguistically diverse students · Special education · Inclusion · Family · Universal Design for Learning · UDL

Introduction

Three-year-old Lea eagerly looks at the computer screen, laughing with delight when she views a short video of herself eating breakfast. The video stops and Lea is given two choices on the screen. She looks at a photo of a bowl of cereal or a pancake. She points to the cereal, letting her mother know what she wants to eat today. Her mother clicks on the photo on the screen, and Lea hears a clip from her favorite song as she watches another short video of herself eating cereal. For Lea, who is unable to communicate with words, the video provides a visual reminder of her morning routine and helps her make her own selection of what she wants to eat for breakfast.

K. Rao (✉) · J. Skouge
University of Hawai'i at Mānoa, Honolulu, USA
e-mail: kavitar@hawaii.edu

In this chapter, we describe ways to involve young children and their families in the process of creating personalized multimedia projects. These projects are simple and creative, combining text, audio, and video, and using everyday technology tools such as the built-in cameras on laptops and mobile devices. Multimedia projects can be designed to provide specific supports for language learning and expressive skills for culturally and linguistically diverse children and for children with disabilities. This chapter presents four vignettes, each one describing a multimedia project that supports specific communication functions and/or social and behavioral skills. Through the vignettes, we provide examples of multimedia projects that can be developed by parents and teachers to support the needs of children with developmental delays and other disabilities. We highlight ways in which multimedia projects allow families and teachers to integrate culture and home language for students from culturally and linguistically diverse backgrounds.

The most important feature of these projects is that the child is involved in creating and interacting with a personalized product. The end result can be appropriate as a way to let a child make choices, practice specific learning objectives, and enjoy language, expression and interaction. The projects celebrate the familiar by including familiar people, places, objects, and activities. The projects give young children a foundation for early language and literacy, each one integrating elements of the surrounding environment that the child knows best. Grounded in the social learning theories of Lev Vygotsky (1978) and Albert Bandura (1997), these projects rely on social construction of knowledge and modeling as a way to support a child in meeting his/her goals. Parents, siblings, teachers, and peers are the stars of short videos within the projects. The children are also featured prominently, as their own self models engaged in role play and practice of emerging knowledge and skill.

Honoring Family, Community, and Culture

Located in the middle of the Pacific Ocean, the state of Hawaii is at a geographic crossroads, as reflected in the cultural and linguistic diversity of its population. In addition to a large Asian population, Hawaii is home to many Pacific Islanders from American Samoa, the Federated States of Micronesia, and the Republic of the Marshall Islands. Many Pacific Islander children grow up as part of an extended family and community of islanders, steeped in the traditional indigenous cultural values of their home islands. Teachers in a typical Hawaii preschool or early childhood classroom may have students speaking 5 or 6 different home languages, including Asian languages such as Ilocano, Tagalog, Chinese, and Vietnamese, and Pacific languages such as Marshallese, Samoan, Tongan, and Chuukese.

In order to honor first language and to integrate students' cultural and linguistic backgrounds as part of their education, we focus on incorporating home language and making cultural connections in these projects. The projects described in this chapter align with principles of effective instruction for diverse students. The Center for Research on Education, Diversity, and Excellence (CREDE) has published five standards for effective pedagogy and learning (CREDE 2004) based on several decades of research with diverse students. Researchers have added two additional standards to the original CREDE standards, based on their work with young children and indigenous learners (Yamauchi et al. 2012) Details on the seven CREDE Standards in Early Childhood can be found on this CREDE Hawaii Project website: http://manoa.hawaii.edu/coe/crede.

The projects we describe align closely to the following CREDE Standards in Early Childhood: Joint Productive Activity, Language Development, Contextualization, Modeling, and Child Directed Activity. The Joint Productivity Activity indicators focus on teachers and students producing together. Collaborative activities with mixed-ability groupings of peers are encouraged as a means to support student learning. The Language and Literacy Development indicators recommend the use of modeling for oral language development and the use of first and second languages in instructional activities. The Contextualization indicators recommend connecting the school curriculum to children's prior knowledge and experiences from their home and community. The Modeling indicators focus on giving children the opportunity to observe and practice behaviors and procedures. The Child Directed Activity indicators focus on giving children the opportunities to generate, develop, and expand on ideas within an activity.

Everyday Technologies

A key element of the projects we describe is simplicity. Using familiar technology tools and software, we strive to make it possible for family members, service providers, and early childhood teachers to create personalized multimedia projects quickly and with ease. The multimedia projects we describe are created using presentation software that is included in computer productivity suites such as Microsoft PowerPoint (available for Mac and Windows operating systems) and Apple Keynote (available for the Mac). Typically, presentation software is used to create slide shows that support speakers who are presenting information to an audience. When used in creative ways, this software has the potential to become a simple multimedia authoring environment. With its ability to combine and display media elements—such as photos, video, audio, and text—presentation software can be used purposefully to transform media into tools of learning and engagement for young children, as we illustrate in this chapter.

Universal Design for Learning and Multimedia Technology

These days, we have an array of creative digital tools at our fingertips. We regularly capture the sights and sounds of our everyday lives, snapping digital photos and taking short videos on our smartphones, tablets, and laptops. When integrated purposefully, these media elements can be turned into powerful and personalized instructional tools for young children.

The Universal Design for Learning (UDL) framework provides a set of principles and guidelines for creating flexible and accessible learning environments (CAST 2013). UDL is based on *universal design*, a term first coined by Ron Mace in the 1980s (Center for Universal Design 2010). Universal design was originally focused on making physical environments accessible to as many users as possible. UDL adds the "learning" component and extends the notion of access to cognitive tasks, focusing on ways to design flexible curricula, resources, and instructional methods to support the learning objectives of a child (Hitchcock et al. 2002).

The UDL framework includes three main principles: (1) provide multiple means of representation, (2) provide multiple means of action and expression, and (3) provide multiple means of engagement. These principles can be applied to instructional goals, methods, materials, and assessments we create for children (Hall et al. 2012). Table 6.1 provides an overview of the nine guidelines that provide more definition to each UDL principle and the even more detailed "checkpoints" under each guideline. (Detailed descriptions of how to apply these checkpoints can be found at http://www.udlcenter.org/aboutudl/udlguidelines.) The projects we describe illustrate the application of these UDL guidelines. While the scope of this chapter does not allow for a detailed mapping of the UDL checkpoints to each project, we provide an overview of the guidelines/checkpoints being applied in each vignette.

The four vignettes in this chapter illustrate how multimedia technologies can be used to create personalized environments that help students communicate, learn, and interact. Each vignette highlights one or more of three communication domains, each relevant for young children with and without disabilities. The three domains addressed by the projects are (1) augmentative communication, (2) social learning, and (3) early literacy. Rather than relying on specialized software or tools that need to be purchased, the projects demonstrate ways in which we can use our everyday technologies creatively to engage young children in constructive and socially-based activities. The creation of these projects requires one or more of the following hardware and software resources:

- laptop or desktop computer
- tablet computer (such as Apple iPad or Sony Nexus)
- presentation software (such as Microsoft PowerPoint or Apple Keynote)
- built-in laptop cameras, smartphones, and/or digital tablets

Project 1—Multimedia Choice Board: Naming My World

Paulava is a 3-year-old with severe physical disabilities and language delays. She demonstrates some receptive language comprehension, but exhibits little or no expressive language. One of her language therapy goals is to learn to express choices by pointing to pictures on a communication board.

Table 6.1 UDL Checkpoints Aligned to Multimedia Projects (NCUDL 2010)

Multiple means of representation
1 *Provide options for perception*
1.1 Offer ways of customizing the display of information
1.2 Offer alternatives for auditory information
1.3 Offer alternatives for visual information
2 *Provide options for language, mathematical expressions, and symbols*
2.1 Clarify vocabulary and symbols
2.2 Clarify syntax and structure
2.3 Support decoding of text, mathematical notation, and symbols
2.4 Promote understanding across languages
2.5 Illustrate through multiple media
3 *Provide options for comprehension*
3.1 Activate or supply background knowledge
3.2 Highlight patterns, critical features, big ideas, and relationships
3.3 Guide information processing, visualization, and manipulation
3.4 Maximize transfer and generalization
Multiple means of action and expression
4 *Provide options for physical action*
4.1 Vary the methods for response and navigation
4.2 Optimize access to tools and assistive technologies
5 *Provide options for expression and communication*
5.1 Use multiple media for communication
5.2 Use multiple tools for construction and composition
5.3 Build fluencies with graduated support for practice/performance
6 *Provide options for executive functions*
6.1 Guide appropriate goal-setting
6.2 Support planning and strategy development
6.3 Facilitate managing information and resources
6.4 Enhance capacity for monitoring progress
Multiple means of engagement
7 *Provide options for recruiting interest*
7.1 Optimize individual choice and autonomy
7.2 Optimize relevance, value, and authenticity
7.3 Minimize threats and distractions
8 *Provide options for sustaining effort and persistence*
8.1 Heighten salience of goals and objectives
8.2 Vary demands and resources to optimize challenge
8.3 Foster collaboration and community
8.4 Increase mastery-oriented feedback
9 *Provide options for self-regulation*
9.1 Promote expectations and beliefs that optimize motivation
9.2 Facilitate personal coping skills and strategies
9.3 Develop self-assessment and reflection

Creating a Personalized Choice Board

Paulava's therapist makes a home-based project that incorporates photos of familiar items and videos of people in Paulava's life. Using a digital camera, Paulava's therapist takes 8 photos of preferred toys, favorite foods, and family members. Using the webcam on her computer, she also takes four short videos of family members, including parents, grandparents, and a sibling, asking each to say, "I love you, Paulava!"

The therapist uses presentation software (e.g., PowerPoint) to create an interactive choice board. She creates several new blank slides and inserts each of the photos and the videos on a separate slide. She has clips of children's music on her computer and knows which ones Paulava responds to with excitement. She places clips of Paulava's favorite songs onto the slides with the photos.

On the first slide of the presentation, she creates a "choice board" to be printed on paper. The choice board is a 4×3 grid (made by inserting a table in PowerPoint) that depicts all of the images from which Paulava will be prompted to choose. She resizes the 12 photos to fit in the grid. Once she has a grid with 12 photos, she prints out this first slide, creating a physical choice board, which she inserts into a plastic sleeve for protection.

Paulava Interacts with the Choice Board

Paulava's parents show her the choice board and prompt her to make choices. For example, they say, "Show me your truck," or "Where is Daddy?" When Paulava points to the correct object or person on the printed choice board, her parents select the corresponding slide on the computer with this image or video. Paulava is delighted by the images, the music, and the videos that pop up once she makes her choices. Upon responding to her parents' questions, she is immediately provided with an engaging reinforcement on screen for making correct choices.

"Paulava, can you show me the picture of Grandma?" Paulava touches her grandmother's picture from among the choices on the grid. Her parents select the slide that has the video of Grandmother smiling, laughing, and saying, "I love you, Paulava." They encourage Paulava to make another choice. "Paulava, which animal says moo?" Paulava touches the cow's picture and her parents click on the slide that has the cow. Paulava is delighted to go to a slide that has a large picture of a cow along with the audio clip of a favorite song, "Old McDonald had a farm. Ee ai. Ee ai. Oh. And on this farm, he had a …"

Educational Objectives

This project provides personalized augmentative communication options for Paulava. She is able to express herself by making simple choices and is immediately rewarded with visual and auditory feedback. The project addresses guidelines related to UDL Principles II and III. For example, the project addresses Guideline 5.1 (use multiple media for communication) and UDL guideline 7.2 (optimize relevance,

> **Step-by-Step Directions: Create a Multimedia Choice Board**
> 1. Take photos of familiar and beloved objects.
> 2. Take short videos of family members expressing a sentiment (such as "I love you") to the child.
> 3. Open a new file using presentation software (such as PowerPoint or Keynote).
> 4. Insert 8 slides and place one digital photo on each slide.
> 5. Optional: Add a short music clip that will interest the child.
> 6. Optional: Add a short text caption.
> 7. Insert 4 slides and place one video clip on each slide.
> 8. On the first slide of the presentation, create a 4 × 3 table and place the 12 photos in the grid. Resize the photos so they fit into the table.
> 9. Print out this first slide and place it in a plastic binder sheet. This is the "choice board" from which the child may select.
> 10. OPTIONAL: If you prefer having a digital choice board, the first slide does not have to be printed. The child may point to the photos on screen.

value, and authenticity). By involving family members in the videos, the project engages those in the child's home and community. For extended family members–such as grandparents, aunts, and uncles–this can be an opportunity to participate actively in supporting a child's developing skills in communication and expression.

Project 2—Social Learning: Video Role Plays

Kimo is a 5-year-old child with autism who is in a full-inclusion kindergarten classroom. Kimo demonstrates delays in the development of his speech and language skills and has trouble taking social cues from others. He becomes agitated during transition times; for example, moving from circle time to centers, recess to lunch, nap to story time, and free play to clean-up. He is engaged by visuals and media, often intently focused on pictures in classroom books.

Planning and Creating the Video Role Plays

Kimo's teacher decides to use role playing and self modeling to help Kimo practice expected behaviors during transition times. Role playing gives Kimo the opportunity to practice target behaviors in an authentic context. Self modeling allows him to practice and model the target behaviors. His teacher starts by identifying key transitions in the daily schedule of her class. Before she develops the role plays, she considers her behavioral expectations for the students during each transition.

For each transition, she asks the students to articulate and demonstrate expected behaviors. Students enjoy stating what they know about expected behaviors and acting them out. Kimo participates with his peers in this activity. Though he does not contribute to the discussion, he listens and acts out the steps with his peers as he is expected to do. After the students practice the desired behavior, the teacher films them modeling appropriate behavior during the transition. She uses the camera on her smartphone to record short video clips depicting about 10–20 s of each transition process. She makes sure Kimo is the focus of her videos. The children are engaged in this role play activity and do not mind the teacher's requests for re-takes.

Kimo Watches the Video Role Plays

After filming the transition activities, Kimo's teacher downloads the video clips onto her laptop and places each video onto a PowerPoint slide. Between each of these slides, she inserts slides with a question related to the next video such as, "What do we do after recess?" or "What do we do after lunch?" When the children view the project together in class, they call out answers to the question and then watch the related video on the next slide.

She also transfers the short videos onto the classroom tablet computer (e.g., iPad). This gives her access to the videos on a mobile device if she needs to review them with Kimo quickly or in different locations. As needed, she can conveniently access a specific video on the tablet to reinforce the behavior just before a transition occurs. The teacher gives Kimo's parents a copy of the PowerPoint file with the videos embedded so they can watch it at home and talk to Kimo about his school day too.

Every day, Kimo sits with the educational assistant at the start of class and reviews the activity sequence along with the teacher's reminder to prepare for the next activity. "Put away your toys. It is time for lunch." Slide by slide, Kimo observes himself engaging in various transition activities, at times choosing to verbalize what he sees on the video and spontaneously commenting as he watches himself. "I wash my hands before lunch."

Step-by-Step Directions: Create Video Role-Play Project

1. Identify a set of target behaviors for a child.
2. Develop role plays of the target behaviors with the child and include peers as appropriate.
3. Film short videos of the child and peers role playing the target behaviors.
4. Place videos on the slides of a presentation software (e.g., PowerPoint or Keynote).
5. OPTIONAL: Add other slides to introduce questions about the activity in the video.
6. OPTIONAL: Put videos on a tablet computer or other mobile device for the child to watch as needed

Educational Objectives

This project provides a means of social learning and positive behavioral support for Kimo. The process of developing the role plays and filming the videos helps make expectations explicit and allows Kimo to practice and reinforce desired behaviors. The project meets several of the guidelines under UDL Principle III. For example, the project provides options for self-regulation, meeting guidelines 9.1 (promote expectations and beliefs that optimize motivation) and 9.2 (facilitate personal coping skills and strategies). The project also meets guideline 8.2 (foster collaboration and community), giving Kimo the opportunity to practice skills alongside his peers. The project integrates collaboration with peers, modeling of behaviors, and opportunities for practice and lets children develop their own ideas within activities as suggested by the CREDE standards of Joint Productive Activity, Modeling, and Child Directed Activity.

Project 3—Identifying Emotional States: Digital Feelings Book

Ms. Arlene teaches a class of 12 kindergartners with varied backgrounds and abilities. Most of her students' families have immigrated to the United States within the past five years. Her culturally and linguistically diverse students speak various languages at home, including Ilocano, Vietnamese, Chinese, Marshallese, and Chuukese. Some of her students have developmental delays and receive special education services for speech and language as well as occupational therapy. Ms. Arlene strives to make her class as inclusive as possible, ensuring that her students participate in activities together, practice language, build social skills, and learn that school is a safe and welcoming place. She decides to create a group project that will help her students learn vocabulary, identify feelings and emotions, practice appropriate social skills, and celebrate their individual personalities in the process.

Taking Photographs for the Feelings Book

Ms. Arlene starts by discussing emotions during circle time. She has prepared index cards listing key emotion words that she wants students to understand. For her first session, students discuss what the words *sad*, *happy*, and *calm* mean. Ms. Arlene asks students to depict each emotion using facial expressions and body language. The students who are generally talkative and outgoing in class call out answers and readily act out the emotions. Ms. Arlene calls on the quieter students and asks them to restate the meaning of the words and act out the emotions. Before long, all the students are actively engaged, using their facial expressions and body language to depict the emotion as they call out and practice the emotion vocabulary words. After the students have practiced ways to depict the words, Ms. Arlene and her classroom assistant take photographs of the students. They organize the students into small groups of three and take photographs of each group depicting the three emotion words.

The next day in circle time, Ms. Arlene introduces three new emotion words and asks students to define and depict them. She introduces the words *silly*, *angry,* and *patient*. Students enjoy making exaggerated expressions as they depict these words, giggling as they watch their peers making similar expressions. Ms. Arlene and her assistant take more digital photos, creating a set of pictures with each small group depicting the new emotion words. The students enjoy the physical nature of this activity, which allows them to stand up, move around, and make choices about how to depict a word using a facial expression and body language.

Creating Videos for the Feelings Book

Ms. Arlene adds a role-playing element to this activity to help students understand the emotion words in context. During the next circle time, she selects two emotion words and asks students what makes them feel that way. For example, she asks the students what makes them *happy* in school. Students offer various examples, such as "playing with friends during center time." Ms. Arlene asks three students to role play "playing with friends" and takes a short video clip of their actions. Over the course of the next few days, Ms. Arlene has various student groups role play short scenarios providing a context for each emotion word (e.g., waiting *patiently* for a classmate to wash hands or feeling *sad* when left out of a game). Students have fun with this activity, collaborating, directing each other, and dramatizing their roles for the video camera.

Creating the Digital Feelings Book

After Ms. Arlene has a collection of photos and videos, she creates a digital Feelings Book by placing the photos and videos onto the slides of presentation software. On a title page, she types in the names of every student in the class. She then places one video role play on a slide followed by a slide which has the text, "How do we feel?" On the next slide, she places the photographs of the groups depicting the emotion word related to the video they just saw. On this page, she types out the emotion word in large font beneath the student group photos.

During the next circle time, Ms. Arlene projects this digital book onto the large screen in the classroom. She sets the stage for the book, telling students they are about to see the Feelings Book that they all made together. The students look at the screen in great anticipation, waiting to see this book they have all helped to create. Ms. Arlene shows the first page, which has the title of the book along with the names of each child. She advances to the next slide, and students watch one of the short video skits. They gasp in delight when they see themselves on screen, and several students call out the names of the three students in the video. "That's me!" says one little girl who is usually very quiet in class. Ms. Arlene proceeds to the next slide with the photos of groups depicting that emotion. In this manner, Ms. Arlene proceeds to go through the whole book, showing each video, asking, "How do we feel?" Students eagerly shout out the answer of the emotion word depicted in the video. She reinforces the word and praises the students for their correct response. In rapt attention, students stare at their photos and re-enact the facial expressions and body language they see on screen. This process reinforces what they have learned in the process of making the short videos and defining the words.

Over the course of the school year, Ms. Arlene adds to the digital Feelings Book as students need to learn about and reinforce how to act in positive and social ways. Ms. Arlene also shares the digital book file with parents. When parents come to visit the classroom, she encourages parents and students to type in the words for the emotions in their first language on the slides in the digital book. In this way, students see their first languages honored along with the English vocabulary in the book.

> **Step-by-Step Directions: Create a Digital Feelings Book**
> 1. Select a set of vocabulary words.
> 2. Have a discussion with students to define each word. Model for students how they can depict words through facial expressions and body language.
> 3. Photograph students depicting the words. The photographs can be taken individually or in small groups, depending on the size of the class and the objective of the activity (individual or whole class).
> 4. Ask students to think about what makes them feel a particular emotion. Ask students to act out a short role play of the situation which makes them feel a particular way. Take a short video (10–20 s) of the role play. This can be done in pairs, small groups, or by individual students.
> 5. Place the videos and photos into presentation software to create a digital book. Add text and short sentences to reinforce vocabulary words.
> 6. As a whole group activity, go through the book together. Have students watch and respond to questions embedded in the digital book.
> 7. OPTIONAL: Engage parents and add home language vocabulary to the book for culturally and linguistically diverse learners.

Educational Objectives

This project addresses early literacy skills and promotes social learning. The project meets the UDL principles of Multiple Means of Representation, providing several options for language including Guidelines 2.1 (clarify vocabulary and symbols), 2.4 (promote understanding across languages), and 2.5 (illustrate through multiple media). The project also provides many options for comprehension including

Guideline 3.1 (activate or supply background knowledge). In addition, the project addresses guidelines under UDL Principle II, such as Guideline 5.3 (build fluencies with graduated support for practice and performance) giving students various ways to learn, express, and practice their understanding of vocabulary words. The processes involved in creating this project align with all of the CREDE standards in Early Childhood that we identified as relevant earlier in this chapter: Joint Productive Activity, Language Development, Contextualization, Modeling, and Child Directed Activity.

Project 4—Read to Me: Digital Storytellers

Mr. Jake is an energetic young educational assistant who loves to come up with creative projects to engage the students in his preschool classroom. He provides support for a teacher in a classroom of six preschool students who range from 3 to 5 years of age. All the students have been assessed as having developmental delays and receive additional speech and language services and/or occupational therapy to meet their specific needs. Many of the students live in extended family settings with their parents, grandparents, and cousins. Mr. Jake comes up with a creative way to bring culture and family into this preschool classroom using video technology and digital storytelling.

Videotaping the Digital Storyteller

Jake decides to create community digital storybooks for his students. He intends to integrate family, community, and culture into this classroom literacy activity. He talks with parents and grandparents when they drop off their children, asking them if they would be willing to be involved in a videotaped reading of classroom storybooks. He assures them that he will help with all technical aspects if they are able to set aside 30 min after school to read a book. Several parents and grandparents readily agree.

Mr. Jake picks a classroom favorite, *The Very Hungry Caterpillar* by Eric Carle. Tiana, the mother of one of his students, has agreed to read this book. Their family is American Samoa and, while Tiana generally speaks Samoan language to her daughter, she is also proficient in English. Tiana stays after school one day, allowing Jake to videotape her reading the book. He asks Tiana to sit in a comfortable chair in the corner of the classroom and places the laptop computer in front of her. He directs her to rehearse the reading, page by page, encouraging her to read with joy and feeling, adding intonation and warmth. After she practices and says she is comfortable, Jake turns on the webcam on the laptop and videotapes her reading. When she finishes, Jake asks her to add one more piece. He helps her formulate some comprehension questions about the story of the very hungry caterpillar in Samoan language (e.g., "What are some of the things that the very hungry caterpillar ate? What did the very hungry caterpillar become?) and asks her if there is anything else she would like to say. He videotapes her asking these questions in Samoan language.

Later, Jake photographs each page of the book. He places the photos on slides in presentation software. On each slide, he places a video clip of Tiana reading the page depicted in the book. At the end of the presentation, he places the short video clips of Tiana asking questions in Samoan language.

Read to Me

In the next class session, Mr. Jake projects the multimedia storybook onto the screen. The children sit in a circle waiting in eager anticipation. He has the classroom copy of *The Very Hungry Caterpillar* with him. He opens the book to the first page, and the children look and talk about the illustration. He then projects the page on the big screen and clicks to play the video embedded on the page. Tiana appears on screen, reading the words. Tiana's daughter is delighted to see and listen to her mother. When they get to the last page of the story and Tiana's mother asks a question in Samoan language, several of the students who speak Samoan shout out answers to her questions.

As the school year progresses, Jake creates several more of these multimedia storybooks, incorporating readings by grandparents and parents of various children in the classroom. In cases where family members do not speak English fluently or are shy to give it a try yet seem interested in the project, Jake offers to help them with the reading as needed. He models sentences by reading them out loud and asks the digital storyteller to repeat after him. He encourages each reader to add a first language piece of his or her own. In this way, Jake ensures that every interested family member gets a chance to be a "digital storyteller" in some way or another.

Step-by-Step Directions: Digital Storytellers in the Classroom

1. Select a classroom book.
2. Recruit a family member to read the story. Give the individual an opportunity to rehearse his/her reading. Prompt the individual to read with joy and expression.
3. Videotape the individual reading. This can be done using the built-in webcam on a laptop or on a smartphone or tablet.
4. Take photos of each page in the book.
5. Place the photos on individual slides in presentation software.
6. On each slide, place a clip of the family member reading that page.
7. OPTIONAL: For linguistically-diverse students, create a short video in which the family member asks questions or says something about the book in the child's first language. Place this video at the end of the presentation.

Educational Objectives

This project addresses early literacy skills and promotes social learning. The project honors home language and brings family members into the classroom, both literally and virtually. These projects can provide a context and opportunity for parents to get involved with classroom activities. For the children, it is a delightful way to see a family member reading to them. The project aligns to guidelines of all three UDL principles. For example, it meets several of the checkpoints under Guideline 3 by providing options for comprehension. The project also addresses Guideline 5.1 (use multiple media for communication) and Guideline 7.2 (optimize relevance, value, and authenticity). The project meets the CREDE standards of Language and Literacy Development and Contextualization by providing personal connections to a school-based literacy activity.

Conclusion

The four vignettes presented in this chapter describe variations on a theme of using presentation software and digital media to create personalized multimedia learning environments. All the projects use similar digital media elements (i.e., photos, video, and text) to reinforce and build communicative contexts and specific skills for children. By design, the projects are flexible and allow parents and teachers to use their own creativity to personalize projects for an individual child or group of children.

The technology tools we use evolve and change rapidly. However, the ideas presented in the vignettes for using the digital media tools in simple and constructive ways transcend the device. Whether today or in 10 years, children will always respond to photos and images of the people and environments that are familiar to them. These elements can always be a springboard for communication, expression, and reflection. Individuals—children and adults alike—learn through role modeling and by practicing and reviewing target skills and behaviors. The projects described in this chapter provide a snapshot of creative technology applications to build community and to promote communication and learning, strategies that can be adapted to new creative technologies that will emerge in the future.

References

Bandura, A. (1997). *Self-efficacy. The exercise of control.* New York, NY: W. H. Freeman.
Center for Applied Special Technology. (2013). About UDL. http://www.cast.org/udl/index.html. Accessed 30 April 2013.
Center for Research on Education, Diversity, and Excellence. (2004). Observing the five standards in practice: Development and application of the standards performance continuum. Research Brief Number 11. Center for Research on Education, Diversity, and Excellence.

Center for Universal Design. (2010). Ronald L. Mace. http://www.ncsu.edu/project/design-projects/udi/center-for-universal-design/ron-mace. Accessed 30 April 2013.

Hall, T., Meyer, A., & Rose, D. (2012). *Universal design for learning in the classroom: Practical applications*. New York, NY: Guilford Press.

Hitchcock, C. G., Meyer, A., Rose, D., & Jackson, R. (2002). Providing new access to the general curriculum: Universal design for learning. *Teaching Exceptional Children, 35*(2), 8–17.

National Center on Universal Design for Learning. (2010). UDL guidelines. http://www.udlcenter.org/aboutudl/udlguidelines. Accessed 30 April 2013.

Vygotsky, L. S. (1978). *Mind in society: The development of higher psychological processes*. Cambridge, MA: Harvard University Press.

Yamauchi, L. A., Im, S., & Schonleber, N. S. (2012). Adapting strategies of effective instruction for culturally diverse preschoolers. *Journal of Early Childhood Teacher Education, 33*(1), 54–72.

Chapter 7
Using Mobile Media Devices and Apps to Promote Young Children's Learning

Sharon Judge, Kimberly Floyd and Tara Jeffs

Mobile phones offer tremendous potential in reaching young children with quality learning opportunities.

S. Judge (✉)
Old Dominion University, Norfolk, USA
e-mail: sjudge@odu.edu

K. Floyd
West Virginia University, Morgantown, USA

T. Jeffs
Loundon County Public Schools, Ashburn, USA

Abstract In this chapter we describe how mobile technologies, with a focus on smart phones, iPod touches, and iPads or other tablet devices and applications (apps), are transforming learning for young children. This chapter discusses young children's experiences and learning with mobile media devices and apps. Key opportunities to seize mobile media devices' unique attributes to improve learning are described. Along with their potential for helping children develop important skills come challenges in using mobile devices for learning that must be addressed. The use of assistive technologies and best practices of Universal Design for Learning provide a viable pathway for needed customization and personalization for young children with disabilities to succeed in using such new and innovative technologies. Finally, implications and insights for education and industry on how to promote young children's learning via mobile devices and apps are addressed.

Keywords Applications (apps) · Disabilities · Media devices · Mobile technologies · Young children

Mobile Learning

Kasey and Kolby are involved in block play during free play in their inclusive setting. Kolby, a 4-year-old with autism, is starting to become frustrated and begins banging the blocks loudly. Kasey, a typically-developing 6-year-old, asks Kolby, "What do you want?" and Kolby uses the iPad app, Proloquo2Go (AssistiveWare 2013), to respond, "I want more big blocks....red blocks." Kasey passes Kolby the large, red blocks, the banging ceases, and the boys begin building together again. Kiki, a 3-year-old with cerebral palsy, is not yet able to grasp and release blocks independently. So, while she plays alongside Kasey and Kolby, she plays with the app, Builder Blocks Preschool (StusApps 2013), on her iPad which allows her to manipulate ABC blocks into towers. This app can be locked so that the tower will not tumble or set in free play mode which will allow the tower to topple from 'gravity.' Kiki giggles with delight as the blocks topple, prompting other children to join her in the activity. Meanwhile, Kasey moves to the manipulative table and begins to play Bridge Basher (Jundroo LLC 2012) on his iPad where he can build virtual bridges and test their strength. Dakota moves beside him and tries to imitate the bridge designs of Kasey by using Legos on the table.

Advances in mobile technologies are showing immense untapped educational potential for young children. In this chapter, "mobile media" refers to smart phones, video iPods, and iPads or other tablet devices. Increasingly important is that mobile media can be designed to allow children to move in and out of overlapping physical, digital, and communicative spaces. In fact, kids today are not referred to as "digital kids" but as "mobile kids" (Shuler 2009a). The portability and ease allows children to use mobile media devices at any time, no matter where they are spending their time. Because of the increasing popularity of mobile media devices among young children (Gutnick et al. 2011; Revelle 2009; Zevenbergen 2007), mobile phones or tablets offer tremendous potential in reaching young children with quality learning opportunities, including facilitating conversations with adults and other learners, encouraging motor skills, and providing ease in navigation and use. The touch screen gives children with introductory motor skills an easy-to-use interface (Buckleitner 2010).

According to the Common Sense Media study (2011), even very young children are frequent digital media users. In a study of 1,384 parents of children ages birth to 8 years, approximately half (52 %) said their children now have access to one of the newer smart mobile devices at home. Furthermore, 11 % of all 0–8-year-olds use a smart phone, iPod, iPad or similar device in a typical day. In addition, this study reports that a third of children ages birth to 8 years have used mobile devices, including 10 % of 0–1-year-olds, 39 % of 2–4-year-olds, and 52 % of 5–8-year olds. The time children spend with these mobile media devices is still very small compared to other media. However, as the cost of mobile media devices decrease, it is anticipated that more families will use them in coming years (Shuler 2009a).

With the proliferation of mobile applications (apps) targeting young children and the tremendous learning affordances of mobile devices for young learners, it is important to consider the role that apps may play in children's learning. The apps market for young children continues to explode with the iTunes store now having a dedicated section of apps for youth. Four years after the opening of the first "app" store, more than a quarter of parents who have children from birth up to age 8 have downloaded apps for their children (Common Sense Media 2011).

With the increased number of young children using mobile media devices, having an accurate understanding of the role this media plays in children's lives is critical for all of those concerned about promoting healthy child development. In 2012, the National Association for the Education of Young Children (National Association for the Education of Young Children, & Fred Rogers Center for Early Learning and Children's Media 2012) revised its position statement regarding the role of technology in today's early childhood classrooms. Of particular importance in this position statement—which is grounded in research, theory, and observations from the field—is that "technology and interactive media are tools that must be used appropriately and intentionally" (p. 3). However, there is limited research on mobile device use among children birth to 11 years of age (Gutnick et al. 2011). In addition, there are key opportunities and challenges in harnessing the potential of mobile media devices to promote children's learning (Shuler 2009a).

Opportunities in Mobile Learning

The Joan Ganz Cooney Center at Sesame Workshop identified five ways mobile learning can change the way children learn (Shuler 2009a). Mobile media devices encourage *seamless learning* (i.e., continuity of the learning experience across different contexts; Looi et al. 2010) and *ubiquitous learning* (i.e., quick and ready access to technologies; Rogers et al. 2005). This "anywhere, anytime" learning promotes situated learning and breaks the barrier between home, school, and after-school (Shuler 2009a). Also, it can promote a seamless 360-degree learning experience that bridges the gap between formal and informal learning environments.

Another benefit of mobile media devices is that they can help advance the goal of achieving digital equity because of their low cost and familiarity. They can also be used to reach underserved children in developing countries since it is estimated that 80% of the world's population lives within range of a mobile network, and the fastest growth rates for mobile networks are in China and Africa (Hoarak 2007). In addition, mobile media devices can encourage new forms of social interaction, collaboration, and communication. Collaboration can occur virtually through web-enabled devices, and numerous communication options are embedded on a mobile media device so that children can communicate through conversation, texting, e-mail, and social-networking applications with both peers and teachers (Field 2005).

Finally, mobile media devices can accommodate many different needs and learning styles. With mobile media devices, children can access information on their own, share information with one another, and take greater control of their own learning. Shuler (2009a) suggested that "there are significant opportunities for genuinely supporting differentiated, autonomous, and individualized learning through media devices" (p. 5). Thus, personalized learning experiences can be offered through mobile media enhanced environments.

Challenges in Mobile Learning

Even with the potential of mobile media devices, there are three broad categories of challenges: (1) social, (2) theoretical, and (3) technological with respect to mobile learning (Shuler 2009a). Social challenges include the amount of "screen time" that children are already exposed to in their lives, the difficulty of monitoring children's access to and sharing of inappropriate content, health concerns that digital media may prevent children from getting physical exercise, and the likelihood of children becoming too distracted by their mobile devices. Of concern are the cultural norms and attitudes toward the use of mobile devices. A 2008 study by the Joan Ganz Cooney Center, in collaboration with Common Sense Media, found that most parents and teachers were questioning the educational value of mobile devices, especially cell phones (Shore 2008).

Theoretical challenges include the issue that no widely-accepted learning theory for mobile learning has been established. According to Rogers and Price (2009), most research to date that has investigated mobile learning has proposed existing learning theories, such as constructivism; others have suggested that new theories are needed. Sharples et al. (2005) propose a framework for theorizing about mobile learning that must be examined against the following criteria:

- Is it significantly different from current theories of classroom, workplace, or lifelong learning?
- Does it account for the mobility of learners?
- Does it cover both formal and informal learning?
- Does it theorize learning as a constructive and social process?
- Does it analyze learning as a personal and situated activity mediated by technology?

Technological challenges include poorly-designed mobile media devices which negatively affect usability and physical features of the device which may prevent an optimal learning experience. Screen size, text entry method, and battery life are the three most noticeable design considerations (Ching et al. 2009). Applications should be built specifically with mobile devices in mind, should operate on as little power as required, and should not require large amounts of text to be entered. In addition, the complexity of the mobile media device market means that the type of mobile device a child may have can range greatly from having many features such as a phone, web browser, MP3 player, GPS, camera, and full-color touch screen to having limited features such as phone and text messaging. Not only having access to a mobile media device but having access to a range of features will account for differentiated access to technology.

Family Engagement with Mobile Media Devices

With the popularity of mobile media devices, a new phenomenon has been observed in grocery stores, restaurants, and crowded airplanes. A report released by the Joan Ganz Cooney Center defined the "pass-back effect" as a parent or other adult "passing" their mobile devices to a child either intentionally for "play" or unintentionally to act as a babysitter while Mom or Dad are engaged elsewhere (Chiong and Shuler 2010). The report presents the results of three studies that support this growing phenomenon. Within the national survey, two-thirds of children ages four to seven have used an iPhone or iPod Touch, and 85% have used one owned by a parent. Given a choice of eight devices, children ranked the iPhone as their favored device for play after the Nintendo DS and the Wii. The report found that children most often use the devices when they are "passed back" by a parent while in a car. In addition, nearly all of the children observed in the studies were adept at using smart mobile devices, even after initial difficulty. In fact, a video posted to YouTube by a father in Singapore (http://www.youtube.com/watch?v=vxlsLzOxxx0&feature=youtu.be) shows his 2-year-old son demonstrating how to use a children's app on his father's new iPhone. However, in most children's apps there are no messages for parents or caregivers on how to have a conversation with young children on the content of the game, nor ways to extend the learning that was the focus of the game.

The explosion of mobile media devices taken together with the "pass-back effect" means that more children than ever before have access to sophisticated internet-enabled devices at younger and younger ages, years before they ever step foot inside a formal education environment. Research has shown that parental guidance, or scaffolding, can improve young children's learning of high quality media educational content, promote language development, and increase engagement in appropriate activities (Fisch 2004). The findings from the Joan Ganz Cooney Center report suggest that parents play important roles in shaping the quality of their children's experiences with mobile media devices (Chiong and Shuler 2010). More specifically, parents' roles were defined as facilitators, teachers, and gatekeepers.

As a facilitator, parents can help their children get started in using the mobile device and explain information to them that they do not understand. As a teacher, parents can extend and elaborate on the relevant information that is communicated. This scaffolding can provide additional motivation for children to continue using the technology. As a gatekeeper, parents can provide rules and regulations about usage of mobile devices. Even with over half of the parents citing child's privacy and online safety as a reason for restricting access to technology, about a third of parents reported that they "rarely" or "never" interact with their child on a smart phone. Thus, due to parental perceptions of the educational value and safety concerns of mobile devices, children do not often engage in meaningful interactions with someone else on the device. However, with the rise of electronic reading, families may be using electronic books (e-books) on mobile devices to promote young children's literacy development (Rainie et al. 2012).

E-books and Parent-Child Reading Interactions

Young children of today are exposed not only to printed books but also to e-books, which they can read independently or with an adult's support. The e-book marketplace is growing rapidly with titles for children. According to the Association of American Publishers, the sale of children's and young adult e-books rose 173.9 % over a 1-year period from 2010 to 2011 (Publishers Weekly 2012). Many e-books are digital versions of classic children's books which were published in a printed format. However, there are important distinctions between basic e-books, enhanced e-books, and apps. Basic e-books digitally replicate the print book while enhanced e-books integrate multimedia features such as animation, music, audio and sound effects, illuminated text, and pop-up graphics. Apps also may exhibit these features but often operate more interactively or as a game. Several examples of free book apps that integrate multimedia features are the *I Love You Little Bird* app (Monroe 2013), *The Velveteen Rabbit* HD (Milbert 2012), and *Put Me In The Story: Personalized Books* app (Sourcebook 2013).

Parents value co-reading because it promotes interactive storytelling, enriches children's vocabularies, and stimulates parent-child conversations, but co-reading e-books may or may not provide the same benefits. Researchers at the Joan Ganz Cooney Center compared parent-child shared reading experiences across print book, basic e-book, and enhanced e-book formats (Chiong et al. 2012). The study participants were 32 pairs of parents and their 3–6-year-old children at the New York Hall of Science's Preschool Place. Each pair read a print book and either an enhanced or basic e-book while researchers videotaped their interactions and took observational notes. The main finding was that there are measureable differences between the ways parent-child pairs interacted with print, basic, and enhanced formats: print books and basic e-books elicited more content-related interactions than enhanced e-books, children recalled fewer narrative details when reading enhanced e-books, and print books were more conducive to building literacy skills, while e-books were more likely to engage children and promote physical interaction. While enhanced e-books were more advantageous for engaging children and prompting physical interaction, they did not add to children's ability to learn and retain the story; instead they distracted them from reading.

To further understand the place e-books have in co-reading with children, Vaala and Takeduchi (2012) conducted a study to survey parents about how they perceived the value of co-reading with the iPad. The survey is based on a group of 462 iPad owners of children between the ages of two and six. The majority (72.5 %) of parents reported using the iPad to co-read with their child; however, these same parents still preferred co-reading with print books, unless they are traveling or commuting with their child. The parents who co-read e-books with their children reported that certain features of the e-books supported early readers, such as clicking on a word to hear it pronounced or word-by-word highlighting as an audio of the text is heard. Other features, however, were considered to be distracting, such as videos and games provided in e-books. Of those parents not co-reading with the iPad, the majority indicated that they preferred to read print books to their children. A third found that it was too difficult to read with a child on an iPad, and nearly as many were concerned that their child would want to use the iPad all the time.

These two e-book studies have important implications for parents, teachers, and designers. Designers of enhanced e-books need to create e-books with co-reading-related activities and design them in a way that allows parents to access and control settings to customize the co-reading experience with their children (Chiong et al. 2012). Parents seem to prefer print books but should be mindful of which kinds of formats they desire for specific times and purposes, whether it is for "fun" or to build literacy skills (Vaala and Takeuchi 2012). For building literacy skills, print books and basic e-books may be a better choice.

Mobile Devices, Apps, and Learning

In January of 2013, Apple announced that its app store had officially hit the 40 billion app download mark. A new study from App Hero (Smith 2013) found that there are over 800,000 apps available in the app store, and 56.2 % of the apps are free. Similarly, the Google Play Store, formerly known as the Android Market, had passed the 700,000 app mark in October of 2012. The number of choices available is staggering, with over 1000 new apps released each day. The mobile app marketplace is growing at a tremendous speed, and recent large-scale studies have documented the use of apps among adults and older children (Purcell et al. 2010; Rainie et al. 2012); however, little research has been conducted with younger children. The following section examines the content and types of apps for young children and how children are using and learning from mobile media devices and apps.

Content and Characteristics of Apps for Young Children

Several studies have been conducted on the types of apps offered to children (Federal Trade Commission 2012; Shuler 2009b, 2012). The Federal Trade Commission (2012) conducted a survey of apps offered for children in the Apple app store and the Android Market. Searching the Apple App Store and the Android Market for the term "kids," they randomly selected 200 apps from each app store and found that education, games, math, spelling, and animals were the most popular app categories. The prices of the apps ranged from free to $ 9.99; however, 77 % of the apps were priced at $ 0.99 or less, and 48 % were free. Free apps were the most frequently downloaded. Of concern is the limited amount of information about the apps' data collection and sharing practices, meaning that parents often cannot determine, before downloading an app, if personal information is collected from children.

Shuler (2009b, 2012) highlights the app explosion, especially for young children, in an iLearn line of market research on the top-selling paid apps in the educational category of the Apple App Store over a 2-year period. Findings indicate that from 2009 to 2011 the percentage of apps for children has risen in every age category, with a decrease in apps for adults. Of the 196 top-selling paid apps in 2011, 58 % were targeted for young children and experienced the greatest growth (23 %). Even more interesting is that 60 % of the top 25-selling apps target young children, strengthening the popular demand for educational apps for children. Similar to the Federal Trade Commission study's (2012) findings, Shuler found that most children's apps are priced at $ 0.99 or $ 1.99. However, over the 2-year period, the average price of children's apps rose by over $ 1.00. The most popular app category was general early learning (47 %), and there were significantly more general early learning apps than the second most popular subject (math, 13 %).

Usage and Learning with Mobile Devices and Apps

Studies indicate that children are quite comfortable and adept in using mobile media devices and apps and that moving from novice to mastery occurs quickly with age-appropriate apps (Chiong and Shuler 2010; Cohen 2011; PBS KIDS 2010). If children had initial usability issues with the device, parents reported that they disappeared after the child played with the device a few times. Observations of young children's use of iPads demonstrated that iPad accessibility and use are relative to the design of the app interface, child's prior digital gaming experience, and the relationship between the app content and the child's developmental level. Overall, using mobile media devices and apps came quite naturally to children.

Evidence also shows that children can learn from apps (Chiong and Shuler 2010; Cohen 2011; PBS KIDS 2010). Children's learning through app play takes several forms involving active exploration, construction of solutions, and learning explicit content. In an evaluation of two educational literacy apps, *Martha Speaks: Dog*

Party and *Super Why*, the majority of children displayed gains in their reading skills and content areas covered in both apps after playing with them (PBS KIDS 2010). The *Martha Speaks: Dog Party* app focuses on vocabulary development for children ages four through seven. Vocabulary gains were made for every age, with the older children gaining the most after playing the app. In contrast, younger children gained the most after playing the *Super Why* app, which aims to increase literacy skills. In addition, this study found that parents perceive apps as educational.

Mobile Learning for Young Children with Disabilities

Mobile media devices provide young learners with an easy-to-use touch interface that offers motivating and engaging learning environments filled with brilliant colors, animations, and sounds that encourage learning and participation. Parents, educators, and related service providers of young children with disabilities often seek out activities and opportunities to increase engagement and participation to ensure that children can reach their potential. Mobile media devices can provide opportunities for inclusion, active participation, and social interactions. It is important to note that a mobile media device itself is not educational; proper integration into curricula and real/authentic tasks can provide meaningful learning experiences (Guernsey et al. 2012).

Strategies for Integration

All children need positive human relationships in order to learn best, and communication is essential to relationship building. Some children and adults need more assistance communicating than others (Bestwick and Campbell 2010). Often children with disabilities lack common experiences and background knowledge that they could share with their peers. Mobile apps can provide an inclusive common ground for children to play, engage, and learn together. Parents, children, and educators can use such technology to strengthen their interactions with each other and improve familiarity with sounds, words, language, and general knowledge (Guernsey et al. 2012). For example, a parent and child can read developmentally-appropriate books together on the iPad that include sounds and interactive activities. Such activities expand the knowledge and learning presented in traditional shared reading times. Rather than carrying a variety of learning toys in the car or on errands, a child can interact with apps that teach the alphabet, letter sounds, and simple words. In classrooms, teachers can utilize iPads and learning apps as a way to supplement and enhance learning and socialization. Speech apps can be programmed to serve as a voice output device for children with delayed or limited speech to use during large group to greet peers, say a repeated line in a story, or even announce the day's weather to the class. There are also speech-to-text apps that allow students with limited fine motor skills to share their thoughts and ideas in a written format, just as their non-disabled peers.

In addition to building communication and opportunities for relationships, mobile apps have been found to engage children in collaborative learning, reasoning, and problem-solving activities that had been thought to be too sophisticated for them to understand and carry out at very young ages (Yelland 2005). One example of this is in the area of math. Virtual manipulatives have been found to have several advantages over physical hands-on manipulatives (Clements and Sarama 2007). Such advantages include: (1) enabling learners to make their knowledge explicit, (2) offering flexibility in the way mathematical concepts are displayed, (3) allowing learners to save their work and retrieve it later, (4) linking the concrete with the abstract both visually and with explicit feedback, and (5) dynamically linking more than one representation of the same concept to encourage problem posing and conjecturing (Clements and Sarama 2007). Specifically, children have virtual manipulatives as well as physical manipulatives in their classroom or home to assist in making the connection from the real object to the more abstract, virtual object. A child can be introduced to tangrams in their classroom or home environment so that they can become familiar with the features of tangram blocks. Then, while traveling in the car when interaction with actual tangrams would not be possible, the child could play the My First Tangrams app and would already have the exposure to the real object for a more meaningful and connected learning experience.

For the young user, it is essential that apps for learning incorporate feature matching. It is essential for success to match the features of the technology to the student needs and/or IFSP or IEP goals. Does the device or app offer flexibility to alter settings to meet different children's needs? Does the app provide opportunities for creative choice making or imaginative expression? The Proloquo2Go app offers a full array of communication and language systems on the iPad. Therefore, if a child has language or communication goals on their IFSP or IEP, the communication system is present with him or her as s/he is interacting with peers or caregivers while still having access to learning games and the freedom to navigate the environment with only an iPad versus also carrying an augmentative communication device.

Learners who use digital media that involves the selection of colors, music, animation, or main characters in a story (to name a few) build fundamental curiosity along with skills involving hypothesizing, problem solving, and positive self-evaluation (Lieberman et al. 2009). Apps are available to build communication skills, pre-literacy skills, pre-math skills, and science skills. Video modeling and social stories through the use of mobile media devices provide just-in-time learning examples that can be used in modeling appropriate behavior and meaningful problem solving in social settings. For example, prior to lining up for lunch at school, a child can view a social story on expected behaviors during lunch with the simple click of a button. Likewise, before interacting with peers on the playground, a child could view a social story on playing on the playground to enhance their experience and communicative opportunities.

Elements of motivation are also essential. Does the app provide enough positive reinforcement to hold the interest of the young user? A software checklist developed through years of research by Boone and Higgins (2007) could be applied in providing guidance in selecting appropriate learning apps. Seven different areas were defined and investigated: (1) instruction, (2) directions and documentation, (3) feedback and evaluation, (4) content, (5) individualization options, (6) interface and screen design, and (7) accessibility. In order to position the child to gain the most from their exposure and to maximize a child's attention and focus to apps, a child must be motivated to interact. Therefore, it is imperative that the caregiver connect aspects on the checklist to the child's interests and developmental levels. Matching a learning app based upon these key features optimizes the likelihood that the app will gain and sustain a child's attention, allowing for greater learning to occur.

Implications

Mobile media devices and apps can bring new learning dimensions to children's everyday activities across different settings. This flexibility means that the educational potential of apps is not just in their content, but also in how they can be used in various contexts to address children's development. Evidence that children learn from well-designed educational apps signals a new challenge to produce quality content and provide guidance for developers. However, too many games and apps do not utilize developmentally-appropriate learning practices. Text-heavy interfaces are often included even in apps for preschool learners, with the assumption that parents will read the content to their children. However, parents participate in media activities with their children only if they find the activities enjoyable (Takeuchi 2011).

The need to create apps that are developmentally appropriate helped drive the development of the Children's App Manifesto with app developers Andy Russell and Daniel Donahoo (Watters 2011). This call-to-action asks parents, educators, marketers, investors, and app developers to think critically about how we can support quality educational digital content. There are a number of websites that provide information that may assist professionals and parents in reviewing and selecting high-quality apps for young children (see Table 7.1). For example, the APPitic directory (http://www.appitic.com) lists more than 3000 apps for education, organized by theme, preschool content area, disability, and other categories.

With the potential that mobile media devices and apps have in promoting children's learning, we must now address the new "app gap" that has developed among young children (Common Sense Media 2011). The app gap seems to be an extension of the traditional "digital divide" as families from low-income backgrounds take longer to embrace certain technologies because of cost considerations. According to the Common Sense Media study (2011), just 14% of lower-income parents had downloaded apps for their children, where as 47% of higher-income parents had done so. The digital divide, though closing, still exists, and the app gap could be having the same effect on children.

The Children's Online Privacy Protection Act (COPPA) of 1998 has been revised because of the concerns about children's ability to understand and evaluate

Table 7.1 Mobile application resources

Mobile applications	URL	Description
App Hero	http://apphero.com/	Free, personalized app recommendations. App Hero learns gathers information about your unique interests, preferences, and characteristics to find apps that best suit your needs
Best apps for kids	http://bestappsforkids.com/category/uncategorized/	Reviews and rates apps that hold potential for facilitating learning
APPitic	http://appitic.com/	Directory of apps for education that have been vetted by Apple Distinguished Educators; categorized by preschool, special education, themes, multiple intelligences, Bloom's Taxonomy, and National Education Technology Standards
Moms with apps	http://momswithapps.com/	Catalog of great children's and family-friendly apps. Search by educational categories and age group to discover new apps and developers
Common sense media	http://www.commonsensemedia.org/mobile-app-lists/free-apps-kids/	Collection of free apps for kids that are categorized by age and rated for learning
Apps4Kids	http://www.apps4kids.net/	Reviews of apps for kids by age, device, content, and enjoyment
Apps in education	http://www.beta.appsineducation.com	Directory of apps for students, teachers, and special education
Bridging apps	http://bridgingapps.org/	Reviews apps and matches apps to goals of people who have special needs
SpedApps2	http://spedapps2.wikispaces.com/	Wiki site maintained by therapists with recommendations regarding apps used with children who have disabilities that are searchable by content
Apps for children with special needs	http://a4cwsn.com/	Reviews apps for children with different types of disabilities and includes video of many of the apps

advertising and commercialization, especially as it pertains to information that is shared with third parties. These revisions were necessitated by advancements in technology since the act's inception, including the creation of mobile media devices and apps. Children's apps and websites will now have to obtain parental consent before gathering photos, videos, or geographic location and before tracking children's online behavior and passing along the data to third party advertising networks. The amendments strengthen children's privacy protections and give parents greater control over the personal information that websites and online services may collect from children under 13. Although changes were very necessary, the recent amendments to the COPPA have sparked some confusion and raised concerns that they will diminish innovative and educational content production. More specifically, many believe the cost and feasibility of compliance with some of the new terms has been massively underestimated by the Federal Trade Commission and will result in many organizations ceasing to create any content for children, especially those under 13 years of age (Family Online Safety Institute 2013). The changes took effect on July 1, 2013 and have required thoughtful consideration on the part of developers, online marketers, and industry.

Finally, mobile media devices and apps have many features that can be customized for young children with disabilities. Smart Phones and mobile touch screen devices have built-in accessibility features. Each new version of mobile operating system becomes more responsive to users' needs and, thus, becomes more accessible. Yet many educators are unaware that some of these accessibility features are already built into their devices and just have to be activated in the settings. There are significant opportunities for genuinely supporting differentiated, autonomous, and individualized learning experiences (Shuler 2009a).

Conclusion

As our youngest of learners begin using digital devices, it is imperative that the whole child is considered when making the determination of goodness of fit. Mobile media devices do not replace the unique learning that occurs dynamically between caregiver or teacher and the child. However, if properly matched and implemented, the utilization is an ideal augmentation of the experiential learning of the child. Although there is limited research on the utility of mobile media devices and apps with young children, there is no doubt that the growth of apps targeted at supporting young children and children with disabilities will continue to grow.

References

AssistiveWare. (2013). Proloquo2Go [iTunes app]. https://itunes.apple.com/us/app/proloquo2go/id308368164?mt=8. Accessed 16 March 2013.

Bestwick, A., & Campbell, J. (2010). Mobile learning for all. *Exceptional Parent, 40*(9), 18–20.

Boone, R., & Higgins, K. (2007). The software checklist: Evaluating educational software for use by students with disabilities. *Technology in Action, 3*(1), 481–492.

Buckleitner, W. (2010). A taxonomy of touch. *Children's Technology Review, 18*(11), 10–11.

Ching, D., Shuler, C., Lewis, A., & Levine, M. H. (2009). Harnessing the potential of mobile technologies for children and learning. In A. Druin (Ed.), *Mobile technology for children: Designing for interaction and learning* (pp. 23–42). Burlington, MA: Elsevier.

Chiong, C., & Shuler, C. (2010). *Learning: Is there an app for that? Investigations of young children's usage and learning with mobile devices and apps*. New York, NY: The Joan Ganz Cooney Center at Sesame Workshop.

Chiong, C., Ree, J., Takeuchi, L., & Erickson, I. (2012). *Print books vs. e-books: Comparing parent-child co-reading on print, basic, and enhanced e-book platforms*. New York, NY: The Joan Ganz Cooney Center at Sesame Workshop.

Clements, D. H., & Sarama, J. (2005). Young children and technology: What's appropriate? In W. J. Masalski (Ed.), *Technology supported mathematics learning environments 67th yearbook* (pp. 51–73). Reston, VA: National Council of Teachers of Mathematics.

Clements, D. H., & Sarama, J. (2007). Effects of a preschool mathematics curriculum: Summative research on the Building Blocks project. *Journal for Research in Mathematics Education, 38*(2), 136–163.

Cohen, M. (2011). Young children, apps and iPad. http://mcgrc.com/wp-content/uploads/2012/06/ipad-study-cover-page-report-mcg-info_new-online.pdf. Accessed 15 March 2013.

Common, S. M. (2011). Zero to eight: Children's media use in America. http://www.commonsensemedia.org/sites/default/files/research/zerotoeightfinal2011.pdf. Accessed 12 March 2013.

Family Online Safety Institute. (2013, January). The implications of the FTC's new COPPA rule. *FOSI Briefs*. http://www.fosi.org/emailers/fosibriefs-jan2013.html. Accessed 1 March 2013.

Federal Trade Commission. (2012). Mobile apps for kids: Current privacy disclosures are disappointing. http://www.ftc.gov/os.2012/02/120216mobile_apps_kids.pdf. Accessed 23 March 2013.

Field, R. (2005). Favourable conditions for effective and efficient learning in a blended faced-to-face/online method. *Proceedings of ASCILITE*. http://www.ascilite.org.au/conferences/brisbane05/blogs/proceedings/23_Field.pdf. Accessed 20 March 2013.

Fisch, S. M. (2004). *Children's learning from educational television: Sesame Street and beyond*. Mahwah, NJ: Erlbaum Associates.

Guernsey, L., Levine, M., Chiong, C., & Severns, M. (2012). *Pioneering literacy in the digital wild west: Empowering parents and educators*. New York, NY: The Joan Ganz Cooney Center at Sesame Workshop.

Gutnick, A. L., Robb, M., Takeuchi, L., & Kotler, J. (2011). *Always connected: The new digital media habits of young children*. New York, NY: The Joan Ganz Cooney Center at Sesame Workshop.

Horak, R. (2007). *Telecommunications and data communications handbook*. Hoboken, NJ: Wiley.

Jundroo LLC. (2012). Bridge Basher [iTunes app]. https://itunes.apple.com/us/app/bridgebasher/id324473106?mt=8. Accessed 23 March 2013.

The kids (books) are alright, says the AAP's monthly statshot. (21 June 2012). *Publishers Weekly*. http://www.publishersweekly.com/pw/by-topic/childrens/childrens-industry-news/article/52632-the-kids-books-are-alright-says-the-aap-s-monthly-statshot.html. Accessed 15 March 2013.

Lieberman, D. A., Bates, C. H., & So, J. (2009). Young children's learning with digital media. *Computers in the Schools, 26*(4), 271–283.

Looi, C. K., Seow, P., Zhang, B., So, H. J., Chen, W.-L., & Wong, L. H. (2010). Leveraging mobile technology for sustainable seamless learning: A research agenda. *British Journal of Educational Technology, 41*, 154–169.

Milbert, S. (2012). The Velveteen Rabbit HD [iTunes app]. https://itunes.apple.com/us/app/the-velveteen-rabbit-hd/id418307824?mt=8. Accessed 10 March 2013.

Minard, A. (2013). My first tangrams HD—A wood tangram puzzle game for kids [iTunes app]. https://itunes.apple.com/us/app/my-first-tangrams-hd-wood/id363843653?mt=8. Accessed 20 March 2013.

Monroe, J. (2013). I love you little bird [iTunes app]. https://itunes.apple.com/gb/app/i-love-you-little-bird/id591847496?mt=8. Accessed 23 March 2013.

National Association for the Education of Young Children, & Fred Rogers Center for Early Learning and Children's Media. (2012). Technology and interactive media as tools in early childhood programs serving children from birth through age 8. http://www.naeyc.org/files/naeyc/file/positions/PS_technology_WEB2.pdf. Accessed 15 Feb 2013.

PBS KIDS. (2010). *PBS KIDS iPod app study: Executive summary*. http://pbskids.org/read/files/iPod_Report_ExecSum.pdf. Accessed 10 March 2013.

Purcell, K., Entner, R., & Henderson, N. (2010). *The rise of apps culture*. Washington, DC: Pew Research Center's Internet and American Life Project. http://pewinternet.org/Reports/2010/The-Rise-of-Apps-Culture.aspx. Accessed 1 March 2013.

Rainie, L., Zickuhr, K., Purcell, K., Madden, M., & Brenner, J. (April 2012). *The rise of e-reading*. Washington, CD: Pew Research Center's Internet & American Life Project. http://libraries.pewinternet.org/files/legacy-pdf/The%20rise%20of%20e-reading%204.5.12.pdf. Accessed 1 March 2013.

Revelle, G. (2009). Mobile technologies in support of young children's learning. In A. Druin (Ed.), *Mobile technology for children: Designing for interaction and learning* (pp. 265–284). Burlington, MA: Elsevier.

Rogers, Y., & Price, S. (2009). How mobile technologies are changing the way children learn. In A. Druin (Ed.), *Mobile technology for children: Designing for interaction and learning* (pp. 3–22). Burlington, MA: Elsevier.

Rogers, Y., Price, S., Randell, C., Stanton-Fraser, D., Weal, M., & Fitzpatrick, G. (2005). Ubi-learning: Integrating outdoor and indoor learning experiences. *Communications of the ACM, 48*(1), 55–59.

Sharples, M., Taylor, J., & Vavoula, G. (2005). Towards a theory of mobile learning. *Proceedings of mLearn 2005*. http://www.mlearn.org.za/CD/papers/Sharples-%20Theory%20of%20Mobile.pdf. Accessed 15 Dec 2012.

Shore, R. (2008). *The power of pow! Wham!: Children, digital media, and our nation's future, three challenges for the coming decade*. New York, NY: The Joan Ganz Cooney Center at Sesame Workshop.

Shuler, C. (2009a). *Pockets of potential: Using mobile technologies to promote children's learning*. New York, NY: The Joan Ganz Cooney Center at Sesame Workshop.

Shuler, C. (2009b). *iLearn: A content analysis of the iTunes app store's educational section*. New York, NY: The Joan Ganz Cooney Center at Sesame Workshop.

Shuler, C. (2012). *iLearnII: An analysis of the education category on Apple's App Store*. New York, NY: The Joan Ganz Cooney Center at Sesame Workshop.

Smith, J. (March 2013). New study pegs Apple's App Store at 800k apps, 56.2 percent of which are free. *Pocket-lint*. http://www.pocket-lint.com/news/50594/new-study-pegs-app-store-at-800k#leftswipe. Accessed 15 March 2013.

Sourcebooks. (2013). Put me in the story-personalized books [iTunes app]. https://itunes.apple.com/us/app/put-me-in-story-personalized/id558177381?mt=8. Accessed 17 March 2013.

StusApps. (2013). Builder Blocks Preschool [iTunes app]. https://itunes.apple.com/us/app/builder-blocks-preschool/id391760918?mt=8. Accessed 18 March 2013.

Takeuchi, L. (2011). *Families matter: Designing media for a digital age*. New York, NY: The Joan Ganz Cooney Center at Sesame Workshop.

Vaala, S., & Takeuchi, L. (2012). *Parent co-reading survey: Co-reading with children on iPads: Parents' perceptions and practices*. New York, NY: The Joan Ganz Cooney Center at Sesame Workshop.

Watters, A. (18 November 2011). The children's app manifesto: Supporting high quality, affordable educational apps. *Hack Education*. http://www.hackeducation.com/2011/11/18/the-childrens-app-manifesto-supporting-high-quality-affordable-educational-apps/. Accessed 15 March 2013.

Yelland, N. (2005). The future is now: A review of the literature on the use of computers in early childhood education (1994–2004). *AACE Journal, 13*(3), 201–232.

Zevenbergen, R. (2007). Digital natives come to preschool: Implications for early childhood practice. *Contemporary Issue in Early Childhood, 8*(1), 19–29.

Chapter 8
Planning, Designing, and Implementing Effective Interactive Portfolios in the Primary Grades: Suggestions for Forming Partnerships among Teachers, Students, and Parents

Esther Ntuli and Lydia Kyei-Blankson

Abstract The use of interactive or e-portfolios among teachers to demonstrate young children's learning is not new. In the last decade, early childhood teachers have tried to use e-portfolios without much success. In this chapter, a step-by-step procedure for developing e-portfolios that effectively show young children's skills in critical thinking, self-evaluation, and emergent literacy is presented. The chapter focuses on e-portfolios that allow for self-evaluation or self-assessment. In addition, criteria for selecting the best artifacts that highlight young children's development or growth over time are outlined and examples of interactive technologies that can be used to develop e-portfolios are provided. Examples of young children's e-portfolios are used to illustrate the concepts discussed in the chapter.

Keywords E-Portfolio · Early childhood teachers · Interactive technologies · Learning · Self-assessment · Emergent literacies · Young children

E-Portfolios and Demonstrating Learning in Early Childhood

Ms. Tee walked up to one of her third grade students, Jane, and started a conversation regarding her performance in class.

    Ms. Tee: How are you doing today, Jane?
    Jane: Good.
    Ms. Tee: You look happy. What's up? Did you have fun with the lesson?
    Jane: Yes, math is one of my favorite subjects. I am doing very well in math and reading. My dad and mum say, if I continue to do well, they will get me a Wii game (smile).

E. Ntuli (✉)
Idaho State University, Pocatello, USA
e-mail: ntulesth@isu.edu

L. Kyei-Blankson
Illinois State University, Normal, USA

Ms. Tee: And how do you know you are doing well?

Jane: My parents went on the Internet to look at my portfolio, and I showed them what I have done so far. It shows that I am doing well in class. I got a "C" last time. Now I have an "A." I showed my dad and mum that I was good at addition and subtraction.

Ms. Tee: That is wonderful! And did you show them the stars on your last math test? I am so proud of you, Jane! Tell your parents to look in your portfolio today. I will leave a note for them in there. I think we can start adding your work in other subjects to the portfolio for your parents to see how well you are doing in them too. That will be nice, right? You can show your work in writing too.

A portfolio is "a purposeful collection of evidence of a child's learning collected over time that demonstrates a child's efforts, progress, or achievement" (McAfee et al. 2004, p. 52). A similar description was put forth by Barrett (2001) as follows: a portfolio is a "purposeful collection of a student's work that exhibits the student's efforts, progress, and achievements in one or more areas" (p. 8). In the same vein, Tierney et al. (1991) describe a portfolio as a systematic collection of documents that reflect what a child does in a classroom. Tierney et al. elaborate on the use of portfolios at the early childhood level by noting that young children's e-portfolios typically are assembled by both teachers and children and, as such, emphasize both process and product. The descriptions presented in these definitions reflect, to a greater extent, paper-based portfolios.

Paper portfolios used by teachers in early education are stored as a collection of evidence of performance in containers such as folders, boxes, drawers, binders, and cabinets (McAfee et al. 2004). Most early childhood teachers use these traditional repositories to store students' work, only to be retrieved during parent-teacher conferencing or when, once in a while, the teacher wants to exhibit evidence of the students' work. While storing documentation of student performance is necessary, it is not very helpful to keep paper copies of students' worked tucked away in boxes or file cabinets because stakeholders are not afforded the ease of accessing and reflecting on the materials or student work. Print copies of student materials may provide evidence of the work completed but may fail to reveal the quality of work or the progress made. A good portfolio should be manageable, easily accessible, and engaging. In addition, effective portfolios make it easy to compare work over time and provide opportunities for stakeholder interaction, assessment, and reflection. Electronic portfolios (or e-portfolios) allow for all of the above. E-portfolios are digitized or web-based portfolios created with technology tools that allow for assessment, feedback, and personal reflection (Lorenzo and Ittleson 2005). E-portfolios can be used as tools for helping children reflect on their work and monitor their own progress.

Conceptual Framework

Teachers of young children need to encourage the development of their students' reflective and self-assessment abilities. Dewey (1938) explained reflection as follows: "To reflect is to look back over what has been done so as to extract the next meanings which are the capital stock for intelligent dealing with further experiences. It is the heart of the intellectual organization and of the disciplined mind" (p. 110). Reflection forms the foundation upon which children learn to make decisions, meet complex challenges, and take responsibility for their actions (Epstein 2003). However, self-assessment is a concept that young children struggle with Liebovich (2012) writes:

> To some, this approach [self-assessment] to assessment may seem an unlikely one for teachers and children to attempt. Children in the U.S. school system have not traditionally been socialized to discuss their work with teachers, parents, or peers, or to critically examine what they learn. Typically, children's work is evaluated by teachers or parents as good/bad and right/wrong. (p. 237)

E-portfolios enhance the ability for teacher, parents, and students to reflect, share, and assess progress over time. As a result, young children develop ownership of their work. When using e-portfolios, young children are able to show what they are able to do in several ways. E-portfolios allow users to collect artifacts in different media types (e.g., audio, visual, text) and to organize these using hypertext links (Barrett 2001). Teachers using e-portfolios also can share feedback in multiple ways using audio, visual, text, or graphics, and they can collaborate with parents in teaching, learning, and assessment of the child. In early childhood education, best practices advocate that parents be consulted when developing young children's individual curriculum, including the development of assessment that guides the curriculum (Copple and Bredekamp 2009). E-portfolios allow for constant interaction among parents, young children, and their teachers and, therefore, need to be well planned and designed for that purpose.

Planning an E- portfolio System and Importance of Partnership with Parents

E-portfolios are one of the best methods for assessing ongoing development or growth among young children (Barrett 2001; June 2004). However, some argue that e-portfolios are not worth the time due to the fact that schools focus too much on yearly test scores (Moritz and Christie 2005). Teachers need to be reminded that the process of learning should not be overlooked (Seitz and Bartholomew 2008). A well-planned e-portfolio system helps students participate in the process of learning. As a result, they attain better scores. Scores alone, such as those produced by standardized assessments, are meaningless to young children, and they are not capable of meeting students' needs. Students engage in reflective thinking about their previous portfolio assignments and map out ways of working hard to become better. When progress is not documented, most young children and families find it difficult to know what to focus on. As teachers plan the design and implementation of e-portfolios in early childhood classrooms, it is essential that they consider the following: (1) the role of the parents in the design and implementation process, (2) the type of e-portfolio system to apply, and (3) the types of artifacts to select for inclusion in the portfolio.

Table 8.1 Appropriate portfolio artifacts (evidence of development and progress)

Artifacts representing development in each subject area

Artifacts related to learning goals of student, teachers, and parents

Artifacts documenting ongoing development over time

A variety of artifacts including teachers' records, parents' records, photos, children's journals, artwork, lists of favorite books, completed checklists, anecdotal records, communications from parents, videos and tapes of child's performance, and children's narratives of science experiments or field trips

Artifacts that can be used for communication with students, parents, and other stakeholders

Artifacts that can be used for assessments and curriculum decisions

Partnership and collaboration with parents is one of the crucial steps that makes the development and use of e-portfolios a success. It is important to note that collaboration between teachers and parents is the cornerstone of effective and successful early childhood education (Eliason and Jenkins 2008; Hedges and Lee 2010). To illustrate the importance of portfolios and collaboration in early childhood, Beaty (2010) notes:

> In early childhood education, teachers do shared observation. Teachers who have initiated shared observation with parents sometimes carry this one step further. They ask parents to participate in helping create a portfolio for their children. (p. 426)

E-portfolios should allow for reflection, and the features in the e-portfolio should provide tools for demonstrating student ability. In selecting e-portfolio systems, teachers need to be mindful of support tools such as Wikis, Edmodo, and Google sites—open source tools which are known to require the user (in this case, young children) to set up an email account in order to log on to the system. For such systems, the teachers would want to involve parents who will monitor and setup the account. It is important that teachers consider sharing tips with parents on how to monitor children as they work on their e-portfolios. Monitoring will include making sure that the young child has the ability to navigate the e-portfolio and work on assignments successfully.

Lastly, teachers need to work with the young children to make decisions about artifacts to select for inclusion in the portfolio. Effective and meaningful portfolios come as a result of planning a portfolio system; the process of planning is done purposefully and continuously. Research indicates that adding portfolio items without planning will lead to the development of an inauthentic assessment system (June 2004; Kingore 1999; Lynch and Purnawarman 2004). Effective portfolios do not come by chance or by luck (Kingore 1999). Kingore urges teachers not to rely on spontaneous moments when wonderful products develop and students rush to their portfolios to include the new treasure. In the same vein, Beaty (2010) cautions that "teachers must provide a framework for collecting items; otherwise the results may become a meaningless hodgepodge" (p. 426). Information presented in Table 8.1 may be used to guide the selection of artifacts for the portfolio.

In the process of determining what artifacts would need to be included in the e-portfolio, the teacher and other stakeholders need to consider the following:

- The purpose of the portfolio
- The audience for the portfolio
- The degree to which the portfolio will allow for interaction

The Purpose of Young Children's Portfolios

Research in the last decade found that portfolios in early childhood education were developed for three purposes: for assessing ongoing child development, for program assessment, and for demonstrating to parents what children are able to do (Beaty 2010; Browne and Gordon 2009; Seitz and Bartholomew 2008). E-portfolios, in particular allow the teacher to meet all three purposes and more.

Teachers use e-portfolios to demonstrate young students' learning and abilities to perform tasks. Apart from using the portfolio for assembling evidence of learning and ability, teachers of young children may use e-portfolios to document a child's developmental progress. Jones and Shelton (2006) explained that "portfolios in which the primary purpose is to facilitate and chart development emphasize work in progress. They foster the development of knowledge, skills, and dispositions that will be employed in subsequent learning and practice contexts" (p. 29). In this kind of a portfolio, teachers may use a child development checklist (see Table 8.2) to guide the collection of artifacts or documentation materials.

E-portfolios may also be used to develop children's reflective processes (Danielson and Abrutyn 1997). Effective e-portfolios allow for two important types of reflection necessary and crucial in developing children's ability to self-reflect and self-assess. By looking at work completed at the beginning of the month, compared to the end of the month, children are able to engage in cumulative reflection on the progress they have made. Those who still have problems in grasping certain concepts are able to see where they need to focus and keep practicing those concepts with the help of their teacher, parents, or even peers who have already mastered the concepts. Apart from cumulative reflection, e-portfolios may be used to help children learn how to reflect on the tasks or evidence they select to be part of the e-portfolio. As they reflect on the selected artifacts, children develop ownership of their work. In the process of reflecting on their work, young children may struggle to find words to describe or analyze exactly how they feel about the evidence they selected. In such cases, the use of reflective statements may be used to help children develop critical thinking skills. For kindergarten through first grade, teachers may add guided reflective statements (see Fig. 8.1) at the end of the e-portfolio artifact to guide thinking.

Table 8.2 Child development checklist

Item	Evidence	Date
1. Self-identity		
2. Emotional development		
3. Social play		
4. Physical growth/motor development		
5. Cognitive/language development		

```
┌─────────────────────────────────────────────────────────────┐
│ Name_____        Date_____              │
│                                                             │
│                     [PORTFOLIO]                             │
│                                                             │
│ I added this in my e-portfolio because:                     │
│                                                             │
│  ○ I am proud of my work                                    │
│  ○ I am the most proud of....                               │
│  ○ I took time and thought hard about my work               │
│  ○ The hardest part was…                                    │
│  _____          │
│  _____          │
│  _____          │
│                                                             │
└─────────────────────────────────────────────────────────────┘
```

Fig. 8.1 Guided reflective statements

Using guided reflective questions such as those in Table 8.3 help young children move beyond one-sentence reflection and engage in higher-order thinking skills such as those recommended in Bloom's Taxonomy.

For older children (i.e. second and third-grade students), the teacher may consider adapting questions such as those offered in Table 8.3 to help guide their reflections.

The Audience of Young Children's Portfolios

There are five audiences for young children's portfolios:

- Teachers
- Parents
- Students
- Students' peers,
- Program evaluators

All stakeholders must have the ability to comprehend the content of the portfolio. Again, stakeholders must be able to participate in assessing progress and provide a basis for evaluating the quality of overall performance (Meisels and Steel 1991). The audience will need to know what to look for in a portfolio, as well as know the aims or purposes of the portfolio (Grace 1992).

Table 8.3 Guided reflection questions for third graders' e-portfolios

Please answer the following questions. Be sure to spell check and use complete sentences

1. As you review your assignments in language arts, science, math, and social studies, what strengths do you see? What evidence do you have of that strength? (The strengths I see are…)
2. What skills do you need to work on? Using your evidence, show the skills you need to work on. (I need to work on…)
3. On a scale of 1–10, with 10 being the best, how would you rate your neatness and organizational skills? What evidence do you have of these skills? (I would rate my neatness as a….)
4. On a scale of 1–10, with 10 being the best, how would you rate your ability to revise your work? What evidence do you have of your capability to revise? (I would rate my ability to revise or make corrections as a…)
5. What is the best activity or project you have done so far in language arts/social studies? What have you liked about this project or activity? (The best project or activity I have done is…)
6. If you could change one thing in math/science/language arts/social studies, what would you change? Why? (Next time I might change…because…)
7. What goals do you have for the next nine weeks to improve in language arts and mathematics? (My goals 7. are…)
8. Explain your plan to achieve these goals? (I will achieve these goals by…)

It is important to note that e-portfolios allow for interactions among the audience more than paper-based portfolios because they are more manageable and easier to manipulate. With permission, e-portfolios allow for easy review across students and even across classes and over time. Parents and teachers need to come to a consensus as to how much interaction should be permitted.

Allowing for Interaction with Young Children's Portfolios

Effective electronic portfolios designed for young children should allow for seven levels of interaction. The first level of interaction should be between the teacher and the portfolio. The second level should be between the student and the portfolio. Third, the portfolio should allow for interaction between the teacher and the student. Next, the student may use the portfolio contents to interact with their peers. Last, the portfolio should allow for interaction with parents, and between the teacher and parents, and between the teacher and program evaluator (see Fig. 8.2).

The teacher should plan for an e-portfolio that allows for interaction and the monitoring of such interactions at different levels. A number of interactive technologies such as Google websites, Wikispaces, PBworks, and Edmodo, to mention a few, allow for interactions at all levels. Figure 8.3 shows a screen shot from a Google website used as an e-portfolio for a first grade class. In this classroom, the teacher was able to manage the site with the use of a course management system. The Google website allows for the interactions previously described in Fig. 8.2.

It must be noted that Google sites are widely used for e-portfolios because they are easy to create. Google accounts are used in universities and in most school districts for email and for easy access to Google apps that allow creating, sharing, and presentation of documents. Google sites also ensure participant privacy, as

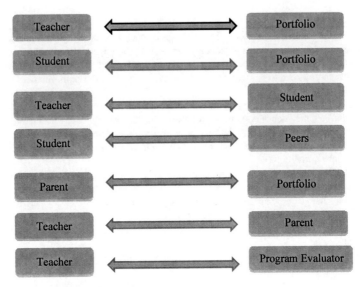

Fig. 8.2 Electronic portfolio interactions

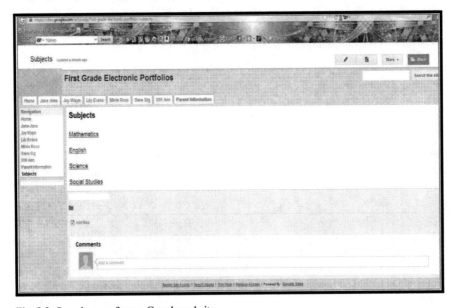

Fig. 8.3 Sample page from a Google website

participants can only interact with the contents of the portfolio if they are invited to do so. Parents may create a Google website on behalf of their child, and the site will be used as an e-portfolio for the class where they display their creative work.

8   Planning, Designing, and Implementing Effective Interactive Portfolios ...

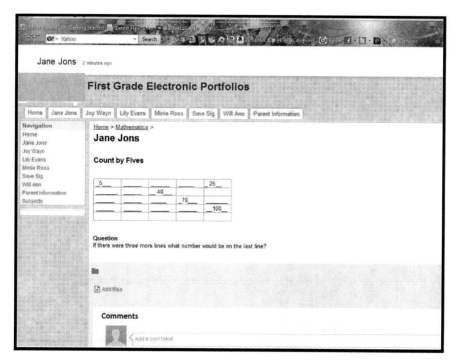

Fig. 8.4 Links to subject areas by student name

Figure 8.3 shows a site that provides easy navigation even for young children. They can navigate this site on their own or with the teacher or a parent's help as they work on their portfolios. After gaining access to the site, all they need to do is click on their names, either on the left navigation bar or on the horizontal navigation bar, to gain access to their portfolios. Parent information can also be accessed through the left navigation bar and the horizontal navigation bar.

When children access their individual e-portfolio, they find links to the different subjects (math, science, reading, etc.). This helps organize the young child's work by subject area. Figure 8.4 shows what one might find under a subject link by clicking on the link to mathematics; the child gets to the page where the mathematics activities can be viewed and reviewed.

Creating Interactive Tabs in the E-Portfolio

The purpose for creating portfolios may be the deciding factor in how to develop interactive tabs. The interactive tabs in an electronic portfolio vary in number depending on the purpose of the e-portfolio. Teachers who want to develop an e-portfolio to document progress of early elementary children (kindergarten through third grade) will be assembling a working portfolio. Teachers may use standards and

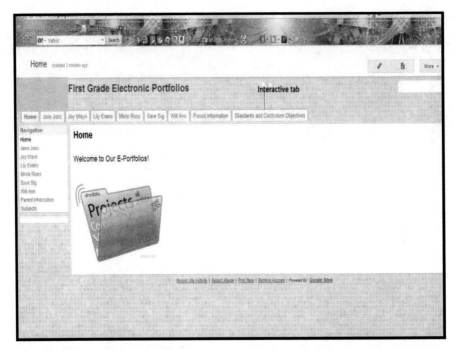

Fig. 8.5 Interactive e-portfolio tabs

curriculum objectives for each subject as a guide to select e-portfolio artifacts. The standards and curriculum objectives should have interactive tabs on the e-portfolio (see Fig. 8.5). The tabs will allow the teacher and other stakeholders (such as parents, program evaluators, etc.) to, not only access the evidence collected easily, but assess the appropriateness of the evidence as well as whether the students are meeting the curriculum objectives.

For a more advanced electronic portfolio assessment system that is geared toward early elementary students, teachers need to consider the following principles as outlined in Table 8.4

Multimodal Feedback and E-Portfolios

Effective instruction requires that the teacher gives students individualized continuous feedback on their portfolios. This strategy is supported in the research on universal design of learning (UDL). UDL requires the teacher to use diverse teaching methods to meet the needs of diverse learners (Chita-Tegmark et al. 2013; Lever-Duffy and McDonald 2011). This also implies that teachers should use multimodal ways of delivering feedback. Instead of the use of written comments or text, teachers may deliver feedback in visual, audio, audio-visual, and interactive forms. Such methods allow children the opportunity to review the materials over and over again because they are interactive and are available at any time. Students can review

Table 8.4 Principles for developing good performance assessments

Set objectives that need to be met with the portfolio.

Determine how the portfolio will be assessed and for what purpose. For example, will the portfolio be used to make transition decisions from one grade level to another?

Design assessment rubrics that match the objectives for the portfolio as well as instruction.

Define the criteria and standards for each assessment rubric item.

Determine the individuals (teachers, students, parents, administrators) who will assess the portfolio.

Provide training where necessary for assessing the portfolios to ensure reliability.

Determine next steps to take after assessing the portfolio. What changes need to be made?

the feedback until they grasp the concept or become confident in their knowledge surrounding the concept. When developing e-portfolios, teachers should consider the use of an interactive tab for feedback. As they listen or watch the feedback, children should also be able to leave comments for the teacher. Children's comments on the feedback help to determine if children comprehend their teacher's suggestions. The decision about when to make the feedback open for children to access depends on the teacher and the purpose of the portfolio. Teachers may use voice thread as one tool to deliver audio-visual feedback because voice thread allows children to leave comments. VoiceThread is a cloud application that allows users to upload media like images, videos, documents, and presentations. Uploading media materials is done asynchronously. In addition, "VoiceThread allows users to have conversations and to make comments using any mix of text, a microphone, a web cam, a telephone, or uploaded audio file" (The Pennsylvania State University 2010, p. 1). Below is a screen shot of a sample VoiceThread (Fig. 8.6).

Fig. 8.6 Audio visual feedback using VoiceThread

Implementation Factors for Transitioning to E-portfolios

Two main approaches to e-portfolios are described in the 2010 United States Department of Education National Educational Technology Plan (NETP) (U.S. Department of Education 2010): a student-managed approach to help students gauge their own learning while demonstrating development to their teachers, parents, and peers and an assessment-driven approach that is used to provide evidence of competencies in relation to learning criteria and standards. The first approach emphasizes process while the second emphasizes product. Irrespective of the approach, it is important to note that certain factors need to be in place to ensure the successful planning, preparation and implementation of e-portfolios. As outlined in Table 8.5, the "implementation strategies and critical success factors" which include administrative support, resources and technological infrastructure (Gathercoal et al. 2002, p. 33), need to be considered prior to, during, and even after implementation of the e-portfolios. Teacher technology competence and skills also play a major role in the transitioning to and maintenance of e-portfolios (Kankaanranta 2001).

Summary

This chapter highlighted the importance of e-portfolios and how e-portfolios can be used in the primary grades to document the evidence of young children learning critical thinking and self-assessment skills. If e-portfolios are planned, designed, and implemented properly, they have the potential to serve as a teaching tool, a learning experience, and an authentic assessment system. E-portfolios may be considered over traditional portfolios for their ease in documenting and evaluating young children's learning; they result in a more professional-looking, highly-revisable document. E-portfolios can easily be evaluated by all stakeholders as they interact with the portfolio content. Also, the evidence presented in e-portfolios is not static, as is the evidence provided in traditional portfolios. In addition, most of the evidence gathered for traditional portfolios is collected randomly without a systematic approach, as traditional portfolios are used mostly for program assessment (for instance, showing alignment of standards and assessments) and for demonstrating evidence of performance at parent teacher conferences.

E-portfolios can promote collaboration among teachers, young children, and their families and may be used as effective teaching and learning tools as stakeholders plan, build, and review the work. Primary teachers and their students are involved in the principles and guidelines for selecting artifacts. E-portfolios help to strengthen the relationships between all stakeholders. Finally, with e-portfolios, teachers are able to deliver developmentally-appropriate interactive feedback using a variety of multimedia techniques.

Table 8.5 Implementation factors for successful transitioning to e-portfolios

Implementation factors	Before implementation	During implementation	After implementation
Administrative support	Administrators are well informed on the use of e-portfolios and are involved in the preparation phase of the e-portfolio idea	Teachers are provided with resources and infrastructure (including time, finances, availability of tools, and technical support) as they implement e-portfolios in their classrooms	Continuous administrative and technical support to help sustain the use of e-portfolios
Teacher technology skills and competence	Teachers need to be engaged in technology professional development to boost instructional technology knowledge	Teachers must align the design of the e-portfolios with educational technology plans and standards	Teachers need continuous update in instructional technology knowledge and strategies as well as knowledge of technology plans and standards
Family commitment	Teacher-parent workshops are needed to share the value of electronic portfolios with parents so they are aware of their role	Parent workshops need to demonstrate how they might support their children at home with access and uploading of materials to the e-portfolio	Rubrics need to be developed for parents to help them assess the effectiveness of the e-portfolio for academic progress or performance
Learner-centered/constructivist pedagogy	Teachers need to prepare learner-centered pedagogy and make sure the strategies and visual and audio tools they plan to apply or select are supported by the e-portfolios	Teachers need to ensure that pedagogy aligns with the web-based portfolio	Teachers need to continue to reflect on their pedagogy and tools to make sure they are supported in the e-portfolio and can be used to demonstrate and/or assess learning

References

Barrett, H. (2001). Electronic portfolios. http://electronicportfolios.org/portfolios/encyclopediaentry.htm. Accessed 6 Nov 2012.
Beaty, J. J. (2010). *Observing development of the young child*. Upper Saddle River, NJ: Pearson Education Inc.
Browne, K. W., & Gordon, A. M. (2009). *To teach well: An early childhood, practicumguide*. Upper Saddle River, NJ: Pearson Education Inc.
Chita-Tegmark, M., Gravel, J. W., Serpa, M., Domings, Y., & Rose, D. H. (2013). Using the universal design for learning framework to support culturally diverse learners. *Journal of Education, 192*(1), 17–22.
Copple, C., & Bredekamp, S. (2009). *Developmentally appropriate practice in early childhood programs serving children from birth through age 8*. Washington, DC: National Association for the Education of Young Children.
Danielson, C., & Abrutyn, L. (1997). An introduction to using portfolios in the classroom. http://www.ascd.org/publications/books/197171/chapters/The-Types-of-Portfolios.aspx. Accessed 10 March 2013.
Dewey, J. (1938). *Experience and education*. New York: Macmillan.
Eliason, C., & Jenkins, L. (2008). *A practical guide to early childhood education curriculum* (9th ed.). Upper Saddle River, NJ: Pearson Education Inc.
Epstein, A. S. (2003). Developing and enhancing thinking skills: How planning and reflection develop young children's thinking skills. *Beyond the Journal~ Young Children on the Web*. http://journal.naeyc.org/btj/200309/Planning&Reflection.pdf. Accessed 8 Oct 2012.
Gathercoal, P., Love. D., Bryde, B., & McKen, G. (2002). On implementing web-based electronic portfolios. *Educause Quarterly, 25*(2), 29–37.
Grace, C. (1992). *The portfolio and its use: Developmentally appropriate assessment of young children*. ERIC Clearinghouse on Elementary and Early Childhood Education ED351150.
Hedges, H., & Lee, D. (2010). 'I understood the complexity within diversity': Preparing for partnership with families in early childhood settings. *Asia-Pacific Journal of Teacher Education, 38*(4), 257–272.
Jones, M., & Shelton, M. (2006). *Developing your portfolio: Enhancing your learning and showing your stuff*. New York, NY: Routledge.
June, A. (2004). Electronic portfolios: Blending technology, accountability & assessment. *T H E Journal, 31*(9), 12–18.
Kankaanranta, M. (2001). Constructing digital portfolios: Teachers evolving capabilities in the use of information and communications technology. *Teacher Development: An International Journal of Teachers' Professional Development, 5*(2), 259–275. doi:10.1080/13664530100200139.
Kingore, B. (1999). *Assessment* (2nd ed.). Austin, TX: Professional Associates.
Lever-Duffy, J., & McDonald, J. B. (2011). *Teaching and learning with technology* (4th ed.). Boston, MA: Pearson Education Inc.
Liebovich, B. J. (2012). *Children's self-assessment*. http://ceep.crc.uiuc.edu/pubs/katzsym/liebovich.html. Accessed 10 Aug 2012.
Lorenzo, G., & Ittleson, J. (2005). An overview of e-portfolios. *Educause Learning Initiative*. http://net.educause.edu/ir/library/pdf/eli3001.pdf. Accessed 14 June 2012.
Lynch, L. L., & Purnawarman, P. (2004). Electronic portfolio assessments in U.S. educational and instructional technology programs: Are they supporting teacher education? *TechTrends: Linking Research & Practice to Improve Learning, 48*(1), 50–56.
McAfee, O., Leong, D. J., & Bodrova, E. (2004). *Basics of assessment: A primer for early childhood educators*. Washington, DC: National Association for the Education of Young Children.
Meisels, S., & Steele, D. (1991). *The early childhood portfolio collection process*. Ann Arbor, MI: Center for Human Growth and Development, University of Michigan.
Moritz, J., & Christie, A. (2005). It's elementary! Using electronic portfolios with young students. In C. Crawford, et al. (Eds.), *Proceedings of Society for Information Technology & Teacher Education International Conference 2005* (pp. 144–151). Chesapeake, VA: AACE.

Seitz, H., & Bartholomew, C. (2008). Powerful portfolios for young children. *Early Childhood Education Journal, 36*(1), 63–68.

The Pennsylvania State University. (2010). *Voice thread: Group conversations around images, documents, and videos.* http://voicethread.psu.edu/. Accessed 8 Nov 2012.

Tierney, R. J., Carter, M. A., & Desai, L. E. (1991). *Portfolio assessment in the reading and writing classroom.* Norwood, MA: Christopher-Gordon.

U.S. Department of Education. (2010). National Educational Technology Plan. http://www.ed.gov/technology/netp-2010. Accessed 18 May 2013.

Part II
Issues and Trends

Chapter 9
Young Children as Multimodal Learners in the Information Age

Nicola Yelland

Children often multitask, such as this 6-year-old playing an electronic game with the television set on.

N. Yelland (✉)
Victoria University, Melbourne, Australia
e-mail: nicola.yelland@vu.edu.au

Abstract This chapter explores the lives of young children in the Information Age and recognizes that they are significantly different because of the ubiquitous presence of new technologies. One of the advantages of new technologies is that they enable children to engage in inquiry and meaning-making in a variety of modes beyond the linguistic. They can incorporate visual, aural, oral, kinesthetic, and spatial modalities to communicate and make sense of the world. In this way, children in the Information Age are multimodal learners and become multiliterate by experiencing and using new technologies in diverse ways. This chapter describes data from empirically-based studies to illustrate the ways in which early childhood pedagogies can incorporate the use of new technologies. These new technologies permeate every aspect of our lives, and young children come to formal learning contexts in the early years of schooling with a wide range of experiences, yet their fluency with new media is often ignored. Traditional media and play are favored, and there are seldom opportunities to playfully explore with new media or even incorporate them into play contexts. Here, these assumptions are interrogated and examples are provided of the ways in which new technologies can offer unique contexts for multimodal learning and meaning-making in the Information Age.

Keywords Multimodal learning · Young children · Digital learning · Early childhood curriculum

Introduction

Lulu (3 years old) is excited about her new iPad and says, "I love my big iPod. Daddy got it for me. It's very BIG!" She turns the iPad around to reveal a picture of a Halloween cat she drew herself. During the next 10 minutes or so, she uses a paint app to produce multiple colored lines, swirls, and squiggles with her fingers and announces proudly, "Look what I did!!"

In the past 20 years we have witnessed dramatic changes in societies, economies, and everyday lived experiences as a result of the ubiquitous presence of new technologies. To name only a few amongst the many, we have seen the mapping of the human genome project begun in 1990 which has enabled the identification of all of the approximately 20,000 to 25,000 genes in human DNA, we have viewed the universe with the Hubble telescope on the Internet, and we have watched wars on TV and seen weapons firing at live targets as if in a video game. Our personal lives have been transformed with the Internet, social media, and other new forms of communications and devices. These devices and the software on them enable us to stay connected to our families and friends in diverse locations, access information and people who can help us with various projects and inquiries, be entertained, move around with the aid of Global Positioning Systems (GPS), and a myriad of other supportive mechanisms. Their use is not restricted to adults. One major report into the role of media in the lives of young people (Rideout et al. 2010) has described childhoods characterized by extensive media use and, for the first time, new patterns and trends in simultaneous multiple media use. The report revealed, for example, "8–18 year olds spend more time with media than in any other activity... an average of more than 7.5 hours a day, 7 days a week" (p. 1). This was an increase of 1 hour a day from their previous report, which was conducted in 2005. It represents a greater amount of time than many adults spend in full-time employment.

The report also noted that 20% of media use by this cohort of 8–18 year olds occurred with mobile devices (mobile phones, iPods, mp3 players, and handheld video games). This allowed the children to not only use the new media more frequently, as they shifted locations during their day, but also enabled them to experience media simultaneously; this made them adept at multi-tasking with various types of media.

Marsh et al. (2005) reported that even younger children (birth to 6 years of age) were "immersed in practices related to popular culture, media and new technologies from birth" (p. 5). This enabled them to become adept at operating the machines and simultaneously build a huge array of skills, knowledge, and understandings about the world in which they live. Participating in media cultures has affected the ways in which children engage with others and impacts what they can do, think, and feel (Marsh et al. 2005). Yet, in the study, parents also reported feeling that their children, while enjoying new media, still maintained "balanced" lives in which they also participated in activities that did not involve the use of new technologies. In fact, the parents were very positive about the role of new media in their children's lives and thought that new media were important to all aspects of their learning. While early childhood practitioners were also generally positive about new media, they did express concern about the perceived amounts of time that children spend on these activities. This is interesting, as there seems to be no information regarding the amount of time being taken away from other "traditional" activities as a result of new media, or if new media is doing children any harm in terms of their overall development and learning. The practitioners who participated in this study also indicated that they wanted more professional learning opportunities to help them incorporate new media into their curricula. They noted that, when new media were used in their classrooms, the children were more engaged and made good progress in speaking, listening, and literacy.

Moreover, we know that children are not passive consumers of media. They self-select media content (e.g. favorite TV shows, DVDs, and music) and mostly initiate the activities, as well as decide how to use the media and when to stop. They are truly new millennials who live in a multimodal world where the impact of new technologies is significant.

All of these studies vary in their use of terminology to describe new technologies. New media and information and communications technologies (ICT) are just a few terms that describe the wide range of devices available for use today as well as the activities that are available on them. Thus, these terms are used interchangeably throughout this chapter depending on the literature being cited and the context of the activity.

It is apparent that new technologies offer new opportunities for learning (Collins and Halverson 2009). They enable interactions with ideas, content, and modalities that were not possible previously. Further, they are not neutral or simply 'tools,' because they *impact* on what people can do as well as providing *contexts* in which *collaborations* and new types of cognitive, social, physical, and emotional experiences are available and offer new potential for engagement in learning. New technologies require us to reconceptualize not only what it means to learn but also the ways in which we organize curriculum and design learning activities in our schools. It begins in the early years.

Early Childhood Pedagogy

It has become a truism that early childhood education is characterized by learning through play (Grieshaber and McArdle 2010; Yelland 2007, 2011). Preschool programs throughout the Western world can be described as being *child-centered* and *play-based* (Qualifications and Curriculum Authority 2000). After preschool, we find that the demands of formal schooling tend to prohibit totally child-centered and play-based programs (Yelland 1999). There is, however, a realization that the first years of school should allow for activities, contexts for learning, and experiences with "concrete materials" before more abstract concepts are explored. This view can be traced back to the work of Piaget, who maintained that early childhood is characterized as "preoperational and concrete operational." In this stage, children must be allowed to manipulate three dimensional objects in order to learn about, and understand, a variety of (mainly logico-mathematical) concepts.

The UK government and a broad base of academic publications have suggested guides for pedagogies that encourage learning via play. Play is regarded as the main vehicle for learning. For example, the Qualifications and Curriculum Authority (2000) has suggested that learning at the Foundation Stage (3–5 years of age) should be characterized by:

> ...opportunities for children to engage in activities planned by adults and also those that they plan or initiate themselves. Children do not make a distinction between 'play' and 'work' and neither should practitioners. Children need time to become engrossed, work in depth and complete activities. (p. 11)

In the United States, developmentally-appropriate practice (DAP) (Bredekamp 1987; Bredekamp and Copple 1997; Copple and Bredekamp 2009) has long been regarded as the base reference for teaching and learning practices in early childhood. It is endorsed by the National Association for the Education of Young Children (NAEYC) and is synonymous with child-centered, play-based curricula in the United States. There was no mention of the use of new technologies in the initial 1987 DAP guide. By 1996 three entries were added after a position statement was released on developmentally-appropriate uses of computers in 1996 (NAEYC 1996). This was a very carefully constructed statement, and despite recognizing that "the potential benefits of technology for young children's learning and development are well documented," (p. 11) it only advocated the use of a limited range of developmentally-appropriate software to be selected by the teacher for young children. The document reiterated that "...computers supplement and do not replace highly valued early childhood activities and materials, such as art, blocks, sand, water, books, exploration with writing materials and dramatic play" (p. 11). In 1996 the view was held that in DAP "...computers should be used in ways that support these existing classroom educational directions rather than distort or replace them" (p. 12). In this way, the stage was set for computers to be an "add-on" to existing practices. An example was provided to suggest that, if children were involved in dramatic play about a shop, they might like to make a sign for the shop with a "banner" computer software program. This activity was considered as DAP since it was "open ended." The policy statement was followed by two articles written by Shade (1996) and Elkind (1996). Shade declared that "the most critical decision a teacher can make is that of software selection." (p. 17) While Elkind, in his "cautionary" note, prophetically stated, "...computers permeate all facets of our lives and are here to stay... I am still a little jarred when I see one among the finger-paints, geraniums, and gerbils of a kindergarten" (p. 22). Elkind invokes Piaget's stage of concrete operations to contend that for a 5-year-old to "click a mouse and manipulate computer icons is probably far in advance of his or her logical comprehension of these actions and symbols" (p. 23).

A later edition of DAP (Copple and Bredekamp 2009) included three entries which reiterated earlier statements made by the NAEYC on the use of computers in early childhood programs, namely that software should be developmentally appropriate and that the use of computers needs to be integrated into existing programs; the implication being that the computers need to *fit in* with rather than challenge existing pedagogies and curricula. More recently, the NAEYC and the Fred Rogers Center have updated their advice to parents and educators (2012) which basically follows the same line: "It is the role and responsibility of the educator to make informed, intentional and appropriate choices about if, how, and when technology and media are used in early childhood classrooms for children from birth through age 8" (p. 11).

In Australia there has been an attempt to standardize approaches to early childhood curricula and pedagogies as documented in *The Early Years Learning Framework for Australia* (Department of Education Employment and Workplace Relations 2009). Play-based learning is advocated as the context for learning through which children organize and make sense of their social worlds as they engage actively with people, objects, and representations. The early years are recognized as a time when children seek to make meaning of the world, and the role of new technologies for meaning-making and expressions of ideas are seen as being an important part of this process. The framework stipulates:

Children use information and communication technologies to access information, investigate ideas and represent their thinking.
This is evident, for example, when children:

- Identify the uses of technology in everyday life and use real or imaginary technologies as props in their play
- Use information and communications technologies to access images and information, explore diverse perspectives and make sense of their world
- Use information and communication technologies as tools for designing, drawing, editing, reflecting and composing
- Engage with technology for fun and to make meaning (p. 44)

The framework recommends that educators can promote this learning, for example, when they:

- Provide children with access to a range of technologies
- Integrate technologies into children's play experiences and projects
- Teach skills and techniques and encourage children to use technologies to explore new information and represent their ideas
- Encourage collaborative learning about and through technologies between children, and children and educators (p. 44)

Pedagogy here is defined as professional practice that builds and nurtures relationships, curriculum decision making, teaching, and learning. Play- based learning refers to a context for learning through which children can organize and make sense of their social worlds as they engage actively with people, objects, and representations. *The Early Years Learning Framework for Australia* adopts a broad view of technologies that includes *all* the digital technologies available and extends this beyond the actual devices to include processes, systems, and environments. In this way, there is an explicit understanding that digital technologies are relevant to the lives of young children in the twenty-first century and need to be incorporated as an integral part of their learning.

Multimodal Learning and Becoming Multiliterate

Multimodality refers to contexts in which modes of communication (linguistic, visual, spatial, aural, gestural/kinesthetic, and linguistic) come together and form resources for meaning making. Multimodal theory (Kress and Van Leeuwen 2001) is concerned with how these coalesce to facilitate or enable learning. Semiotic (meaning making) resources that are multimodal are critical for learners to be able to represent and understand their learning with new technologies. Their existence challenges traditional conceptualizations of literacy that are based in the language of the printed text and enable a wide variety of multimodal forms of expression and understandings. Jewitt (2003) stated, "New technologies make different kinds of cultural forms available like computer games and websites" (p. 9). She also warned, "How a technology contributes to learning depends on how it is used; a technology is not inherently good or bad" (p. 29). Thus, the recommendations that DAP software will enhance learning cannot go unchallenged. It is not just by virtue of playing with computer activities that benefit learning in the twenty-first century. It is the way in which the software is designed to utilize the semiotic resources available so that learners can make the most meaning from the combinations and use them to connect and build on their understandings. New ways of combining modalities in media enable different forms of engagement with ideas that were not possible with old technologies and, thus, impact on the h*ow* and *what* of learning. The various combinations influence the ways in which concepts can be represented and interpreted by learners and give them access to a whole new range of knowledge-building opportunities. These combinations seem to occur naturally in learning scenarios with new technologies in informal or out-of-school environments. What can we learn from these?

These new contexts require a rethinking of pedagogies for teachers of the twenty-first century (Yelland 2007). When pedagogies are viewed as knowledge processes, (Cope and Kalantzis 2000; Kalantzis and Cope 2008; Yelland et al. 2008a) it is possible for teaching to be regarded as a design experience in which the learners are provided with a framework for linking the current experience to their existing knowledge base (from the *known* to the *new*), where conceptualizations and conjectures move from *naming* to *theorizing*, and where there are opportunities for *analyzing* (functionally and critically) and *applying* (appropriately and creatively). These all constitute learning scenarios in which new technologies are regarded as opportunities for transformative pedagogies to be deployed and build on the pedagogy of multiliteracies (New London Group 1996). This chapter provides examples of how this can be achieved in early childhood education.

Pathways to New Learning

The implications of research in digital (Lankshear and Knobel 2008) and new literacies (Lankshear and Knobel 2003; Pahl and Rowsell 2006) on practice indicate that one way to encourage multiliteracies is to observe and learn what children are doing with new technologies in out-of-school contexts. Another is to work with teachers using a pedagogy of multiliteracies as a framework. I have done this in a number of research projects with colleagues that generated substantive outcomes in terms of changed practice (Hill et al. 2002; Hill et al. 2001; Yelland et al. 2008b). What follows are examples of some of the ways in which we were able to do this in research projects with teachers and young children.

Millennial Children and Multiliteracies

Making Films

Sarah introduced both still and digital video cameras to her 3-year-old kindergarten group in the western suburbs of a large Australian city. Most parents of the children were unemployed or working part-time in "blue-collar" jobs. Only a few owned a computer or a digital camera, but they did have other technologies in the home such as TVs, DVD/video machines, and a range of "white" goods (refrigerator, microwave). About three quarters of them had mobile phones. Sarah had worked as a teacher for 7 years and had what she called a "traditional play-based kindergarten program." That is, it was structured around indoor and outdoor play-based activities planned around the children's interests.

Sarah knew how to use the two cameras and had previously taken and printed out selected digital photos of kindergarten life to share with the parents on her notice board. She was a bit tentative about using the cameras with the children in her class. She was worried they might drop and break them and that the children would not be able to use them appropriately or effectively. Initially, she sat the children on the carpet and explained to them that they would each take turns over the next week to use both types of cameras, and she explained the differences between them. The children had seen the cameras before, so they knew what they could do and were excited that they were being "allowed" to use them. None of them indicated that they had previously used a camera. Sarah demonstrated how to use each camera and then said the children would be able to use them to film what they thought "might be interesting to them or others." Different ways of introducing the cameras to the children were discussed, and the whole-class approach was chosen for the introduction, to be followed up by small groups sharing the camera. In their small groups, the children could discuss what might make a good shot, or action, to record and collaborate about how to organize the shoot. Sarah knew the members of the class well, and she knew who would need more time than others and who could be left alone to explore. There was no hard and fast "rule" for doing this. The children needed to know how to use the cameras from a technical standpoint before they could appropriate it for their own purposes.

Over the next week, the children took photos and movies around the classroom. For Sarah, this meant relinquishing her traditional program in which all the children were either inside or outside at a given time. This was made easier because the author was there for the research project, but Sarah could also call upon her teacher aide for assistance if she felt that the group needed supervision outside or inside. There were photographs of faces, activities, and locations as well as movies of children playing.

Sarah held sharing sessions in which the children talked about what they had done and expanded their stories with examples and other stories. She introduced the notion of different representations (e.g., drawings) of what the children had seen and experienced in their daily interactions and what they were viewing on the cameras. In this way, the different modalities were being introduced to them at an early age and becoming part of their repertoire for the various concepts they were encountering.

In playing with the cameras, Sarah hoped that the children would use them as their "eyes to the world"—their immediate environs. She also hoped that the children would, not only talk about the places they had chosen to "capture" digitally, but also think about the sounds, how they moved, and other ways of telling stories about their images.

These are playful explorations (Yelland 2010) in which the children were exploring and discovering knowledge and skills in a context of adult-supported and scaffolded learning. It is very different from traditional forms of play that are frequently described in the literature. It began with some structure and included specific technical scaffolding (Yelland and Masters 2006). As the children became more adept with the operation of the media, they were able to make more informed decisions as they extended their explorations. Sarah noted that she gave the children as much scope as she had done in traditional play-based scenarios, yet she was initially concerned that she was directing them too much and structuring what they were doing. Gradually, she felt that the scaffolding she provided (in terms of the technical capabilities of, for example, *how* to take a photo that was not directly pointing into the sun) was important to the process, and she became used to this new role as their teacher.

Feedback from the parents was very positive. They felt that their children were much more engaged with focused conversations. The children talked about concepts and ideas as they were experiencing them and were very animated. A number of parents talked about wanting to purchase digital cameras with a video feature to build on the activities that Sarah had initiated. This was difficult for many in terms of the cost, but they planned carefully since they thought the cameras had great potential to add value to their lives in ways they had not thought possible.

Making Music

Another teacher, Claire, wanted to consider extending modalities to the aural and visual by music making with her children. They were used to playing with musical instruments in their play-based program as part of indoor activities. In fact, when the weather was fine, they could play outside. Claire wanted to extend this work with new (visual/aural) modalities that computer-based music making afforded.

She introduced *Super Dooper Music Looper* (Sony 2003) to the whole group, showing them what was available and asking for questions. The discussion included comments about how the program used instruments like the ones they were used to playing with in the kindergarten to those they had heard in other places, like pianos or violins. The children then explored the synthesized sounds by taking turns and talking about the new "labels" they had given to the manufactured sounds—like "bubbles" and "check it out." The latter was a sort of male-voiced rap version of the words repeated the number of times that the child said them into the microphone.

The making of music with *Super Dooper* was easily integrated into indoor play time. The children loved making musical compositions with it in their small groups of three or four and enjoyed saving and replaying their creations with the whole group in class sharing times. The role of the teacher here was to scaffold the learning so she could extend their thinking and language to link the electronic instruments with those they had already used in the center. The children compared the sounds of the traditional instruments to those that were available on the computer and not in the "real world" (like the simulated bubble sounds that could be coordinated to form a rhythm). What struck the author as a "non-musical" observer were the ways in which the music created via the computer sounded more sophisticated and a closer approximation to a melody than the sounds made with traditional instruments. These on-computer music experiences enabled the children to become composers of music rather than just consumers, and certainly this aspect warranted further investigation.

Making Advertisements

In a multiage (6 and 7-year-old) class, the children were asked to design and create an advertisement for a new product that was a sports/health drink. They worked in self-selected groups ranging from 4 to 6 members and started by thinking about what type of product they wanted to create and how they might advertise it. In the first instance, after the task was explained to the whole group, the children watched and talked about advertisements that they had seen and liked. They frequently decided that they needed a jingle and some action to accompany it and, since the product was a sports drink, they all thought that some action shots of children doing sports were necessary. One group decided to call their product "Speedo" and, with the guidance of one of the teachers, began to create a storyboard of ideas. Once this was done, they started to plan the filming of sequences and make a list of the props they needed before the filming could commence. The class had been introduced to digital cameras before, so this was not their first time using them. After the filming, one of teachers, Jill, showed each group how to edit using *iMovie*. She gradually participated and advised them less frequently as they became more proficient. This was time consuming, but the children were enthusiastic and became fluent editors very quickly. They became adept at taking turns editing the various scenes. This work took place over a 3-week time span. The teachers and children had twice-weekly sharing sessions where they discussed their progress and the strategies they had tried which had been successful as well as those that did not work so well. In this way, the children were able to learn from each other. When the children were ready, they showed the advertisement to one of the teachers who made her final comments before all the advertisements were unveiled in a special preview to which all the school was invited.

The two teachers of the multiage class were willing to try things out, and this was mirrored in the behavior of the children in their group. Their roles changed as the children became more confident with the tasks, and their scaffolding techniques shifted and diminished as the 3 weeks passed. They used some didactic pedagogies to teach new skills, but generally their techniques were related to supporting the children to actively engage with concepts and skills. The project took place in Term 3 of a four-term school year; therefore, many of the processes regarding how to work together effectively were already in place. The teachers had indicated that, at the start of the year, they spent a great deal of time with the children explaining procedures and processes. By the second term, this was paying off in terms of encouraging the children to be autonomous learners and taking the lead in their own learning. They also stated that, as a result of the project, the children had become more interested in the use of new technologies for learning and that everyone should have this opportunity. This supports what many teachers have reported regarding a lack of opportunity to find out how new technologies impact *what* and *how* the curriculum is taught. Experienced teachers reported that they felt pressure to "cover" content and perform in national tests. It was only after "having a go" with technology that the teachers realized twenty-first century learning with new technologies could be accommodated in their enacted curriculum.

Conclusions

The examples cited here represent "pockets of innovation" that document alternative ways of designing learning in the early years. They encapsulate the use of new technologies to promote multimodal learning that are possible for dynamic learning in the Information Age. Yet whole-scale change remains elusive, and children in our classrooms seem trapped in a time warp. Teachers still maintain that it is difficult for them to find the time to figure out what they might do to extend their pedagogical repertoires (Jewitt 2003; Marsh et al. 2005; Plowman and Stephen 2005). Tinkering with curricula has not worked; and while accountability and testing regimes are the flavor of the era, transformative practices in schools remain increasingly out of reach. If education and schooling are the keys to successful societies and economies, then all these issues need to be addressed as a matter of urgency.

Two news items caught the author's attention within 2 days of each other a few years ago. The first was a report on Sky News about a new heart analysis machine that enabled medical practitioners to take cross sectional photographs of the heart and turn them into a 3D model. The report suggested that this new machine would change the way in which doctors are trained, since there would no longer be a need to cut up organs or cadavers.

The second report came from the inquiry into the Iraq war in the United Kingdom. Sir Peter Spencer (Chief of Defense Procurement) stated, with regard to using up-to-date equipment in the army:

> It is not acceptable in my view for people to be trained to the top of their professional competence with the best equipment available and then ... have it taken off them. That is demoralizing from a soldier's point of view... Frankly you can't uninvent things. When soldiers know how new technology has enabled them to do a job, you can't take away the new technology and say, 'Just do it the old-fashioned steam-driven way'. That's not on.
> Iraq Inquiry transcripts. July 28 2010 (lines 11–21)

In the first example, it is evident that new technologies are revolutionizing the ways in which doctors are trained and able to carry out their job. In the second, users have access to new technologies in one context and have these technologies taken away in another context. It is possible to imagine analogies here with education, teachers, and students, and ask, "Are pre-service teacher education students being prepared to teach students for the twenty-first century? And, are we asking students in schools to forget what they do in their everyday lives as they come to learn in schools and use heritage technologies in enacted curriculum?"

If educators contend that schooling fulfills both cultural and economic imperatives, why are heritage curricula, traditional pedagogies, and "old" ways of doing things privileged? The contention seems to be that there are "basics" everyone needs to know in order to succeed in learning and life, and they are content-based and need to be learned and stored in our memories to be recalled immediately. The realization that it is easy to look up most of this information quickly, and that is a valuable skill in itself, is often eclipsed by the persistent misconception that learning consists of students recalling facts under examination conditions. The twenty-first century skills argument (Partnerships for the 21st Century 2008) has shown that this is no longer a viable view and that we need to reconsider what constitutes the focus for schooling in contemporary times. Industrial-age curricula are responsible for the increasing number of secondary students who are disenfranchised and bored with schooling—many of them opting out of traditional schools and becoming engaged in informal learning contexts (out of school) with new technologies (Partnerships for the 21st century 2008). This needs to be addressed as a matter of urgency and must begin in the early years.

References

Bredekamp, S. (1987). *Developmentally appropriate practice in early childhood programs serving children from birth through age 8*. Washington, DC: NAEYC.
Bredekamp, S., & Copple, C. (Eds.). (1997). *Developmentally appropriate practice in early childhood programs. Revised Edition*. Washington, DC: NAEYC.
Collins, A., & Halverson, R. (2009). *Rethinking education in the age of technology: The digital revolution and schooling in America*. New York: Teachers College Press.
Cope, W. W., & Kalantzis, M. (2000). *Multiliteracies: Literacy, learning and the design of social futures*. Melbourne: Macmillan.
Copple, C., & Bredekamp, S. (2009). *Developmentally appropriate practice in early childhood programs serving children from birth through age 8*. Washington, DC: NAEYC.
Department of Education Employment and Workplace Relations. (2009). Belonging, being and becoming: The early years framework for Australia. Barton, ACT: Commonwealth of Australia. http://files.acecqa.gov.au/files/National-Quality-Framework-Resources-Kit/belonging_being_and_becoming_the_early_years_learning_framework_for_australia.pdf. Accessed 19 July 2014.
Elkind, D. (1996). Young children and technology: A cautionary note. *Young Children, 51*(6), 22–23.
Grieshaber, S., & McArdle, F. (2010). *The trouble with play*. Maidenhead, UK: OUP.
Hill, S., Yelland, N. J., & Thelning, K. (2001). *Children of the new millennium: Young children learning with ICT*. Barton, ACT: Australian Research Council.
Hill, S., Yelland, N. J., & Mulhearn, G. (2002). Children of the new millennium: Young children learning with ICT. *The International Journal of Learning, 12*, 236–248.
Jewitt, C. (2003). *Technology, literacy and learning. A multimodal approach*. London: Routledge.
Kalantzis, M., & Cope, W. W. (2008). *New Learning*. Melbourne: Oxford University Press.
Kress, G., & Van Leeuwen, T. (2001). *Multimodal discourse: The modes and media of contemporary communication*. London: Hodder.
Lankshear, C., & Knobel, M. (2003). *New literacies: Changing knowledge and classroom learning*. Buckingham, UK: Open University Press.
Lankshear, C., & Knobel, M. (2008). *Digital literacies: Concepts, policies and practices* (Vol. 30). New York: Peter Lang Publishing Inc.
Marsh, J., Brooks, G., Hughes, J., Ritchie, L., Roberts, S., & Wright, K. (2005). *Digital beginnings: Young children's use of popular culture, media and new technologies*. Sheffield: University of Sheffield.
NAEYC. (1996). NAEYC position statement: Technology and young children—ages three through eight. *Young Children, 51*(6), 11–16.
NAEYC & Fred Rogers Centre. (2012). Technology and interactive media as tools in early childhood programs serving children from birth through age 8. Retrieved from http://www.naeyc.org/files/naeyc/file/positions/PS_technology_WEB2.pdf. Accessed 19 July 2014.
New London Group. (1996). A pedagogy of multiliteracies. *Harvard Educational Review, 60*(1), 66–92.

Pahl, K., & Rowsell, J. (2006). *Understanding the new literacy studies in the classroom.* London: Paul Chapman.

Partnerships for the 21st Century. (2008). *21st century skills, education & competitiveness: A resource and policy guide.* Washington, DC: The Partnership for 21st Century Skills.

Plowman, L., & Stephen, C. (2005). Children, play, and computers in pre-school education. *British Journal of Educational Technology, 36*(2), 145–157.

Qualifications and Curriculum Authority. (2000). *Curriculum guidelines for the foundation stage.* London: Qualifications and Curriculum Authority.

Rideout, V. J., Foehr, U. G., & Roberts, D. F. (2010). *Generation M2: Media in the lives of 8 to 18 year olds.* Menlo Park, CA: Kaiser Family Foundation Study.

Shade, D. D. (1996). Software evaluation. *Young Children, 51*(6), 17–21.

Sony. (2003). *Super Dooper Music Looper.* Palo Alto, CA: Sony Creative SoftwareInc.

Yelland, N. J. (1999). Reconceptualising schooling with technology for the 21st Century: Images and reflections. In D. D. Shade (Ed.), *Information technology in childhood education annual* (pp. 39–59). Virginia: AACE.

Yelland, N. J. (2007). *Shift to the future: Rethinking learning with new technologies in education.* New York: Routledge.

Yelland, N. J. (2010). New technologies, playful experiences and multimodal learning. In I. R. Berson & M. J. Berson (Eds.), *High tech tots: Childhood in a digital world* (pp. 5–22). Charlotte, NC: Information Age.

Yelland, N. J., & Masters, J. (2006). Rethinking scaffolding in the information age. *Computers and Education, 48*(3), 362–382.

Yelland, N. J. (2011). Reconceptualising play and learning in the lives of children. *Australasian Journal of Early Childhood, 36*(2), 4–12.

Yelland, N. J., Cope, W. W., & Kalantzis, M. (2008a). Learning by design: Creating pedagogical frameworks for knowledge building in the 21st century. *Asia Pacific Journal of Teacher Education, 36*(3), 197–213.

Yelland, N. J., Lee, L., O'Rourke, M., & Harrison, C. (2008b). *Rethinking learning in early childhood education.* Milton Keynes, UK: Open University Press.

Photo Credit: Melanie Lucas

Chapter 10
Universal Design for Learning and Technology in the Early Childhood Classroom

Craig Blum and Howard P. Parette

Abstract Instructional technology (IT) integration hinges on several principles: (a) the technologies should align well with the curriculum, (b) the choice of technology should be based on how well the tool serves classroom learning and teaching needs, and (c) teachers must ensure opportunities for all children to participate and learn in the technology-rich environment. To serve the needs of all young children in a technology-supported curriculum, a framework known as "universal design for learning" (UDL) proves helpful. Early childhood curricula that employ UDL principles are proactive and designed to provide young children with multiple means of (a) engagement, (b) action and expression, and (c) representation. Varying strategies and materials are used in assessments, goals, curricula content, the classroom environment, instructional methods and materials, and interactions with children. Technology use affords early childhood education professionals the opportunity to create such accessible classroom settings. This chapter explores the relationship between information literacy, technology literacy, and universal design for learning in early childhood education. Vignettes illustrating practical classroom applications are presented.

Keywords Early childhood · Universal design for learning · Technology integration · Readily-available technology · Diversity · Inclusion · Response to Intervention (RtI)

Shatoya is a young child enrolled in preschool who has been identified as having a developmental delay and a vision impairment on her IEP. She enjoys interacting with her peers, but sometimes has difficulty communicating needs or commenting during play activities. The other students in the class like her and are always willing to help her with classroom tasks she needs to complete. Shatoya seems to like to listen to other children during literacy activities, particularly those that involve the computer. She also appears to like activities that emphasize beginning sounds, though she sometimes becomes frustrated when she doesn't understand what is taking place in these emergent literacy activities, and, on those occasions, will cry or become angry. When placed in a group setting, she is sometimes distracted by other children and their work and will stop working on her own assigned task. Shatoya

---

C. Blum (✉) · H. P. Parette
Illinois State University, Normal, USA
e-mail: cblum@ilstu.edu

often has a 5- to 10-s delay before she responds to instructions. She enjoys performing various classroom duties, especially those that have multi-step directions or numerous materials that have to be organized before completing the assigned task. Unfortunately, Shatoya's distractibility interferes with her completion of these duties. The teacher has begun using a classroom schedule to help children decide what activity is next and where the students are to go for each activity; however, Shatoya has trouble seeing the schedule. She enjoys participating in emergent reading activities, but she cannot see the words in the books.

Today's early childhood learning environments are undergoing rapid change due, in large part, to the presence of technology. Integration of technology into the classroom can help address the complex and diverse needs of children like Shatoya. Most education professionals working with young children once believed that technology was suspect as a characteristic of developmentally-appropriate practice (DAP), i.e., it could interfere with active learning that needs to take place in child-centered early childhood programs that provided authentic learning activities (National Association for the Education of Young Children 1996). Even today, many early childhood education professionals frequently perceive technology to support "passive activity" at best, and, at worst, to be an inhibiter to meaningful engagement in rich play and social activities essential to children's development. More innovative twenty-first century education professionals, including library media specialists, who work with young children, now have an expanded and more accepting understanding of the role of technology in today's classroom settings.

New personalized technologies such as tablets and smartphones, wireless technology, and technologies associated with software development and the Internet have not only revolutionized the relationship that education professionals have with technology, but these current and emerging tools have become an active part of young children's play and learning in the home and school (Parette 2011). Young children are exposed to technology early in industrialized nations (Parette et al. 2013b; Peurling 2012; Simon and Nemeth 2012) and, even before entering kindergarten, have learned to navigate and interact with websites, apps, and other types of technology. Child-friendly touchscreen interfaces, in particular, have made it easier for young children to have direct and meaningful contact with many technologies. The presence and use of technology by today's young children is increasingly being driven by the marketplace. For example, more than 60 % of apps used on hand-held devices are directed at young children (Shuler 2009; Travers and More 2013).

In addition to supporting play and social activity in the home, the personalized nature of technology has made parents and education professionals much more comfortable with their use in the daily lives of children; it also has increased interest in finding innovative uses to better educate children (Parette and Blum 2013a; Peurling 2012; Simon and Nemeth 2012). In fact, the expansion and personalization of readily-available technology that is integrated into children's daily life has now been considered developmentally-appropriate practice or DAP (National Association for the Education of Young Children (NAEYC) 2012; Parette and

Blum 2012; Parette et al. 2010). DAP means that activities and materials used in the delivery of the curriculum are individual appropriate, age appropriate, and socially and culturally appropriate (NAEYC 2009). This presents challenges to education professionals who must (a) make decisions about how technology is used in a developmentally-appropriate manner and (b) attend to how it may be effectively and efficiently connected to the curriculum using planned early childhood classroom activities that link learning standards and instructional objectives, instructional strategies, and assessment approaches (Parette and Blum 2013a). The ultimate goal of this connection is to ensure "meaningful" curricular access that supports diverse learners in early childhood settings. Universal design for learning (UDL) provides a framework to guide such curriculum development and implementation.

The Role of the Teacher in Fostering Inclusion

The attitudes and perceptions of teachers are consistently identified as important factors in the inclusion of children with disabilities (Avramidis et al. 2000; Brady and Woolfson 2008; Ernst and Rogers 2009; Hammond and Ingalls 2003; McGregor and Campbell 2001; Sze 2009). Too often, teachers and administrators focus on the disabilities of the child and respond reactively when a particular deficit interferes with the social or academic functioning of the child. Simply reacting to deficits and ignoring strengths is problematic. UDL is far more proactive—emphasizing strengths and eliminating barriers before they occur. A paradigm shift from deficit-reactive to ability-proactive can lead to academic and social success.

Kluth (2003) sees the role of the teacher as an educational leader and stresses how attitudes, beliefs, and the actions of teachers are crucial to the success of students in an inclusive environment. The teacher's perspective on his or her role in supporting the child with autism has a profound effect on the success of that child. Kluth (2003) suggests that educators make an attitudinal shift from seeing *differences* that pose difficulties as something that needs fixed or changed to fit the classroom environment to seeing *differences* as something to be desired and valued. Differences can serve as valuable assets on which to capitalize when planning for instruction and socialization. Fully recognizing the strengths, interests, and challenges of the individual requires the teacher to develop a supportive and authentic relationship with the child. Students know when and if the teacher believes they can learn and achieve (Kluth 2003). Even with the most positive, proactive attitudes and expectations, teachers can experience disappointment and frustration without thoughtful and appropriate planning for transition and sustained support.

The Role of UDL in Today's Early Childhood Classrooms

Early childhood education professionals have increasingly focused on the potential of UDL to help all young children participate in the curriculum (Lieber et al. 2008; Stockall et al. 2012; van Kraayenoord 2013). There are three major principles integral to the UDL framework: multiple means of (1) engagement, (2) action and expression, and (3) representation (Rose and Meyer 2002). Each of these principles has distinct implications for how technology is used and how learning is supported.

Engagement refers to how the design and delivery of a planned classroom activity can be used to (a) recruit the child's interest in the activity, (b) provide the child with multiple options for sustaining his or her effort and persistence, and (c) enhance the child's self-regulatory behavior. Children are motivated by many different types of activities. For example, some may prefer working individually, in a small group, or a whole-group setting. Some children will prefer more structure and teacher involvement in the classroom activity, while others will prefer greater independence, spontaneity, and opportunity for self.

Action and expression refers to varying the ways in which young children can express what they have learned during a planned classroom activity and/or through participation in other early childhood classroom settings. Some young children may be able to communicate well orally while others may prefer drawing. Young children not only vary in the means of expression that are most effective for them but also in terms of how comfortable they may be in expressing themselves in different settings (e.g., small group, large group, with a parent, different teachers, different children).

Representation refers to how the education professional and young children are allowed to present information and content in classroom activities. Children differ in the ways they perceive and comprehend information that is presented to them; thus, there is no single means of representation that will be effective for all young children. For example, children with physical disabilities, problem solving and organizational challenges, and language barriers all approach classroom learning tasks very differently. Multiple representations are used because they allow students to make connections within, as well as between, concepts.

In the most basic sense, UDL is a framework that guides decision making about curriculum design, instructional practices, and assessment strategies. Much of curricular design is targeted to a particular group of students and planned to deliver a specific type of content. Some curricula have been modified by special education teachers to meet the unique needs of young children. When UDL principles are applied to any curriculum, the goal is to maximize access that, in turn, creates meaningful learning outcomes for young children. One of the known benefits of applying UDL principles is that they can be used be used to create learning contexts that enhance children's interest in the curriculum as they acquire the knowledge and skills required for mastery of desired educational outcomes (Lieber et al. 2008).

But to better understand the implications of UDL and what it means for the early childhood education professional, the complexity of the classroom learning environment must also be considered in the context of "systems" that are present. The following section presents an overview of the role of understanding systems in curriculum planning and implementation when UDL principles are being considered.

Technology Considerations and UDL When incorporating technology into any planned classroom activity, UDL principles should be an important consideration (Division for Early Childhood and the National Association for the Education of Young Children 2009). Parette et al. (2013b) noted that today's technologies "are flexible, digital, shared, dynamic, and interactive, and the use of such technologies aligns with UDL principles" (p. 10). When UDL principles are combined with these features of personalized technology in the classroom, leanners connect with the curriculum in ways that may have been previously limited. For example, when wireless Internet is connected to personalized devices and interactive whiteboards (e.g., SMART Board), opportunities are present to connect children with a global and culturally-diverse world.

Information and Technology Literacy

Information literacy refers to an individual's ability to find, retrieve, analyze, and use information (American Library Association 1997–2013; Heider 2009). Technology literacy refers to a set of skills wherein varying technologies are used to support learning, personal productivity, decision making, and daily life (International Society for Technology in Education n. d.). Given the exponential increase in both availability and use of personalized and readily-available technologies in our society, young children have unprecedented access to interactive technology which can help shape both their information and technology literacy development (Blum et al. 2011; Parette et al. 2010; Wartella et al. 2010). Use of smartphones, tablet devices, and personal computers—all of which are typically connected to the Internet—provide the potential of harnessing massive amounts of computing power that allows for global interaction and immense information being available to young children.

Tablet devices are portable and have touch interfaces that are particularly accessible to young children. Not only do such personalized technologies expand children's ability to interface with information in new ways (e.g., Internet and apps), but the twentieth-century format of traditional text-based books has morphed into an electronic, or "e-book" format, that has garnered considerable interest by education professionals, parents, and young children (Buckleitner 2011; Zucker et al. 2009). These books are now widely available and are typically either no- or low-cost to consumers. Parette et al. (2013a) recently conducted a features analysis demonstrating that "expert-rated" no-cost e-books frequently have many of the same features as low-cost e-books. However, they did note that the number of features alone should not be considered in choosing an e-book for young children; rather, the e-book's connection to learning goals, curriculum, and pedagogy are critical in any final evaluation of utility.

Fig. 10.1 EXPECT IT-PLAN IT-TEACH IT framework for technology integration in the early childhood classroom. (© 2013, H. P. Parette, & C. Blum. Used with permission)

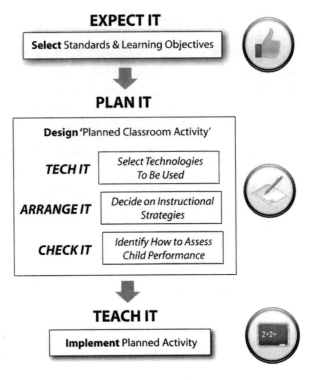

EXPECT IT-PLAN IT-TEACH IT

Information and Technology Literacy

In order for young children to develop higher levels of information and technology literacy competence, they must use technology in play, during planned learning activities in the early childhood classroom, and at home. The EXPECT IT-PLAN IT-TEACH IT child-centered model of technology integration (Parette and Blum 2013; see Fig. 10.1) provides early childhood education professionals with a framework to support technology integration. A goal of using this framework is to support the development of information and technology literacy among young children. The framework is standards-based (EXPECT IT) and focused on developing and delivering child-centered planned activities throughout the day and at home.

One underlying issue when considering technology integration and information and technology literacy is decision making regarding what is developmentally appropriate (National Association for the Education of Young Children and Fred Rogers Center 2012). EXPECT IT should be connected to meaningful learning outcomes for young children. Further, planned activities should move beyond the engaging nature of technology alone. The National Education Technology Standards for Students (NETS-S) provide guidance for development of planned technology-supported classroom activities which build literacy skills among young children (International Society for Technology in Education [ISTE] 2007).

There are six NETS-S standards that can be incorporated with any state early learning standards: (a) Creativity and Innovation; (b) Communication and Collaboration; (c) Research and Information Fluency; (d) Critical Thinking, Problem Solving, and Decision Making; (e) Digital Citizenship; and (f) Technology Operations and Concepts. In fact, it is not uncommon that states have either considered the NETS-S standards and blended them into their early learning standards or have a separate set of technology standards based on NETS-S. Each of the NET-S standards can be modified or clarified to develop an expectation in EXPECT IT that is developmentally appropriate.

Admittedly, young children are quite capable of key aspects of critical thinking essential to information and technological literacy (Epstein 2008). An example of how critical thinking can be supported is presented in the following vignette:

Ms. Corona instructs Carmen, a 5-year-old girl, in her pre-K classroom. In a joint parent conference with Carmen, Ms. Corona discovers that Carmen's favorite television show is 'Dog with a Blog.' Ms. Corona has surveyed the families in her class about their use of technology and media in the home. Ms. Corona asks Carmen's parents if their daughter is familiar with the Web site for the show. Carmen's parents have a laptop computer, but are unsure whether Carmen should have access to it. Ms. Corona explains that Carmen uses the classroom computer regularly, and that the school has a partnership with the local community library down the street. A library media specialist visits the class weekly and works with the teachers and children at the community preschool. Ms. Corona also mentions that the school has a book and media fair where children can purchase books and learn about e-books and other Internet applications for young children that can be accessed at home. Ms. Corona has prepared a simple instruction sheet for Carmen to use at home. It has instructions for her parents on one side and visual instructions with simple words on how to search for 'Dog with a Blog' on the other side. Carmen can use the computer keyboard to independently type in 'Dog with a Blog,' and she knows how to find the correct link that leads her to the Web site for her show and the activities. Ms. Corona encourages her parents to do this with Carmen, talk about the activities she is doing, and even have a friend play with her.

The preceding vignette illustrates how Ms. Corona helps parents create opportunities for communication and collaboration (working with peers); research and information fluency (conducting a search); and technology operations and concepts (use of a Web site and laptop). It further illustrates how partnerships can be created, even in a community preschool with limited resources. It should be noted that keyboarding is not an objective but *incidental* to a technology-supported, planned classroom activity. Young children enjoy working with technology independently, including typing on the keyboard. In today's marketplace, there are keyboards designed specifically for young children, e.g., having large keys, color-coded keys, and enlarged print on keys; however, many young children are still capable of using the standard keyboard in technology-supported planned classroom activities. In activities that require use of a keyboard, young children may often need assistance

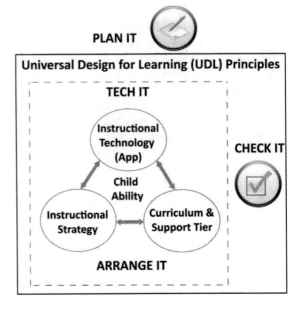

Fig. 10.2 PLAN IT: The dynamic relationship of TECH IT to instructional strategies, curriculum, and support tier (ARRANGE IT), and CHECK IT and Universal Design for Learning (UDL). (© 2013, H. P. Parette & C. Blum. Used with permission)

with letter identification in their initial keyboarding attempts. Sometimes the letters they learn in school look different than the text on the computer keyboard, or they may not have had enough repetitions to find a particular letter.

EXPECT IT helps the education professional identify the outcomes desired for the young child; PLAN IT is where technology integration planning occurs. *Intentionality* is a cornerstone of early childhood education (Copple and Bredekamp 2009). In other words, early childhood environments are not *random* play-engaging activities, but they are rich *child-centered* activities that create learning opportunities for young children. PLAN IT is a process that allows the early childhood education professional to specifically connect a classroom activity to EXPECT IT. It creates intentionality in how technology is used to support information and technology literacy. Using the EXPECT IT-PLAN IT-TEACH IT approach, the library media specialist may be focused on an activity in the library, or more likely, an activity within the classroom, or both. Young children learn much better when they interact with technology through play and exploration (Bischke et al. 2013; NAEYC and Fred Rogers Center 2012). Hence, focusing on the use of information and technology literary skills during center-based or other small-group learning activities is crucial. In the PLAN IT phase, the early childhood education professional and library media specialist must consider TECH IT (i.e., the selection of technology used in the planned activity), ARRANGE IT (i.e., the instructional strategies used in the activity), and CHECK IT (i.e., the assessment methods used to determine whether learning has occurred, see Fig. 10.2).

During PLAN IT, the education professional's attention is focused on the young child's ability and the developmentally-appropriate use of technology within the planned activity. An array of strategies can be incorporated to ensure EXPECT IT is accomplished by young children in the learning environment. Common instructional strategies include various forms of scaffolding (e.g., prompting and signals), exploratory play, modeling, interactive discussions, problem solving (i.e., creating opportunities for it and guiding young children through it with scaffolding), and embedding technology within natural daily routines (e.g. using a SMART Board to check in for attendance; Blum and Parette 2013).

Other important considerations are (a) the curriculum and how the children are progressing when participating in its delivery and (b) available response to intervention (RtI) tier (Blum and Parette 2013). Many early childhood programs now employ some form of RTI wherein students who are at-risk or have identified individual needs have been screened (National Professional Development Center on Inclusion 2012). Consideration of the unique needs of these children is essential because it identifies areas for specialized instruction or needs for unique applications of technology to support children's participation in the curriculum.

Each of these considerations becomes part of the reflective thinking exhibited by the early childhood education professional and library media specialist as they plan a classroom activity or sets of activities. A final consideration is CHECK IT, the assessment component that is directly connected to EXPECT IT. There is an array of traditional assessment approaches and technology tools used to support assessment that are helpful to evaluate the instruction. The CHECK IT component is a four step process: (a) ask an evaluation question, (b) choose an evaluation strategy, (c) use the evaluation strategy in an authentic manner, and (d) make decisions based on the data (Meadan et al. 2013). Digital cameras, smartphones, and tablet computers enable instantaneous capture of children's use of information and technology literacy skills during planned classroom activities. Apps designed for use on tablet computers are particularly important given the increasing presence of the iPad in twenty-first-century early childhood classroom settings. One unique app is Educreations (Educreations, Inc. 2013), a free app having numerous UDL features that allows young children to upload pictures and drawings, as well as to draw and record their thoughts (Parette and Blum 2013b). Young children can import pictures found on the Internet and insert them into screens in Educreations while telling a story about the picture. The picture can be "expanded" if children draw on the screen while talking about the picture. Other similar apps having UDL features include Doodlecast for Kids (zinc roe 2011); and Doodlecast Pro (zinc roe n. d.). Such apps are powerful because they create unique, permanent product records of children's language and allow them to demonstrate information and technology literacy using the UDL principle of multiple means of expression.

The final phase of the technology integration framework is implementation of the planned activity, or TEACH IT. On the surface, implementation appears to state the obvious, i.e., that a planned activity could be smoothly and effectively delivered to young children. However, when integrating technology, the potential exists for many barriers to successful delivery that may not have been anticipated. It is important that the early childhood education professional adhere to the plan that has been developed. This is referred to as *fidelity* (Blum and Parette 2013).

Typically, in many early childhood classroom settings, there are multiple education professionals involved in the EXPECT IT phase. All individuals involved in the TEACH IT process need to reflect with one another on how well the technology is being integrated, while also jointly deciding on whether the planned activity steps should be adhered to or changed. Even the most prepared early childhood educator may need to refine the plan. The library media specialist needs to consult with all early childhood education professionals and not assume that delivery of the planned activity is effective. Follow-up collaborative meetings are essential, as well as discussions of data collected during the CHECK IT process. Several people looking at work products and other data collected can help improve the technology integration and outcomes associated with the planned activity.

Considering UDL in Teaching Information and Technology Literacy

A key assumption of the EXPECT IT-PLAN IT-TEACH IT framework is that UDL principles are considered in the process of technology integration. As previously noted, application of UDL principles in this process creates (a) multiple means of representation to enhance access to curriculum; (b) multiple means of engagement to foster motivation; and (c) multiple means of action and expression enabling various approaches to physically do things needed to engage the curriculum, express oneself, or use technology to manage and self-regulate information. Because many of today's technologies appropriate for use in early childhood classrooms are dynamic, interactive, shared, and flexible (Parette et al. 2013b), they play a unique role in ensuring that UDL principles can be implemented.

Numerous Web 2.0 tools are designed to accomplish many of the goals inherent in information and technology literacy. Web 2.0 tools permit collaboration, social connection, sharing, cooperation, communication, and democracy. Common Web 2.0 tools such as *VoiceThread* (VoiceThread LLC 2013), *MindMeister* (MeisterLabs 2013), podcast tools, and other technologies have an array of applications with young children. Additionally, apps and e-books can be used in unique and creative ways to foster similar information and technology literacy skills. The flexibility of these tools, as well as the features within the hardware itself (e.g., text-to-speech and accessibility features within the operating systems) allow young children to access the curriculum in ways that were previously thought cumbersome or inefficient. The Center for Applied Special Technology (CAST) has a free UDL lesson plan builder at http://lessonbuilder.cast.org/. The CAST Web site also has a wealth of resources and examples that the library media specialist and the early childhood education professional can explore together. There are specific examples of lesson plans that adhere to UDL principles with links to teacher reflections on the planning process. The lesson plan builder offers tips on how to adhere to UDL principles.

McPherson (2009) documented how early childhood education professionals used blogging tools to create a connected, international collaborative effort on the life cycle of butterflies. Utilizing similar tools, library media specialists can expand the frequently limited access early childhood educators have to libraries and librarians.

When considering UDL principles, planning is a key characteristic of effective development of a technology-supported classroom activity. While some technologies and curricula for young children have features of UDL principles, library media specialists must collaborate with other early childhood education professionals to ensure that these principles are used in developing planned activities which focus on information and technology literacy skill development. The EXPECT IT-PLAN IT-TEACH IT framework was designed to be a practical, activity-based approach to technology integration. It incorporates elements of traditional lesson planning while ensuring that technology is part of the everyday experience in the early childhood classroom. EXPECT IT-PLAN IT-TEACH IT considers the connections among between available technology, instructional strategies, and the curriculum in order to integrate technology effectively. While CAST points out that technology is not requisite to implement UDL principles (Rose et al. 2011), the nature of digital and Web-based tools is such that they are more flexible, interactive, and dynamic, thus making UDL much easier to achieve. Hence, the EXPECT IT-PLAN IT-TEACH IT framework is a natural fit for library media specialists and early childhood education professionals to embed UDL principles during PLAN IT. As noted in Fig. 10.1, all instruction begins with EXPECT IT. Consistent with UDL principles, these expectations are not modified, but access is enhanced using UDL principles. Each row in Table 10.1 presents a PLAN IT consideration accompanied by examples of how each UDL learning principle might be applied. Although a few exemplars are noted, it should be recognized that UDL is a complex framework about which entire books are available. It is important that library media specialists consult more extensive resources regarding the principles, especially the CAST website.

In Table 10.1 there is sometimes an overlap between instructional strategies and the curriculum. This is because instructional methods and curriculum are frequently harnessed together. When planning any form of instruction, educators start out considering technology, instructional strategies, and curriculum separately. However, once the planned activity is developed, technology, instructional strategies, and curriculum start to merge into a learning experience that is child-focused. Incorporating the UDL principles into the EXPECT IT-PLAN IT-TEACH IT technology integration model only enhances the child-centered, activity-based approach. One additional consideration in the EXPECT IT-PLAN IT-TEACH IT framework of technology integration is the tier of support, or response-to-intervention (RtI) tier (Blum and Parette 2013). In RtI, young children are screened for academic or behavioral needs and identified for early intervention that matches their needs. The more intense the need, the higher the tier. Most RtI models are considered three-tier models of support. The first tier responds to the core curriculum and typically-developing children. The second tier responds to children who are at-risk but need only modest intervention. The third tier targets children who require intensive intervention to address needs that could not be met using a tier 2 intervention. In the UDL framework, RtI is important because instructional strategies vary as the intensity of supports

Table 10.1 TECH IT's & ARRANGE IT's connection to UDL

PLAN IT	Multiple Means of Representation	Multiple Means of Action and Expression	Multiple Means of Engagement
TECH IT: *Technology*	Identify technology features that allow for flexible representations (e.g., visual support; text-to-speech; highlighting of text)	Identify technology that allows for flexible responses (e.g., respond with drawing or picture; respond with a voice recording; respond by selecting a picture on an app or using a Web 2.0 tool)	Identify technology features that support multiple means of engagement (e.g., apps that give mastery feedback, allow for choice, and are relevant and authentic to young children's learning)
ARRANGE IT: *Instructional strategies*	Embed different means of representation with the strategy (e.g., visual vs. auditory prompting or scaffolding)	Embed opportunities for different means of physical expression within the strategy (e.g., during interactive discussions allow for responses using assistive technology or drawing of responses). Consider strategies that foster executive functioning (e.g., teach and model problem solving)	Embed choice, authenticity, mastery feedback, community, reflection and other elements of engagement within the instructional strategy (e.g., in guided discovery, follow the child's interest, have interactive reflective discussions on why it is important to learn something, and embed learning opportunities during natural routines)
ARRANGE IT: *Curriculum*	Consider different options for representation connected to the curriculum (e.g., present the life cycle in a graphic organizer; allow children to touch real objects associated with vocabulary)	Consider different means of action and expression tied to the curriculum (e.g., use paper visual schedules to promote routine-related tasks; allow assistive technologies to support fine motor tasks connected to curriculum; allow expression of curricular goals through pictures, graphs)	Consider expanding choice, connecting to authentic and meaningful experiences, and reflection on learning within the curriculum (e.g., use real items and food to recruit interest in a lesson on food; expand the lesson by going to a store; reflect on why students need to learn about food, and rate self-knowledge)

provided to children change (Cates et al. 2011). In EXPECT IT-PLAN IT-TEACH IT, RtI is reflected in curricular changes and the corresponding instructional strategies that are connected to them. Intensifying instructional supports typically does not lead to curricular changes in early childhood classrooms; however, if a student is significantly behind his or her peers, UDL may enhance curricular access but will most likely require pairing with specialized educational supports (Peterson-Karlan et al. 2013).

VoiceThread: A Readily Available Technology Having UDL Features

Today's early childhood education classrooms often have some available technology that education professionals can use to deliver their curricula. A computer with Internet access should be a key component of the technology infrastructure (Parette et al. 2013d; Simon and Nemeth 2012) to provide depth of the learning experiences afforded young learners when using the computer. To maximize the potential of both these tools, an LCD projector or interactive whiteboard (e.g., Promethean Board, SMART Board) have increasingly been integrated into many early learning settings (Simon and Nemeth 2012; Parette et al. 2013b) and play an important role in curriculum delivery. Of particular importance, LCD projectors and interactive whiteboards that are connected to computers having Internet access enable access to a broad array of other readily-available technologies that are free or low cost (Parette et al. 2010, 2011, 2013c).

One example of a free Web 2.0 technology having UDL features is *VoiceThread* (VoiceThread LLC 2007–2011). This tool has an array of uses in an early childhood classroom (Gillis et al. 2012). In the most general sense, *VoiceThread* might be described as a multimedia slide show tool that displays images, documents, and videos (Brunvand and Byrd 2011). Its potential lies in the ability of both the young child or education professional to create and upload content, explore slides, and construct comments using voice, text, audio file, video, or doodling (drawing). Gillis et al. (2012) have described features of *VoiceThread* and how it can be used with young children for emergent literacy activities.

In the case of Shatoya, whose learning characteristics were described previously, *VoiceThread*'s UDL features enable her teacher, Ms. Jones, to plan a classroom activity connected to an EXPECT IT learning standard (Demonstrate an emerging understanding of spoken words, syllables and sounds [phonemes]), and related learning objective (matches pictures to beginning sounds—"p," "c," "d," and "b"). Once that decision is made, she proceeds to PLAN IT. In collaboration with the library media specialist, Ms. Obadia, she selects a TECH IT tool—*VoiceThread*—for the planned activity because she knows that it has many features that allow her and the students in her classroom to represent content, i.e., both her instructional content and the students' subsequent work products and thinking/understanding about the beginning sounds 'p,' 'c,' 'd,' and 'b,' in a number of ways. The library media specialist and teacher discuss how much Shatoya likes computer-based activities, and the big screen format enabled by use of her LCD projector and wall-mounted screen will support her engagement. Since *VoiceThread* allows students to "act" and express themselves using text, audio, video, or drawing by doodling, Ms. Obadia points out to Ms. Jones that there is great flexibility in how the children will communicate their knowledge and skills regarding the beginning sound instruction both to her and to one another during the planned activity. Shatoya has problems communicating orally, but she likes to draw. *VoiceThread*'s features, enabling her to upload drawings and record either her voice or a video, or doodle while making comments about her drawings, will allow Shatoya, and all students, to have choices about comments they wish to make. Finally, Ms. Jones shares with Ms. Obadia that she can design the planned activity using *VoiceThread,* her computer webcam, and her LCD projection system in such a way that children will be engaged at multiple levels.

Having made the decision to use *VoiceThread* in the planned activity, Ms. Obadia and Ms. Jones then make an ARRANGE IT decision and choose the specific instructional strategies to be used when teaching "p," "c," "d," and "b." Ms. Jones suggests *direct instruction,* which will allow her to present each of the four letters and a picture representing each of the beginning sounds, in sequence, on four *VoiceThread* screens. She can present *models* of the sound and how it is produced, followed by having children repeat her modeling of the beginning sound. She can then return to each of the four letter screens and have the class respond to her question, "What is the beginning sound?" wherein she can listen to the choral responses provided and correct any inaccurate sound pronunciations by the students. Students will then be presented with a series of *VoiceThread* screens presenting only pictures (pen, cat, ball, and dog) and asked to name the sound with which each picture begins. This is both part of the direct instruction process in ARRANGE IT and a part of CHECK IT, or assessing children's performance on the learning objective for the planned activity. Additionally, Ms. Obadia and Ms. Jones decide, after the direct instructional component of the lesson, she will use a guided discovery strategy to ask students to draw a picture of something having each of the beginning sounds. She will ask students to choose between uploading their picture to VoiceThread and making an audio comment about it, or recording a video of themselves showing and talking about their picture. Providing students with these options supports multiple means of engagement and provides the teacher with the representation of content (i.e., the students' images and their explanations) in several formats. Additionally, when the children view the VoiceThread later (in a big screen format), they hear both audio *and* see images/video—multiple means of expression—that have been captured. Permanent products in varying forms are present to document the children's work, i.e., hard copy drawings, uploaded pictures of children's work, audio explanations of work provided by children, and/or video footage of children commenting on their work. Ms. Obadia tells Ms. Jones that, when the children come to the library, they will expand on this lesson by talking about letter sounds on VoiceThread related to stories read in e-books.

The previous example illustrates the immense potential of current and emerging technologies having UDL features that allow young children and education professionals to integrate technology using the EXPECT IT-PLAN IT-TEACH IT framework in a flexible manner that supports and enhances access to curriculum by all learners. Education professionals will only be limited by their creativity with regard to how these technologies can be used in tandem with UDL principles to support curricula in twenty-first-century classroom settings.

Conclusion

UDL is a frontier of education in the twenty-first century. This chapter outlines how early childhood media specialists can integrate technology into their instruction. Use of UDL with the technology integration framework sets the stage for instruction to be connected to outcomes for all young children. While the EXPECT IT-PLAN-IT-TEACH-IT technology integration framework was developed in the United States, its basic principles are broad enough that it can be employed internationally.

Likewise, UDL is designed to cut across cultural barriers. Cultures and nation-states may have unique worldviews that influence their instruction of young children. Even so, in working with UDL and the technology integration framework described in this paper, the media specialist needs to consider how their culture views the instruction of young children and the role of the media specialist. Saito-Kitansako (2012) conducted a case study using UDL in first and third grade in Japan. Teachers who adopted UDL principles effectively into their classroom found alignment between UDL principles and the Japanese learning philosophy of collectivism. Internationally, media specialists wishing to employ UDL and the EXPECT IT-PLAN-IT-TEACH-IT framework should work within their context and philosophy.

When employing UDL in nation-states, it is necessary to consider both global and local contexts. For example, it is now considered a human right for girls, as well as boys, to have access to education (UNESCO 2005). This global standard, as well as UNESCO's guidelines to inclusion were essential when considering the development of policy and practice of inclusion in counties like Brunei Darussalam (a small country in South East Asia on the Island of Borneo) (Fitzgerald 2010). Media specialists need to consider the global context, the local context, and striking a balance between current values and accessibility to education and technology to achieve outcomes for young children. Global values of accessibility may be counter to some parochial world views. Finding ways for stakeholders to draw meaning consistent with local cultural norms, as well as values of the global community that promote equity and accessibility, is essential. Opening up dialogues about technology and accessibility with teachers, parents, and community partners can facilitate this goal.

As important as UDL and the technology integration framework is to obtaining educational outcomes and accomplishing educational equity, it is noteworthy that young children need supervision when using technology to accomplish educational goals. Most devices are relatively safe, but young children must be kept away from electrical areas. Covers are available to make it difficult for young children to access outlets that are plugged into the wall. Sturdy, protective covers for devices such as iPads are also useful. Most importantly, the media specialist needs to introduce technology as a tool for learning and the expectations when using it. When media specialists model for young children how to use technology tools, they are quite capable of using them safely with proper supervision.

In addition, schools should supervise children while they are accessing the Internet and set up firewalls to prevent children from stumbling upon inappropriate material. While young children are vulnerable, they also can be made resilient and empowered when taught media literacy. Much like we teach young children healthy eating, we can also protect young children by teaching them about a healthy media diet. It is noteworthy that a media diet does not mean to be media free, but rather to be in a media-rich environment with interactions that are healthy and developmentally appropriate. In many cultures, the concept of "media free" is unrealistic because the culture has embraced technology; hence, activities such as media-free weeks do not encourage young children to become discriminating users of technology and media but encourage abstinence, a failed goal from the start. Children should not only be consumers of technology but creators in their use of technology. Ensuring young children use interactive technology as part of their imaginary play and artistry is an important part of safe and developmentally-appropriate practice. When media specialists provide young children with safe, developmentally-appropriate, universally-designed learning environments that integrate technology with intentionality (i.e., EXPECT IT-PLAN IT-TEACH IT), the environments that young children learn in will be enhanced and consistent with a twenty-first-century global community.

References

American Library Association. (1989). *Presidential committee on information literacy. Final report*. Chicago, IL: Author. http://www.ala.org/acrl/publications/whitepapers/presidential.

American Library Association. (1997–2013). Introduction to information literacy. http://www.ala.org/acrl/issues/infolit/overview/intro.

Bischke, C. C., Watts, E. H., & Parette, H. P. (2013). Integrating technology to support play. In H. P. Parette & C. Blum, *Instructional technology in early childhood: Teaching in the digital age* (pp. 199–225). Baltimore, MD: Brookes.

Blum, C., & Parette, H. P. (2013). Using instructional strategies in early childhood classrooms (ARRANGE IT). In H. P. Parette & C. Blum, *Instructional technology in early childhood: Teaching in the digital age* (pp. 51–72). Baltimore, MD: Brookes.

Blum, C., Parette, H. P., & Travers, J. (April 2011). *Future of instructional technology in early childhood special education*. Presentation to the Council for Exceptional Children 2011 Convention and Expo, Washington, DC.

Brunvand, S., & Byrd, S. (2011). Using VoiceThread to promote learning engagement and success for all students. *Teaching Exceptional Children, 43*(4), 28–37.

Buckleitner, W. (2011). The children's e-book revisited. *Children's Technology Review, 19*(1), 6–10.

Cates, G. L., Blum, C., & Swerdlik, M. E. (2011). *Effective RTI training and practices: Helping school and district teams improve academic performance and social behavior*. Champaign, IL: Research Press.

Copple, C., & Bredekamp, S. (2009). *Developmentally appropriate practice in early childhood programs serving children from birth through age 8*. Washington, DC: NAEYC.

Division for Early Childhood & National Association for the Education of Young Children. (2009). Early childhood inclusion. http://www.naeyc.org/files/naeyc/file/positions/DEC_NAEYC_EC_updatedKS.pdf.

Educreations, Inc. (2013). Teach what you know. Learn what you don't. http://www.educreations.com/.

Epstein, A. S. (2008). An early start on thinking. *Educational Leadership, 65*(5), 38–42.

Exec. Order No. 13227. (2002). *Federal Register, 67*(27), 6157. http://www.gpo.gov/fdsys/pkg/FR-2002-02-08/pdf/02-3337.pdf.

Fitzgerald, K. W. (2010). Enhancing inclusive educational practices within secondary schools in Brunei Darussalam. *Journal of the International Association of Special Education, 11,* 48–55.

Fletcher, J. D., & Tobias, S. (2005). The multimedia principle. In R. E. Mayer (Ed.), *The Cambridge handbook of multimedia learning* (pp. 117–133). Cambridge, MA: Cambridge University Press.

Gillis, A., Luthin, K., Parette, H. P., & Blum, C. (2012). Using *VoiceThread* to create meaningful receptive and expressive learning activities for young children. *Early Childhood Education Journal, 40,* 203–211.

Heider, K. L. (2009). Information literacy: The missing link in early childhood education. *Early Childhood Education Journal, 36,* 513–518. doi:10.1007/s10643-009-0313-4.

Individuals with Disabilities Education Improvement Act, 20 U.S.C. § 1400 *et seq.* (2004).

International Society for Technology in Education. (2007). National educational technology standards for students. www.iste.org/standards/nets-for-students.

International Society for Technology in Education. (n. d.). NETS for students. Profiles for technology literate students. http://daytlc.edublogs.org/files/2012/05/NETS_S-Profiles-1zfeu3t.pdf.

Lieber, J., Horn, E., Palmer, S., & Fleming, K. (2008). Access to the general education curriculum for preschoolers with disabilities: Children's school success. *Exceptionality, 16*(1), 18–32.

Loveless, A., & Dore, B. (2002). *ICT in the primary school.* Berkshire, UK: Open University Press.

McPherson, S. (2009). A dance with the butterflies: A metamorphosis of teaching and learning through technology. *Early Childhood Education Journal, 37,* 229–336. doi:10.1007/s10643-009-0338-8.

Meadan, H., Blum, C., & Parette, H. P. (2013). Check it: Assessment and evaluation in technology-supported early childhood classrooms. In H. P. Parette & C. Blum, *Instructional technology in early childhood: Teaching in the digital age* (pp. 73–94). Baltimore, MD: Brookes.

MeisterLabs. (2013). Mind mapping. Brainstorming. The leading online mind mapping software. http://www.mindmeister.com/.

National Association for the Education of Young Children. (1996). *Technology and young children-ages 3 through 8. A position statement of the National Association for the Education of Young Children.* http://www.naeyc.org/about/positions/pdf/PSTECH98.pdf.

National Association for the Education of Young Children. (2009a). *Developmentally appropriate practice serving children from birth through age 8. A position statement of the National Association for the Education of Young Children.* http://www.naeyc.org/files/naeyc/file/positions/PSDAP.pdf.

National Association for the Education of Young Children. (2009b). *Developmentally appropriate practice in early childhood programs serving children from birth through age 8. A position statement of the National Association for the Education of Young Children.* http://www.naeyc.org/files/naeyc/file/positions/PSDAP.pdf.

National Association for the Education of Young Children & Fred Rogers Center for Early Learning and Children's Media. (2012). Technology and interactive media as tools in early childhood programs serving children from birth through age 8. http://www.naeyc.org/files/naeyc/file/positions/PS_technology_WEB2.pdf.

National Professional Development Center on Inclusion. (2012). Response to intervention (RTI) in early childhood: Building consensus on the defining features. http://npdci.fpg.unc.edu/sites/npdci.fpg.unc.edu/files/resources/NPDCI-RTI-Concept-Paper-FINAL-2-2012.pdf.

Parette, H. P. (November 2011). *Readily available technology integration in early childhood education: Lessons learned.* Paper presented at the Assistive Technology Industry Association (ATIA)-Chicago Annual Meeting, Chicago, IL.

Parette, H. P., & Blum, C. (2013a). *Instructional technology in early childhood classrooms: Helping all children learn.* Baltimore, MD: Brookes.

Parette, H. P., & Blum, C. (April 2013b). *Using readily available technologies to facilitate scaffolding in early childhood classrooms*. Presentation to the Council for Exceptional Children 2013 Convention and Expo, San Antonio, TX.

Parette, H. P., Quesenberry, A. C., & Blum, C. (2010). Missing the boat with technology usage in early childhood settings: A 21st century view of developmentally appropriate practice. *Early Childhood Education Journal, 37*, 335–343.

Parette, H. P., Blum, C., & Luthin, K. (2013a). *Integrating recommended e-books into planned preschool classroom activities: An examination of features*. Manuscript submitted for publication.

Parette, H. P., Blum, C., & Quesenberry, A. C. (2013b). The role of technology for young children in the 21st century. In H. P. Parette & C. Blum, *Instructional technology in early childhood: Teaching in the digital age* (pp. 1–28). Baltimore, MD: Brookes.

Parette, H. P., Blum, C., & Travers, J. (April 2013c). Effective teaching using technology in the UDL-supported early childhood classroom. Presentation to the Council for Exceptional Children 2013 Convention and Expo, San Antonio, TX.

Parette, H. P., Peterson-Karlan, G. R., & Blum, C. (2013d). Integrating technology in early childhood classrooms. In H. P. Parette & C. Blum, *Instructional technology in early childhood: Teaching in the digital age* (pp. 29–50). Baltimore, MD: Brookes.

Peterson-Karlan, G. R., Parette, H. P., & Blum, C. (2013). Technology problem solving for children with disabilities. In H. P. Parette & C. Blum, *Instructional technology in early childhood: Teaching in the digital age* (pp. 95–147). Baltimore, MD: Brookes.

Peurling, B. (2012). *Teaching in the digital age. Smart tools for age 3 to grade 3*. St. Paul: Redleaf Press.

Rose, D. H., & Meyer, A. (2002). *Teaching every student in the digital age: Universal design for learning*. Alexandria, VA: Association for Supervision and Curriculum Development.

Rose, D. H., Gravel, J. W., & Domings, Y. M. (2011). *UDL unplugged: The role of technology in UDL*. Wakefield: National Center on UDL. http://www.udlcenter.org/resource_library/articles/udlunplugged.

Saito-Kitansako, Y. (2012). Applying principle of universal design for learning to early elementary math classes in Japan: A case study (Doctoral Dissertation). Retrieved from ProQuest, UMI Dissertations Publishing. (3506052).

Shuler, C. (2009). iLearn: A content analysis of the iTunes App Store's education section. http://joanganzcooneycenter.org/Reports-21.html.

Simon, F., & Nemeth, K. (2012). *Digital decisions. Choosing the right technology tools for early childhood education*. Lewisville, NC: Gryphon House.

Siraj-Blatchford, J., & Whitebread, D. (2003). *Supporting information and communications technology in the early years*. Glasgow, UK: Open University Press.

Stockall, N. S., Dennis, L., & Miller, M. (2012). Right from the start: Universal design for preschool. *Teaching Exceptional Children, 45*(1), 10–17.

Travers, J., & More, C. M. (2013). TECH IT: Obtaining, evaluating, and using instructional technology innovations in early childhood. In H. P. Parette & C. Blum (Eds.), *Instructional technology in early childhood: Teaching in the digital age* (pp. 227–247). Baltimore, MD: Brookes.

UNESCO. (2005). Guidelines for inclusion: Ensuring access to education for all. Paris: United Nations Educational, Scientific and Cultural Organization.

van Kraayenoord, C. E. (2013). School and classroom practices in inclusive education in Australia. *Childhood Education, 83*, 390–394.

VoiceThread LLC. (2013). VoiceThread: Conversations in the cloud. http://voicethread.com/.

Wartella, E., Schomburg, R. L., Lauricella, A. R., Robb, M., & Flynn, R. (2010). *Technology in the lives of teachers and classrooms: Survey of classroom teachers and family child care providers*. Latrobe: The Fred Rogers Center for Early Learning and Children's Media. www.fredrogerscenter.org/media/resources/TechInTheLivesofTeachers.pdf.

zinc roe. (2011). Doodlecast for kids. http://www.zincroe.com/news/show/doodlecast_for_kids.

zinc roe. (2013 n.d.). Doodlecast Pro. http://www.zincroe.com/portfolio/show/doodlecast_pro.

Zucker, T. A., Moody, A. K., & McKenna, M. C. (2009). The effects of electronic books on pre-kindergarten-to-grade 5 students' literacy and language outcomes: A research synthesis. *Journal of Educational Computing Research, 40*(1), 47–87.

Chapter 11
Developmentally-appropriate Technology and Interactive Media in Early Childhood Education

Olivia N. Saracho

Contemporary children's toys often are media-influenced; this 2-year-old is pretending to be a singer.

Abstract Society is relying, to a considerable extent, on the field of early childhood education to change in the areas of technology and interactive media. Young children understand their world through manipulatives, playing with digital and non-digital technology, and interactive media. The purpose of this chapter is to describe the status of technology at the international level and to provide a framework on developmentally-appropriate practices in technology and interactive media. First,

O. N. Saracho (✉)
University of Maryland, College Park, USA
e-mail: ons@umd.edu

K. L. Heider, M. Renck Jalongo (eds.), *Young Children and Families in the Information Age,* Educating the Young Child 10, DOI 10.1007/978-94-017-9184-7_11,
© Springer Science+Business Media Dordrecht 2015

the chapter describes how technology has become an international major development and how the International Society for Technology in Education (ISTE), the leading professional international organization, has established standards on the effective use of technology at all educational levels. Then, outcomes on the technology developments in several countries are described. Next, the chapter provides an overview on children and technology along with several vignettes. Then it presents the status of technology in the schools and homes. The chapter then describes NAEYC'S Position Statement on Technology and Interactive Media; discusses developmentally-appropriate new media literacies based on Jenkins' (*Confronting the challenges of participatory culture: Media education for the 21st century, 2006*) paradigm; explains families' use of interactive media; addresses internet safety with appropriate interventions; and provides recommendations for families and early childhood educators on developmentally-appropriate practices of technology and interactive media.

Keywords Digital media · Developmentally-appropriate practices · Early childhood education · Families · Interactive media · NAEYC position statement · Technology

Developmentally-appropriate Technology and Interactive Media in Early Childhood Education

Technology and interactive media are an integral part of young children's lives. They easily use digital devices that are quickly becoming the tools of the culture at home, at school, at work, and in the community (Rideout et al. 2011). Technology devices that are used for communication, cooperation, social networking, and user-generated content have transformed the conventional culture. These devices have transformed the way (a) families contend with their daily lives and search for entertainment, (b) teachers manage materials in the classroom with young children and communicate with families, and (c) teacher education and professional development (Jackson 2011a, b) prepare teachers. The purpose of this chapter is to describe the status of technology at the international level and to provide a framework on developmentally-appropriate practices in technology and interactive media for both families and early childhood educators.

Global Communication: Young Children and Technology

In today's world and education, technology has become a major development to advance the fluctuating educational system. The International Society for Technology in Education (ISTE) is the leading professional organization that is devoted to improving learning and teaching by improving the effective use of technology at all educational levels in pre-kindergarten through 12th grade and teacher education. The ISTE membership consists of (a) individual members from more than 80 countries worldwide, 80 affiliate organizations, six affiliate regions, and 60 corporations worldwide. ISTE members communicate with peers and meet in different mediums to discuss the challenges and enthusiasm of teaching and participating in a community that guides the transformation of educational technology. More than 100,000 education leaders and developing leaders throughout the world are ISTE members. They have joined forces to address educational issues of national and global scope (ISTE 2012). All members are focusing on the ISTE Standards to meet the needs of students, teachers, and school leaders. The ISTE Standards establish a standard of excellence in leading practices for learning and teaching in technology education. The ISTE Standards encourage students to (a) develop their higher-order thinking skills, (b) prepare to compete and succeed in obtaining their professional occupation, (c) learn in online settings, (d) have school experiences in digital learning, and (e) become digital age professional models for working, collaborating, and decision making (ISTE 2012).

Members from the United States, including the Commonwealth of Puerto Rico, and numerous other countries including Norway, Costa Rica, Malaysia, Japan, Australia, the Philippines, Micronesia, Korea, and Turkey are adopting the ISTE Standards as their information and communication technologies (ICT) frameworks in their schools (ISTE 2012). In addition, countries are conducting research studies to examine their status with educational technology.

Research on Educational Technology to Confront the Challenge in Several Countries

Research results and information concerning the progress of educational Information Technology (IT) throughout the world show that, in several developed and developing countries, a broad range of programs have been organized to activate the schools with educational equipment such as computers and the Internet (Hamidia et al. 2011). Researchers are focusing on how other countries have technological access to (a) provide opportunities for involvement and (b) develop cultural competencies and social skills. Countries all over the world are beginning to focus their attention on *new media literacies* (Jenkins et al. 2009). This term will be discussed in detail in a later section. Outcomes for some of these studies and examples of the technology developments in several countries are described in the following sections.

Australia In Australia, technology in early childhood education is considered to be an innovative curriculum discipline. Resources that support technology teaching in schools have increased for children whose ages range from 3 to 8 years. Fleer (2000) examined the children's participation in technology education in a child care program. She specifically observed how they planned, created, and evaluated their activities. She showed how young children planned lists and designs. The majority of the children were able to make the transition from oral planning to 2-D designs. Fleer (2000) concludes that a profile of the children's technological experience can identify the characteristics of their technological process and guide the children's learning.

Israel Studies on young children's programming strategies identified important features on the process by which to develop programs. Levy and Mioduser (2010) showed how young children from Israel mastered, constructed, and understood intelligent rule-based robot behaviors. They found that young children were able to replicate these behaviors with rules and could communicate their knowledge up to a specific level of difficulty. In relation to their methods of engagement, the children conducted intensive and extended playful investigations. In addition, the children systematically and comprehensively examined the robot's playful behaviors. They also exhibited three types of transitions in their understanding of the system such as: (a) adjustment to the formal language; (b) synchronization of several spatial views; and (c) shifting from observing rules as a one-time incident to their observation of the periodic and persistent explanations of a process. Furthermore, similar studies on child-robot interaction support that children are able to isolate and manage spatial perspectives (e.g., the robot's, observer's). Levy and Mioduser (2010) suggested that in the future, researchers need to focus, design, and test several forms of support for learning within the design of the computational environment.

The Center of Educational Technology in Israel designed a kindergarten multimedia curriculum to promote young children's (4–7 years old) mathematical concepts and skills about numbers and operations to engage them in self-regulated learning. The multimedia curriculum consists of six stages which are grounded on a different level of mathematical computational skill. Weiss et al. (2006) used this multimedia curriculum to examine the effects of learning mathematics. They found that engaging with multimedia in kindergarten affects the children's mathematical skills. The children's performance was remarkably high for all three levels of mathematical computational skills because of their active engagement; participation in groups; frequent interaction and feedback; and connections to real world contexts.

Hong Kong Recently, in an attempt to reform education systems, several North American, European, and Asian societies put into practice educational vouchers to transmit the course of public money to families or schools (Li et al. 2008; Yuen 2007). Debate on the use of vouchers has prompted studies that have examined the effects of vouchers on preschool education (Levin and Schwartz 2007). In 2007, after two decades of early childhood curricula and pedagogy reform, Hong Kong decided to put into practice an incentive method by initiating a preschool voucher program, which they called the Pre-primary Education Voucher Scheme (PEVS). Their goal was to provide affordability, accessibility, and accountability (3As) in early childhood education. The PEVS had three distinctive characteristics: (1) discriminating against profit kindergartens, (2) promoting the teachers' professional development, and (3) limiting the parents' choice to only non-profit schools. The Hong Kong voucher program is among a small number of national-scale preschool vouchers in the world. Hui et al. (2010) examined the perceived effects and modifications caused by PEVS. They conducted a large-scale survey of the most influential stakeholders in Hong Kong: parents, principals, and teachers.

Their outcomes showed that (1) most of the respondents had positive responses to the 3As of early childhood education; (2) there were major differences among the stakeholders (parents, teachers and principals) in relation to school types (profit or non-profit), eligibility, and familiarity, such as parents and teachers were more positive than principals about the PEVS; (3) the parents, particularly those from nonprofit/eligible kindergartens had more positive reactions than others; and (4) the principals and teachers described several implementation problems. The study indicated that the stakeholders' point of view was very positive toward the PEVS. The parents and kindergarten personnel who received the vouchers had positive remarks on the policy, which suggests that the voucher system is a worthwhile attempt to support the 3As of early childhood education.

Conclusion

The aforementioned studies indicate that reasonable and promising technology can be used with young children in a multimedia environment. It seems that there is a need to design several multimedia environments that focus on technology. Studies on new technologies for children suggest new ways to work with them including the design process. It is important to collaborate with young children and become partners in designing technologies including those in the developing world. Approaches need to support the design of mobile and social technology that addresses the endless curiosity of children and their search for meaning. Cooperative inquiry also needs to expand and evolve (Guha et al. 2013).

Children and Technology

Very young children have become consumers, creators, and distributors of media, tools, and technology. They may become separated into "digital natives" and "digital immigrants." Technological exploration through play may encourage children and adults to work together in their learning development. The following situations provide examples of children's experiences with technology.

Situation 1

In a first grade classroom, children rotate through a variety of centers. A group of four children approaches the math center, which is stationed at the interactive whiteboard (IWB) this week. The children have been investigating money during the past few weeks, and this center provides an extension to these investigations. At the top of the IWB, there is a picture of a quarter labeled "25 Cents." Below it are pictures of pennies, nickels, and dimes that can be moved around the board and duplicated, depending on the activity. One child presses a picture of a horn, activat-

ing an audio file that asks the children to make 25 cents in a variety of ways using the coins on the IWB. The children work together to use the pennies, nickels, and dimes to create sets of 25 (Linder 2012, p. 26).

Situation 2

Andy, who is 4 years old, and his mother sit in front of a laptop. Andy clicks on the Skype icon on the desktop using a child's mouse that his parents purchased for him. Andy's mother points to her father's name in a contact list that appears and says, "Click on Papa's name." Andy makes the selection and then follows his mother's prompt to "click on Video Call." Andy enthusiastically moves the cursor to a green Video Call button and clicks. A ringtone is heard and then a familiar face appears on the screen. "Hi, Andy," his grandfather says, as Andy smiles and reaches to hug the image on the screen (Parette et al. 2013, p. 2).

Situation 3

Three children sit excitedly around the computer. Their teacher, Miss Janirys, says, "I wonder what Miss Liz and Miss Cindy have for us today." Miss Cindy and Miss Liz are at a conference in California. She clicks on a picture of an elephant seal sleeping on the sand. Next to it is an avatar photo of Miss Liz. Miss Janirys clicks on a photo of Miss Liz, and the children listen to what she posted for them earlier in the day. Miss Liz says, "This is an elephant seal. Elephant seals don't have any ears, and an elephant seal is so big it could never fit in your mommy's or daddy's car." Miss Janirys turns to the children. "Who would like to tell Miss Liz something?" They all bounce at the chance.

Miss Janirys helps Juanita write, "What do elephant seals eat?" Tommy asks to speak into the microphone. He says, "An elephant seal won't fit into your grandma's or grandpa's or Aunt Bonnie's or Angelo's car." It's Shea's turn next. She says, "Why does an elephant seal have no ears? How can it hear with no ears? Because I can hear when I have ears."

The children scamper off to the other centers, knowing they can check back for their responses from Miss Liz and Miss Cindy all the way across the country. They are excited to hear what their teachers have to say. Later in the day, they get their answers. Miss Liz answers Juanita's question about what elephant seals eat and reaffirms that elephant seals would not fit in anyone's car. She adds, "Elephant seals would even weigh more than the car." Miss Cindy adds, "The elephant seals do not have ears; you are absolutely right. What they have are little holes on either side of their head, and the little holes are just like ears that allow them to hear."

Great question. I like the way you are thinking!" (Fantozzi 2012, p. 42).

Situation 4

While eating breakfast, 3-year-old Sean opens an application (or "app"), Teach Me Toddler, on his father's iPad and immediately becomes engaged in practicing letters, numbers, and shapes. A little mouse provides voice prompts to find something on the screen, and a checkmark appears when Sean makes an appropriate choice. After breakfast, Sean goes to the family computer and clicks on an icon for Zac Browser, an engaging browser designed for young children. When the browser launches, Sean is delighted to see the screen change to an undersea world where an animated submarine has become his cursor. Guiding the submarine to a games menu at the bottom of the screen, Sean smiles as his submarine changes to an animated butterfly, which he then directs to an icon representing a game called ABC Instruction. After clicking the Play button, an arrow prompts Sean to trace the letters of the alphabet (Parette et al. 2013, p. 1).

The situations presented above show how a broad range of technologies are infused in young children's daily experiences. The present generation of children depends on technology. Technology's progress makes it easy to use, customize, and obtain at reasonable prices. Technology has attracted the attention of early childhood education researchers and educators. Its use has increased in early childhood and family settings. Many, like the National Association for the Education of Young Children and the Fred Rogers Center for Early Learning and Children's Media at Saint Vincent College (NAEYC and the Fred Rogers Center 2012), have raised concerns about technology's role in the education of young children (Parette et al. 2010). They believe that early childhood programs and families need to use developmentally-appropriate technology methods.

At home, young children regularly experience the use of computers and associated technologies. Family members use different technologies in a variety of ways in their everyday experiences. Thus, technology has become a part of young children's school, community, and family life. Many of these technologies seem to have a potential for learning, but it is important to determine how and whether such technologies make a difference in children's learning and development (Parette et al. 2010).

Many families purchase computer toys to motivate their children to practice spelling, arithmetic, and eye-hand coordination, although children use them in a different way. When they use the computer toys, children usually theorize, hypothesize, and think through an emerging way of interpreting several facets of the world such as causality, life, and consciousness. Children initiate their interpretation of the world in relation to what they know best, which is themselves. However, the computer is different. Although it is a novel entity, children seem to believe that computers are able to think and possess a psychological existence, even if they are only objects (Turkle 2005).

Status of Technology in School and Homes

Presently, young children live in a world that is surrounded by an enormous selection of technologies. All day, they are absorbed in technologies when they participate in home and community activities, get ready for school, engage in classroom activities, and interact with others in the world around them. The commercial toys children use in play activities and the different kinds of entertainment media they use in their homes are usually technology-based. Young children's technology usage continues to increase, and most families permit their children to retrieve and participate with web-based interactive games and activities that are developmentally-appropriate for young children. Additionally, young children observe that their families repeatedly use their mobile phones and other handheld devices. They also observe families using mobile phones and handheld devices on television programs and movies. Children's observations and inferences lead them to understand the role of technology in their lives, which influences and structures their development (Parette et al. 2013).

Early childhood education programs are progressively using more technology to promote young children's learning (Shillady and Parikh 2012). The first technology device in children's homes was the television, which was followed by videos and computers. During the twentieth century, technological developments included the radio, television, videocassette recorder (VCR), microwave oven, air conditioner, refrigerator, personal computer, and Internet. Children use electric toys to play tic-tac-toe, videogames with missiles that are threatened by attacking asteroids, and challenging "intelligent" programs (Turkle 2011).

Today's children use advanced technology, such as tablets, e-readers, and smartphones, at an early age (Gutnick et al. 2011; Rideout 2011). They are experiencing a rapid shift in a digital age that differs from the age of their parents and grandparents. An assortment of technologies is found in children's homes and schools. Such technologies and media can reinforce their learning and adult-child relationships.

Technology is a tool that offers young children opportunities to develop their cognitive, social, emotional, physical, and linguistic abilities. Although it concentrates on the young child's individual needs, it does not substitute human interaction. Developmentally-appropriate experiences with technology can provide young children with extraordinary learning possibilities. Both child development and technology professionals (e.g., Cooper 2005; Copple and Bredekamp 2009) believe that developmentally-appropriate practices need to be used with technology. Children can acquire computer skills that help them learn reading, writing, and mathematics concepts. However, an early childhood education component in technology that is developmentally-appropriate is necessary to help young children acquire their ability to learn and succeed in school.

Developmentally-appropriate Practice in Technology

Early childhood educators need to seriously consider the value of using developmentally- appropriate technology with young children and become knowledgeable on how to carefully use it with them. They need to integrate technology education into the early childhood education curriculum to help young children become well informed about the nature, power, and limitations of technology. When young children work on the computer, teachers need to (a) be close by, (b) interact with children, and (c) offer opportunities for peer-to-peer learning (McManis and Gunnewig 2012). Turkle (2005) believes that computers are more than "tools," because they are integrated in the children's social and psychological lives. Her view goes beyond using computer games and spreadsheets to discover how the computer influences children's awareness of themselves, of one another, and of their relationship with the world.

Young children can be provided with enjoyable and engaging shared experiences that optimize success in their learning, development, and relationships with both adults and their peers. Young children can design Web interfaces (Bilal 2003) and Web portals (Large et al. 2003). All design experiences must be developmentally-appropriate. Both children and teachers need to collaborate in developing any design (Bilal 2003; Large et al. 2003). When teachers use children as design partners, children perceive that teachers respect their intelligence and creativity, which stimulates their interest. In technology, children's developmental needs are considered when teachers use responsible, well-considered design, and high-quality content selections (Cooper 2005).

Technology tools are used for communication, collaboration, social networking, and user-generated substance that has modified the everyday culture. Specifically, technology tools have changed the way (a) families deal with their everyday lives and search for entertainment, (b) teachers use classroom materials with young children and communicate with families, and (c) university professors prepare teachers and plan their professional development (Barron et al. 2011; Jackson 2011a, b; Wahi et al. 2011).

Researchers, parents, and early childhood professionals have an ambiguity about how technology, such as electronic and screen-based tools, can best be integrated in the early childhood curriculum next to the conventional non-digital tools, equipment, and manipulatives. Fortunately, professional organizations have developed position statements to guide families and early childhood programs in using developmentally-appropriate practices in technology. These position statements are described in the following sections.

Position Statement on Technology and Interactive Media

Interactive media surrounds children in today's world. The effortless use of digital devices has become the culture at home, at school, at work, and in the community (Berson and Berson 2010; Chiong and Shuler 2010; Couse and Chen 2010; Rideout et al. 2011). Technology and media are now vastly different from those of 15 years ago and are far more widespread. Children are growing up in a media-rich world that is shifting at highspeed. Nine-month-old children spend almost an hour a day watching television or DVDs; 5-year-olds are pleading with parents to let them use their iPhones; and 7-year-olds are using the computer several times a week to play games, do homework, or find out what their avatars are doing in their preferred virtual worlds (Rideout 2011).

The National Association for the Education of Young Children and the Fred Rogers Center for Early Learning and Children's Media at Saint Vincent College (NAEYC and the Fred Rogers Center 2012) published a position statement titled, *Technology and Interactive Media as Tools in Early Childhood Programs Serving Children from Birth through Age 8*, to offer critical and innovative assistance to early childhood programs on the effective implementation of media and technology.

The position statement by NAEYC and the Fred Rogers Center (2012) suggests ways to appropriately and intentionally use current technology to network with individual children and their families. It provides principles to guide the appropriate use of technology and interactive media as tools in early childhood programs that serve children from birth through 8 years of age. Examples of these principles include:

- Developmentally-appropriate teaching practices must always guide the selection of any classroom materials, including technology and interactive media. Appropriate use of technology and media depends on the age, developmental level, needs, interests, linguistic background, and abilities of each child (p. 5).
- Interactions with technology and media should be playful and support creativity, exploration, pretend play, active play, and outdoor activities (p. 6).
- Assistive technology must be available as needed to provide equitable access for children with special needs (p. 9).
- Technology tools can be effective for dual-language learners by providing access to a family's home language and culture while supporting English language learning (p. 9).
- Early childhood educators need training, professional development opportunities, and examples of successful practice to develop the technology and media knowledge, skills, and experience needed to meet the expectations set forth in this statement (p. 10).

This position statement demonstrates the positive capability of using technology and media in ways that are grounded in principles of child development to make sure that the use of technology is developmentally-appropriate for young children.

This position statement represents the continuous shift in the digital age and guides families and early childhood educators on how to apply technology and interactive media to promote young children's cognitive, social, emotional, physical, and linguistic development. Technology and media provide children with opportunities to communicate, access information, and participate in interactive play. Theoretically, such uses of technology and media promote their cognitive and social development (Johnson 2010). It offers the positive capacity to be used to individually connect children and their families. In addition, it recommends online learning experiences that are effective, engaging, and empowering and that support young children's learning. These experiences provide symbolic, technological, and multi-modal ways of meaning making.

Developmentally-appropriate New Media Literacies

New Media Literacies (NMLs) are "a set of cultural competencies and social skills that young people need in the new media landscape" (Jenkins 2006, p. 4), which Blanchard and Moore (2010) proclaim, "provide valuable information about the digital media environments that surround preschoolers as they develop emergent literacy skills" (p. 5). Policy and pedagogy need to concentrate on fostering social skills and cultural competencies for children of different social, economic, and ethnic backgrounds to succeed in preschool, grade school, and beyond.

Studies on young children and media need to examine the children's social, physical, intellectual, cultural, and emotional development in relation to experiences with media of various formats (e.g., mass, digital, non-digital). Many believe that more valid and scholarly research must be conducted on how digital technology affects (positively or negatively) young children's development (NAEYC and the Fred Rogers Center 2012) before generalizing on the impact of technology (Alper 2013). Studies show conflicting results, which confuse educators and families. Examples of negative and positive results are described below.

Negative Results on the Value of Technology in Children's Development

Some studies show negative results. The television's background (American Academy of Pediatrics 2011; Kirkorian et al. 2009) may affect children's eyes, while sedentary use of screen media (American Academy of Pediatrics 2011) is linked to obesity (Birch et al. 2011; Schepper 2011). Intensive media use also generates irregular sleeping patterns, behavioral problems, lack of focus and attention, a low academic performance, slow socialization and language development, and an increased quantity of time young children are sitting in front of screens (American Academy of Pediatrics 2011; DeLoache et al. 2010; Tomopoulos et al. 2010). The first NAEYC (1996) position statement offered moderate support for the use of technology in developmentally-appropriate practices. Regrettably, early researchers voiced several different concerns about technology and its role in young children's lives including violence in the media, the effect of long hours of watching television, and additional matters that were compounded with the instructional uses of technology. Presently, early childhood education professionals have become better aware and more accepting about the role of technology in young children's lives.

The position statement on *Developmentally Appropriate Practice in Early Childhood Programs Serving Children from Birth through Age 8* by Copple and Bredekamp (2009) states that "with children spending more time in adult-directed activities and media use, forms of child play characterized by imagination and rich social interactions seem to be declining" (p. 15). However, this position statement needs to redefine the term "media" in relation to meaningful play experiences and developmentally-appropriate practices based on child development and learning, individual differences, and children's social and cultural contexts because technology and media have changed and advanced during the last decade. According to Schomburg and Donohue (2009):

> Too often we equate "technology" with electronic media only. Yet… technology is a term that can apply to any tool that helps us… to work… to learn… to play. […] We might think of technology as providing digital manipulatives for children… tools that serve the same purpose as Froebel's gifts or the Montessori materials… or any of the other materials that we provide for young children in our programs. Technology provides us with digital tools for learning. We should be asking: What can children learn from these tools? What can they DO with these tools? (p. 3)

There are three important issues concerning the negative effects of media and technology on young children: (1) media and technology decrease the time in learning and development activities; (2) two-dimensional screen media essentially impinges on the brain's development; and (3) screen media content may include violence, stereotypes, and advertising. Such issues indicate that early childhood educators need guidance to be able to make knowledgeable decisions on the best way to incorporate media and technology into the early childhood education curriculum (NAEYC and the Fred Rogers Center 2012). However, several researchers report some positive outcomes.

Positive Results on the Value of Technology in Children's Development

Although critics have released numerous warnings against television and computers and their negative effects on children's learning, Wainwright and Linebarger (2006) state that the scholarly literature shows that what is important is the educational substance of the content rather than the format in which it is presented. Several educational television shows, websites, and other digital media are worthwhile, although some of them lack educational value or are educationally worthless.

Various studies on children's media support the belief that screen media is inherently harmless. The United States Department of Education, the Corporation for Public Broadcasting (CPB), Public Broadcasting Service (PBS), and the Ready To

Learn Partnership (RTLP) funded the "Ready to Learn" initiative to use the most recent research about the most effective ways for children, especially those from low income families, to enhance their reading skills. The initiative's goal was to prepare 2- to 8-year-old children to become ready to read. Results from the studies on the "Ready to Learn" initiative indicate that television programs and electronic resources that are carefully designed to integrate effective reading instruction are positive and powerful tools for teaching and learning (Corporation for Public Broadcasting 2011; Tandon et al. 2011). According to Parette et al. (2010), when teachers become familiar with technology and provide children with opportunities to use it in the classroom, positive results with children can be expected, which provides convincing support for its use in the classroom.

In conclusion, some literature on young children and media has emphasized (a) the negative effects of mass media and (b) essential methods to protect young children from any hazardous effects. Yet, Alper (2013) states that this literature seldom presents the social, physical, intellectual, cultural, and emotional development that children may achieve from experiences with media of numerous formats (e. g., mass, digital, non-digital, or otherwise). The quantity of time children use technology and media is important; however, the way children use technology and media should be considered in assessing their effectiveness and appropriateness (Christakis and Garrison 2009; Tandon et al. 2011). The results of these studies may be positive.

New Media Literacies Framework

Young children discover their world through manipulatives and engaging in both digital and nondigital technology. For example, digital e-books and print books are different but share similar characteristics. Young children work, learn, and play using both digital and non-digital media that have possibilities for extending their applications. Alper (2013) adapts an existing framework of the New Media Literacies (NMLs) paradigm, as set forth by Jenkins (2006), to early childhood education. The NMLs paradigm has a two-fold value for young children: (1) offers more flexible definitions of "media" and "technology" that includes both digital and non-digital forms that represent young children's surroundings and (2) offers opportunities to explore the possible positive effects of media and technology. To understand the effects of technological innovation on child development, it is important to explore how children repetitively make meaning in translating concepts between media (e.g., paper, clay, digital photography, video). Jenkins (2006) adds, " ...new literacies almost all involve social skills developed through collaboration and networking. These skills build on the foundation of traditional literacy, research skills, technical skills, and critical analysis skills taught in the classroom" (p. 4). Progressively, more educators are concerned about the consequences that interactive media and technology have in families' lives (Chesley 2005).

Families and Interactive Media

Innovative consumer technologies are infiltrating children's homes at an accelerated speed and basically altering the way families live, work, play, and communicate. Families buy digital media for their children and supervise its use based on their perceptions of it. At home, children have different kinds of media: 98% have at least one television set at home, 72% have a computer, 67% have a video player/recorder, 44% have game players, 41% have a smartphone, 21% have new media devices such as a video iPod, and 8% have the newest platforms such as an iPad or other tablet device (Rideout 2011). In addition, 42% of children under the age of 8 have a television in their bedroom, a rate that ranges from 30% for 0–1-year-olds, 44% for 2–4-year-olds, and up to 47% for 5–8-year-olds (Rideout et al. 2010).

National surveys indicate that computer and Internet use at home is increasing (U.S. Census Bureau 2012). Families with children whose ages range from 4 to 14 years of age use 11 consumer electronic devices (NPD Group 2009), which indicates that children are spending a large portion of their waking hours texting friends from mobile phones, playing video games, listening to their iPods, and visiting websites like Facebook and Webkinz. Children ranging from 2 to 4 years of age spend less than an hour a day with screen media, whereas children ranging from 5 to 8 years of age spend approximately 3 hours daily (Rideout 2011).

Several of these technologies (e.g., the Internet, video games, e-books, cell phones) provide families and their children new opportunities for learning at home. Families are shifting as they become aware of the importance of technology in their children's learning and future success. For example, Takeuchi (2011) reports the results of two parallel studies that document the way families with young children incorporate digital media in their daily lives. Their major findings consist of the following:

- Forces (e.g., occupation, culture) outside of the home shape children's experiences with digital media.
- Families prefer participating in activities with their children that involve older media such as watching television or playing board games.
- Families value each digital medium differently. They consider computer-based activities to be the most valuable for young children's learning, whereas they consider mobile telephones to be the least valuable for learning.
- Families are concerned about the effects digital media might have on young children's healthy development, such as interfering with their physical exercise and their online safety and privacy.
- Most families assume that their children are safe, especially when children use laptops, MP3 players, and handheld gaming devices outside the home.
- Almost two-thirds of families limit their children's use of media.

Takeuchi's (2011) outcomes suggest contemporary trends in the kinds of media young children are using at home and the families' perceptions concerning raising children in a digital age. The following are examples of these contemporary trends:

- Digital media influences the families' routines, play, and learning patterns
- Families' perceptions concerning the role of digital media in young children's development
- Families' attitudes toward technology
- Families' values, routines, and structures that determine young children's experiences in using digital media
- Families and children's use of media jointly and independently

Families assume an active role in establishing young children's relationship with media and reinforcing their emerging skills and competencies. Contemporary media technologies permit families to control the flow of media that enters their lives. However, families frequently express that they are inundated with the media that children experience on a daily basis. They are also concerned about the risks involved when young children use media. Livingstone and Bober (2005b) conclude, "Opportunities and risks go hand in hand…The more children experience one, the more they also experience the other" (p. 3). Instead of restricting selections to protect young children from risks, families need to help children become proficient in using the media to prevent problems. They can teach young children about the tools available to them for reducing online risks. This will ensure a safer experience for younger internet users (Livingstone and Bober 2005a). Families need to have the fundamental information that can assist them to cope with both the increasing media choices and the malfunctions of conventional attempts at gatekeeping. They need to consider ways to reduce children's risks related to media exposure and concentrate on its potential to educate them. Livingstone and Bober (2005b) provide several suggestions to avoid any risks. For example, they recommend that families:

- Teach children knowledge that is essential to evaluation of subject matter
- Use high-quality online sources of advice for families and young children
- Ease the transition from only receiving to also generating subject matter
- Reject inappropriate online involvement
- Attempt to prevent children's contact with objectionable subject matter and provide appropriate interventions
- Develop websites that promote children's internet literacy

These recommendations are an attempt to help families and children reduce or attend to such risks. However, Livingstone and Bober (2005b) believe that risks are not an ethical panic and do not justify harmfully restricting limit young children's internet use. They need to experience the numerous benefits of the Internet. They need to access the Internet and develop the abilities to use it. Nonetheless, since young children encounter risks that are prevalent, worrying, and problematic, families need to attend to these risks and provide an appropriate intervention.

Internet Safety: Guiding Young Children

Currently, children's technological world helps them connect and network with their teachers, peers, and parents through a range of digital devices, such as cell telephones (feature phones and smartphones), computers, BlackBerry devices, tablets, e-readers, iPads, and iPods. In the twenty-first century, young children need guidance in navigating and staying safe in a world that is inundated with technology and information (Kolb 2013). The Internet is an important part of life and a dominant resource, which helps young children to learn and communicate in many new ways. Young children are constantly surrounded by online technology and using the Internet (NAEYC and the Fred Rogers Center 2012). The Internet's impact on young children's social development continues to increase. They have endless access to social network websites (such as Facebook and Twitter) and apps, media sharing platforms (such as YouTube, Instagram, and Tumblr), immediate messaging submissions (such as Skype or Facebook Chat), online gaming, mobile phone data use, and Short Message Service (SMS), which is a text messaging service element of the telephone, web, or mobile communication systems (Queensland Government 2013). Cell phones are one of the most common and accessible devices and have rapidly become an important function of a child's social life, and anything that takes up so much time and interest definitely merits scrutiny (Kolb 2013). According to Seiter (2005), "The Internet is more like a mall than a library; it resembles a gigantic public relations collection more than it does an archive of scholars" (p. 38). In addition, "The World Wide Web is a more aggressive and stealthy marketeer to children than television ever was, and children need as much information about its business practices as teachers and parents can give them" (Seiter 2005, p. 100). According to the Australian Communications and Media Authority (ACMA 2010), there are threats when using the Internet. The Internet can expose young children to inappropriate content including images, text, or games that are sexually explicit or offensive, violent, or promote activities that are risky or illegal. Various websites sponsor severe political, violent, racist, or sexist interpretations. This content can be retrieved through website browsing, newsgroups, shared in peer-to-peer networks, or sent by email or instant messaging services.

Children need to learn how to use the Internet safely to have a positive online experience. Children need to be provided with a safe space where they are able to learn the skills to become citizens and consumers who can analyze communications from self-interested contributors. They need to be able to distinguish truth from misrepresentation as they initiate their experimentation with innovative methods of imaginative communication and community contribution (Jenkins et al. 2009).

Currently, children can develop and preserve relationships through face-to-face and/or cyber communications. Some Internet users will not encounter difficulties, although ensuring that children are safe and understand these risks is important (ACMA 2010). In addition, unexpected problems also emerge (Jenkins et al. 2009). For instance, a national fear concerning predatory behavior toward children has motivated the use of safer guidelines and supervision of their practice (Parette et al.

2010). These technological devices provide young children with many opportunities to interact with both other children and adults. The immediate responses sometimes motivate children to use this technology as a means to harass and intimidate others. Children can use the Internet to immediately send out any information to a huge number of people. Since they have a feeling of anonymity, they are able to e-mail material or details to others under a fabricated name. They simply post negative or damaging remarks with impunity. This also gives them the chance to compose and write cruel messages which inflict emotional and psychological suffering on other children. The following are some examples of harmful messages:

- sending or posting abusive, threatening, humiliating or harassing messages via text, social networking sites, or email
- uploading embarrassing or degrading images or videos involving other children (including fight videos)
- taking and sending sexually explicit images of other children using mobile phone or web applications
- using social networking sites or blogs to post Photoshopped photographs or inappropriate messages about other children or school staff
- imitating others or assuming a child's identity, then sending and posting material which damages their social status or relationships with others (Queensland Government 2013, p. 4).

When children experience cyberbullying (e.g., teasing, spreading online rumors, distributing unsolicited or intimidating messages, or offensive material), they can learn how to gain control of the situation. For example, families can:

- Encourage children to avoid responding to these types of messages.
- Teach children ways to block bullies.
- Maintain a record of the harassing messages and any responses to discover the individual who is sending them.
- Maintain a record of unknown usernames and passwords.
- Encourage children to immediately tell a parent or teacher about any intimidating messages. Since it is illegal, it can be reported to the police.
- Inform the website administrator (webmaster) to remove the content of the website (ACMA 2010).

Young internet users need to learn ways to stay safe and enjoy using the internet. The following are examples of rules that young children can follow:

- Be cautious about who to trust online. Although new friends can be exciting, it is possible that they may not be who they say they are.
- Avoid sharing your password.
- Keep a private profile to have your personal information unrevealed.
- Avoid reading messages from strangers, because they may be insulting messages, have viruses, or attempt to sell something.
- Inform your parents or teacher if a message troubles you with language, pictures, or anything scary on the Internet (ACMA 2010).

Social computing can be enjoyable, motivating, and educational; but online environments for children must be safe. Children are naturally social individuals who like to interact and are occasionally lured to reveal private information. However, it is important to respect children by permitting them to have the essential autonomy to develop in an online social environment (Guha et al. 2013).

Summary

Technologies all over the world have the capacity to promote young children's learning in educational environments and are of special meaning to early childhood education professionals. Conversations concerning the role of technology are embedded in the recent understanding of *developmentally appropriate practice* (DAP). This expression relates to the teacher's understanding about (1) the way young children develop and learn; (2) the individual child's strengths, needs, and interests; and (3) young children's social and cultural environment (NAEYC and the Fred Rogers Center 2012).

In 2012, NAEYC and the Fred Rogers Center for Early Learning and Children's Media at Saint Vincent College revised the 1996 position statement on technology titled, *Technology in Early Childhood Programs Serving Children from Birth through Age 8* (NAEYC 1996), placing a stronger emphasis on its role in DAP in early childhood education classrooms. The position statement from the NAEYC and the Fred Rogers Center (2012), *Technology and Interactive Media as Tools in Early Childhood Programs Serving Children from Birth through Age 8,* defines technology broadly but primarily focuses on principles and practices related to current technologies (Parette et al. 2013).

Contemporary media can offer children opportunities to use cinematic and virtual reality to examine their inner fantasies of control and empowerment over their real-world environment. Media can introduce characters, objects, and events that help children develop in a distinctive, meaningful world where they can play mentally. It is important to examine the formal educational environment and the relationship between school and home settings for media literacy and the successful development for very young children and their families (Alper 2013). As the field of early childhood education considers its future, NAEYC and the Fred Rogers Center (2012) recommend that families and early childhood educators:

1. Select, use, integrate, and evaluate technology and interactive media tools in intentional and developmentally appropriate ways, giving careful attention to the appropriateness and the quality of the content, the child's experience, and the opportunities for co-engagement.
2. Provide a balance of activities in programs for young children, recognizing that technology and interactive media can be valuable tools when used intentionally with children to extend and support active, hands-on, creative, and authentic engagement with those around them and with their world.

3. Prohibit the passive use of television, videos, DVDs, and other non-interactive technologies and media in early childhood programs for children younger than 2, and discourage passive and non-interactive uses with children ages 2 through 5.
4. Carefully consider the screen time recommendations from public health organizations for children from birth through age 5 when determining appropriate limits on technology and media use in early childhood settings. Screen time estimates should include time spent in front of a screen at the early childhood program and, with input from parents and families, at home and elsewhere (p. 11).

The NAEYC and the Fred Rogers Center (2012) position statement offers an all-purpose assistance to educators and children's families on developmentally-appropriate practices with technology and interactive media. It is both educators' and children's families' responsibility to make informed, intentional, and appropriate decisions concerning if, how, and when to use technology and media with young children. Technology and interactive media supplement rather than substitute other valuable early childhood educational activities (e.g., creative play, outdoor experiences, social interactions with peers and adults). Technology and interactive media are valuable tools that need to be used with a purpose to foster active, hands-on, creative, authentic participation, and communication with children all over the world. Educators need to professionally assess the use of technology and media as a learning tool. They need to emphasize active participation instead of passive, noninteractive uses (NAEYC and the Fred Rogers Center 2012).

Technology and interactive media have the potential to increase learning and communication in the family environment. Unraveling the possibilities in digital media requires a more vigorous national dialogue about the families' responsibilities in helping their children use the technological tools of their age group. Takeuchi (2011) concludes that helping family members assume these responsibilities demands extensive new thinking by producers, the research community, and policymakers. Such attempts need to be considered in a period of rapid transformation where families have become more important in planning a stimulating and energetic route for all of their children's success.

Children under 6 years of age are ready to learn literacy and social skills. Families can help them develop their technological abilities. Daily, families assume major responsibilities in helping young children (a) make important selections when they use media and (b) foresee the ramifications of their selections. Families tend to become fearful and anxious about new forms of media that are foreign to them. Families can read some books that can guide them in making appropriate selections and using media with their young children. Examples of these books are:

1. Brooks-Young, S. J. (Ed.) (2010). *Teaching with the tools kids really use: Learning with web and mobile technologies.* Thousand Oaks, CA: Corwin Press.
2. Dell, A.G., Newton, F., & Petroff, J. (2011). *Assistive technology in the classroom: Enhancing the school experiences of students with disabilities.* (2nd ed.) Boston, MA: Allyn & Bacon.
3. Scheibe, C. & Rogow, F. (2012). *The teacher's guide to media literacy: Critical thinking in a multimedia world.* Thousand Oaks, CA: Corwin (NAEYC 2012).

In addition, several internet sites offer current information, resources, and discuss issues related to the position of media in children's lives (Jenkins 2006). Examples of these internet websites and resources include:

1. **Diigo Group (http://groups.diigo.com/group/ecetech)** has blogs, others' postings, and links to early childhood education technology articles.
2. **Fred Rogers Center for Early Learning and Children's Media at Saint Vincent College (www.fredrogerscenter.org)** helps build "bridges between early learning and children's media." It has a variety of resources (e.g., issue briefings, online support community; database links to key organizations, publications, media sources of early learning and children's media; Fred Rogers' speeches, personal correspondence, digital audio and video television programs; curriculum toolkits with assignments, in-class activities, syllabi, research links, videos).
3. **Technology in Early Childhood [TEC] Center at Erikson Institute (www.teccenter.erikson.edu)** provides up-to-date news and blog posts, forthcoming center events, free webinar series, and lectures on early childhood studies in education and technology (NAEYC 2012).

It is essential to consider the context in which digital and non-digital tools and content support or hinder young children's development. They may interact with digital and non-digital technologies, which need to be used in a way that promotes young children's socio-emotional, physical, cultural, and cognitive development. It is essential to develop partnerships with academics, policy-makers, and early childhood educators in order to acquire natural ways to emphasize and enhance present teacher and family practices in technology (Alper 2013). Future and present early childhood educators need to become lifelong learners. Teachers need to know how to use both digital and nondigital devices with children in developmentally-appropriate ways. They need to select the best digital device that is available to provide children with developmentally-appropriate experiences.

References

Alper, M. (2013). Developmentally appropriate new media literacies: Supporting cultural competencies and social skills in early childhood education. *Journal of Early Childhood Literacy, 13*(2), 175–196.

American Academy of Pediatrics. (2011). Policy statement: Media use by children younger than 2 years. *Pediatrics, 128*(5), 1–7.

Australian Communications and Media Authority. (2010). *Cybersmart guide for families*. Melbourne Vic: Australian Communications and Media Authority.

Barron, B., Cayton-Hodges, G., Bofferding, L., Copple, C., Darling-Hammond, L., & Levine, M. H. (2011). *Take a giant step: A blueprint for teaching young children in a digital age*. New York: Joan Ganz Cooney Center at Sesame Workshop. http://www.joanganzcooneycenter.org/Reports-31.html. Accessed 15 Dec 2013.

Berson, I. R., & Berson, M. J. (2010). *High-tech tots: Childhood in a digital world*. In I. R. Berson & M. J. Berson (Eds.), *Research in global child advocacy*. Charlotte, NC: Information Age Publishing.

Bilal, D. (2003). Draw and tell: Children as designers of web interfaces. In M. J. Bates & R. J. Todd (Eds.), *ASIST 2003: Humanizing information technology: From ideas to bits and back:*

Proceedings of the 66th ASIST Annual Meeting, October 19–22, 2003, Long Beach (pp. 135–141). Medford, NJ: Information Today.

Birch, L. L., Parker, L., & Burns, A. (Eds.). (2011). *Early childhood obesity prevention policies.* Washington, DC: National Academies Press.

Blanchard, J., & Moore, T. (2010). *The digital world of young children: Impact on emergent literacy.* Mill Valley, CA: Pearson Foundation.

Chesley, N. (2005). Blurring boundaries? Linking technology use, spillover, individual distress, and family satisfaction. *Journal of Marriage and the Family, 67*(5), 1237–1248.

Chiong, C., & Shuler. C. (2010). *Learning: Is there an app for that? Investigations of young children's usage and learning with mobile devices and apps.* New York: The Joan Ganz Cooney Center at Sesame Workshop. http://pbskids.org/read/files/cooney_learning_apps.pdf. Accessed 15 Dec 2013.

Christakis, D. A., & Garrison, M. M. (2009). Preschool-aged children's television viewing in child care settings. *Pediatrics, 124*(6), 1627–1632.

Cooper, L. Z. (2005). Developmentally appropriate digital environments for young children. *Library Trends, 54*(2), 286–302.

Copple, C., & Bredekamp, S. (Eds.). (2009). *Developmentally appropriate practice in early childhood programs serving children from birth through age 8* (3rd ed.). Washington, DC: NAEYC.

Corporation for Public Broadcasting. (2011). *Findings from ready to learn 2005–2010.* Washington, DC: Author. www.cpb.org/rtl/. Accessed 15 Dec 2013.

Couse, L. J., & Chen, D. W. (2010). A tablet computer for young children? Exploring its viability for early childhood education. *Journal of Research on Technology in Education, 43*(1), 75–98.

DeLoache, J. S., Chiong, C., Sherman, K., Islam, N., Vanderborght, M., Troseth, G. L., Strouse, G. A., & O'Doherty, K. (2010). Do babies learn from baby media? *Psychological Science, 21*(11), 1570–1574.

Fantozzi, V. B. (2012). Exploring elephant seals in New Jersey: Preschoolers use collaborative multimedia albums. *Young Children, 67*(3), 42–49.

Fleer, M. (2000). Working technologically: Investigations into how young children design and make during technology education. *Journal International Journal of Technology and Design Education, 10*(1), 43–59.

Guha, M. L., Druin, A., & Fails, J. A. (2013). Cooperative inquiry revisited: Reflections of the past and guidelines for the future of intergenerational co-design. *International Journal of Child-Computer Interaction, 1*(1), 14–23.

Gutnick, A. L., Robb, M., Takeuchi, L., & Kotler, J. (2011). *Always connected: The new digital media habits of young children.* New York, NY: The Joan Ganz Cooney Center at Sesame Workshop.

Hamidia, F., Ghorbandordinejadb, F., Rezaee, M., & Jafarid, M. (2011). A Comparison of the use of educational technology in the developed/developing countries. *Procedia Computer Science, 3,* 374–377.

Hui, L., Wong, J. M. S., & Wang, X. C. (2010). Affordability, accessibility, and accountability: Perceived impacts of the pre-primary education vouchers in Hong Kong. *Early Childhood Research Quarterly, 25*(1), 125–138.

International Society for Technology in Education. (2012). Global reach local impact. https://www.iste.org/about-iste. Accessed 15 Dec 2013.

Jackson, S. (2011a). Learning, digital media, and creative play in early childhood. *Spotlight on digital media and learning* (blog), March 24. Chicago, IL: MacArthur Foundation. http://spotlight.macfound.org/featured-stories/entry/learning-digital-media-and-creative-play-in-early-childhood. Accessed 15 Dec 2013.

Jackson, S. (2011b). Quality matters: Defining developmentally appropriate media use for young children. *Spotlight on digital media and learning* (blog), March 16. Chicago, IL: MacArthur Foundation. http://spotlight.macfound.org/blog/entry/quality-matters-defining-developmentally-appropriate-media-use-for-young-ch/. Accessed 15 Dec 2013.

Jenkins, H. (2006). *Confronting the challenges of participatory culture: Media education for the 21st century.* Chicago, IL: The John D. and Catherine T. MacArthur Foundation.

Jenkins, H., Clinton, K., Purushotma, R., Robison, A. J., & Weigel, M. (2009). *Confronting the challenges of participatory culture: Media education for the 21st century.* Cambridge, NY: MIT Press.

Johnson, G. M. (2010). Young children's Internet use at home and school: Patterns and profiles. *Journal of Early Childhood Research, 8*(3), 282–293.

Kirkorian, H. L., Pempek, T. A., Murphy, L. A., Schmidt, M. E., & Anderson, D. R. (2009). The impact of background television on parent-child interaction. *Child Development, 80*(5), 1350–1359.

Kolb, L. (2013). *Help your child learn with cell phones and web 2.0.* Washington, D. C.: International Society for Technology in Education.

Large, A., Beheshti, J., Nesset, V., & Bowler, L. (2003). Children as designers of Web portals. In M. J. Bates & R. J. Todd (Eds.), *ASIST 2003: Humanizing information technology: From ideas to bits and back: Proceedings of the 66th ASIST Annual Meeting*, October 19–22, 2003, Long Beach (pp. 142–149). Medford, NJ: Information Today.

Levin, H. M., & Schwartz, H. L. (2007). Educational vouchers for universal pre-schools. *Economics of Educational Review, 26*, 3–16.

Levy, S. T., & Mioduser, D. (2010). Approaching complexity through planful play: Kindergarten children's strategies in constructing an autonomous robot's behavior. *International Journal of Computers for Mathematical Learning, 15*(1), 21–43.

Li, H., Wong, J. M. S., & Wang, X. C. (2008). Early childhood education voucher in Hong Kong: An internet study of the public views. *International Journal of Early Childhood, 40*(2), 49–63.

Linder, S. M. (2012). Interactive whiteboards in early childhood mathematics: Strategies for effective implementation in pre-K-grade 3. *Young Children, 67*(3), 26–35.

Livingstone, S., & Bober, M. (2005a). *UK children go online*. London: Economic and Social Research Council.

Livingstone, S., & Bober, M. (2005b). *UK children go online: Final report of key project findings*. London: Economic and Social Research Council.

McManis, L. D., & Gunnewig, S. B. (2012). Finding the education in educational technology. *Young Children Home, 67*(3), 14–24.

National Association for the Education of Young Children. (1996). Position statement: Technology and young children: Ages three through eight. *Young Children, 51*(6), 11–16.

National Association for the Education of Young Children. (2012). Resources for technology and young children: New tools and strategies for teachers and learners. *Young Children, 67*(3), 12–13, 58.

National Association for the Education of Young Children and the Fred Rogers Center for Early Learning and Children's Media. (2012). *Technology and interactive media as tools in early childhood programs serving children from birth through age 8*. Joint position statement issued by the National Association for the Education of Young Children and the Fred Rogers Center for Early Learning and Children's Media at Saint Vincent College. Washington, DC: NAEYC; Latrobe, PA: Fred Rogers Center for Early Learning at Saint Vincent College.

NPD Group. (2009). Kids' use of consumer electronics devices such as cell phones, personal computers, and video game platforms continue to rise. https://www.npd.com/wps/portal/npd/us/news/press-releases/pr_090609a/!ut/p/c5/04_SB8K8xLLM9MSSzPy8xBz9CP0os3g3b1NTS98QY0MLPxMXA09Lf0unULNQAyMTU_1I_SjjeBc3Sw8PN28TQ4sgSwsDT1d_QxfPoAAjC0sj_YLsQEUAzUQEmA!!/. Accessed 15 Dec 2013.

Parette, H., Quesenberry, A., & Blum, C. (2010). Missing the boat with technology usage in early childhood settings: A 21st century view of developmentally appropriate practice. *Early Childhood Education Journal, 37*(5), 335–343.

Parette, H., Blum, C., & Quesenberry, A. C. (2013). The role of technology for young children in the 21st century. In H. P. Parette & C. Blum (Eds.), *Instructional technology in early childhood teaching in the digital age* (pp. 1–28). Baltimore, MD: Brookes Publishing Co.

Queensland Government. (2013). *Cybersafety and cyberbullying: A guide for parents and caregivers*. Department of Education, Training and Employment. http://education.qld.gov.au/studentservices/behaviour/qsaav/docs/cyberbullying-cybersafetyprintfriendlyguide.pdf. Accessed 15 Dec 2013.

Rideout, V. J. (2011). *Zero to eight: Children's media use in America*. San Francisco, CA: Common Sense Media.

Rideout, V. J., Foehr, U. G., & Roberts, D. (2010). *Generation M2: media in the lives of 8- to 18-year-olds*. Menlo Park, CA: Henry J. Kaiser Family Foundation.

Rideout, V. J., Lauricella, A., & Wartella, E. (2011). *Children, media, and race: Media use among white, black, Hispanic, and Asian American children*. Evanston, IL: Center on Media and Human Development, School of Communication, Northwestern University.

Schepper, R. (2011). Introducing let's move! Child care: Tools for child and day care centers and family-care homes. *Let's move* (blog), June 8. http://www.letsmove.gov/blog/2011/06/08/introducing-let%E2%80%99smove-child-care-tools-child-and-day-care-centers-and-family-care-h. Accessed 15 Dec 2013.

Schomburg, R., & Donohue, C. (2009). *Rationale for revising the NAEYC Young Children and Technology Statement*. Latrobe, PA: Fred Rogers Center for Early Learning and Children's Media.

Seiter, E. (2005). *The internet playground: Children's access, entertainment, and mis-education*. London: Peter Lang.

Shillady, A., & Parikh, M. (2012). New tools and strategies for teachers and learners. *Young Children, 67*(3), 10–12.

Takeuchi, L. (2011). *Families matter: Designing media for a digital age*. New York, NY: Joan Ganz Cooney Center.

Tandon, P. S., Zhou, C., Lozano, P., & Christakis, D. A. (2011). Preschoolers' total daily screen time at home and by type of child care. *Journal of Pediatrics, 158*(2), 297–300.

Tomopoulos, S., Dreyer, B. P., Berkule, S., Fierman, A. H., Brockmeyer, C., & Mendelsohn, A. L. (2010). Infant media exposure and toddler development. *Archives of Pediatrics & Adolescent Medicine, 164*(12), 1105–1111.

Turkle, S. (2005). *The second self: Computers and the human spirit*. Cambridge, MA: MIT Press.

Turkle, S. (2011). *Alone together: Why we expect more from technology and less from each other*. New York, NY: Basic Books.

U.S. Census Bureau. (2012). *Computer and internet use*. Washington, DC: U.S. Department of Commerce, Economics and Statistics Administration.

Wahi, G., Parkin, P. C., Beyene, J., Uleryk, E. M., & Birken, C. S. (2011). Effectiveness of interventions aimed at reducing screen time in children. *Archives of Pediatrics & Adolescent Medicine, 165*(11), 979–986.

Wainwright, D. K., & Linebarger, D. L. (2006). *Ready to learn: Literature review. Part 1: Elements of effective educational TV*. Philadelphia, PA: Annenberg School for Communication, University of Pennsylvania; American Institutes for Research. http://pbskids.org/read/files/BOBPARTI-ElementsofSuccessfulEdTV.PDF. Accessed 15 Dec 2013.

Weiss, I., Kramarski, B., & Talis, S. (2006). Effects of multimedia environments on kindergarten children's mathematical achievements and style of learning. *Educational Media International, 43*, 3–17.

Yuen, G. W. K. (2007). Vouchers in Hong Kong: A new milestone of early childhood education. *Contemporary Issues in Early Childhood, 8*(4), 355–357.

Chapter 12
Could Computer Games-based Problem Solving Positively Affect the Development of Creativity in Young Children? A Mixed Method Case Study

Georgios Fessakis, Dimitrios Lappas and Elisavet Mavroudi

Abstract The widespread uses of Information and Communication Technologies (ICT) by children, in combination with the importance of developing creativity in society, justifies the necessity for educational research regarding the impact of ICT on children's creativity, even from preschool age. A current research direction concerns the verification of developmentally-appropriate, effective, and efficient learning activities that utilize ICT to cultivate creativity. This paper presents a case study of the influence that the use of an open-ended problem-solving digital game, under the teacher's guidance, has on kindergarten children's creativity. The research design includes the observation of children's interaction with the software, as well as the measurement of children's creativity and self-efficacy, before and after the use of the game. The analysis of the research data reveals that, within the framework of the specific learning intervention, the use of the game significantly improved both the children's skill of producing alternative solutions (fluency) and their self-efficacy regarding playing games of a specific kind. The results of the research could be of interest to creativity researchers, educators aiming at fostering students' creativity through the use of ICT, and parents/guardians who wish to engage their children in creative ICT activities.

Keywords Creativity · ICT · Problem-solving software · Digital games

Introduction

Children playing with the Crayon Physics game are faced with the problem of the screenshot, presented in Excerpt 1, Fig. 12.1. Their goal is to guide the red ball on the left so it touches the star on the right, making drawings that then behave like objects and can influence the ball's movement. This rather unusual, for traditional kindergartens, interactive learning situation has the potential of triggering creative problem-solving thinking by children, as the following dialogue excerpt reveals. Could playing such games cultivate children's creativity?

G. Fessakis (✉) · D. Lappas · E. Mavroudi
Learning Technology and Education Engineering Lab, School of Humanities,
University of the Aegean, Rhodes, Greece
e-mail: gfesakis@rhodes.aegean.gr

K. L. Heider, M. Renck Jalongo (eds.), *Young Children and Families in the Information Age*, Educating the Young Child 10, DOI 10.1007/978-94-017-9184-7_12,
© Springer Science+Business Media Dordrecht 2015

Excerpt 1
Creative Problem Solving by Children under the Guidance

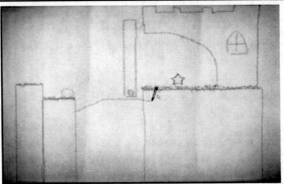

Teacher:	What do we have here, kids?
Yiorgos:	A bridge. (He draws a bridge and pushes the ball, which stops in front of the raised drawbridge.)
Teacher:	Why hasn't it made it to the star, Yiorgos? moving?
Yiorgos:	It needs more power, I guess.
Teacher:	Is there anything that has prevented the ball from
Kenta:	Yes, this is it! (pointing to the red, raised drawbridge)
Teacher:	Does this remind you of anything?
Yiorgos:	No.
Kenta:	Yes! It reminds me of a door that could be lowered
Teacher:	Great! So, go on, think.

Fig. 12.1 Screenshot of one of the problems presented to the children

Recent advances in the research on creativity and ICT-enhanced learning, along with the gradual development of a knowledge-based society, have played a key role in the formation of the belief that creative thinking is important for both the mental wellness and the professional success of individuals (Torrance 1995). From social and financial views, creativity is considered an essential precondition when it comes to innovation, and its development constitutes an official political goal (European Commission 1998). The development of creativity, therefore, as an important factor for social and financial prosperity, is justified as a high priority for modern educational systems (Partnership for 21st Century Skills 2009).

Creativity is not an innate talent possessed only by a few gifted people. Instead, as it is claimed by modern psychology, creativity can be cultivated through appropriate education and practice methods (Sefertzi 2000). This perspective challenges educational systems to take over the important role of developing the creative potential of each individual and, consequently, of society as a whole. At the same time, an increasing number of new computational tools, capable of supporting the creative process by both strengthening various well known techniques (e.g. brainstorming) and introducing new ones, have been developed (Sefertzi 2000).

In order to explore the feasibility of developing the creative potential of young children through the utilization of ICT, research is required to identify and examine the impact of several factors (e.g., best practices, software types, instructional guidance, and learning approaches). Towards this direction, this chapter describes a case study on the effect of an open problem-solving digital game on the creativity of 4–6-year-old children. The rest of the paper is divided into two main parts—theoretical and empirical. In the theoretical part, a definition of the creativity concept is provided first; then the relation of creativity to preschool education, to problem solving, and to ICT is reviewed. In the empirical part, the research questions, the conditions, the methodology, and the data analysis are presented. The chapter concludes with a discussion and implications of the study findings.

The Concept of Creativity in Education

Creativity is a complex concept with many definitions. For the purpose of this study, we have adopted a definition that comprises the main views of creativity researchers (Csikszentmihalyi 1999; Gardner 1993; Runco 1997, 2000; Sternberg and Lubart 1996). According to their definition, the term "creativity" means the process of producing a work, of any kind (e.g. artifact, device, idea), that is considered remarkable and original within the framework of a community.

According to the above definition, originality is a fundamental requirement for creativity. The scope of originality could be (1) individual (an individual creates something for the first time for him/herself), (2) group (an individual creates something original in the framework of a group), or (3) global (an individual creates something for the first time in human history). By expanding the scope of originality to include (1) individual and (2) group, creativity becomes a skill possessed by everyone rather than being restricted to groundbreaking inventions by a few "select" people. Seeking in particular to describe this view, the term "democratic" creativity was first coined by the National Advisory Committee on Creative and Cultural Education in 1999 to state that all students can be creative in personal or group (e.g. class) level. This democratic view of creativity is more important for education systems, and this is primarily why it has also been adopted in this study.

According to Torrance (1966, 1974, 2001), creativity depends mainly on divergent thinking ability which can be analyzed by examining four main characteristics of human responses to problems: (1) **fluency** (the number of relevant responses), (2) **flexibility** (the number of different categories in responses), (3) **originality** (the number of unusual yet relevant ideas, as determined by statistical infrequency), and (4) **elaboration** (the number of details used to extend a response). The above characteristics are the basis for the most widely-used measurements of creativity, an example of which is the Multidimensional Stimulus Fluency Measure (MSFM) test (Moran et al. 1983), which has been used within the framework of this study and is briefly described in the following sections.

Creativity may be practiced and developed through the use of tested teaching techniques (Mansfield et al. 1978; Parnes and Brunelle 1967; Rose and Lin 1984; Taylor 1972). Beyond the direct instruction of creativity techniques, education can influence other factors that contribute to the development of creativity. More specifically, according to Sternberg and Lubart (1991), there are six main factors that converge to form creativity: *intelligence, knowledge, thinking styles, personality, motivation,* and the *environment*. In addition, education can also affect self-efficacy which, according to Sternberg (1996), is an essential factor for cultivating creative thinking. Self-efficacy is defined as the "beliefs in one's capabilities to mobilize the motivation, cognitive resources and courses of action needed to meet given situational demands" (Wood and Bandura 1989, p. 408). Self-efficacy is considered to be important for creativity because persons with high self-efficacy tend to possess more initiative, take risks more easily, and engage in experimentation with persistence more often; thus, the odds are that they will come up with more creative ideas and solutions.

Creativity and Preschool Education

Creative thinking is one of the most important abilities that can be developed during the preschool years (Wheeler et al. 2002). Typically, according to Horakova (2004), 3–6 years old is the ideal age for children to develop self-efficacy, a factor that affects creativity. Creativity flourishes during kindergarten, as evidenced by the amount of time that children devote to drawing, creating, experimenting, and exploring. The amount of creative thinking that is observed at this age is fairly impressive. Resnick (2007) pointed out the distinction between the development of creative thinking skills that takes place in preschool education, and that of any other educational level, and proposed that the kindergarten approach to learning should be extended to students of all ages since it is ideally suited to the needs of contemporary society. According to Resnick (2007), children in kindergarten exhibit a pattern of action and thinking which can be described as the iteration of the following steps: (1) **imagine** what they want to do, (2) **create** a project based on their ideas, (3) **share** their ideas and creations with others, (4) **reflect** on their experiences, and (5) **imagine new ideas**.

Creativity in general, and in kindergarten in particular, has two main faces; the first one concerns the process of producing art and personal expression (artistic creativity), while the second one relates to the process of defining and/or solving problems (creative problem solving). The latter is the focus of this study, as will become clear in the following section.

Creative Problem Solving and ICT

In contemporary kindergarten, technological material may be used in addition to traditional materials (e.g., building blocks, drawing/painting materials, musical instruments) for cultivating children's creativity. The use of ICT may influence not only the artistic creative activities, but also the actions involving creative problem solving. While the utilization of ICT is obvious in most artistic activities (e.g. usage of drawing and music software), the use of ICT in ways that facilitate the development of students' problem-solving creative ability is not straightforward. Clements (1995) describes two contrasting perspectives of the relation between ICT and creativity. According to the first perspective, the mechanistic-algorithmic nature of ICT lacks any creative potential and, thus, ICT use comes in contradiction with the aim of developing creativity. The second view considers ICT a valuable tool for increasing creativity of artists, musicians, writers, and scientists. Clements' (1995) studies on the influence of LOGO (Papert 1980) programming language on child creativity reported mixed results, thus leaving the issue open. More specifically, according to Clements, it seems that the use of computer programming sometimes reinforces, but at other times weakens, children's creative potential. It should be pointed out, though, that Clements' findings derived from studies carried out on quite early versions of LOGO that did not constitute particularly pleasant and attractive environments for children, which makes these findings limited in scope. The recent development of open, exploratory, interactive, and developmentally-appropriate learning environments makes it necessary to conduct new studies that focus on contemporary approaches (Fessakis et al. 2013).

Furthermore, Haugland (1992) studied the influence of closed-behavioristic educational software on children's creativity and argued that the prolonged use of software of this type may destroy children's creative potential by prematurely strengthening convergent thinking through exclusive exposure to problems with one correct answer. At that time, Haugland (1992) asserted that software of this type weakened the intrinsic motivation for learning by substituting it with an external reward; she further noted that, when children were allowed to choose for themselves, they showed a preference for software of closed type. Such early findings emphasize the responsibility that educators and guardians share in promoting the beneficial use of ICT. In addition, the spread of internet availability in kindergartens gives opportunities for creative teaching through learning activities that combine the use of software and real artifacts in an authentic communication context (Fesakis et al. 2011).

Summarizing the above, it appears that research on the utilization of ICT for the development of the capacity for creative problem solving still has a long way to go. More specifically, technological advances in digital learning environments aimed at young children, if combined with creativity techniques, bring new possibilities for pedagogical applications that have not been studied in depth so far. Moreover, it is interesting to explore factors such as the role of the teacher/guardian in the course of learning activities and the impact of social interaction among participants throughout the creative activity.

Research Rationale

In an attempt to explore the feasibility of using ICT to facilitate the development of creative potential in preschoolers, a case study based on an award-winning problem-solving digital game, called *Crayon Physics Deluxe* (Purho 2009), has been designed and conducted. (This is the game illustrated in Fig. 12.1.) This specific game was chosen because it is considered both developmentally appropriate and engaging for young children; it also incorporates a number of features that could foster problem-solving creativity. *Crayon Physics Deluxe* presents players with a series of problems of increasing complexity. More specifically, at each level of the game, a red ball and a star appear simultaneously on the computer screen but on a different background scene. The object of the game is for the player to guide the ball to touch the star. Obstacles, gaps, and other challenges may appear in between, though. Aside from being able to give the ball a slight "nudge" to the left or the right, the player cannot manipulate it directly. What she/he must do is think of and draw objects to push and carry the ball, overcome the obstacles, and move the ball forward until it reaches the star. Children can draw whatever two-dimensional shape they can imagine using the mouse or even their finger if the appropriate input device is available (e.g. Interactive White Board, tablet pc). The objects on the projected screen are subject to the law of gravity when they are not "pinned." There is no restriction on the number of attempts, and the player is permitted to delete objects and retry the same level as many times as she/he wishes. If the ball finally reaches the star, the star takes off and goes to the sky. The player then continues to the next game level. The total number of stars in the sky constitutes the score of the user.

It must be stressed that *Crayon Physics* does not constitute a simulation in the formal sense of the term but rather a game microworld (Papert 1980) because all objects exhibit solid-state attributes. As a consequence, some inconsistencies to the corresponding physical world appear (e.g. the user may see a box standing on a cloud). That is to say, the knowledge content of the game should not be considered formal physics but rather a series of logic puzzles in which loose gravity laws rule the objects' behaviour in the microworld. The familiarization of the user with gravity laws comes more as a "side effect" of the software use rather than an explicit learning goal of the game designers. *Crayon Physics* is considered age-appropriate for children ages 6 and up, working without guidance. In our kindergarten case study, the teacher's mediation made the game accessible to younger children.

Most of the puzzles can be solved in more than one way, giving students the opportunity to employ divergent thinking and express fluency in the specific problem genre. In general, the puzzles of the game meet the criteria set by Goffin and Tull (1985) and, thus, are suitable for fostering creativity. Indicative problem situations of the game are presented in Fig. 12.2.

In Fig. 12.2, the ball and the star are grounded on top of the battlement of a castle. If we just give the ball a slight nudge to the right, it will not reach the star;

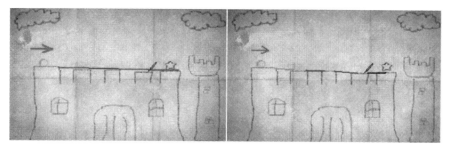

Fig. 12.2 Sample problem solving on *Crayon Physics Deluxe*

it will fall in the gap between the merlons. One solution is to draw a long line (a bridge) to join the merlons where the ball and the star are standing. The ball will move over and across this line and will eventually hit the star. A second option is to join the interim battlements with small lines (bridges) so that the ball moves to the star by passing over each little bridge.

The aim of the research is to investigate whether problem-solving activities, set in the context of the specific game and conducted under the guidance of the teacher, are achievable and engaging in the first place, and also whether such activities could be used to enhance the creative potential of children. More specifically, the study seeks to enhance our understanding of what children can achieve in such learning situations, to estimate the influence of the software on children's creativity, and finally, to outline the appropriate role of the parent/guardian/teacher in the process of guidance.

Methodology

The research methodology chosen is the case study approach, which is considered more suitable for an exploratory research design with the aim of gaining a better understanding of a complex situation under specific conditions (Merriam 2009). The case study methodology resides in the qualitative/subjective educational research approach which seeks to understand and interpret complex social phenomena in terms of their participants' views, in contrast to the scientific paradigm. The aim of which is the creation of theoretical models that can be tested through formal experimentation. A case study concerns the in-depth observation of a specific, well-defined instance of people (e.g. a child, a class, a school) in realistic context. Case studies often enable the illustration of general principles from the study of distinct instances (Cohen et al. 2000). In this study, the case of young children (4–6 years old) attending a typical semi-urban kindergarten in Greece is examined with the aim of investigating the extent to which computer game-based, problem-solving activities under the guidance of a teacher may impact the development of their creativity and self-efficacy. As it will be analyzed in detail below, the study examines the value of the learning intervention as well. The unit of the study is an ecosystem made up of children pairs, the teacher, the game, and the learning activities. Our research is an exploratory case study (Yin 2011) which focuses on the exploration of research questions posed without prior statement of specific propositions.

Research Questions

In order to explore the role of ICT in facilitating the development of creativity in young children, the following questions were posed:

Q.1: Is problem solving through the use of the specific game feasible and attractive for children?
Q.2: Does the use of the software game have an impact on the development of children's creativity?
Q.3: Does the use of the software game have an impact on the development of children's self-efficacy?
Q.4: How does the teacher's role during the problem-solving process facilitate the development of creativity?

Participants

The participants were 10 children of the 19th public Kindergarten of Rhodes. Kindergartens in Greece serve 4–6-year-old children. The participants' demographics are summarized in Table 12.1, where children are referred to with pseudonyms. The research protocol conforms to the ethical guidelines of the European Union. The children were chosen randomly from the class and were also arbitrarily paired.

Process and Research Data Collection

The research was implemented on January 20, 21 and 24, 2011. Pairs P1 and P2 were treated on Jan/20, pairs P3 and P4 on Jan/21, and pair P5 on Jan/24. The research was conducted in the kindergarten teachers' office where each pair used the software on a laptop computer, separated from the rest of the class, under the guidance of the researcher. The researcher (the second author of the paper), who is also a licensed kindergarten teacher, was not the regular teacher of the class. For each pair, the whole session had been organized as a sequence of five discrete stages. In the first stage, the initial (before the intervention) levels of creativity and self-efficacy of each child were measured through the use of appropriate tests. In the second stage, the initial knowledge of the children on the problem domain was assessed individually. In other words, the first and the second stages consisted of

Table 12.1 Research participants' data

Pair	Child	Sex	Age (Years:Months)
P1	Kenta	Female	5:6
	Yiorgos	Male	5:3
P2	Efie	Female	5:3
	Konstantinos	Male	5:11
P3	Tsampika	Female	5:9
	Sotiria	Female	5:10
P4	Mechalis	Male	5:7
	Nikoletta	Female	5:1
P5	Kiki	Female	4:3
	Yiannis	Male	4:10

pre-tests. In the third stage, each pair of children was introduced to the learning scenario through the use of a story. In the fourth stage, the children were engaged in problem-solving processes using the digital game. Post-tests for creativity and self-efficacy were conducted in the final, fifth stage using the same tests as in the first stage. In the following sections, each stage is presented in detail along with the research data collection tools.

1st Stage: Introductions and Pre-tests

In the first stage, after a short introduction of himself, the researcher conducted the tests to measure the children's creativity as well as their computer games-related self-efficacy. The researcher recorded the answers provided by the children along with notes about their reactions.

Preschool children's creativity was assessed by the *Multidimensional Stimulus Fluency Measure* (MSFM) test (Moran et al. 1983). MSFM can be applied to young children since it uses visual and tactile stimuli and requires verbal responses. Children's responses are scored in terms of fluency and originality only. For the application of the MSFM test, a process similar to the one described by Aguirre and Conners (2010) was followed. More specifically, three subtests were applied, namely: *Instances, Patterns,* and *Uses*. In the *Instances* subtest, children were asked to name instances of round things and red things. In the *Patterns* subtest, children were required to give possible interpretations for two simple three-dimensional styrofoam shapes. In the last subtest, *Uses*, children were asked to name uses for a couple of common objects: a box and paper.

The usual method of measuring self-efficacy is to present students with problems that are similar to the ones that they will be required to solve in the intervention (Bong and Skaalvik 2003). Thus, in the context of this research, the children were asked to answer the questions: (1) *If I give you some plasticine, do you believe that you can make a little man/woman out of it?* (in order to estimate the level of their self-efficacy in problem solving, in general) and (2) *If I let you play a computer*

Fig. 12.3 Sample screenshot shown to children in stage 2

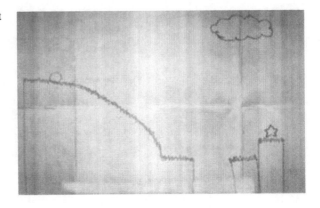

game, do you believe you can win? (in order to estimate children's level of self-efficacy with regard to the use of computer games).

2nd Stage: Pre-test on Children's Ability to Solve Problems Involving Movement in a Gravity Field

Through a computer presentation incorporating snapshots from the software, the children watched a series of selected problems for which the researcher asked them to predict what kind of movement the objects in the images would make if they were released. For example, the exact question for the problem depicted in Fig. 12.3 was: *Can this red ball move if nobody pushes it? If yes, where will it go?* The purpose of this test was the investigation of the children's initial knowledge about movement of objects in the gravity field of earth. The researchers chose to use screenshots from the software so that the problems would be similar to those of the game. The children's responses were recorded on individual interview sheets promptly following each interview.

Table 12.2 shows the answers that the children gave to the specific problem.

The tests carried out in the 1st and 2nd stages were individually answered by all participants.

Table 12.2 Sample answers of children for the problem of Fig. 12.3

Child	Answer
Kenta	In the gap
Yiorgos	On the other side of the gap
Efie	Into here (showing the gap)
Konstantinos	Down
Tsampika	It will go like thiiiiiis (pointing to the gap)
Sotiria	Inside the hole
Mechalis	It will touch here and here (showing the gap)
Nikoletta	Here (showing the gap)
Kiki	It will fall
Yiannis	It will get into here (showing the gap)

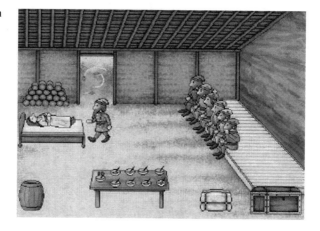

Fig. 12.4 A screenshot from the digital version of the learning scenario

3rd Stage: Introducing the Learning Scenario

In an attempt to make the problem solving more meaningful and to motivate and engage children in the research activities, a story-based learning scenario was designed. The story is an adaptation of the fairytale *Snow White and the Seven Dwarfs* by the Grimm brothers (Grimm and Grimm 1857). The adaptation concerns the end of the story; more specifically, in order to wake up Snow White, the prince has to collect the stars that had fallen on earth using the apple. Through this script, the children developed empathy for the role of the prince as they tried to help him achieve his goal. A digital narration of the fairytale was created with the use of *Story Maker 2* software (SPA Software 2005; see Fig. 12.4).

The digital storytelling technique adopted in this stage was enthusiastically received by children, enabled them to actively participate in the narration and, at the same time, practice computer mouse skills. During this stage, the researcher was taking notes about the reactions of the children.

4th Stage: Problem Solving through the Use of the Computer Game

This is the main stage of the research process during which children get engaged with solving problems by playing with the *Crayon Physics Deluxe* game under the guidance of the teacher. The teacher's role during this phase is crucial because she/he can formulate the children's interactions and retain their engagement in the game in case of frustration. By guiding them through appropriate questions, as well as through suggestions to consider alternative solutions for the same problem, the teacher may stir children's imagination and, thus, foster creativity.

For the collection of the research data in this stage, the screen of the computer, along with children's interactions with the software and their speech, were recorded with the use of computer screen capturing software.

5th Stage: Post-tests of Creativity and Self-efficacy

Finally, the teacher repeated the tests of self-efficacy, creativity, and problem solving, given at the 1st stage, in order to compare the results and document any significant difference.

Research Results and Findings

The main results of the research data analysis are presented in this section per research question.

Q.1: Is problem solving through the use of the specific game feasible and attractive for children?

The children's reactions and their eagerness to play, as well as their engagement, reveal that they found the game very attractive. After the completion of the research, the game remained available for all the children in the kindergarten, and the teacher informed the researchers that it was the choice of many children from then on, for the rest of the school year.

As far as the feasibility of the problem solving by children is concerned, Table 12.3 shows that most of the pairs (P1–P4) managed to solve 14 problems/ levels and gather 14 stars in 44–71 min. After level 14, the puzzles become too complex for the children, at least when they are experiencing the game for the first time. Pair P5, comprised of younger children, solved 10 levels in 38 min and, in general, experienced more difficulties than the rest of the groups. The average time of the groups' engagement with the software was about 53 min. Excerpt 2 is indicative of what children can achieve while using the game (Fig. 12.5).

Q.2: Does the use of the software have an impact on the development of children's creativity?

All participating children underwent the MSFM creativity test before and after the use of the software; the scores of the test are shown in Table 12.4.

For the purpose of the statistical analysis of the results, four variables have been defined, namely the Fluency Before and After (FB and FA respectively) and the Originality Before and After (OB and OA respectively). Based on the Shapiro-Wilk tests results: (1) (S-W(FB)=0.916; $p = 0.322$; $\alpha = 0.05$) (2) (S-W(FA)=0.955; $p = 0.727$; $\alpha = 0.05$) (3) (S-W(OB)=0.918; $p = 0.338$; $\alpha = 0.05$) (4) (S-W(OA)=0.905;

Table 12.3 Levels solved by each pair

Pair	Levels/stars	Duration of the session in minutes
P1	14	63
P2	14	52
P3	14	71
P4	14	44
P5	10	38

Excerpt 2

Indicative Example of Children's Interaction with the Game

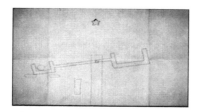

Researcher:	So tell me, what should we do here?
Yiannis:	Ah a stone!
Researcher:	Where will we put it?
Yiannis:	Here. (with his finger pointing over the right edge)
Researcher:	Why there?
Yiannis:	So that it goes...here! (pointing to the star)
Researcher:	You mean the ball?
Yiannis:	Yes! (smiling)
Researcher:	If we put the stone over here, how is the ball supposed to reach the star?
Yiannis:	It will turn like this...(showing the movement of the catapult)

Fig. 12.5 Screenshot of the puzzle that triggered the dialogue above

Table 12.4 Results in the MSFM creativity test

	Kenta	Yiorgos	Efie	Konstantinos	Tsampika	Sotiria	Mechalis	Nikoletta	Kiki	Yiannis
Fluency Before (FB)	16	9	13	16	21	21	14	10	10	15
Fluency After (FA)	16	13	15	21	19	23	19	11	14	21
Originality Before (OB)	21	14	16	26	32	35	20	15	10	16
Originality After (OA)	18	24	22	36	21	32	32	17	15	32

$p = 0.246$; $\alpha = 0.05$), we may consider, at a reasonable safety level ($\alpha = 0.05$), that all the variables follow the normal distribution. We can thus apply parametric tests of significance for the differences in mean values, and for the variance, before and after the intervention. In particular, the statistical analysis of the data reveals that:

A. There is a statistically-significant increase in the average fluency (from $a_{fb} = 14.5$ to $a_{fa} = 17.2$) since the t-test for two paired samples/Lower-tailed test gives t(FB-FA)$=-3.36$, $df=9$, $p=0.004$. This could be attributed to the teacher who insisted on the production of alternative solutions as well as on the software. The reduction of the standard deviation of the fluency of samples (from $s_{FB}=4.249$ to $s_{FA}=3.967$), although not statistically significant [Fisher's F-test/Two-tailed test: F(FB-FA)$=1.148$, $df1=df2=9$, $p=0.841$], supports the value of fluency increase finding, given that means are affected by outliers.

B. When it comes to originality, the increase in the mean of samples (from $a_{OB}=20.5$ to $a_{OA}=24.9$) is not statistically significant, since the t-test for two paired samples/Lower-tailed test gives t(OB-OA)$=(-1.69$, $df=9$, $p=0.063$). The reduction in the standard deviation of the Originality variable (from $s_{OB}=8.141$ to $s_{OA}=7.505$) in this case as well, although not statistically significant [Fisher's F-test/Two-tailed test: F(OB-OA)$=1.177$, $df1=df2=9$, $p=0.812$], strengthens the means difference. Therefore, the intervention with the particular computer game does not seem to make a significant change in the originality of the children's solutions to the specific problems class. Any contrary finding would nevertheless be rather strange, since neither the total duration of the children's involvement with the software, nor the children's ages, are conducive to the statistically-significant increase in originality for the solutions of the specific problems class. It is definitely not possible to attempt a generalisation of this result beyond the context in which this study took place—for example, in the case of a long-term use of the software under the guidance of teachers and/or the parallel application of other interventions (e.g. the use of experiential activities).

Finally, it was observed that a second solution to the same problem was suggested not only by students with high fluency score, but also by students with low fluency score (according to the MSFM test). Furthermore, original solutions were suggested not only by children of high originality score, but also by children of low score (according to the MSFM test). However, there is a quantitative difference in the number of multiple and original solutions that derived from children of high creativity score in comparison to the rest of the children. In other words, the essential difference among the children, as far as fluency and originality of solutions are concerned, is quantitative and not qualitative.

Considering these results in relation to the research question of whether the software affects the creativity of children, we can claim that, according to the findings, the software use under appropriate teacher guidance has the potential of increasing children's fluency early on. As far as the originality is concerned, no significant increase has been observed within the framework of this case study. Yet, the effects of the long-term use of game on originality remains an issue for further investigation.

Q.3: Does the use of the software have an impact on the development of children's self-efficacy?

Students underwent two self-efficacy (SE) tests before and after the use of the software (Table 12.5).

In Table 12.5, we have four self-efficacy variables which correspond to the rows of the table. More specifically, the variables are: self-efficacy in general problem solving before and after (SPB and SPA) as well as self-efficacy in computer games before and after (SGB and SGA). In order to test whether a statistically-significant change exists before and after the intervention, we treat the variables as binary (0$=$No, 1$=$Yes), (adopting the less optimistic interpretation: *I do not know*$=0$) so

Table 12.5 Results in the self-efficacy test

	Kenta	Yiorgos	Efie	Konstantinos	Tsampika	Sotiria	Mechalis	Nikoletta	Kiki	Yiannis
SE in General Problem Solving Before (SPB)	1	1	1	0	1	1	0	0	1	1
SE in General Problem Solving After (SPA)	1	1	1	1	1	1	1	1	1	1
SE in Computer Games Before (SGB)	0	1	0	0	1	1	1	1	1	0
SE in Computer Games After (SGA)	1	1	1	1	1	1	1	1	1	1

as to be able to apply the McNemar test. Applying the McNemar test to Table 12.5, we have the following results:

A. The application of the McNemar test, (Exact p-value)/Lower-tailed test to SPB and SPA variables ($Q=3$, $Zobserved=-1.732$, $p=0.125$), indicates an increase in general self-efficacy from 7/10 to 10/10 which is not statistically significant. It should be pointed out, though, that the children of the sample already had sufficiently-high self-efficacy results and a statistically-significant change should, therefore, not be expected. Given that it is common for children to exhibit high levels of self-efficacy (Bandura and Schunk 1981), the increase in self-efficacy in this case could be interpreted as positive evidence because the learning activity contributed to a further increase of the already high self-efficacy of the children.

B. On the other hand, as far as the computer game is concerned, the change in self-efficacy appears statistically significant, as the McNemar test (Exact p-value/Lower-tailed test) in SGB and SGA variables shows ($Q=5$, $Zobserved=-2.236$, $p=0.031$). We could, therefore, draw the conclusion that the particular intervention described in this paper seems to increase children's self-efficacy with regard to the use of the computer game. This is significant, because children with high self-efficacy are not easily discouraged by difficulties and failures in an activity. Instead, they remain strongly involved in it because they believe that they will eventually manage to work things out.

Q.4: How does the teacher's role during the problem-solving process facilitate the development of creativity?

During the problem-solving process, at the outset of each new activity, the teacher would use appropriate questions to lead the children through recognising and defining the problem to be sure they had detected the obstacles and had obtained a full grasp of the situation. Later on, during their engagement with the game, whenever the children seemed to face difficulties, the teacher preferred to guide them through questions rather than provide them with suggestions of how to solve the problem. Following are some of the common thought-provoking questions employed by the teacher: (1) *Why can't the ball go to the star?* (2) *Is there anything close to the ball that could help us?* (3) *What was wrong with your design?* (4) *How did you think about that?* (5) *Do you think there could be another way to help the ball reach the star?* The teacher encouraged the children to experiment with alternative solutions. Furthermore, he commented on the children's successful choices and prompted them to explain their thinking. After each unsuccessful trial, the teacher asked the children to describe what went wrong and analyse their solutions, a technique that could lead them to try new, improved solutions. An indicative dialogue, revealing the facilitating role of the teacher, is provided in Excerpt 3. The teacher also encouraged collaboration among children. On the other hand, in order to prevent frustration and discouragement brought on by possible unsuccessful attempts, he was supportive by helping them analyze and understand their mistakes throughout the activities. Finally, in cases of repeated unsuccessful efforts, the teacher would demonstrate possible solutions. Without the teacher's presence and guidance, the children would, most likely, have given up and stopped searching for alternative solutions even if the software had been "easier" for the kindergarten children to use (Fig. 12.6).

Excerpt 3

A Dialogue Excerpt Revealing the Facilitating Role of the Teacher

Tsampika:	*I think that this needs something.*
Teacher:	*Like?*
Tsampika:	*You need to put little lines here. (pointing to the gaps)*
Teacher:	*Why is that so?*
Tsampika:	*Because there are gaps.*
Researcher:	*Sotiria, what do you think?*
Sotiria:	*We need to put little lines.*
Teacher:	*Could there be another way?*
Sotiria:	*Hmmm. It can jump here and here.(pointing to the battlement)*
Teacher:	*That's right! It could also go this way.*

Fig. 12.6 A screenshot of the puzzle to which the dialogue above refers

Conclusions

Creativity constitutes an integral part of life and evolution of human species, not only on personal but also social levels. The interest of experts, educators, and parents is now turning more and more to the development of creativity, starting from the preschool age. Many studies on the development of creativity, as well as on the implementation of special techniques that foster its cultivation through activities that exploit the use of appropriate educational material, have been conducted. Yet, the introduction of ICT in every section of human life has turned the discussion of the development of creativity in a different direction, which provokes new questions from parents and educators.

The above questions constituted the focal point of the present research, within the framework of which creative problem solving in a digital environment was experimentally tested. The software used throughout the study, together with the support provided by the teacher, contributed to the development of a creative approach to problem solving by preschoolers. In particular, the study indicates a positive effect on the development of preschoolers' fluency in solutions. A positive effect was also indicated in the improvement of the children's self-efficacy in relation to the use of computer games. Within the short duration of the study, we did not have a statistically-significant increase in the originality of the solutions, which seems to require a better knowledge of the problems domain than the participant children had or could develop in the framework of the study. Yet, the increase of the children's fluency combined with the increase in their self-efficacy promises positive results with respect to the cultivation of creativity in preschool. Finally, the non-statistically significant increase in the number of original solutions produced by the participating children should not detract from the fact that the researchers observed innovative solutions from children, regardless of the initial assessment of their creativity. In other words, from a qualitative point of view, the intervention provided opportunities for students to demonstrate creative solutions.

In general, the authors have the conviction that this particular kind of software, under appropriate teacher's guidance, may benefit the development of problem-solving skills and the creative potential of children in a pleasant and intriguing manner. Teacher's guidance is considered a key precondition for an effective and efficient use of the software towards this direction; which means that a different approach, such as the typical case where children would just get their computer time and work independently or with a partner, is not likely to yield similar positive results. *Crayon Physics,* along with the guidance of the teacher, helped form an attractive, engaging learning environment for the cultivation of creative problem-solving ability of the children, in an enjoyable way.

References

Aguirre, K., & Conners, F. (2010, Spring). Creativity and intelligence in preschoolers: Preliminary findings. *The University of Alabama McNair Journal, 10,* 1–7. http://graduate.ua.edu/mcnair/journals/2010/Aguirre.pdf.

Bandura, A., & Schunk, D. H. (1981). Cultivating competence, self-efficacy, and intrinsic interest through proximal self-motivation. *Journal of Personality and Social Psychology, 41,* 586–598.

Bong, M., & Skaalvik, E. M. (2003). Academic self-concept and self-efficacy: How different are they really? *Educational Psychology Review, 15,* 1–40.

Clements, D. (1995). Teaching creativity with computers. *Educational Psychology Review, 7*(2), 141–161.

Cohen, L., Manion, L., & Morrison, K. (2000). *Research methods in education* (5th ed.). London: Routledge (Falmer Press).

Csikszentmihalyi, M. (1999). Implications of a systems perspective. In R. J. Sternberg (Ed.), *Handbook of creativity* (pp. 325–339). Cambridge, MA: Cambridge University Press.

European Commission. (1998). *Innovation management techniques in operation.* Luxembourg: European Commission.

Fesakis, G., Sofroniou, C., & Mavroudi, E. (2011). Using internet for communicative learning activities in kindergarten: The case of the "shapes planet." *Early Childhood Education Journal, 38*(5), 385–392. doi:10.1007/s10643-010-0422-0.

Fessakis, G., Gouli, E., & Mavroudi, E. (2013). Problem solving by 5–6 years old kindergarten children in a computer programming environment: A case study. *Computers & Education, 63,* 87–97. doi:10.1016/j.compedu.2012.11.016.

Gardner, H. (1993). *Creating minds.* New York, NY: Basic Books.

Goffin, S., & Tull, C. (1985). Problem solving encouraging active learning. *Young Children, 40,* 28–32.

Grimm, J., & Grimm, W. (1857). *Kinder- und Hausmärchen.* English edition: Grimm, J., & Grimm, W. (1857). *Children's and households fairy tales* (Vol. 1, 7th ed., pp. 264–273). Göttingen: Dietrich.

Haugland, S. (1992). The effect of computer software on preschool children's developmental gains. *Journal of Computing in Childhood Education, 3,* 15–30.

Horakova, S. (2004). *Self-efficacy of preschool children. Summary of the dissertation project.* Prague: Charles University. http://www.uky.edu/~eushe2/Pajares/tezeaj2.pdf.

Mansfield, R. S., Busse, T. V., & Krepelka, E. G. (1978). The effectiveness of creative training. *Review of Educational Research, 48*(4), 517–536.

Merriam, S. B. (2009). *Qualitative research: guide to design and implementation* (2nd ed.). San Francisco: Jossey-Bass Publishers.

Moran III, J. D., Milgram, R. M., Sawyers, J. K., & Fu, V. R. (1983). Original thinking in preschool children. *Child Development, 54,* 921–926.

National Advisory Committee on Creative and Cultural Education. (1999). *All our futures: Creativity, culture and education.* London: Department for Education and Employment.

Papert, S. (1980). *Mindstorms.* New York, NY: Basic Books.

Parnes, S. J., & Brunelle, E. A. (1967). The literature of creativity. *Journal of Creative Behavior, 1*(1), 52–104.

Partnership for 21st Century Skills. (2009). Framework for 21st century learning. http://www.p21.org/documents/P21_Framework_Definitions.pdf. Accessed 16 Feb 2011.

Purho, P. (2009). Crayon Physics Deluxe. [Computer Software]. http://crayonphysics.com/. Accessed 16 Feb 2011.

Resnick, M. (2007). All I really need to know (about creative thinking) I learned (by studying how children learn) in kindergarten. *Proceedings of the 6th ACM SIGCHI Conference on Creativity and Cognition.* Washington, DC: ACM.

Rose, L. H., & Lin, H. T. (1984). A meta-analysis of long-term creativity training programs. *Journal of Creative Behaviour, 18*(1), 11–22.

Runco, M. A. (1997). *Creativity research handbook: vols. 1–3*. Creskill, NJ: Hampton Press.

Runco, M. A. (2000). Creativity: Research on the process of creativity. In A. E. Kazdin (Ed.), *Encyclopedia of psychology: Vol. 2* (pp. 342–346). Washington, DC: American Psychological Association.

Sefertzi, E. (2000). Creativity. Luxemburg, European Union, Report Produced for the EC funded project. *INNOREGIO: Dissemination of Innovation and Knowledge management Techniques*.

SPA Software. (2005). StoryMaker v2. [Computer Software] http://www.questaslimited.co.uk/SPA/demostorymaker.html. Accessed 16 Feb 2011.

Sternberg, R. J. (1996). Investing in creativity: Many happy returns. *Educational Leadership, 53*, 80–84.

Sternberg, R. J., & Lubart, T. I. (1991). Creating creative minds. *Phi Delta Kappan, 72*, 608–614.

Sternberg, R. J., & Lubart, T. I. (1996). Investing in creativity. *American Psychologist, 51*, 677–688.

Taylor, C. W. (1972). Can organizations be creative, too? In C. W. Taylor (Ed.), *Climates for creativity* (pp. 1–15). New York, NY: Pergamon Press.

Torrance, E. P. (1966). *Torrance tests of creative thinking: Norms technical manual* (Research Ed.). Princeton, NJ: Personnel Press.

Torrance, E. P. (1974). *Norms-technical manual: Torrance tests of creative thinking*. Lexington, MA: Ginn & Co.

Torrance, E. P. (1995). *Why fly?* Norwood, NJ: Ablex.

Torrance, E. P. (2001). *Experiences in developing creativity measures: Insights, discoveries, decisions*. Manuscript submitted for publication.

Wheeler, S., Waiter, S., & Bromfield, C. (2002). Promoting creativity thinking through the use of ICT. *Journal of Computer Assisted learning, 18*, 367–378.

Wood, R., & Bandura, A. (1989). Impact of conceptions of ability on self-regulatory mechanism and complex decision making. *Journal of Personality and Social Psychology, 56*(3), 407–415.

Yin, R. K. (2011). *Applications of case study research*. Thousand Oaks, CA: Sage.

Chapter 13
The Impact of Popular Media on Infant/Toddler Language Development: Research-based Recommendations for Working with Families

Melissa Calderon

Abstract The rapid growth of television programs and DVDs marketed to infants and toddlers has changed the context of early learning experiences. Many of these products make educational claims that attract families with the intent of using the content to increase their child's language development. Social development theory explains the importance of a child's interactions with other adults and children in order to gain knowledge about their world. Current research on young children's language development and media usage provides a variety of research-based conclusions that are contingent upon the child's age and the content of the program. Early education professionals are in a position to inform families about current research findings on the dangers of passive screen media usage before the age of 2 as well as the potential benefits of later viewing. Recommendations for infant-centered early language experiences and media usage are provided to assist families in making age-appropriate choices for their young child's early language experiences.

Keywords Media · Infants · Toddlers · Young children · Language development · Expressive language · Receptive language · Infant DVDs · Parent-child interactions

Young Children's Media Usage

Ashley's 2-year-old daughter, Leah, is cared for by various family members during the weekdays. Leah is allowed to watch several hours of television while she is in their care. When Ashley returns from her long day, she rewards Leah's good behavior by allowing her to watch more television. This time also allows Ashley to complete household chores while Leah is entertained in front of the television. Ashley believes that Leah can learn more from the screen than she can from watching her mother. Ashley is satisfied with her decision to use media for her stated purposes.

Jessica, the mother of 18-month-old Sadie, allows her daughter to watch about 3 h of television per day. Her mother believes it is very important to read the packaging of each DVD and examine the content of all television programs. She believes that Sadie will be more prepared for school if she continues to view the videos. Jes-

M. Calderon (✉)
Community College of Allegheny County, Pittsburgh, PA
e-mail: mgunter@iup.edu

sica believes there is a great deal of learning that her daughter can gain by simply viewing the content on the screen. She also feels confident that she is building a smarter baby and is proud of the investment she has made in infant DVD products.

Both of these parents use popular, heavily-advertised children's media for different reasons. Leah's family uses television media for entertainment and as a reward for appropriate behaviors. Sadie's mother has chosen specific programming content with the intent of increasing her child's preparation for future schooling. In these vignettes, infants and toddlers under the age of 2 are watching screen media for several hours a day. Scenarios such as these raise questions concerning the potential learning benefits or harm, if any, to children under 2 years of age who view screen media. Families and early childhood professionals need access to resources regarding the impact of early media viewing on learning and development.

The American Academy of Pediatrics (AAP) (2012) clearly states that parents of children under the age of 2 should be discouraged from allowing their children to use electronic media. Children over the age of 2 should be limited to less than 2 h of screen time per day. The organization supports current research on early brain development that suggests the need for social interactions in order to promote healthy development. These interactions provide for the physical, cognitive, social, and emotional development of the young child.

Other organizations offer similar recommendations. The White House Task Force on Childhood Obesity (2010) supports the AAP recommendations for no use of screen media before the age of 2. While the AAP recommends no more than 1–2 h of screen time for children over 2 years, the Task Force on Childhood Obesity recommends no more than 30 min–1 h for children ages 2–5. The stringent recommendations made by the task force demonstrate the attempts being made to change children's sedentary behaviors while promoting children's engagement in a more active lifestyle. These reasons are also influencing other nations to create recommendations on children's media use. The Australian Department of Health and Ageing (DoHA 2011) issued recommendations in the *Get Up and Grow* publication for children birth to 5 years. The department stated that infants and toddlers under the age of 2 should not be exposed to any form of screen time. Children 2–5 years of age should be limited to less than 1 h per day.

In the U.S., it is estimated that a majority of infants under the age of 2 spend an average of 1–2 h per day viewing infant DVDs and television programs (Rideout 2013; Rideout et al. 2006). Research has found a significant increase in young infants' screen media usage including television, DVDs, video games, and computers (Anderson and Pempek 2005). Several studies conducted in other countries have also reported an increase in young children's screen media use including iPads, iPhones, notebooks, and similar viewing devices (Sigman 2012; Skouteris and McHardy 2009). A study conducted in the United Kingdom (UK) reported that children ages birth to six were watching 2 h and 6 min of screen media per day. This data suggests that young children living in the UK are exposed to approximately the same amount of screen media as those living in the United States (US). Data analysis of a longitudinal study found that approximately 86 % of infants in the UK have watched television or DVDs before the age of 2 (Marsh et al. 2005).

Considering the high levels of use at early ages, it is possible that many parents and professionals agree with the use of infant media. Adults may rely on information provided by the immense amount of marketing material promoting media for infants and toddlers. This chapter begins by reviewing the current trends in popular media usage by young children and examining the impact of this usage on language development. Next, Lev Vygotsky's social development theory is presented as a guide to understanding how infants and toddlers gain language abilities through interactions with adults and other children in their environment. These interactions contribute to a young child's receptive and expressive language development. Heavily-marketed popular media for infants and toddlers under the age of 2 often make claims about the product increasing the child's vocabulary skills. This chapter will present and discuss research studies examining relationships between media usage and the domains of language development in young children. The chapter concludes with an understanding of the family's role in providing age-appropriate language interactions and safe media viewing experiences. Recommendations are presented to guide families in making developmentally-appropriate choices for media use and infant-centered language experiences embedded in the young child's environment.

DVD Marketing for Language Development

A rising number of infant DVDs and television programs are marketed to infants and toddlers. The DVD market includes *Baby Einstein, Brainy Baby, Baby Genius, Baby Superstar,* and *SoSmart! Baby Beginnings.* In 2006, cable and satellite providers launched a 24-h channel called *BabyFirstTV.* Infants and toddlers from birth to 36 months are increasingly exposed to these types of programs.

Marketing companies typically make claims regarding their products' ability to increase young children's cognitive development. Language skills are a domain of development that is typically mentioned on the packaging of these products. Several research studies have examined young children's language development in relation to the content of the programming viewed. Currently, there are no research-based findings that suggest young children under the age of 2 acquire language skills from infant-directed programming (Linebarger and Walker 2005; Zimmerman et al. 2007). In response to these research findings, the French broadcast authority announced in 2008 that it would ban television programs targeted at audiences under the age of 3. Included in the list of programs to be banned were *BabyFirstTV* and *BabyTV.* The organization used research findings from many US studies that have shown no benefits in language or other developmental areas for young children under 2 years of age who watch television or DVDs. Other studies have found, with increased television and DVD use, young children report more sleep disturbances, decreased attention spans, and increased excitability (Barr 2008; Ollivier 2008). While reviewing research on current media usage, it is important to begin by examining how young children construct knowledge during their first few years of life.

The Role of Social Interactions in Language Development

Early education professionals have become concerned, over recent years, with the amount of media viewed by infants and toddlers. One reason for this concern is the understanding of how children learn during the first few years of life. Social development theorist Lev Vygotsky (1962) believed children construct their knowledge of language from interactions with adults and other children in their environment. Interactions take place between the child (learner) and a More Knowledgeable Other (MKO) which can include individuals who are older or younger than the child. The MKO must have a greater ability in understanding or performing a certain task.

A fundamental idea in Vygotsky's theory on social development and learning is the Zone of Proximal Development (ZPD). Vygotsky describes the ZPD as a metaphorical area between a person's actual knowledge or developmental level, as determined by their performance during an independent problem solving task, and the person's level of potential knowledge or development during a task that is assisted by a MKO (Vygotsky 1978). Within this metaphorical area are skills that the learner is in the process of gaining through maturation and assistance by the scaffolding techniques of a MKO. Vygotsky places an emphasis on the social dialogue used between the learner and MKO during instruction and cognitive growth.

The social interactions and scaffolding that take place in the ZPD provide a framework for understanding the process of language development. Young children need a MKO to provide labels for objects and actions within their environment. This labeling process enhances children's receptive vocabulary development. Receptive language skills include the young child's ability to listen and understand what is being orally communicated. Expressive language skills can be observed when the child uses previously-learned knowledge from a MKO to communicate orally or through writing. Receptive language skills develop earlier than expressive (Lickliter 2001; Ouellette 2006). As young children grow, they listen to words repeated in their environment, remember the words, and then eventually reproduce the words they have heard.

The child's vocabulary is a blend of receptive and expressive language skills. Vocabulary is often assessed by the number of words children know and use when they listen or orally communicate. Young children use vocabulary words as labels to identify familiar and unfamiliar objects or concepts in their environment. Vocabulary skills are gained by interacting with adults and other children. The theoretical framework of children gaining language from a MKO places an emphasis on the need for a live person scaffolding the child's learning. Many families choose to use popular media as a way to contribute to their child's vocabulary skills. Parents and educators need to consider Vygotsky's theory when exposing young children to media.

Review of Media Research

The History of Baby Einstein

The first video made for infants was created in the basement of Julie Aigner-Clark's home in 1996. The former teacher created a VHS video for her infant daughter that included art, music, and poetry. Julie Aigner-Clark stated that her intentions were to make a video that would provide an opportunity for the two of them to explore the world together while sharing in her appreciation for humanities and the arts. On January 31, 1997, the first infant video was sold in over 36 retail stores. In 1998, Julie Aigner-Clark and her husband sold a portion of the *Baby Einstein Company* to *Artisan Entertainment* and a second portion to *Family Home Entertainment* in 2000; which resulted in a 20% reallocation of the *Baby Einstein Company's* total profits. The *Walt Disney Company* bought the remaining 80% of the *Baby Einstein Company* in 2001 (Baby Einstein 2013b).

Marketing Claims

Since its inception in 1997, the *Baby Einstein Company* has evolved into a multimillion dollar company. A study by Garrison and Christakis (2005) reviewed marketing data of infant videos and found that three-quarters of the top 100 DVDs made educational claims. Many times the educational claims are insinuated in the title, such as *Baby Einstein* and *Brainy Baby*. DVDs may also state educational claims on the packaging. For example, the cover of the *Brainy Baby Left Brain* DVD states that the video inspires logical thinking while displaying a picture of a math formula. The packaging also claims that the video stimulates children's cognitive growth while teaching them language, sequencing, and how to analyze information. Several other infant DVDs have made educational claims as well. The infant DVD *Baby Einstein Language Nursery* is targeted for infants as young as 1 month and states that the video enhances the child's engagement and learning potential (Garrison and Christakis 2005). Many families believe the educational claims made by infant DVDs and rely on this type of media as a way to support their young child's development. Families do not realize that most marketing research conducted on infant DVDs, which drives the development of these products, is linked to how long an infant will pay attention to the stimulus on the screen rather than what the infant has learned from viewing the content (Krcmar 2010).

Associations between Young Children's Language Skills and Media Usage

Researchers have questioned whether paying attention to content on the screen is as beneficial to development as paying attention to a real-life stimulus providing the same content. Studies using children under 2 years of age revealed that infants directed their attention to the real-life stimulus more often when compared to the screen-based stimulus. In addition, infants were more likely to imitate the actions of the live stimulus following a 24-h delay (Barr and Hayne 1999).

Infants and toddlers learn best through experiences with people in their environment. Researchers have placed an emphasis on the importance of other individuals repeating words several times before the child learns the word. Typically, words are not repeated within the viewing time frame of a television program. A slight variation to the lack of word repetition occurs when programs are replayed. However several researchers have found no significant difference in receptive or expressive language skills after repeatedly watching the same program several times a week for 6 weeks (Ross et al. 2009). Interestingly, infants and toddlers have displayed gains in receptive and expressive language development when exposed to a live child or adult who repeats words in the child's presence (Krcmar et al. 2007). Infants and toddlers learn best from a MKO. Limitations in cognitive abilities make it difficult for them to learn from the content delivered on the screen. An opportunity for greater learning potential can be found when the same type of content is experienced by the infant interacting with others.

Research examining the use of a live stimulus for learning supports children's ability to gain language skills. A study conducted by Krcmar et al. (2007) assessed the language acquisition of nonsense words such as *keeg*, *doot*, and *sas* in children ages 15–24 months. Infants were given four modes of delivery for the nonsense words which included (1) an adult presenting the word while the child was paying attention, (2) an adult presenting the word while the child was not paying attention, (3) an adult on the screen presenting the word, and (4) the word being presented by the television program the *Teletubbies*. Each word was associated with an object that infants and toddlers may have viewed but had not labeled. Findings from the study displayed a significant difference in vocabulary knowledge between young children who viewed the adult *in vivo* and those who viewed the *Teletubbies* and the adult on the screen. Although the difference was not significant, infants and toddlers who were paying attention to the live adult presenter displayed a slight increase in knowledge of nonsense words compared to those children who were not paying attention. Infants and toddlers in the group exposed to the adult live stimulus gained the highest number of words, whereas those in the *Teletubbies* group displayed the lowest number of nonsense words (Krcmar et al. 2007). Families of young children need to be made aware of the findings on vocabulary development and the *Teletubbies* program. This program targets preverbal children before they have gained a significant amount of receptive language from interactions with others in their environment. Infants and toddlers need the opportunity to learn from a live adult or child in order to attach labels to objects and understand word meanings.

A previous study conducted by Linebarger and Walker in 2005 also found no language benefits from infants watching the *Teletubbies* program. The study examined the impact of television program content on young children's knowledge of vocabulary words and expressive language skills. Data were collected in 3-month increments beginning when participants were 6 months old and ending at 30 months of age. The results displayed differences in language development depending upon the age of the child and content provided. Several television programs were associated with increased vocabulary knowledge and expressive language skills for children over the age of 30 months. The programs *Dora the Explorer*, *Blue's Clues*, *Arthur*, *Clifford*, and *Dragon Tales* provide opportunities for language modeling while decreasing the amount of distracting stimuli on the screen. Linebarger and Walker (2005) found positive effects from those programs that used child-directed speech to elicit a response from the viewer. Responses included having the child point, repeat, and answer questions. This style of content requires the child to become an active participant while they analyze, encode, and synthesize the incoming information. It is important to emphasize that the benefits of these programs on language skills were only seen in children over the age of 30 months. It is possible that children at this age have acquired enough experiences with receptive language skills to support vocabulary and expressive language development through different modes of delivery beyond real-life experiences.

The Linebarger and Walker (2005) study also found several television programs that were considered to have minimal or negative impacts on language development for children less than 30 months of age. Infants and toddlers who viewed the *Teletubbies* program had lower scores in vocabulary knowledge and expressive language skills at all age points. *Barney & Friends* also displayed an association between viewing the program's content and lower vocabulary knowledge. This research is important for families in the US as well as other countries. A 2005 survey of young children's viewing habits in the UK revealed that *Teletubbies* and *Barney & Friends* were among the top ten choices for children under the age of 2.

In the Linebarger and Walker (2005) study, viewing *Sesame Street* at 30 months of age was associated with a small decrease in expressive language skills and revealed no impact on vocabulary knowledge. The *Sesame Street* program has been promoted for its potential benefits to increasing vocabulary skills in older children. However, the findings in this study suggest a lack of evidence regarding the developmental benefits of infants and toddlers viewing programs that are considered appropriate for older children.

Linebarger's previous work also displayed an association between older children's literacy skills and television programming. In 2000, Linebarger reported on a research study examining kindergartners' literacy skills after viewing 17 half-hour episodes of the television show *Between the Lions*. A second group of kindergarten children did not view the program. The results displayed significant increases in language skills for those children that viewed the program when compared to the control group. Viewers had significant increases in letter-sound correspondence and reading ability scores. Children who viewed the program were also more likely to visit the library and bookstores. Differences were also observed within the classroom setting. The children who viewed the television program *Between the Lions* spent more time during free play writing notes, letters, and creating stories. The program has been documented as providing significant benefits in learning literacy concepts especially for those children in kindergarten.

A portion of the study was also conducted with first grade participants. The results displayed a significant increase in phonetic awareness; however, other literacy areas were not significantly different from the control group. Researchers suggested that a ceiling effect could have been created and more advanced skills need to be presented in the content of the program (Linebarger 2000). These findings point to the critical time periods when the content of media can benefit children's language development and when it becomes ineffective in promoting literacy skills.

Although there is a considerable amount of research on the benefits of television programming for children over the age of 2, parents of viewers under the age of 2 should be cautioned in the use of media. Infants and toddlers are still in the beginning process of learning language and need rich experiences using their receptive language abilities. At this age, they have decreased skills in expressive areas such as communication, which is often needed for a more interactive learning experience involving media.

A research study by Zimmerman et al. (2007) examined the association between infants' and toddlers' levels of communication and media usage. Over 1,000 families located in Minnesota and Washington completed the *MacArthur-Bates Communicative Development Inventory* (CDI). The results displayed a 16.99 point decrease in communicative language development in infants and toddlers aged 8–16 months who watched 1 h of DVDs such as *Baby Einstein* and *Brainy Baby* in comparison to infants who did not view DVD videos. An analysis of the results displayed an association between the number of hours viewed per day and language development. Other variables that were examined included parents reading and telling stories to their children daily as well as listening to music several times a week. Examination of the CDI data results displayed a 7.07 increase from the normed score as a result of the parent reading to the 8–16-month-old child. Story telling was associated with a 6.47 increase from the normed score on the CDI measurement tool, while listening to music did not result in a significant increase (Zimmerman et al. 2007). The results of this study indicate the increase in language development that can be attributed to parent-child interactions, such as reading and storytelling. An equally important finding is the negative impact on language development that occurs when infants and toddlers ages 8–16 months passively view 1 h of infant DVDs.

A study in 2009, also examined *Baby Einstein* videos for their potential language benefits in young children. The *Baby Wordsworth* video by the *Baby Einstein Company* is specifically designed to enhance infant and toddler vocabulary. This video features a cat that provides associations between words and objects around the home (Baby Einstein 2013). Participants aged 12–25 months were divided into two groups. The experimental group was given specific instructions to allow their infants to view the video five times during a 2-week period for 6 weeks total. The control group was instructed to continue with their typical routines for the 6-week duration of the study. Receptive and expressive language skills were assessed in both groups of participants. The results displayed no significant difference between the control group and the experimental group even after repeated exposures to the words in the video (Ross et al. 2009). This research complements past findings that suggest infants and toddlers do not gain language skills while passively viewing screen media. Although other studies have found decreased receptive and expressive language in infants and toddlers after viewing screen media, this study found no significant difference between both groups. The lack of a significant difference may be due to the repetition of the same words in the video over the 6-week time frame in the experimental group.

Anderson et al. (2001) found strong predictors of school readiness and vocabulary development for children over the age of 2 who are exposed to educational programming that is continually replayed, thereby repeating the same words. This study found the greatest gains for participants who were considered early viewers, ages 2–3. The strength of the impact decreased with children who were considered late viewers, after the age of 4. This may be due to the need for more advanced cognitive strategies in learning vocabulary. Repetition of viewing can result in rehearsing, storing, and retrieving information which can lead to an increase in the future use of the word. It is also possible that words heard from screen media may be repeated by children under the age of 2, although some young children may lack an understanding of the content or meaning of the word.

Researchers compared the amount of time young children in Canada spent watching television and their vocabulary skills in several languages. The languages that were assessed included monolingual English or French and bilingual English and French. The researchers also divided viewing time into the categories of quality and quantity. The results indicated that the amount of viewing time was not significantly related to vocabulary skills. However, the poor quality of some programming content was directly related to lower levels of vocabulary skills in each language. Content that was considered poor quality included programming that was intended for adults and the television being on in the background while children play. Other factors, such as the child viewing the program alone or early ages of first time use, were also associated with lower vocabulary skills. The children who were English speaking or bilingual demonstrated the lowest vocabulary gains in comparison to the monolingual French speaking groups of participants (Hudon et al. 2013). These findings suggest differences in the impact of screen content on vocabulary skills depending on the language being presented.

After examining the evidence suggesting that infant DVDs and television programs provide no discernible positive effects on infants' language development, action must be taken to ensure families gain access to this important information. Families make decisions about their young child's media exposure for many reasons. The vignettes presented in the beginning of this chapter demonstrate the lack of knowledge families have concerning the potential harms of passive media usage. Professionals in the field of early childhood education need to be a source of information regarding the dangers of media exposure for children under the age of 2. Early education professionals can also provide suggestions for positive language experiences that shape young children's development. Families are a significant factor in the contribution of these early language experiences and need to be educated on the impact of popular media on young children's language development.

The Family's Role in Young Children's Language Development and Media Usage

In young children, the ability to use language is learned primarily through interactions with adults and other children in their environment (Weizman and Greenberg 2002). The family environment has an influence on the receptive and expressive language skills of infants and toddlers. Families need an awareness of media research in order to make appropriate choices regarding their young child's language experiences. The ploys of marketing and the lack of information on early child development may lead families to choose media in an attempt to provide the young child with language skills. The vignettes presented in the beginning of this chapter are examples of infants and toddlers spending several hours of their day watching television programs. Families need resources that provide evidence-based research regarding media usage in the first years of life. Recommendations for early language experiences can help families in creating age-appropriate environments and interactions that stimulate vocabulary growth.

Recommendations for Infant-Centered Early Language Experiences

The theoretical framework and research provided in this chapter support the role of adults in young children's early language experiences. Families need access to information on how to promote early language skills without the use of media. Oftentimes, the experiences infants require are inexpensive and rely more on interactions than expensive toys and videos. Routine activities such as feeding, changing diapers, and bathing contribute to 90% of social exchanges between infants and adults (Hardman et al. 2011). These interactions support language skills by connecting words and actions in the environment. A sense of trust can also be instilled as the infant experiences familiarity in these repetitious language exchanges over time.

Researchers have used data related to the social influences of early language development to create recommendations for families of young children (Tamis-LeMonda et al. 2006). These recommendations include the idea that language skills are enhanced when adults interacting with young children use a form of infant-directed speech called *motherese*. During these vocal interactions, the adults will use simple words and sentences that are phrased in a high-pitched manner. Research suggests that the use of *motherese* increases the likelihood of the child responding to the adult therefore enhancing vocabulary development. Various research studies have found that *motherese* is common in many countries all over the world (Nonaka 2004; Trainor and Desjardins 2002).

Tamis-LeMonda et al. also recommends that adults interacting with infants and toddlers respond expressively in a manner that is attuned to what the child is uttering. During these interactions, it is beneficial to extend a young child's words or gestures in an effort to increase their language development. Infants naturally point to objects and use gestures within the first year of life. Adults interacting with infants and toddlers can make use of pointing and gesturing as a way to gain the child's attention and to help them understand the words that are being said.

Other research studies have found growth in language development and emergent literacy through participation in learning activities such as reading and shared storytelling. During these experiences, young children gain a greater concept of print awareness as well as becoming exposed to formal sentence structures. Both of these activities increase the young child's positive attitude towards literacy (Payne et al. 1994; Senechal et al. 1996; Snow and Dickinson 1990; Raikes et al. 2006).

Recommendations for Infant and Toddler Media Usage

Many families state that their young child does not continually watch the television. Oftentimes, the television is on in the background as the child is playing. Families may change the television to a program of their choice and content level because they believe the child is not viewing the program. A research study in 2008 examined the effects of background television while infants and toddlers were engaged in play. Participants aged 12–36 months were videotaped for 1 h while playing. The television was on for 30 min out of the hour time frame and displayed the program *Jeopardy!* The number of times the young child looked at the program while playing was counted. The results indicated a significant increase in screen viewing during the first 6 min. This behavior gradually declined as the child became habituated to the content. Researchers also examined toy engagement and found a significant decrease in the amount of time focused on toys while the television was on in the background. Infants and toddlers were also more likely to switch to another toy or play activity after looking at the television (Schmidt et al. 2008). This finding suggests that the television being on during play disrupts the child's schema and attention to play. Young children look at the television and then forget what they were playing. This disruption is taking away from valuable play time. Families need to be aware of the child's attention to the television being played in the background. Infants and toddlers may also be viewing content that is inappropriate. Considering the importance of play in young children's lives and the disruption that television creates during play, the simple answer for families is to turn off the television.

Many parents will not restrict the use of media in very young children. In these cases, the best recommendation is for parents to participate in co-viewing the program. During and after the viewing time, parents can repeat and extend the educational content that is provided on the screen. The parent-child interactions taking place during viewing times are beneficial to the child's learning.

A study by Alan Mendelsohn et al. (2010) examined the impact of co-viewing and found language increases at 14 months of age for those young children who viewed and discussed the content of the educational programs. Young children who engaged in more passive television experiences without an opportunity for co-viewing displayed less receptive and expressive language skills at 14 months. These results were found for families considered to be of low socio-economic status with children at-risk for school failure. Almost half of the participants in this study were English Language Learners (ELL) with Spanish as their native language. This study emphasizes the benefits of co-viewing and parent-child interactions for the child's maximum learning potential when engaging in media viewing.

Parents living in the UK were surveyed on how often they participated in co-viewing television or DVDs with their child. Of the parents interviewed, 33% watch the program with the child most of the time and 34% co-view about half of the time. Only 6% of parents reported viewing television with their young child all of the time. Researchers also examined parent's attitudes towards their young child's use of media. Overall, parents responded favorably to questions regarding the benefits of media use for young children. Approximately 79% of parents believed that television was a beneficial part of their child's language development.

In an effort to promote the awareness of healthy media use, the National Association for the Education of Young Children (NAEYC) and the Fred Rogers Center for Early Learning and Children's Media at Saint Vincent College (2012) have created a joint position statement on young children's media usage. Recommendations are made for children ages birth to 8 years. Both parties in the position statement recommend limiting the use of media programs for children under the age of 2. When considering the use of media devices, recommendations are centered on developmentally-appropriate experiences that encourage parent-child interactions and relationships. For example, infants and toddlers can view digital photos and videos along with participating in webcam services where they can interact with family members not living in their home. Opportunities for media exposure should be thoughtfully planned to provide more hands-on interactive learning and less passive viewing of a screen.

A research team in Australia compared data from the Longitudinal Study of Australian Children and the recommendations for use of screen time as stated by the Department of Health and Ageing. While taking into account these two sets of data, researchers separated the children's screen time into the content categories of active and passive. The categories reflect the variety of screen time experiences available depending on the content of the program. By providing this categorization, professionals can gain a more accurate view of children's screen time. The researchers in this study concluded that the majority of television and DVD use is passive viewing. They also found that children use television and DVDs more often than video games and computers. When comparing screen time and the stated recommendations, researchers found that children under the age of five were exceeding the Department of Health and Ageing's maximum time limit on screen use per day (Sweetser et al. 2012). Parents and professionals need to be aware of the difference between active and passive media experiences. Research has displayed benefits with older children engaging in active media experiences. It is also important to remember that infants and toddlers are typically unable to fully interact with active screen media in the same ways they would interact with an adult or child (Linebarger and Walker 2005).

Around the world, young children are using media at an alarming rate. Many professional organizations have become aware of the current trends towards increases in media usage and decreases in other activities. One organization that supports limiting children's use of media is the Campaign for a Commercial-Free Childhood (CCFC). Each year, in the beginning of May, the CCFC hosts an annual event that encourages children, families, and communities to turn off their screens and engage in more active community experiences (CCFC 2013).

Recommendations for Safe Media Use

Young children are exposed to a variety of influences that shape their understanding of the world. A common concern is keeping the child safe while using media. Safety can become compromised in a variety of ways. Researchers from the Fred Rogers Center for Learning and Children's Media at Saint Vincent College collaborated with professionals in the field of education in order to create a common framework that can be used as a guide to help parents and educators make appropriate decisions regarding digital media in the lives of young children. The first principle of this framework explains the importance of promoting the child's development by keeping them safe while using media. The selected media should promote active engagement and address the needs of the whole child. Media experiences need to include nurturing interactions between adults and children while enhancing creativity and exploration. Parents and professionals should ensure that the media content chosen is appropriate for the child's development. The content on the screen in the child's presence, including background television, should not be harmful to the child's emotional or psychological development. Content should not be violent or sexual in nature. Media of any form should not be used to exploit or intimidate children. The privacy and safety of all children should be respected at all times. Additionally, parents and professionals should limit the amount of advertising young children are exposed to on a daily basis (Fred Rogers Center 2012).

The recommendations listed in this chapter can guide parents and professionals working with children in selecting developmentally-appropriate experiences. Table 13.1 displays additional resources for families of young children. These resources present current information for families in order to provide positive media exposure at an age-appropriate level.

Table 13.1 Resources for families

Name of organization	Description	Website
American Academy of Pediatrics	Provides recommendations and resources to families regarding children's age-appropriate interactions with media	www.aap.org
Campaign for Commercial-Free Childhood	Information for early educators in a download specifically addressing young children's technology use in the early education classroom	www.commercialfree-childhood.org
	Parent resources aimed at providing information on the marketing schemes of products and the increase of inappropriate media	
Children Now	Addresses the impact of media in the lives of young children including children's health and education in association with media viewing	www.childrennow.org
Common Sense Media	The educators' tab provides information for ways to help families make appropriate media choices	www.commonsense-media.org
	Professional development opportunities are also presented	
	Results of the most recent data from the *Zero to Eight Studies* on children's media usage are available	
The Henry J. Kaiser Family Foundation	Conducts ongoing research studies focusing on the effects of electronic media on children ages zero to six	www.kff.org
PBS Parents	Provides advice for families on the dangers of media content. Media exposure of children ages birth to 18 is addressed along with ways for the family to remain involved	www.pbs.org/parents/

Summary

Early interactions shape the language development of infants and toddlers. Families serve as important role models and facilitators in early language acquisition. There has been an increase in the number of families in the US using media to provide language experiences for infants and toddlers. Several studies have also found increases in young children's viewing of DVDs and television programs in other countries. All families need access to the information presented in this chapter regarding the lack of developmental benefits for infants and toddlers under 2 years of age who passively view screen media. Programs are marketed toward an audience that is preverbal and in the process of gaining language skills. Families need to be aware of current research that does not support the educational claims made by these companies. Additionally, educating families on child development is a critical step towards adults making appropriate media decisions. It is important for families to be educated on the development of infants and toddlers. The need for interactions with others in the first few years of life is essential for infants and toddlers who are gaining an understanding of their world. Verbal exchanges between caregivers and infants form the foundation for receptive and expressive language skills. These interactions help infants and toddlers create labels for objects and experiences in the environment. Families with this knowledge can help their young children engage in beneficial language experiences.

Professionals in the field of education are in a unique position to inform families about age-appropriate activities and experiences. Workshops, parent meetings, handouts, newsletters, parent-teacher conferences, and open house events are all ways to distribute this information to families. Early childhood educators can use the research provided in this chapter to inform families of the dangers of passive media usage for infants and toddlers under the age of 2. As a result, families can use this information to make age-appropriate decisions regarding early language experiences and media usage.

References

American Academy of Pediatrics. (2012). Electronic media and children. http://www.aap.org/en-us/advocacy-and-policy/aap-health-initiatives/Pages/Electronic media-and-children.aspx?nfstatus=401&nftoken.

Anderson, D. R., & Pempek, T. A. (2005). Television and very young children. *American Behavioral Scientist, 48*(5), 505–522.

Anderson, D. R., Huston, A. C., Schmitt, K. L., Linebarger, D. L., & Wright, J. C. (2001). Early childhood television viewing and adolescent behavior: The recontact study. *Monographs of the Society for Research in Child Development, 66*(1), 1–147.

Australian Government Department of Health and Ageing (DoHA). (2011). *Get up and grow: Healthy eating and physical activity for early childhood–family book*. www.health.gov.au/internet/publications/publishing.nsf/Content/gug-family-toc.

Baby Einstein. (2013a). Products. http://www.babyeinstein.com/en/products/product_explorer/.

Baby Einstein. (2013b). Our story. http://www.babyeinstein.com/en/our_story/history/.

Barr, R. (2008). Attention to and learning from media during infancy and early childhood. In S. L. Calvert & B. J. Wilson (Eds.), *Blackwell handbook of child development and the media* (pp. 143–165). Malden, MA: Blackwell.

Campaign for a Commercial-Free Childhood. (2013). Screen-free week. http://www.commercialfreechildhood.org/screenfreeweek.

Christakis, D. A., Zimmerman, F. J., DiGiuseppe, D. L., & McCarty, C. A. (2004). Early television exposure and subsequent attentional problems in children. *Pediatrics, 113*(4), 708–713.

Garrison M., & Christakis, D. (2005). *A teacher in the living room? Educational media for babies, toddlers, and preschoolers*. Menlo Park: Kaiser Family Foundation. (Publication # 7427).

Hardman, M. L., Drew C. J., & Egan, M. W. (2011). *Human exceptionality* (10th ed.). Belmont, CA: Wadsworth Cengage Learning.

Hart, B., & Risley, T. R. (1995). *Meaningful differences in the everyday experience of young American children*. Baltimore, MD: Paul H. Brookes.

Hudon, T. M., Fennell, C. T., & Hoftyzer, M. (2013). Quality not quantity of television viewing is associated with bilingual toddlers' vocabulary scores. *Infant Behavior & Development, 36*(2), 245–254.

Krcmar, M. (2010). Assessing the research on electronic media, cognitive development, and infants. *Journal of Children and Electronic Media, 4*(2), 119–134.

Krcmar, M., Grela, B., & Lin, K. (2007). Can toddlers learn vocabulary from television? An experimental approach. *Media Psychology, 10*(1), 41–63.

Kuhl, P.K., Tsao, F. M., & Liu, H. M. (2003). Foreign-language experience in infancy: Effects of short-term exposure and social interaction on phonetic learning. *Proceedings of the National Academy of Sciences of the United States of America, 100*(15), 9096–9101.

Lickliter, R. (2001). The dynamics of language development: From perception to comprehension. *Developmental Science, 4*(1), 21–23.

Linebarger, D. L., & Walker, D. (2005). Infants' and toddlers' television viewing and language outcomes. *American Behavioral Scientist, 48*(5), 624–645.

Marsh, J., Brooks, G., Hughes, J., Ritchie, L., Roberts, S., & Wright, K. (2005). *Digital beginnings: Young children's use of popular culture, media and new technologies*. Sheffield: University of Sheffield, Literacy Research Centre. http://arrts.gtcni.org.uk/gtcni/bitstream/2428/DigitalBeginningsReport.pdf.

Mendelsohn, A. L., Brockmeyer, C. A., Dreyer, B. P., Fierman, A. H., Berkule-Silberman, S., & Tomopoulos, S. (2010). Do verbal interactions with infants during electronic media exposure mitigate adverse impacts on their language development as toddlers? *Infant and Child Development, 19*(6), 577–593.

Nonaka, A. M. (2004). The forgotten endangered languages: Lessons on the importance of remembering from Thailand's Ban Khor sign language. *Language and Society, 33*(5), 737–767.

Ollivier, C. (2008). France bans broadcast of TV shows for babies. *USA Today*. http://usatoday30.usatoday.com/life/television/news/2008-08-20-france-tv_N.htm.

Ouellette, G. P. (2006). What's meaning got to do with it: The role of vocabulary in word reading and reading comprehension. *Journal of Educational Psychology, 98*(3), 554–566.

Payne, A. C., Whitehurst, G. J., & Angell, A. L. (1994). The role of home literacy environment in the development of language ability in preschool children from low-income families. *Early Childhood Research Quarterly, 9*(3–4), 427–440.

Raikes, H., Pan, B. A., Luze, G., Tamis-LeMonda, C. S., Brooks-Gunn, J., Constantine, J., Tarullo, L. B., Raikes, H. A., & Rodriguez, E. T. (2006). Mother-child book reading in low-income families: Correlates and outcomes during the first three years of life. *Child Development, 77*(4), 924–953.

Rideout, V. J. (2013). *Zero to eight: Children's media use in America 2013*. San Francisco: Common Sense Media. http://www.commonsensemedia.org/research/zero-to-eight-childrens-media-use-in-america-2013.

Rideout, V. J., Hamel, E., & Kaiser Family Foundation. (2006). *The media family: Electronic media in the lives of infants, toddlers, preschoolers and their parents*. Menlo Park, CA: Henry J. Kaiser Family Foundation.

Schmidt, M. E., Pempek, T. A., Kirkorian, H. L., Lund, A. F., & Anderson, D. R. (2008). The effects of background television on the toy play behavior of very young children. *Child Development, 79*(4), 1137–1151.

Senechal, M., LeFevre, J. A., Hudson, E., & Lawson, P. (1996). Knowledge of storybooks as a predictor of young children's vocablary. *Journal of Educational Psychology, 88*(3), 520–536.

Sigman, A. (2012). Time for a view on screen time. *Archives of Disease in Childhood, 97*(11), 935–942.

Skouteris, H., & McHardy, K. (2009). Television viewing habits and time use in Australian preschool children. *Journal of Children and Media, 3*(1), 80–89.

Snow, C. E., & Dickinson, D. K. (1990). Social sources of narrative skills at home and at school. *First Language, 10*(29), 87–103.

Sweetser P., Johnson, D., Ozdowska, A., & Wyeth, P. (2012). Active versus passive screen time for young children. *Australasian Journal of Early Childhood, 37*(4), 94–98.

Tamis-LeMonda, C. S., Cristofaro, T. N., Rodriguez, E. T., & Bornstein, M. H. (2006). Early language development: Social influences in the first years of life. In L. Balter & C. S. Tamis-LeMonda (Eds.), *Child psychology: A handbook of contemporary issues* (2nd ed., pp. 79–108). New York, NY: Psychology Press.

Trainor, L. J., & Desjardins, R. N. (2002). Pitch characteristics of infant-directed speech affect infants' ability to discriminate vowels. *Psychonomic Bulletin & Review, 9*(2), 335–340.

Vygotsky, L. S. (1962). *Thought and language*. Cambridge, MA: MIT Press.

Weis, R., & Cerankosky, B. C. (2010). Effects of video-game ownership on young boys' academic and behavioral functioning: A randomized, controlled study. *Psychological Science, 21*(4), 463–470.

Weizman, E., & Greenberg, J. (2002). *Learning language and loving it: A guide to promoting children's social, language, and literacy development in early childhood settings* (2nd ed.). Toronto: The Hanen Centre.

Zimmerman, F. J., Christakis, D. A., & Meltzoff, A. N. (2007). Associations between electronic media viewing and language development in children under age 2 years. *Journal of Pediatrics, 151*(4), 364–368.

Chapter 14
Participatory Youth Culture: Young Children as Media and MOC Makers in a Post-millennial Mode

Marissa McClure and Robert W. Sweeny

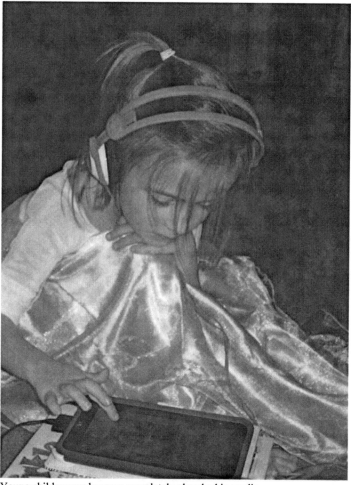

Young children can become completely absorbed in media.

Abstract This chapter looks to early childhood learning that is informed by and presented through an understanding of the convergence of contemporary networked digital technologies and young children's digital lives as media makers. Very young learners have at their disposal a vast media landscape that, when compared with earlier media forms, allows for unprecedented opportunities for making, engagement, and interaction. These opportunities are often accompanied by challenges to notions of creativity, originality, and appropriateness for young children. Online, fan-based media also allow for forms of collaboration between children and adults that challenge traditional modes of mentorship, parenting, and pedagogy. As artists and art educators who work with young children and youth, the authors present observations and analyses of young children working in out-of-school settings, creating traditional artwork, composing digital games, and constructing interactive vignettes that can inform the in-school practices of educators in multiple disciplines who work with young children.

Keywords Art education · Digital technology · Participatory culture · Social media · Early childhood education

"What's Up LEGO Fans? It's Jang Here."

Frantic music ends with a boom as the "brought to you by Jang" tagline slurps to the bottom of the YouTube viewer. A black background recedes as a shiny blue plastic humanoid figure and a man's hand takes its place. The hand belongs to Lego Jang, a San Francisco-based Internet user interface designer and Lego hobbyist, who introduces the blue plastic figure LEGO Hero Factory MOC Specimen 7E. To the participants in the vast and deeply-networked online LEGO culture, MOC means "my own creation." Pronounced "mock," MOCs are built by LEGO fans without instructions, and are often modifications of existing LEGO builds. In this case, MOC Specimen 7E is made from parts from the LEGO Hero Factory series which is billed as consisting of members of the galaxy's most heroic peace-keeping organization and from parts from the LEGO Bionicle series whose story was told through DC Comics. After making Specimen 7E, Jang shares its backstory as a kind of "mad scientist who has been experimenting with different hybridizations of biological and mechanical beings," and adds, "It's a made-up creature." Now that he's created Specimen 7E, he can make other characters and creatures that could be made by that same mad scientist.

M. McClure (✉)
The Pennsylvania State University, University Park, USA
e-mail: mam1068@psu.edu

R. W. Sweeny
Indiana University of Pennsylvania, Indiana, USA

Four-year-old Porter views and listens to Lego Jang each time he has an opportunity to interact with his father's iPhone or a friend's iPad. He memorizes and recites Jang's MOCs, always starting with the catch phrase, "Let's begin the build." He diligently saves the money he earns from chores to purchase LEGO Hero Factory heroes in small, inexpensive sets. Occasionally, he makes the heroes according to the instructions that accompany them in photos, but he spends most of his time not only making his own creations but inventing the narratives that support and surround them. His MOCs infiltrate his play spaces at home and at school, his relationships with his friends and the adults around him, and his drawings and writings.

Like the young children playing with Superheroes whom Anne Haas Dyson (1997) described, Porter's engagement with MOCs and with Lego Jang is multimodal. He also works deftly between children's and adult's toy and digital cultures. LEGOs are as often entertainment and art media for adults as they are for children, and Jang's channel, an adult channel, undoubtedly appeals to other children like Porter even if it is not intentionally children's programming. This raises questions of how adults in the child's home, care settings, and school settings interact with content that children may be using but that is not made for children. We believe, following the guidelines established by the Early Childhood Art Educators (ECAE), that the adult's role is a responsive one which values young children's diverse abilities, interests, questions, ideas, and cultural experiences, including popular culture (2006). At the same time, we acknowledge that even very young children are capable of using digital media in subaltern ways as they actively create and re-create kindercultures (Thompson 2006) that subvert adult surveillance.

As Henry Jenkins (2007) has repeatedly observed, Porter's engagement with the iPhone screens and the digital networks they represent is not passive. While Jenkins wrote his essay "Going Bonkers!" about his kindergarten son's and five kindergarten friends' viewing of *Pee-Wee's Playhouse* in response to media panic surrounding children's non-educational television viewing, his conclusions are equally applicable to our own research and observation of young children interacting with networked digital media. Jenkins found that television viewing, itself, was a form of play, networked and linked with and to other forms of play. He found that children's television viewing lacked the textual imperative of adults' television viewing. In essence, each viewing becomes a MOC that may borrow elements from the scriptwriter's intentions but inevitably becomes intertwined in multiple modes of media, making, friendships, and shared play experiences. In this case, the viewing becomes less about interpreting a plot but more about affect and feeling. This type of viewing supports other scholars' conclusions that children's engagement with new media is embodied and interactive (Ito et al 2009; Walkerdine 2007). Within this context, young children are not mere consumers of media but media producers who actively confront, construct, create, and re-create a participatory youth culture.

Young Children's Roles in Participatory Youth Culture

Even very young learners today are becoming familiar with digital technologies in many forms that may range from the iPads that appear in early childhood classrooms to family members' smart phones, to GPS technology, and so forth. These networked digital experiences offer young learners new opportunities for engagement, allowing users to interact with a friend across the room or across the country, view a webpage that increasingly reflects and responds to the personalities of the users, and use programs that extend beyond the confined spaces of the classroom or the home.

These contemporary experiences relate less to specific media processes and technologies and more to what we will refer to as *participatory youth culture*. According to media scholar Henry Jenkins, participatory youth culture describes a culture in which young people not only consume but also produce media. Building from Jenkins' work and art educator Brent Wilson's work, early childhood art educators have looked at young children's play and media using both new and traditional media as participatory youth cultures (Schulte 2011; Thompson 2006; Wilson 1974, 1976, 2007). In this chapter, we will use this term to discuss possibilities for culturally-relevant and socially-responsible educational practices that respond to the complexity of contemporary digital technologies and young children's interactions with them. Through examples drawn from our research practices, we will argue that contemporary digital media offer educators the opportunity to rethink traditions within the field of early childhood education, to develop new pedagogical strategies, and to rethink the ways that young children use digital technologies.

At a moment when digital technologies are infiltrating all aspects of daily life, it may be relevant to look to technological modes of interaction that are collaborative, dynamic, and socially-engaged. As artists—an art educator and an early childhood art educator—we see that this process will inevitably push education further from a traditional center than many find comfortable. As we will argue, this decentering can be productive. In the creative and critical acknowledgement of participatory youth culture, educators, families, and those involved with young children can build upon these three aspects of contemporary digital media: social interaction, mobile application, and personal augmentation or the ability to move things around oneself to personalize the experience.

Participatory Youth Culture is Social

The recent events in Northern Africa and the Arab Peninsula have once again raised the issue of the political potency of social media. While some may debate the direct effect that Twitter and Facebook play in political change, what cannot be debated is the general impact that social media represents. Some recent statistics demonstrate this: worldwide, there are 500 million on Facebook, 60 million on LinkedIn,

57 million on MySpace, and 5 million on Twitter. As the Pew Research Center (2010) states, nearly three quarters (73 %) of online teens and an equal number (72 %) of young adults currently use social networking sites. Unfortunately, young children are not included in these statistics. While there are ample informal accounts of young children's use of digital media and social networking sites (e.g., Stout 2010), no studies have looked at young children as a population of media users or makers. In addition, these statistics do not reveal *how* young people use these social media sites. In this chapter, we are especially concerned with young children's social media usage, which does not often appear in statistics but has been the focus of much recent educational research (e.g., NAEYC 2011). In many of these cases, young children may be using social media with family members or in classrooms with teachers, or they may be the subject of posts that include photographs, videos, and comments with or without their consent. In this chapter, we are most interested in the ways in which young children use digital media outside of school or outside of direct adult instruction. As art educators, we use the term "voluntary" (Wilson 2007) to describe these interactions with media—adults may provide media devices but children determine their own usage. Porter's viewing of Lego Jang is an example of this.

The widespread use of social media is not limited to young people in the United States; networked digital technologies are changing the social landscape of countries the world over. In countries that are heavily networked, such as South Korea and Japan, these technologies have led to new forms of literature written and read on cellular phones (Onishi 2008), along with treatment programs for those with a dependency on electronic media (Gluck 2008). South Korea, for example, recently put into effect a nightly ban on online gaming for users under 18 (Bosker 2010). These responses to social media hint at an uneasiness with certain groups as users. This discomfort extends to early childhood, where concerns have been raised about the appropriateness of online content, amount of "passive" screen time, amount of indoor versus outdoor time, and a fear of social disengagement. Such responses echo reactions to media for young children throughout the twentieth century, including fearful responses to radio and television and the subsequent push to censor young children's experiences and make them educational, not entertaining (Jenkins 2007).

Social media allows users to not only take in and reconfigure information, but also produce content just as easily, as Henry Jenkins (2007) has persuasively suggested in his research on participatory culture. Socially-networked sites designed for young children, such as Club Penguin and Webkinz, allow even the youngest users to generate content on the web. Yet young children do not only participate as media producers on platforms designed expressly for them. On social networking sites such as Facebook, YouTube, Instagram, and Flickr, young children may either generate content with assistance from family members or appear as the subjects in content created by family members. There are even hashtags on Instagram that denote photographs depicting kids: #family and #baby are two of the site's most popular, as is #adorable which is frequently used in posts of children. Bloggers compiled this list of hashtags that could either be used by or about kids: #kids, #kid,

#baby, #babies, #instakids, #instababy, #play, #happy, #smile, #instacute, #igbabies, #tiny, #little, #1nstagramtags, #child, #children, #childrenphoto, #love, #cute, #adorable, #instagood, #young, #sweet, #pretty, #handsome, #little, #young, #family, and #baby. Older children may be savvy enough to work around age barriers by creating and hiding false accounts or having family assistance in so doing (Boyd 2011). In any of these cases, young children may generate content collaboratively by directing their own actions, the actions of others, or interacting with older friends and family members.

For example, some of the most watched video pieces on YouTube feature young children as primary subjects. *David after Dentist*, which has been viewed more than 119 million times, features a young boy who is under the influence of nitrous oxide after a dental treatment. The video has generated countless remixes and made David and his father social media celebrities. Another well-known video, *Charlie Bit My Finger*, in which an infant bites his slightly older brother, has been viewed more than 500 million times. Charlie has his own channel, where viewers can purchase t-shirts or download apps. These videos feature what we might call "typical" or "cute" antics of young children. Another popular video, *3-Year-Old Crying Over Justin Bieber*, with 29 million views, features a young girl who is crying—not an action typically captured by snapshots or shared by families—because she can't see Justin Bieber.

While we might question the young child's agency in any of these videos, there are others in which children play more pivotal roles. The site *FunnyorDie* features the "film" *The Landlord* (2007) in which actor Will Ferrell interacts with the director's 2-year-old daughter, Pearl. Pearl plays a mean landlord, who drinks, curses, and humiliates the adult who is behind on his rent. Such examples cause us to confront multiple assumptions about young children's roles in digital media and the pedagogical implications of these roles. Are young children knowing participants? Are they being exploited? Are they collaborators with adults? Do they realize the power and reach of digitally-networked social media? How do they use this power? As makers? As participants? As viewers?

We would like to make a distinction between these instances and other examples of user-generated content that are made by young children. Children often make these products with assistance from adults or older family members (siblings) but generate the content themselves and appear as actors and directors. Two particularly illustrative examples include *The Scared Is Scared* (2013), film collaboration between a college student and a 6-year-old, and *Axe Cop* (2009), a series of graphic novels and a YouTube channel in which a 5-year-old storyteller and his 29-year-old cartoonist brother tell the story of a cop transformed by an axe and his crime-fighting adventures. Artists like photographers Christian Boltanski and Wendy Ewald also collaborate with children. Boltanski's collaboration, *Favorite Objects*, with young children at the Lycee Chicago involved photographing the children's favorite objects, including stuffed toys. Ewald has been collaborating with children through photographs that children make themselves since 1979 (Ewald 2000). While the video pieces we discussed above seem to involve adults creating roles for young children, in a variation of what we see as traditional adult/child or even teacher/student relationships, these examples illustrate the immense expressive and pedagogical potential of collaboration. They can be seen as examples of networked learning, of co-learning, and of adult and children co-constructing knowledge (e.g., Reggio Children 2004; Wilson 2007) together as media producers and participants in a shared culture.

The visual qualities of social media are typically not emphasized when discussing the social impact of these technologies. However, it seems that this should be the first place for art educators to begin the discussion, as social media offers the user the ability to interact in environments that are graphically-dense and visually-stimulating. Digital media allows young children to participate in networks of co-production, creating forms of expression that are widely-viewed and slickly-produced. These media forms also allow young people to engage in modes of production in increasingly-mobile ways.

Participatory Youth Culture is Mobile

Digital media is ubiquitous, embedded, embodied, and in motion. It is found in our phones, our shoes, our teddy bears, our bodies, and our Barbies. Developments in the miniaturization of circuits and lenses, and the replacement of videotape with flash memory, have allowed technologies of visuality, such as video cameras, to shrink to the point of invisibility. This has allowed for the recording of previously-clandestine spaces in the home and in the school.

Public education is, of course, public. As such, public education operates within complex networks of visuality, of seeing and being seen, of acting out and hiding from sight. Public spaces in general incorporate numerous visualities. From early Greek descriptions of the Agora, to urban areas organized according to sitelines, to descriptions of cities as visual texts (de Certeau 1984), the social order is at least partially defined and maintained through visual means (Lyon 1995).

Spaces of public schooling are no different. Educators often take into account the relationship between what is learned and where learning takes place, going back to at least John Dewey. Reform efforts such as the Open Classroom movement in the United States sought to allow students to directly structure both learning and the learning environment, although in this example the results were often chaotic and far from conducive to the educational process.

As we have previously discussed, networked digital technologies have restructured public spaces, blurring boundaries between the personal and the public through social media. They have also allowed for the blurring of the physical and the digital in numerous ways. One of the revisions most relevant to the discussion of participatory youth culture can be seen in mobile digital media, where public space is used as the field of play. In so-called "big games" such as *PacManhattan* and *PlaceStorming* v.2.0. (McGonigal 2006), the visual immersion of videogames is blended with the physical immersion of the environment as the video arcade becomes the public park.

Mobile networked devices for children, such as the Nintendo DS series, allow young users to, not only generate content to be shared via various social media platforms, but also facilitate interaction among users in real space. The built-in software, *Street PassMii Plaza*, allows DS users to locate and interact locally with one another's Miis in a virtual plaza. Users' Miis can also participate in some DS games and can interact with Wiis at home. Several large educational sites, including PBSKids, the Fred Rogers Center Early Learning Environment, and Jumpstart, develop mobile apps for young children to use on their own or family members' iPhones, iPods, and iPads.

The ability for young children to produce media forms while they are on the move has created new possibilities for the interrogation of personal space. At the same time, these technologies raise issues concerning the civil liberties of young people, as seen in the community resistance to radio frequency identification cards in Sutter, California schools (Zetter 2005). Digital media allow the user to interact and engage with space in new ways, changing the subjectivity of the user in the process.

Participatory Youth Culture is Personal

Digital media are often thought of as being cold, inert, inactive, and devoid of life. This is especially apparent in current discussions about the dangers of screen time or passive media consumption for young children (NAEYC 2012). In their joint position statement on technology and interactive media, NAEYC and the Fred Rogers Center stress the importance of active, supported, adult participation with young children using digital media in educational settings. These forms of support are meant to allay fears that young media users will become increasingly withdrawn, falling into dangerous cyberspaces where child predators lurk behind every screen name.

Identity within a participatory youth culture is fragmented and flickering. Individuals shift between social media platforms, video production, and text messages, each shift representing a unique facet of the individual user. The schizophrenic subject of Deleuze and Guattari (2004) can be visualized as a series of interconnected nodes that refuse to conform to the structure of the centralized network. In much the same way, young children's learning has been characterized as an affective assemblage (Olsson 2009) in which children move in between adult-directed and child-directed forms of media making and play.

Young children are often seamlessly able to negotiate complex roles through their interactions with digital media in the same manner that governs their use of more traditional forms of media in early childhood: drawing, blocks, and dramatic play, for example. In our research with young children and digital video, we have found children engage in processes of play with digital media in ways that are familiar, not distant, to us (McClure 2013). Five-year-old Malachi and 29-year-old Ethan might use YouTube to tell *Axe Cop*'s story, but his narrative is one that has populated school yards and playrooms since the years in which Paley (2004) and

Davies (2003) first wrote about young children's play. YouTube might not be an educational app, but in the story of *Axe Cop*, Ethan engages in multi-modal literacy in the way that Dyson (1997) has so eloquently described. The co-creators of *The Scared Is Scared* use the video sharing platform, *Vimeo*, in ways in which educators in the past have used readers' theater. In other examples we have studied in art classrooms (McClure 2013), preschool children who are using digital video to record both scripted and unscripted play episodes have assumed the roles of directors, actors, and critics alongside the roles of chasers, rescuers, and game-players.

Pedagogical Potentials of Participatory Youth Culture

If educators acknowledge the ways that digital technologies intersect with notions of artistic production in childhood, then perhaps the practices described in this chapter can inform future pedagogical approaches. In particular, we are drawn to examples of interaction between participatory youth culture and collaboration with adult culture and young children's voluntary uses of digital media as media makers as examples of possible pedagogical models. For example, art educator Brent Wilson (2007) has vividly described scenes of adults and young people drawing together in in-school and out-of-school settings. We envision this collaboration could extend to adults and young children producing new media art—digital video, video games, locative media—together and sharing their productions via social networks. Such an approach to pedagogy aligns with contemporary concepts of negotiated curriculum including the project approach (Katz and Chard 2000), co-construction of knowledge (Project Zero and Reggio Children 2004), and pedagogical practices informed by Deleuze and Guattari (Olsson 2009). Similarly, educators who emphasize the narrative in learning (Egan 1989) and fantasy play (Duncum 1985; Paley 2005) might provide voluntary experiences for young children to incorporate digital media into their narratives, as Porter does with his Lego MOCs. Both of these pedagogical practices diverge from educator-centered introduction of digital media experiences (e.g., digital flash cards on an iPad) in order to explore the expressive potentials of digital media as expressive media: visuality, networked possibilities, and deeply affective and embodied learning. Participatory youth culture is an ever-changing landscape. Young learners will certainly not pause for educators, researchers, and families to determine the best practices for digital media use. We must be flexible, mobile, and skeptical, even as we celebrate the educational possibilities in the video game, the app, and the webpage.

References

Boltanski, C. (1997). Favorite objects. http://www.lyceechicago.org/lycee/web/artists/boltanski_swf/boltanski_flash.html.
Bosker, B. (2010). South Korea imposes midnight ban to combat addiction. Huffington Post. http://www.huffingtonpost.com/2010/04/12/south-korea-imposes-midni_n_534782.html.

Boyd, D. (2011). Why parents help tweens violate Facebook's 13+ Rule. *Huffington Post.* http://www.huffingtonpost.com/danah-boyd/tweens-on-facebook_b_1068793.html.

Davies, B. (2003). *Frogs and snails and feminist tales: Preschool children and gender.* New York, NY: Hampton.

Deleuze, G., & Guattari, F. (2004). *A thousand plateaus: Capitalism and schizophrenia* (Trans: Massumi, B.) (2nd ed.). Minneapolis, MN: University of Minnesota Press (Original work published 1980).

Duncum, P. (1985). The fantasy embeddedness of girls' horse drawings. *Art Education, 38,* 42–46.

Dyson, A. (1997). *Writing superheroes: Contemporary childhood, popular culture, and classroom literacy.* New York, NY: Teachers College Press.

Early Childhood Art Educators. (2006). Art: Essential for early learning. Early Childhood Art Educators Issues Group and National Art Education Association position paper. http://www.arteducators.org/community/committees-issues-groups/ECAE_Position_Statement.pdf.

Egan, K. (1986). *Teaching as storytelling: An alternative approach to teaching and curriculum in the elementary school.* Chicago, IL: University of Chicago Press.

Ewald, W. (2000). *Secret games: Collaborative works with children, 1969–1999.* Durham, NC: Center for Documentary Studies at Duke University.

Ito, M., Herr-Stephenson, B., Perkel, D., & Sims, C. (Eds.). (2009). *Hanging out, messing around, and geeking out: Kids living and learning with new media.* Cambridge, MA: MIT Press.

Jenkins, H. (2007). *The wow climax: Tracing the emotional impact of popular culture.* New York, NY: NYU Press.

Katz, L., & Chard, S. (2000). *Engaging children's minds: The project approach.* Norwood, NJ: Ablex.

McClure, M. (2013). The monster and lover girl: Preschool children's digital video production. *Studies in Art Education, 55* (1),18–34.

National Association for the Education of Young Children (NAEYC), & Fred Rogers Center for Early Learning and Children's Media at Saint Vincent College. (2012). Technology and interactive media as tools in early childhood programs serving children from birth through age 8. http://www.naeyc.org/content/technology-and-young-children.

Olsson, L. (2009). *Movement and experimentation in young children's learning: Deleuze and Guattari in early childhood education.* London, England: Routledge.

Paley, V. (2005). *A child's work: The importance of fantasy play.* Chicago, IL: University of Chicago Press.

Schulte, C. M. (2011). Verbalization in children's drawing performances: Toward a metaphorical continuum of inscription, extension, and re-inscription. *Studies in Art Education, 53*(1), 20–34.

Stout, H. (2010, October 15). Toddlers' favorite toy: The iPhone. *New York Times,* 15 October. http://www.nytimes.com/2010/10/17/fashion/17TODDLERS.html?pagewanted=all.

Thompson, C. (2006). The "Ket" aesthetic: Visual culture in childhood. In J. Fineberg (Ed.), *When we were young: New perspectives on the art of the child* (pp. 31–43). Berkeley, CA: University of California Press.

Urwin, C. (1995). Turtle power: Illusion and imagination in children's play. In C. Bazalgette & D. Buckingham (Eds.), *In front of the children: Screen entertainment and young audiences* (pp. 127–140). London, England: British Film Institute.

Walkerdine, V. (2007). *Children, gender, and video games: Towards a relational approach to multi-media.* New York, NY: Palgrave Macmillan.

Wilson, B. (1974). The superheroes of JC Holz: Plus an outline of a theory of child art. *Art Education, 27*(8), 2–9.

Wilson, B. (1976). Little Julian's impure drawings: Why children make art. *Art Education, 17*(2), 45–61.

Wilson, B. (2007). Art, visual culture, and child/adult collaborative images: Recognizing the other-than. *Visual Arts Research, 33*(2), 6–20.

Zetter, K. (2005). School RFID plan gets an "F." *Wired Online.* http://www.wired.com/politics/security/news/2005/02/66554.

Chapter 15
Young Children at Risk of Digital Disadvantage

Genevieve Marie Johnson

Abstract It is increasingly apparent that children who engage with digital technologies under certain conditions and in specific ways demonstrate numerous cognitive, emotional, and social advantages. Conversely, children who do not have access to emerging technologies or those who engage with technology in unhealthy ways are digitally disadvantaged. For example, children who play video games for extended periods of time and those who use the internet to isolate rather than network are at risk of social and emotional problems. The Ecological Techno-Subsystem and Techno-Microsystem provide a comprehensive conceptual framework by which to organize and interpret the large body of research on the developmental consequences of technology use during the early years of life. Such a theoretical and evidence-based foundation provides for specific interventions aimed at minimizing early childhood digital disadvantage. For example, public library internet access programs focused on promoting digital information, communication, and recreation literacy may be specifically directed toward young children residing in disadvantaged communities.

Keywords Young children · Risk · Technology · Child development · Digital divide · Digital exclusion · Digital disadvantage

Variation in Early Childhood Digital Experience

Our school has a class set of iPads which are signed out of our library by teachers on a period-by-period basis. I was excited to use the iPads with my first grade students to review and reinforce the mathematical concepts of shape and ordering on the basis of size. In preparation, I had ensured that the iPads had the appropriate icons on the desktop so the children could easily access the applications. "Boys and girls," I started, "I have something special for you, so listen carefully and look at me. These are …" I was interrupted by several children overcome with excitement and delight as they saw the iPads I was about to distribute. A few children began to laugh aloud and vibrate with anticipation. I noticed that some children

G. M. Johnson (✉)
Curtin University, Perth, Australia
e-mail: g.johnson@curtin.edu.au

K. L. Heider, M. Renck Jalongo (eds.), *Young Children and Families in the Information Age*, Educating the Young Child 10, DOI 10.1007/978-94-017-9184-7_15,
© Springer Science+Business Media Dordrecht 2015

appeared confused as they glanced from the iPads to the other children and then to me. Before I could continue, one child shouted "iPads!" and another implored loudly, "Me please, Miss Smith, me first!" As the iPads were distributed, some children immediately scrolled the screen as they searched for applications while other children appeared increasingly confused and disoriented. As the lesson progressed, most of my time was spent helping children who were unfamiliar with the iPad technology. The children who were the most comfortable with the technology spent the most time identifying shapes and organizing shapes on the basis of size. My lesson included, for some children, digital remediation and, for other children, curriculum acceleration.

Early childhood teachers frequently observe variation in children's background experiences and routinely scaffold instruction to allow all students to move toward mastery of learning objectives. The disparity in out-of-school exposure to digital technologies, however, is particularly evident and immediately consequential in school-based use of new technologies. In teaching her first-grade mathematics lesson, Miss Smith was taken aback by the extreme variation in her students' capacity to interact with iPad applications. Those children who were digitally competent were at a learning advantage; those children who were digitally challenged may have been further disadvantaged by decreased opportunities to engage with enriching mathematics applications. Indeed, based on an increasingly-convincing body of research evidence (Johnson 2012a), the use of digital technology during the early years has a powerful effect on child developmental outcomes. However, because young children in technologically-advanced nations are highly dependent upon adults for access to innovation, children vary widely in their experiences with digital technology, and this is particularly true before mandated school attendance (Johnson 2010a).

This chapter starts with a historical interpretation of adult anxiety regarding young children and technological innovation. Ecological theoretical models of the effect of digital technology use on child development are reviewed and promoted including the Techno-Subsystem and Techno-Microsystem. Recent research findings on the effect of digital technology use on young children's development and learning are synthesized. Based upon that research synthesis, a definition of early childhood digital disadvantage is proposed, that is, digital experiences that are insufficient or inadequate relative to those of developmental peers. From an ecological perspective, digital disadvantage is potentially addressed through support for families, schools, and communities.

Technological Innovation and Young Children: A Historical Analysis

Most typically, fear and suspicion surround the introduction of new technologies, particularly with respect to the young (Johnson 2006); the more vulnerable the youth, the greater parental fear of exposure to the unknown. For example, when microwave ovens first became popular, there was widespread fear that warming baby food with the new technology would cause cancer. As has been the case with every technological innovation, especially those with which parents and teachers have limited personal experience, there is fear that the innovation will actually cause physical harm (e.g., screen media damages eye sight), expose children to risk (e.g., the internet is a depository of uncensored pornography), and displace healthy activities (e.g., playing videogames reduces outdoor play). In an evolutionary context, such parental fear of exposing children to the unknown has, no doubt, served the species very well.

In the history of technology, innovation is typically first embraced by socially privileged young adults such as male university students of high socioeconomic status (Johnson 2007). Over time, the use of the new technology fans out across the population in predictable patterns. In the case of personal computers with internet connectivity, for example, over the course of two decades, internet use increased both up and down the age range; that is, users became progressively older (Erickson and Johnson 2011) and progressively younger (Johnson 2010a). Simultaneously, as personal computers and internet connectivity became more available and thus more affordable over the course of two decades, progressively more individuals—irrespective of social situation—became digitally connected (Broadband Commission for Digital Development 2012). Indeed, internet connectivity is increasingly perceived as essential for participation in a democracy (Hargittai 2008). The *digital divide*, the first term used to describe social disparity in computer use and internet access (Graham 2011), is unlikely to close because, as new technologies emerge, there are predictable differences in access, especially early access in the processes of popularization of the innovation. This is currently the case with emerging telephone technology where learning and communication advantages are associated with full keypad touchscreen smartphones as opposed to traditional alphanumeric multi-press keypad cell phones (Kent and Johnson 2012).

In an increasingly digitalized society, young children commonly use a range of digital technologies, most notably, television, video games, the internet (Hofferth 2010) and, most recently, cell phones (Divan et al. 2012) and technology-based toys (Gibbons 2012). Based on a large representational sample of American parents of children aged 0–6 years, on a typical day, 2, 13, and 16 % for ages 0–2, 3–4, and 5–6, respectively, played video games (an average of 55 min). Approximately 4 % of 0 to 2-year-olds, 20 % of 3 to 4-year-olds, and 27 % of 5 to 6-year-olds used a computer on a typical day (an average of 50 min at the keyboard) (Vandewater et al. 2007). In 2009, 78 % of 5 to 7-year-olds in Britain had home access to the internet, and 84 % had home access to a video game console (Ofcom 2009). In a sample of Canadian 6 to 8-year-olds, 49 % reported using the internet to play games *sometimes* while 32.5 % reported using the internet to play games *often* (Johnson 2010a). According to the Australian Bureau of Statistics (2009), 60 % of 5 to 8-year-old children use the internet, and 2 % use mobile phones. In 2010, the Swedish Ministry of Culture reported that 25 % of Swedish children 2–5 years of age use computers several times every week (Lindahl and Folkesson 2012). Roberts and Foehr (2008) observed that digital media consumption spikes during the late preschool period, decreases during the early school years, and then rises again at approximately 8 years of age. Due to maturational processes, all environmental experiences during infancy and early childhood, including use of digital technologies, are of considerable consequence to child developmental and learning outcomes (Johnson 2010b; Sprenger 2010).

The pediatric recommendation that very young children should not be exposed to screen media and digital technologies may be interpreted in the context of the history of technological innovation. The digital revolution created devices which were quickly adopted by young people (e.g., video games) but with which adults had no experience and thus no understanding. The evolutionary predisposition to protect the young from the unknown may, at least to some extent, be responsible for the common, but frequently unfounded, assumption that digital technology is harmful to young children (Boice and Tarone 2011). Currently, there are two conflicting anxieties surrounding young children and digital technology; first, that the use of such technology may harm children, for example, by exposure to inappropriate content and, second, that children who do not have experiences with these same technologies will be socially and educationally disadvantaged (Johnson 2012a).

For more than 100 years, facilitation of the processes of child learning and development has been guided by theory and research (Keil 2000). In evaluating the developmental consequences of young children engaging with digital devices, ecological systems theory (Bronfenbrenner 1997, 2005) provides a comprehensive conceptual framework by which to organize and interpret relevant empirical evidence and pave the way for the best possible treatment of young children.

The Ecological Techno-Subsystem and Techno-Microsystem

There is a reciprocal and spiraling interaction between child development and elements of the child's environment. For example, as infants develop the ability to manipulate objects in their environment, their manipulation of those objects affects their subsequent development. To illustrate, as an infant shakes a rattle, there is increased understanding of sounds and objects and increased ability to use the muscles in hands and arms. Such increased understanding and ability affect subsequent infant interactions with objects in the environment. All experiences, particularly experiences involving the infant's sensory input and motor movement, influence the course of that infant's development. Not surprisingly, parents and caregivers are eager to provide infants with a range of stimulating and safe environmental experiences including toys and playful adult interactions. As children mature, their capacity to interact with elements in their environment correspondingly increases. Those environmental interactions, in turn, affect patterns of continuous maturation and development. Parents and teachers are eager to provide the maturing child with a range of stimulating and safe environmental experiences including books, games, community exploration, and supervised peer interactions.

Socio-cognitive theorists (Piaget and Inhelder 1973; Vygotsky 1978) propose a reciprocal and spiraling relationship between cognitive capacity and environmental stimulation; that is, cognitive capacity causes the individual to seek out stimulating experiences, which in turn increase cognitive capacity, which causes the individual to seek out more stimulating experiences, and so on. In comparing standardized measures of cognitive ability with patterns of internet use, Johnson (2008) reported that cognitive test scores were consistently greater for frequent users, as opposed to infrequent users, both in general and with respect to specific applications such as online communication. Although correlation does not establish causation, it may be that "cognitive capacity causes the individual to use Internet applications, use of Internet applications causes increased cognitive capacity, which in turn causes the individual to seek out more stimulating Internet applications, and so on" (p. 2103).

Ecological theory provides a comprehensive view of environmental influences on learning and development by situating the child within a system of relationships affected by multiple levels of the surrounding environment (Johnson 2010c). Bronfenbrenner (1977) organized the contexts of development into five nested environmental systems, with bi-directional influences within and among these systems. The *microsystem* refers to direct or immediate interactions (i.e., family, peers, and school). The *mesosystem* is comprised of connections between immediate environments (e.g., home-school interactions). The *exosystem* includes settings that indirectly affect child development (e.g., parent's workplace). The *macrosystem* refers to social ideologies and cultural values that affect the developing child (e.g., child protection services and childcare regulations). The *chronosystem* highlights the effect of time on all systems and all learning and developmental processes (e.g., innovative technologies). As Bronfenbrenner (2005) expanded his theoretical model, he proposed a bio-ecological perspective which viewed the child's biology (e.g., genetic predispositions) as part of the microsystem.

Ecological theory (Bronfenbrenner 1977, 1979) emerged prior to the digital revolution and the developmental impact of then available technology (e.g., analogue television) was conceptually situated in the child's microsystem. To counter this, Johnson and Puplampu (2008) proposed the *ecological techno-subsystem*, a dimension of the microsystem, which includes child interactions with both human (e.g., communicator) and nonhuman (e.g., hardware) elements of digital technologies. Further, they argued that the developmental impact of using digital technologies during childhood is, theoretically, mediated by techno-subsystem interactions which occur in the microsystem (Fig. 15.1). To illustrate, in industrialized nations, elements of children's microsystem (e.g., home and school) are affected by cell phones (e.g., communication with peers). School internet portals are mesosystemic because they connect home and school by allowing parents online access to their children's homework assignments, attendance records, and grades. Parent use of the internet at work, an element of the exosystem (an environment in which the child does not directly participate), may indirectly affect children's home internet access which may ultimately impact on child development and learning (Johnson 2010c). The macrosystem reflects selective cultural endorsement of uses of digital technology (i.e., for school learning and family communication).

Fig. 15.1 Ecological Techno-Subsystem (Johnson and Puplampu 2008)

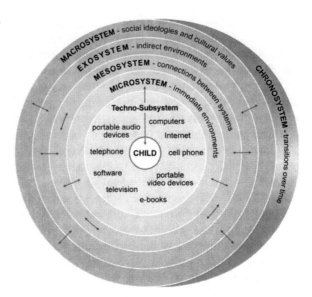

While the techno-subsystem highlights the importance of technology in children's learning and development, it fails to provide a precise description of the mechanisms of influence. As presented in Fig. 15.2, the *techno-microsystem* includes the bio-ecology of the child (i.e., cognitive, social, emotional, and physical development) which unfolds in response to various uses of digital technologies across various microsystemic contexts. The microsystem rings surrounding the developing child should be considered as fluid, and the descriptors in the rings are for purposes of illustration. That is, child developmental outcomes are typically conceptualized in terms of domains which include social, emotional, cognitive, and physical. But child development is holistic (e.g., physical development includes brain changes, and brain changes affect and are affected by cognitive development). Further, use of digital technology may also have a range of intentions and outcomes (e.g., iPad applications often provide children with both information and recreation). Nonetheless, the ecological techno-microsystem provides a conceptual framework for organizing dimensions of child learning and development in relation to digital technologies for communication, information, and recreation mediated by home, school, and community opportunities and constraints. "Theoretically, the techno-microsystem has the capacity to, for example, coordinate children's learning experiences across home, school, and childcare environments, protect children from harmful at-home online experiences by community-based web-awareness initiatives, and prioritize school-based hardware for children without home connectivity" (Johnson 2010b, p. 35).

Fig. 15.2 Ecological Techno-Microsystem (Johnson 2010b)

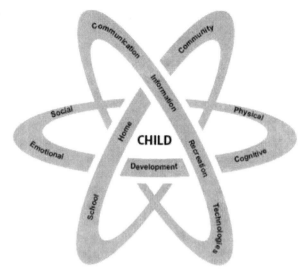

The Effect of Digital Technology on Young Children

The developmental value or liability of any environmental experience may best be determined from an ecological perspective, that is, in the context of the opportunities and constraints that define available environmental experiences from which a child, parent, caregiver, or teacher may select. Obviously, a child should not ingest any substance that may be contaminated unless, of course, there are no other options, as may be the case in situations of starvation and draught. If a mother is experiencing acute gastrointestinal distress, it is better for her young child to view many educational videos and extensively play digital games rather than experience limited environmental stimulation for several days. Scientific research, unfortunately but understandably, provides information on general trends in populations and rarely considers the complexity of individual situations. It is thus that the ecological techno-microsystem may provide a practical focus on the individual child-in-context while simultaneously providing a theoretical structure on which to organize the empirical evidence regarding the effect of digital technology on young children. Indeed, research findings concerning the educational and developmental consequences of using small screen technologies during early childhood are collectively complex and subject to interpretation (Johnson 2009; Livingstone 2009).

One in six Australian children aged 6–7 years has a television in his/her bedroom (Rutherford et al. 2010). Is this good or bad? Based on a comprehensive review of recent research, Mitrofan et al. (2009) concluded that there was insufficient, contradictory, and methodologically-flawed evidence on the association between television viewing and aggression in children. Likewise, television viewing after 3 years of age has not been linked to attention problems (Zimmerman and Christakis 2007). Similarly, Moses (2008) reviewed the research on the effect of television on young children's literacy and concluded that moderate amounts of television viewing were beneficial for reading. The content of programs viewed by children was important. Programs that aim to promote literacy in young children positively impacted early literacy skills, and there were limitations to the existing literature. Research that takes into account program content generally finds that educational programming is associated with positive academic outcomes while entertainment programs are negatively associated (Brown and Marin 2009). Gentzkow and Shapiro (2008) used heterogeneity in the timing of television's introduction to different local markets to identify the effect of preschool television exposure on standardized test scores during adolescence. Their findings suggested that an additional year of preschool television exposure raised average adolescent test scores by about 0.02 standard deviations. For reading and general knowledge scores, the positive effects were largest for adolescents from households where English was not the primary language, whose mothers had less than a high school education, and for nonwhite children. However, after reviewing 50 years of research, Schmidt and Anderson (2007) noted that a relation between television viewing and reading achievement past the early school years could not be established. From an ecological perspective, research findings support the conclusion that, in environments where young children have many choices of cognitive stimulation, moderate viewing of educational programs facilitates development. In environments where young children have limited choices of cognitive stimulation, extended viewing of educational programs may be necessary to facilitate cognitive development.

Consistent with research on the effect of television on young children, the educational and developmental consequences of playing video games are collectively complex and again subject to multiple interpretations (Steinkuehler 2010). DeBell and Chapman (2006) concluded that computer use promotes cognitive development in children, "specifically in the area of visual intelligence, where certain computer activities—particularly games—may enhance the ability to monitor several visual stimuli at once, to read diagrams, recognize icons, and visualize spatial relationships" (p. 3). In contrast, Johnson (2009) reported that at-home, online learning and communicating (but not playing and browsing) were associated with advanced child development in expressive language and metacognitive planning. Lee et al. (2009) found that, among young school-aged children, time spent reading was negatively related to time spent playing video games. Swing et al. (2010) reported an association between playing video games and increased attention problems during childhood. Focus group interviews with children revealed the perception of overarousal and loss of awareness of surroundings during video game playing (Funk et al. 2006). Anderson et al. (2007) concluded that "no matter how many risk and protective factors the child already has, playing violent video games still adds additional risk for future increased aggressive behaviour" (p. 141). Nonetheless, the learning of 4 to 5-year-olds was reportedly maximized by a combination of traditional teaching methods and interactive video games (Hong et al. 2013). Schotland and Littman (2012) clearly established the learning benefits of video games for teaching complex concepts to 4 to 6-year-olds. From an ecological perspective, research findings support the conclusion that, in environments where young children have many choices of cognitive stimulation, moderate playing of educational video games facilitates development. In environments where young children have limited choices of cognitive stimulation, extended playing of educational video games may be preferable to other repetitive activities.

Research findings on the relationship between internet and computer use and child learning and development appear to be more uniformly positive than those associated with video gaming. Kumtepe (2006) observed that computer literate kindergarten children were rated by their teachers as demonstrating better social skills than children who were less computer proficient. Cole and Hilliard (2006) reported that reading skills in a sample of third grade students increased more with web-based than with traditional literacy instruction. In comparing traditional and computer-assisted remedial reading interventions, the enduring effectiveness of digital learning tools was apparent (Saine et al. 2010). A meta-analysis undertaken by Cavanaugh et al. (2004) confirmed a positive relationship between internet use during childhood and school achievement. One explanation for this is that the internet, although rich in graphic display, is primarily a text-based medium and therefore "the more a child uses the Internet, the more he/she reads" (Jackson et al. 2007, p. 188). Fiorini (2010) concluded positive and enduring cognitive benefits of computer use during early childhood with evidence of associations with proactive social behavior. In a comprehensive review of the literature, McCarrik and Li (2007) concluded that young children who used computers, compared to those who did not, demonstrated significant and global developmental superiority. From an ecological perspective, internet and computer use facilitate a range of positive developmental outcomes during early childhood, although physical and social interaction must not be limited. As previously argued, "Current anxiety surrounding children's Internet use should be for those whose cognitive processes are not influenced by the cultural tool" (Johnson 2006, p. 570).

Unlike technologies such as the internet, television, and video games, cell telephones are a relatively recent childhood phenomenon, and research is just emerging. Given historical patterns of digital technology penetration, younger children might reasonably be expected to increasingly use cell phones. Bond (2010) indicated a possible explanation for this. Cell phones are viewed by children as essential to supporting relationships and offering security and reassurance. Mezei et al. (2007) reported a strong relationship between cell phone ownership during childhood and duration of time spent watching television and playing computer games, although no relationships to attention or obesity emerged. According to Cameron and Hutchison (2009), young children's telephone-mediated language can, under certain circumstances, be more generative, explicit, and elaborative than previously believed. From an educational perspective, using cell phones to learn is expected to increase among all age groups (Kim et al. 2008). Smart phones may be particularly beneficial as they have applications for young children which support the development of emergent literacy (Blanchard and Moore 2010). Young children's increasing engagement with cell telephones, text messaging, and similar communications technologies might well be harnessed for pedagogical purposes in emergent literacy (Gillen et al. 2005). "In contrast to teacher reports, recent research suggests that use of textese (i.e., idiosyncratic written conventions used in text messaging) is positively associated with Standard English literacy skills during childhood" (Johnson 2012b, p. 1). From an ecological perspective, cell phone use during the early years has the potential to facilitate child development if used to increase communicative opportunities.

Digital technology has had a strong influence on children's toys and the nature of play (Spatariu et al. 2012). "In today's digitally-intense world, young children represent a key target demographic for digital consumer electronic devices" (Gibbons 2012, p. 4). There are now laptop computers for infants and toddlers, electronic talking books, animated stuffed animals and dolls, digital cameras for very small hands, and battery-driven toys including infant rattles and crib mobiles (Wooldridge and Shapka 2012). The toys listed on the Parent's Choice Awards (2009) included toys with electronic and computer components including a night-vision camcorder, a laptop device that teaches spelling and counting, remote control devices, board games with electronic features, and a robotic insect. The buzzword at the 2012 Toy Fair was *augmented reality*. Many of the exhibitors introduced toy cars, puzzles, board games, and other playthings that work with iPads or other handheld devices. The idea is that, rather than replace the physical toy, digital applications enhance play and increase toy sales. Several toy companies have launched entire product lines based on this concept, including Mattel's Apptivity, Spin-Master's Appfinity, Hasbro's zAPPed, and WowWee's AppGear brands, while others launched one or more individual augmented-reality items (Raugust 2012). Because popular use of such toys is relatively recent, the effect of their use on child development and learning has yet to be systematically investigated. It seems likely, however, that use of such toys will soon be linked to positive developmental outcomes for children, perhaps because only children who are socially advantaged have opportunities to engage with new high-tech toys. From an ecological perspective, because technical competence is culturally-valued and because technology-enhanced play experiences often stimulate problem-solving, memory, and communication, electronic toys likely facilitate child development and learning particularly in the context of a wide range of varied environmental opportunities. Young children without a wide variety of culturally-valued and stimulating environmental experiences are unlikely to develop to their maximum genetic potential (i.e., bio-ecology). With respect to technologically-advanced societies, while it is possible that a young child without digital experiences might develop normally, in general, it seems quite unlikely.

Young Children at Digital Disadvantage

Consider a 5-year-old starting kindergarten having never watched television, never talked on a telephone, and never listened to recorded nursery rhymes. Such restricted experiences would make it difficult for the child to feel comfortable in the increasingly digitalized early childhood education classroom (Gibbons 2012).

Equally, such a child may have difficulty interacting effectively with other children whose conversation includes television characters and electronic toys. However, 50 years ago, few children viewed television, talked on telephones, and listened to recorded nursery rhymes. In understanding child development, there are few absolutes because developmental expectations reflect culture, and cultural nuances change over time (i.e., the ecological chronosystem) particularly in technologically-advanced societies. From an ecological perspective, developmentally-ideal environmental experiences can only be conceptualized in the context of available opportunities which differ widely across children. If all children enjoyed an equal variety of culturally-endorsed environmental opportunities, the author's recommendation would be that all children experience, for example, during the first year of life, auditory stimulation in the form of consistent communicative partners who provide ample age-appropriate language including singing, rhymes, naming, explanation of relationships between objects, and pairing vocabulary with visual and tactical experiences. Since all children do not have access to such a communicative ideal, digital recordings may provide some level of audiological stimulation in some situations. During the seventh year of life, to continue the example, a child would benefit from familiar and trusted communicative partners and communicative modes including text-based (e.g., email to grandparents), video-based (e.g., Skype with relocated playmates), and digitally-mediated (e.g., cell phone calls to working parents). Such digital experiences, in the context of a variety of physical activities and face-to-face human interaction, may be considered ideal.

But extreme digitalization of experience, particularly of certain types, according to the research evidence, is not in the best interest of young children, except perhaps in the most extreme and unusual circumstances where environmental opportunities are severely restricted. During the early years, exposure to and use of digital technologies may best be conceptualized as environmental experiences that reside within a context of a wide range of culturally-valued and age-appropriate experiences that simultaneously maximize child physical, cognitive, social, and emotional developmental potential (i.e., bio-ecology). To illustrate, a child may feel emotionally comforted by cell phone contact with parents (Bond 2010), but such contact should augment, not replace, direct and intense personal contact with parents. Most young children would benefit from playing educational video games (Schotland and Littman 2012), but no young child should be exposed to prolonged use of violent video games (Anderson et al. 2007; Funk et al. 2006). A young child with high needs for cognitive stimulation would benefit from digital multitasking during quiet time (e.g., listening to a talking book while practicing concepts with an iPad application). Thus, digital disadvantage during the early years is not a binary state but, rather, a matter of degree. In technologically advanced nations, digital disadvantage is manifest by the degree to which young children lack digital experiences that are culturally-valued, age-appropriate, and normative. Digital disadvantage may include, for example, isolated and excessive television viewing and video gaming which will not, generally, maximize child developmental outcomes.

Addressing Digital Disadvantage: The Role of the Family

Young children, most typically, reside in families, and the characteristics of those families, from an ecological theoretical perspective, determine the degree of digital advantage or disadvantage. Within the context of the family, two issues particularly influence the quality and quantity of young children's digital experiences: physical access and patterns of *co-use* (a term preferred over terms such as monitoring or supervision). As evidenced by the mounting literature on the digital divide, not all children have home access to digital communication and information technologies (Livingstone and Helpsper 2007). Family socioeconomic status, including parent education and family income, is at the heart of the digital divide (Krebeck 2010), and such family characteristics are linked to patterns of young children's use of technology. Indeed, numerous researchers have concluded that differences in access to emerging technologies tend to reinforce and replicate existing social inequalities (Dutton and Helsper 2007; Eynon 2009). In a comprehensive cross-sectional and longitudinal analysis of technology use among children 5–8 years of age, Lee et al. (2009) reported that family income significantly predicted children's use of new technologies such as personal computers. Correspondingly, higher parental education has frequently been associated with decreased television viewing by children (Australian Communications and Media Authority 2009; Baxter and Hayes 2007). Thus, perhaps not surprisingly, young children who are socially advantaged in terms of family characteristics are also digitally advantaged by virtue of the same family characteristics. Technology co-use, however, adds another dimension to the digital advantage—disadvantage continuum.

Co-use is a general term used to refer to the social sharing or cooperative use of digital technologies (Johnson 2012a). With respect to young children and digital technology, co-use with a more mature partner facilitates the development of digital competencies while simultaneously protecting the child from digital risk (e.g., inappropriate content and excessive use). Cho and Cheon (2005) surveyed families and found that parents' perceived control, obtained through shared web activities and family cohesion, reduced children's exposure to negative internet content. Lee and Chae (2007) reported a positive relationship between parental mediation techniques (i.e., website recommendation and internet co-use) and children's educational attainment. Yoon (2003) observed that cell phone use extended parental control because contact and monitoring of children was always available. From a developmental perspective, young children's digital experiences are always improved when shared with a partner who explains, extends, questions, confirms, monitors, and adjusts to maximize the cognitive, social, and emotional benefits of the digital interactions. This is equally true of television viewing and video gaming. The role of the family is unchanged following the digital revolution. That is, families remain directly responsible for maximizing the developmental outcomes of children during the early years. Parents make choices on behalf of young children and those choices, if possible, should provide children with a wide range of culturally-valued and age-appropriate experiences. In this regard, excessive use of digital devices should be avoided. Varied environment experiences will include, as the child grows, increased use and co-use of digital technologies that facilitate concept development, social interaction, and emotional security. As families consider childcare options, the digital opportunities available to young children should be considered.

Addressing Digital Disadvantage: The Role of the Childcare Provider

Many parents of young children rely on various forms of non-family childcare in order to engage in paid employment, run a business, increase educational attainment, or because it is deemed in the best interest of the child (Ansari and Winsler 2013). Research has clearly established that high quality child care does not harm children and, in fact, often complements parenting to maximize child developmental outcomes (Bekkhus et al. 2011; Gimenez-Nadal and Molina 2013). While high-quality care is typically described in terms of staff-child ratios and child health and safety, recent focus group interviews conducted with low-income parents of children aged 2–5 years in Baltimore revealed parents' desire that their young children experience digital technologies while in care settings (Forry et al. 2012). Apparently, parents understand the importance of young children developing information and communication technology (ICT) literacy. According to Morrison (2008), when child care professionals support children's use of computer technology in their centers, it helps children to develop skills such as the use of a keyboard and basic computer software. "It also assists children to build learning concepts around computer use and digital media over time. This will ultimately help children to function in learning environments where skills involving computer use are beneficial and/or necessary" (p. 15). *Computer Gym* is an online site that provides weekly computer-based lessons to pre-school children at childcare centers. Initial lessons of the program "focus on early computer skills such as mouse control and movement, confidence and social skills on the computer. All children will also do activities with an emphasis on self and relationships as well as early literacy and numeracy topics" (Computer Gym 2013, p. 1).

Despite parental desire and increasingly-available opportunities, many child care centers remain reluctant to include digital devices in young children's play and learning. This may be a manifestation of continued fear of exposing the young to the unknown, a common pattern in the history of technological innovation, as previously discussed. It may also reflect misunderstanding of the nature of recent digital innovation. The American Academy of Pediatrics recommends limiting screen time to 1–2 h of quality programming per day for preschool-age children (Tandon et al. 2011). Such a recommendation, however, refers most obviously to television. Many current uses of digital technology, although they include a small screen, are highly interactive. For example, the internet is not like other media in as much as it is used primarily for communicating, information gathering, and playing games rather than for passively experiencing narratives (Johnson 2009). iPads are promoted as extremely useful for young children (Dixon 2011) because tablets' mobile capability, touch screen, and intuitive operation make the devices appealing to many, and are especially valuable to children with special needs (Johnson 2013). From an ecological perspective, there are few absolutes in terms of maximizing child developmental outcomes. There are numerous situations in which young children may benefit from playing with iPad applications in childcare centers, particularly if the center is their only opportunity to gain familiarity with small screen interactive applications. The child care provider may function as a mechanism of increased social equity as long argued by the proponents of early intervention programs for young children at risk (Lipscomb et al. 2013). Since all children in industrialized nations attend school at a relatively young age, 4–5 years, the school has the capacity to reduce digital disadvantage.

Addressing Digital Disadvantage: The Role of the School

According to Spatariu et al. (2012), "each generation of children come to early childhood programs with increasingly different experiences and exposure to technology" (p. 24). Arguing the importance of ICT in early childhood education, a recent report by UNESCO claimed that "research done on the learning of North American and European children has discovered that as much as 80 percent of knowledge they gain by the age of 11 is learned from the non-print media outside the classroom" (Kalaš 2010, p. 7), although methodological details were not provided. In addition to the critical role of technology in informal knowledge acquisition, young children are highly motivated to interact with digital devices. For example, Course and Chen (2010) reported that preschool children, 3–6 years of age, preferred drawing on tablet computers rather than using paper and pencil. In many studies of preschool children, learning with computers was associated with better achievement in literacy, mathematics, and science compared to traditional learning activities (Vernadakis et al. 2005). Unfortunately, there is often considerable disparity between the technological skills of early childhood educators and the digital learning needs of their young students (Lindahl and Folkesson 2012). Fortunately, curriculum standards in advanced nations mandate digital competencies during the early school years. For example, 5-year-old children in Australia are expected to "construct texts using software including word processing programs" and "understand concepts about print and screen, including how books, film and simple digital texts work, and know some features of print, for example directionality" (Australian Curriculum, Assessment and Reporting Authority 2013, para. 1). Thus, school-based use of digital technology during the early years facilitates mastery of curriculum concepts as well as increases culturally-valued digital literacy.

Addressing digital disadvantage in the early childhood classroom requires technologically-competent early childhood educators who have access to required software and digital devices. Increasingly, early childhood teacher preparation programs include courses directed toward interpreting curriculum in the digital context

(Thomas and Spencer Cooter 2012). Teachers of young children must integrate digital experiences into the school day in a variety of ways, including: ICT and the outdoor environment, using computers and software, ICT and creativity, using a smart board, and using digital cameras and scanners (E2BN 2008). Digital experiences are easily integrated into a play-based curriculum that supports key areas of learning such as collaboration, communication, exploration, and socio-dramatic play (Siraj-Blatchford and Siraj-Blatchford 2006). In personalizing learning experiences, children who are digitally literate may benefit from non-digital experiences including physical building blocks and traditional early childhood musical instruments. Children who are digitally illiterate may require extensive exposure to, for example, iPad applications and internet websites, although a range of sensory, motoric, social, and cognitive experiences during the school day are ideal for all young children. According to Zevenbergen and Logan (2008), computer access in early childhood settings should be improved in order to reduce digital divides among early childhood learners. Early childhood teachers may provide parents with information on age-appropriate use of digital devices and emphasize the importance of presenting young children with a range of experiences and opportunities. Out-of-school parental reinforcement of young children's school-based skills and concepts should include, as may be appropriate, parent-child co-access of teacher-recommended websites and co-use of recommended software and applications. In some cases, parents may be able to borrow digital devices from schools; but among the most digitally and socially disadvantaged, the provision of devices becomes a community responsibility.

Addressing Digital Disadvantage: The Role of the Community

Ideally, young children should enjoy a variety of environmental opportunities that include home- and school-based experiences with small screen digital devices that facilitate concept formation, social interaction, and emotional security, among other positive developmental outcomes. When home access and age-appropriate use are lacking, the early childhood classroom provides digital learning opportunities and the early childhood teacher provides digital guidance and direction to parents of young children. There are many situations, however, when family circumstances require more than the early childhood classroom teacher can reasonably provide. In such situations, a community-based effort is required which may include, for example, programs that provide access to digital devices and internet connectivity.

In technologically-advanced societies, the provision of internet access is increasingly viewed as central to the mission of the public library (Kinney 2010). In a 2002 survey of Australian public libraries, approximately one-third reported providing internet training specially targeting children. Forty-seven percent provided websites for children that linked to recommended material, 16% provided separate terminals for children, 72% required parental consent for children to use the internet, and 26% required a parent to be with children using the internet (Australian Library and

Information Association 2010). In 2012, a public library in Wisconsin was among the first to lend iPads in large numbers. "Demand for the iPads was high for quite some time after their introduction, and at one point the number of holds remained around 400" (Price 2012, para. 4). A Connecticut public library recently introduced an eTot program for 2 and 3-year-old children and their caregivers. The head children's librarian explains, "As I hand out the iPads, we recite an iPad poem based on the nursery rhyme 'One, Two Buckle My Shoe.' As we read the book app together, I alert everyone to any interactivity on the screen, to make sure no one misses these features. When the reading is finished, we open another app—generally an educational or entertaining title, and I offer the adults a few pointers on using it. After that everyone is free to explore whatever they like" (Wall 2013, para. 7). While such initiatives are currently enjoyed by socially-advantaged children, specifically targeting the digitally disadvantaged should constitute a priority and may require library out-reach programs.

In organizing the impact of environmental experiences on the developing child, the Ecological Techno-Subsystem (Johnson and Puplampu 2008) is surrounded by nested systems, including the macrosystem, which includes social ideologies and cultural values. It could be argued that the provision of connectivity is as much a public responsibility as is the provision of a safe supply of drinking water. Internet connectivity and devices such as iPads with children's ebooks (Chiong et al. 2012) and educational applications can hardly be considered frivolous in the current highly-digital and seemingly democratic context. Community-based programs that specifically target young children at digital disadvantage might include home visits from volunteers who update software applications and provide role models of digital literacy for both young children and their parents.

Summary and Conclusion

There is a reciprocal and spiraling interaction between child development and elements of the child's environment. The Ecological Techno-Microsystem (Johnson 2010b) emphasizes the importance of direct digital experience in children's development because such experience is normative and because such experience, under some conditions, facilitates positive social (e.g., communication), emotional (e.g. security), and cognitive (e.g., problem solving) developmental outcomes. From a developmental perspective, young children at digital risk are those whose digital experiences are insufficient or inadequate relative to other children of the approximate developmental status (i.e., peers). Once children start school, reducing digital disadvantage becomes possible, but many schools lack the resources necessary to ensure digitally-enriching experiences for all children, particularly those who do not enjoy such experiences at home. The provision of class sets of emerging digital devices and the digital up-skilling of early childhood teachers would function to provide all children with digital advantages.

Johnson (2010c) examined the relationships between family socioeconomic status and children's internet use and cognitive development. Reportedly, family socioeconomic status accounted for 5–7 % of differences in child cognitive-developmental test scores. In contrast, indices of home internet use during childhood accounted for up to 29 % of differences in child cognitive-developmental test scores. Structures of social equalization (e.g., public education, quality child care, preschool interventions, and prenatal programs) have not proven entirely effective in erasing differences in the quality of children's environments, particularly home and community environments. While family access to food and housing may have improved in recent decades, access to technological innovation is restricted to families with considerable disposable income. As society moves forward, technological progress is not uniformly experienced. But if any group must not be left behind, it is the youngest, the most vulnerable and, without question, the most important to the future of that society.

References

Anderson, C. A., Gentile, D. A., & Buckley, K. E. (2007). *Violent video game effects on children and adolescents*. New York, NY: Oxford University Press.

Ansari, A., & Winsler, A. (2013). Stability and sequence of center-based and family childcare: Links with low-income children's school readiness. *Children and Youth Services Review, 35*(2), 358–366.

Australian Bureau of Statistics. (2009). Children's participation in cultural and leisure activities. Catalogue Number 4901.0. http://www.abs.gov.au/ausstats/abs@.nsf/mf/4901.0. Accessed 15 July 2014.

Australian Communications and Media Authority. (2009). *Use of electronic media and communications: Early childhood to teenage years: Findings from growing up in Australia: The longitudinal study of Australian children (3 to 4 and 7 to 8-year-olds) and media and communications in Australian families (8 to 17-year-olds), 2007*. Canberra: NSW.

Australian Curriculum, Assessment and Reporting Authority. (2013). Foundation year: English year level description. http://www.australiancurriculum.edu.au/FoundationYear. Accessed 15 July 2014.

Australian Library and Information Association. (2010). Survey of internet access in public libraries, 2002 report. http://www.alia.org.au/members-only/advocacy/internet.access/report.html#5.7. Accessed 15 July 2014.

Baxter, J., & Hayes, A. (2007). How four-year-olds spend their days: Insights into the caring context of young children. *Family Matters, 76*, 34–43.

Bekkhus, M., Rutter, M., Maughan, B., & Borge, A. (2011). The effects of group daycare in the context of paid maternal leave and high-quality provision. *European Journal of Developmental Psychology, 8*(6), 681–696.

Blanchard, J., & Moore, T. (2010). *The digital world of young children: Impact on emergent literacy*. Arizona State University. College of Teacher Education and Leadership. Pearson Foundation. http://www.pearsonfoundation.org/literacy/research/emergent-literacy.html. Accessed 15 July 2014.

Boice, J. D., & Tarone, R. E. (2011). Cell phones, cancer, and children. *Journal of the National Cancer Institute, 103*(16), 1211–1213. doi:10.1093/jnci/djr285.

Bond, E. (2010). Managing mobile relationships: Children's perceptions of the impact of the mobile phone on relationships in their everyday lives. *Childhood, 17*, 514–529.

Broadband Commission for Digital Development. (2012). The state of broadband 2012: Achieving digital inclusion for all. International Telecommunication Union and the United Nations Educational, Scientific and Cultural Organization. http://www.ericsson.com/res/docs/2012/the-state-of-broadband-2012.pdf. Accessed 15 July 2014.

Bronfenbrenner, U. (1977). Toward an experimental ecology of human development. *American Psychologist, 32,* 513–531.

Bronfenbrenner, U. (1979). *The ecology of human development: Experiments by nature and design.* Cambridge, MA: Harvard University Press.

Bronfenbrenner, U. (2005). *Making human beings human: Bioecological perspectives of human development.* Thousand Oaks, CA: Sage.

Brown, B., & Marin, P. (2009). Adolescents and electronic media: Growing up plugged in. *Child Trends, 29,* 1–11.

Cameron, C. A., & Hutchison, J. (2009). Telephone-mediated communication effects on young children's oral and written narrative. *First Language, 29*(4), 343–367.

Cavanaugh, C., Gillan, K., Kromrey, J., Hess, M., & Blomeyer, R. (2004). *The effects of distance education on K–12 student outcomes: A meta-analysis.* Naperville, IL: Learning Point Associates.

Chiong, C., Ree, J., Takeuchi, L., & Erickson, I. (2012). Comparing parent-child co-reading on print, basic, and enhanced e-book platforms. The Joan Ganz Cooney Center. http://www.joanganzcooneycenter.org/wp-content/uploads/2012/07/jgcc_ebooks_quickreport.pdf. Accessed 15 July 2014.

Cho, C. H., & Cheon, H. J. (2005). Children's exposure to negative Internet content: Effects of family context. *Journal of Broadcasting and Electronic Media, 49,* 488–509.

Cole, M. J., & Hilliard, V. R. (2006). The effect of web-based reading curriculum on children's reading performance and motivation. *Journal of Educational Computing Research, 34,* 353–380.

Computer Gym. (2013). Term 1: Me, my family & friends. http://www.computergym.com.au/home.asp. Accessed 15 July 2014.

Couse, L. J., & Chen, D. W. (2010). A tablet computer for young children? Exploring its viability for early childhood education. *Journal of Research on Technology in Education, 43*(1), 75–98.

DeBell, M., & Chapman, C. (2006). Computer and internet use by students in 2003. National Center for Educational Statistics. U.S. Department of Education, Washington, DC. http://nces.ed.gov/pubs2006/2006065.pdf. Accessed 15 July 2014.

Divan, H. A., Kheifets, L., Obel, C., & Olsen, J. (2012). Cell phone use and behavioural problems in young children. *Journal of Epidemiology and Community Health, 66*(6), 524–529.

Dixon, D. (2011, October 11). School matters: The future of apps in the classroom. The ASHA Leader. http://www.asha.org/Publications/leader/2011/111011/School-Matters–The-Future-of-Apps-in-the-Classroom.htm. Accessed 15 July 2014.

Dutton, W. H., & Helsper, E. (2007). *The 2007 OxIS survey: The Internet in Britain.* Oxford Internet Institute. University of Oxford.

E2BN. (2008). ICT in the early years. East of England Broadband Network. http://ictearlyyears.e2bn.org/index.php. Accessed 15 July 2014.

Erickson, J., & Johnson, G. M. (2011). Internet use and psychological wellness during late adulthood. *Canadian Journal of Aging, 30*(2), 197–209.

Eynon, R. (2009). Mapping the digital divide in Britain: Implications for learning and education. *Learning, Media and Technology, 34*(4), 277–290.

Fiorini, M. (2010). The effect of home computer use on children's cognitive and non-cognitive skills. *Economic of Education Review, 29,* 55–72.

Forry, N., Simkin, S., Wessel, J., & Rodrigues, K. (2012). Providing high quality care in low-income areas in Maryland: Definitions, resources, and challenges from parents and child care providers' perspectives. Regional Economic Studies Institute. Townsend University. http://www.childtrends.org/files/child_trends-2012_11_27_RB_providing.pdf. Accessed 15 July 2014.

Funk, J. B., Chan, M., Brouwer, J., & Curtiss, K. (2006). A biopsychosocial analysis of the video-game-playing experience of children and adults in the United States. *Studies in Media and Information Literacy Education, 6*(3), 79. http://www.utpjournals.com/simile/issue23/Funk1.html. Accessed 15 July 2014.

Gentzkow, M., & Shapiro, J. M. (2008). Preschool television viewing and adolescent test scores: Historical evidence from the Coleman study. *The Quarterly Journal of Economics, 123*(1), 279–323.

Gibbons, A. N. (2012). The impact of technology on early childhood education: Where the child things are? Adults, children, digital monsters and the space between. In S. Blake, D. Winsor, & L. Allen (Eds.), *Technology and young children: Bridging the communication-generation gap* (pp. 1–23). Hershey, PA: Information Science Reference.

Gillen, J., Accorti-Gamannossi, B., & Cameron, C. A. (2005). 'Pronto, chi parla?' ('Hello, who is it?') Telephone as artefacts and communication media in children's discourses. In J. Marsh (Ed.), *Popular culture, media and digital literacies in early childhood* (pp. 242–272). London: Routledge Falmer.

Gimenez-Nadal, J. I., & Molina, J. A. (2013). Parents' education as a determinant of educational childcare time. *Journal of Population Economics, 26*(2), 719–749.

Graham, M. (2011). Time machines and virtual portals: The spatialities of the digital divide. *Progress in Development Studies, 11*(3), 211–227.

Hargittai, E. (2008). The digital reproduction of inequality. In D. Grusky (Ed.), *Social stratification* (pp. 936–944). Boulder, CO: Westview Press.

Hofferth, S. L. (2010). Home media and children's achievement and behavior. *Child Development, 81*(5), 1598–1619.

Hong, J-C., Tsai, C-M., Ho, Y-J., Hwang, M-Y., & Wu, C-J. (2013). A comparative study of the learning effectiveness of a blended and embodied interactive video game for kindergarten students. *Interactive Learning Environments, 21*(1), 39–53.

Jackson, L. A., Samona, R., Moomaw, J., Ramsay, L., Murray, C., Smith, A., & Murray, L. (2007). What children do on the internet: Domains visited and their relationship to socio-demographic characteristics and academic performance. *CyberPsychology and Behavior, 10*, 182–190.

Johnson, G. M. (2006). Internet use and cognitive development: A theoretical framework. *E-Learning and Digital Media, 3*(4), 565–573.

Johnson, G. M. (2007). College student internet use: Convenience and amusement. *Canadian Journal of Learning & Technology, 33*, 141–157.

Johnson, G. M. (2008). Cognitive processing differences between frequent and infrequent Internet users. *Computers in Human Behavior, 24*, 2094–2106.

Johnson, G. M. (2009). At-home Internet behavior and cognitive development during middle childhood. *Technology, Instruction, Cognition, and Learning, 6*, 213–229.

Johnson, G. M. (2010a). Young children's internet use at home and school: Patterns and profiles. *Journal of Early Childhood Research, 8*, 282–293.

Johnson, G. M. (2010b). Internet use and child development: The techno-microsystem. *Australian Journal of Educational and Developmental Psychology, 10*, 32–43.

Johnson, G. M. (2010c). Internet use and child development: Validation of the ecological techno-subsystem. *Educational Technology & Society, 13*, 176–185.

Johnson, G. M. (2012a). Learning, development, and home digital media use among 6 to 8 year old children. *Problems of Psychology in the 21st Century, 1*, 6–16.

Johnson, G. M. (2012b). Comprehension of Standard English text and digital textism during childhood. *Internet Journal of Culture, Language and Society, 35*(1), 1–6.

Johnson, G. M. (2013). Using tablet computers with elementary school students with special needs: The practices and perceptions of special education teachers and teacher assistants. *Canadian Journal of Learning and Technology, 39*(4), 1–12.

Johnson, G. M., & Puplampu, P. (2008). Internet use during childhood and the ecological techno-subsystem. *Canadian Journal of Learning and Technology, 34*, 19–28.

Kalaš, I. (2010). Recognizing the potential of ICT in early childhood education: Analytical survey. UNESCO Institute for Information Technologies in Education. Moscow. http://iite.unesco.org/pics/publications/en/files/3214673.pdf. Accessed 15 July 2014.

Keil, F. C. (2000). The origins of developmental psychology. *Journal of Cognition and Development, 1*(3), 347–357.

Kent, S. P., & Johnson, G. M. (2012). Differences in the linguistic features of text messages send with an alphanumeric multi-press keypad mobile phone versus a full keypad touchscreen smartphone. *Scottish Journal of Arts, Social Sciences and Scientific Studies, 6*(2), 50–67.

Kim, P., Miranda, T., & Olaciregui, C. (2008). Pocket School: Exploring mobile technology as a sustainable literacy education option for underserved indigenous children in Latin America. *International Journal of Educational Development, 28,* 435–445.

Kinney, B. (2010). The internet, public libraries, and the digital divide. *Public Library Quarterly, 29*(2), 104–161.

Krebeck, A. (2010). Closing the digital divide: Building a public computing center. *Computers in Libraries, 30*(8), 12–15.

Kumtepe, A. T. (2006). The effects of computers on kindergarten children's social skills. *Turkish Online Journal of Educational Technology, 5,* 52–57.

Lee, S. J., & Chae, Y. G. (2007). Children's Internet use in a family context: Influence on family relationships and parental mediation. *CyberPsychology and Behavior, 10,* 640–644.

Lee, S. J., Bartolic, S., & Vandewater, E. A. (2009). Predicting children's media use in the USA: Differences in cross-sectional and longitudinal analysis. *The British Journal of Developmental Psychology, 27*(1), 123–143.

Lindahl, M., G., & Folkesson, A. M. (2012). Can we let computers change practice? Educators' interpretations of preschool tradition. *Computers in Human Behavior, 28*(5), 1728–1737.

Lipscomb, S. T., Pratt, M. E., Schmitt, S. A., Pears, K. C., & Kim, H. K. (2013). School readiness in children living in non-parental care: Impacts of Head Start. *Journal of Applied Developmental Psychology, 34*(1), 28–37.

Livingstone, S. (2009). Half a century of television in the lives of our children. *The Annuals of the American Academy of Political and Social Science, 625,* 151–163.

Livingstone, S., & Helpsper, E. (2007). Gradations in digital inclusion: Children, young people and the digital divide. *New Media & Society, 9,* 671–696.

McCarrick, K., & Li, X. (2007). Buried treasure: The impact of computer use on young children's social, cognitive, language development and motivation. *AACE Journal, 15*(1), 73–95.

Mezei, G., Benyi, M., & Muller, A. (2007). Mobile phone ownership and use among school children in three Hungarian cities. *Bioelectromagnetics, 28,* 309–315.

Mitrofan, O., Paul, M., & Spencer, N. (2009). Is aggression in children with behavioural and emotional difficulties associated with television viewing and video game playing? A systematic review. *Child: Care, Health and Development, 35,* 5–15.

Morrison, T. (2008). Computers in child care. *Putting Children First, 27,* 14–16.

Moses, A. M. (2008). Impacts of television viewing on young children's literacy development in the USA: A review of the literature. *Journal of Early Childhood Literacy, 8,* 67–102.

Ofcom. (2009). UK children's media literacy. London: UK. http://stakeholders.ofcom.org.uk/market-data-research/media-literacy/medlitpub/medlitpubrss/uk_childrens_ml/. Accessed 15 July 2014.

Parent'sChoiceAwards.(2009).Parents'choiceawardswinners:Toys.http://www.parents-chioce.org. Accessed 15 July 2014.

Piaget, J., & Inhelder, B. (1973). *Memory and intelligence.* New York, NY: Basic Books.

Price, G. (2012). Eau Claire, Wisconsin public library says iPad lending project a major success. *InfoDocket Library Journal.* http://www.infodocket.com/2012/11/14/eau-claire-wisconsin-public-library-says-ipad-lending-project-a-major-success. Accessed 15 July 2014.

Raugust, K. (2012). Technology at the forefront of upbeat toy fair. *Publishers Weekly, 259*(8), 6–7.

Roberts, D., & Foehr, U. (2008). Trends in media use. *Future of Children, 18*(1), 11–37.

Rutherford, L., Bittman, M., & Biron, D. (2010). *Young children and the media: A discussion paper.* West Perth, WA: Australian Research Alliance for Children and Youth.

Saine, N. L., Lerkkanen, M. K., Ahonen, T., Tolvanen, A., & Lyytinen, H. (2010). Predicting word-level reading fluency outcomes in three contrastive groups: Remedial and computer-assisted remedial reading intervention, and mainstream instruction. *Learning and Individual Differences, 20,* 402–414.

Schmidt, M., & Anderson, D. (2007). The impact of television on cognitive development and educational achievement. In N. Pecora, J. Murry, & E. Wartella (Eds.), *Children and television: Fifty years of research* (pp. 65–84). Mahwah, NJ: Lawrence Erlbaum.

Schotland, M., & Littman, K. (2012). Using a computer game to teach young children about their brains. *Games for Health Journal, 1*(6), 442–448.

Siraj-Blatchford, I., & Siraj-Blatchford, J. (2006). *A guide to developing the ICT curriculum for early childhood education*. Staffordshire: UK Trentham.

Spatariu, A., Peach, A., & Bell, S. (2012). Enculturation of young children and technology. In S. Blake, D. Winsor, and L. Allen (Eds.), *Technology and young children: Bridging the communication-generation gap* (pp. 24–48). Hershey, PA: Information Science Reference.

Sprenger, M. (2010). *Brain-based teaching in the digital age*. Alexandria, VA: ASCD.

Steinkuehler, C. (2010). Video games and digital literacies. *Journal of Adolescent and Adult Literacy, 54*, 61–63.

Swing, E. L., Gentile, D. A., Anderson, C. A., & Walsh, D. A. (2010). Television and video game exposure and the development of attention problems. *Pediatrics, 126*, 214–221.

Tandon, P. S., Zhou, C., Lozano, P., & Christakis, D. A. (2011). Preschoolers' total daily screen time at home and by type of child care. *The Journal of Pediatrics, 158*(2), 297–300.

Thomas, K., & Spencer Cooter, K. (2012). Early childhood teachers: Closing the digital-divide. In S. Blake, D. Winsor, & L. Allen (Eds.), *Technology and young children: Bridging the communication-generation gap* (pp. 126–150). Hershey, PA: Information Science Reference.

Vandewater, E. A., Rideour, V. J., Wartella, E. A., Huang, X., Lee, J. H., & Shim, M-S. (2007). Digital childhood: Electronic media and technology use among infants, toddlers, and preschoolers. *Pediatrics, 119*(5), 1006–1015.

Vernadakis, N., Avgerinos, A., Tsitskari, E., & Zachopoulou, E. (2005). The use of computer assisted instruction in preschool education: Making teaching meaningful. *Early Childhood Education Journal, 33*(2), 99–104.

Vygotsky, L. S. (1978). *Mind in society: The development of higher mental process*. Cambridge, MA: Harvard University Press.

Wall, C. (2013). eTots: A public library iPad program for preschoolers. Southington Library & Museum, Connecticut. http://littleelit.com/2013/01/31/etots-a-public-library-ipad-program-for-preschoolers-from-slj/. Accessed 15 July 2014.

Wooldridge, M. B., & Shapka, J. (2012). Playing with technology: Mother–toddler interaction scores lower during play with electronic toys, *Journal of Applied Developmental Psychology, 33*(5), 211–218.

Yoon, K. (2003). Retraditionalizing the mobile young people's sociality and mobile phone use in Seoul, South Korea. *European Journal of Cultural Studies, 6*(3), 327–343.

Zevenbergen, R., & Logan, H. (2008). Computer use by preschool children: Rethinking practice as digital natives come to preschool. *Australian Journal of Early Childhood, 33*(1), 37–44.

Zimmerman, F. J., & Christakis, D. (2007). Associations between content types of early media exposure and subsequent attentional problems. *Pediatrics, 120*, 986–992.

Chapter 16
Cybersafety in Early Childhood: What Parents and Educators Need to Know

Kelly L. Heider

With proper guidance, young children can take advantage of the learning opportunities technology provides.

Abstract The internet provides wonderful learning opportunities that were not available to previous generations; however, there are also drawbacks to allowing young children to use internet-capable technology. This chapter identifies the specific dangers associated with online play and learning; reviews the international laws, government regulatory practices, and professional standards that protect children

---

K. L. Heider (✉)
Indiana University of Pennsylvania, Indiana, USA
e-mail: kheider@iup.edu

K. L. Heider, M. Renck Jalongo (eds.), *Young Children and Families in the Information Age,* Educating the Young Child 10, DOI 10.1007/978-94-017-9184-7_16,
© Springer Science+Business Media Dordrecht 2015

from online dangers; and provides tips and resources that parents and educators can employ/access to ensure that young children use technology safely and responsibly.

Keywords Early childhood · Online dangers · Cybersafety · Cyberethics · Cybersecurity · Information literacy

A False Sense of Security in a Virtual World

It's a rainy Sunday morning, and 6-year-old Ania asks her mother if she can use her laptop to play in Panfu—a virtual, online world where children create panda bear avatars to navigate an island world full of tree houses, games, and exciting adventures! In Panfu, there's even an underwater school where avatars go to learn math, German, and English.

Ania's mother is well-acquainted with Panfu. Before allowing Ania to create an account, she clicked on the site's link for parents and read every bit of information that was provided, including the benefits of avatar play as well as the risks. She felt comfortable allowing Ania to play on Panfu when she discovered that the site employs a child welfare officer, a data protection expert, and a team of moderators who are trained to monitor chats in several languages. So, she quickly agrees to allow her daughter to play online since playing outside is not an option.

After about 30 min of play, Ania meets up with another avatar who asks where she lives and where she goes to school. Ania's mother had reviewed the Panfu rules (which include never revealing personal information) with Ania before allowing her to create an account but, in the excitement of play, Ania forgets these rules and gives her new friend both her address and the name of her school. Ania's mother, who is busy catching up on laundry, has no idea that her daughter may now be in danger. Although Panfu, like many other virtual, online worlds for children, has security measures in place, these measures depend, in large part, on young children remembering to follow the rules. Unfortunately, children make mistakes and sometimes forget the rules.

The first chapter of this book began with a discussion of virtual worlds and their benefit to children's cognitive development. By viewing children's online play through Bronfenbrenner's (1979) ecological systems theory and Vygotsky's (1978) sociocultural theory, Jones and Park present a very strong case for the integration of virtual worlds, virtual field trips, and tele-collaborative projects into early childhood education. In fact, many of the authors in this book present research and theories that support the use of information and communication technology (ICT) in the education of young children. However, very little has been mentioned about the dangers associated with young children using these technologies. This chapter will: (1) identify the specific dangers associated with online play and learning; (2) review the international laws, government regulatory practices, and professional standards that protect children from online dangers; and (3) provide tips and resources that parents and educators can employ/access to ensure that young children use technology safely and responsibly.

Dangers Associated with Online Play and Learning

Grey (2011) warns parents and educators that "although ICT offers children wonderful opportunities for learning, it exposes them to risks and dangers unknown to previous generations" (p. 77). She describes four risks associated with children's ever-growing access to ICT:

1. inappropriate contact (e.g. stalking and grooming)
2. inappropriate content (e.g. violence and pornography)
3. commercialism (i.e. unwanted marketing and advertising aimed at young children)
4. negative culture (e.g. cyberbullying and infringement of copyright laws)

Inappropriate Contact

In the scenario provided at the beginning of this chapter, Ania's mother is lured into a false sense of security by the safety claims posted on a virtual world website. According to Panfu (Goodbeans 2014), a user who is caught violating the website's policies will have his/her account locked for up to 24 h. If violations persist, the user's membership may be terminated. It is likely that Panfu's moderators would have locked the account of the user who asked for the name of Ania's school and her address; however, at that point, the damage may have already been done and Ania could possibly become the victim of an online predator. Online predators often stalk their victims or use *grooming* to build trust, set up a meeting, manipulate, or seduce a child (North Carolina Department of Justice 2014). Ey and Cupit (2011) define *grooming* as "seducing children by feigned attention, affection, kindness and empathy" (p. 55). Sexual predators find grooming online much easier than "face-to-face" grooming because they can hide their true identities. By pretending to be another child, predators are able to gain trust and get information about a child's support system and daily routines. If a predator feels that a child is vulnerable, he/she may use flattery, gifts, threats, or intimidation to exert control (Parents Protect, 2014). In addition, "pedophiles routinely introduce pornography to set the stage for abuse. Children of all ages are curious about sex, and it is not difficult to hold their attention with this material" (Wooden 2014, para. 14). Many adults would be surprised to know how easy it is for a child to stumble upon pornography while surfing the Internet.

Inappropriate Content

Both legal adult pornography and illegal child pornography are just a click away on the Web. In fact, children don't have to be looking for sexually explicit material to find it. By simply clicking on the wrong link or misspelling a web address, children can find themselves looking at a website with inappropriate content (National Center for Missing and Exploited Children 2014). Besides sexually explicit material, children may also stumble upon sites that glorify risky or illegal behavior and violence.

> The American Academy of Pediatrics recognizes exposure to media violence...as a significant risk to the health of children and adolescents. Extensive research evidence indicates that media violence can contribute to aggressive behavior, desensitization to violence, nightmares, and fear of being harmed. (American Academy of Pediatrics 2001, p. 1222)

Dr. Eugene Beresin, the Director of Child and Adolescent Psychiatry Residency Training at Massachusetts General Hospital and McLean Hospital, claims that, "before age 4, children are unable to distinguish between fact and fantasy and may view violence as an ordinary occurrence" (2013, para. 3). Although there is more evidence on the effects violent television programming has on youth, studies are beginning to emerge on the incidence of violence on the Internet and the impact of violent video games. According to Dr. Beresin, "the fact that the child gets to act out the violence, rather than to be a passive observer, as when viewing television or movies, is especially concerning to experts" (2013, para. 4). Equally concerning to experts is the effects of commercialism on young children.

Commercialism

Unable to distinguish between commercials and regular programming on television, children under the age of four or five are susceptible to persuasion and misleading advertising (Kunkel 2001). Greenfield (2004) argues that it is even more difficult for young children to distinguish between regular Web content and commercials on the Web. It is not until age seven or eight that children begin to realize that the purpose of commercials is to sell products (Kunkel 2001).

Two broad categories of online advertising practices pose threats to children—invasion of privacy and deception. Invasion of privacy includes: (1) eliciting personal information from children through the use of prizes, games, and surveys; (2) monitoring children's online activities and compiling detailed personal profiles; and (3) designing personalized advertising aimed at individual children. Deception includes: (1) designing advertising environments to capture children's attention for extended periods of time; (2) seamlessly integrating advertising and content; and (3) creating product "spokes-characters" to develop interactive relationships with children (Montgomery and Pasnik 1996).

Greenfield (2004) contends that there is another developmental issue raised by the marketing of products to young children on the Internet—the socialization of materialism.

> Consumer socialization keeps the economy going, but, from the point of view of human values, is this what we want for our children's development: to measure identity and success in terms of possessions and, particularly, branded possessions? (Greenfield 2004, p. 753)

Furthermore, online advertising often leads to conflicts between parents and their children. If parents deny their children the material possessions they see in online advertisements, children may become upset or resentful. "This is not a positive developmental experience for the child; nor is it an ideal condition of socialization when a parent has to fight such an all-persuasive socializing environment as the Internet" (Greenfield 2004, p. 754). Like commercialism, negative online culture can also hinder the positive development of young children.

Negative Culture

Negative online culture can take many forms including cyberbullying and internet piracy. According to KidsHealth (2014), cyberbullying is "the use of technology to harass, threaten, embarrass, or target another person" (para. 4). Although most research on cyberbullying focuses on children from ages 9–18, cyberbullying can begin as soon as children start using the Internet (iKeepSafe 2014), and it can take many forms including: text messages, tweets, videos posted to YouTube, comments to photos posted on Instagram, or responses to status updates on Facebook. Young children who are cyberbullied may suffer from anxiety, depression, and other stress-related disorders (KidsHealth 2014). Unfortunately, it is often difficult to identify a cyberbully because, on the Internet, bullies can hide behind screen names and avatars (Rivers and Noret, 2009).

Less threatening to the health and welfare of children, but just as serious, is the negative online culture of internet piracy. Schwartz (2001) argues:

> As children have access to computers earlier and earlier in their educational careers, experts in piracy, hacking and other forms of Internet mischief say that any effort to tackle the illicit trade in digital goods—including video games, computer software, music and even movies—should be looking at a younger crowd. (p. C1)

According to Farber, children who illegally download music and videos and see nothing wrong with it become the internet pirates of the future (as cited in Schwartz 2001).

In the summer of 2012, major internet service providers in the U.S. began warning users to stop downloading illegally-copied material. Users are warned a few times before legal action is taken. Whether children are knowingly downloading pirated material, or clicking on a link just because they want to listen to a song or watch a movie, does not matter. Parents can be held accountable for their children's actions. Therefore, it's very important that young children be taught computer ethics, including positive internet culture, as soon as they begin using the Internet (Owens 2012).

International Laws, Government Regulatory Practices, and Professional Standards that Protect Children from Online Dangers

Protecting children from online dangers can be a daunting task for both parents and educators. Parents and teachers simply cannot monitor children's activity on the Internet 24/7. Darlington (2010) contends:

> In the context of homes, PCs—or, increasingly other Internet access devices like game consoles or mobile phones—are not always in the living room but often in a bedroom or study and, in any event, a parent cannot be expected to stand over the child at all times. In the context of schools, a teacher may have up to 30 children using computers at the same time and again cannot be monitoring the usage by every child on a continuous basis. Therefore, while parents and teachers must exercise responsibility, they should be assisted by other approaches including the taking down of sites with criminal content and the filtering of sites with offensive or inappropriate content. (para. 20)

In recent years, several international laws and government regulatory practices (see Table 16.1) have been developed to protect children from online dangers.

Table 16.1 International cybersafety laws/regulatory practices. (Source: Australian Institute of Family Studies 2014; Collins 2013; Dinning 2013; Information Commissioner's Office 2014; National Academy of Sciences 2003; Pusey and Sadera 2011; Sky News 2013)

Country	Law/regulation	Description
Australia	Australian Communications and Media Authority (ACMA)	Works with consumers and other stakeholders in the communications industry to achieve active self–regulation and co-regulation
		Acts to ensure compliance with license conditions, codes and standards, and the collection of both federal and state laws that apply to internet content
Canada	Nova Scotia Cyber Safety Act of 2013	Gives greater powers and responsibilities to principals and school boards through amendments to the Nova Scotia Education Act
		Parental responsibility for cyberbullying in some circumstances
		Creation of a cyber investigative unit
		Victims of cyberbullying may apply for protection order from the court
		New statutory tort of cyberbullying which permits individuals to sue for damages or obtain an injunction
New Zealand	Communications (New Media) Bill of 2012	A penalty of up to 3 years in jail for inciting someone to commit suicide through internet, texting, or any other means
		Using a communications device to cause harm (sending or posting any message that is "grossly offensive, indecent, obscene or menacing" or "knowingly false") is punishable with up to 3 months in jail or a $ 2,000.00 fine
United Kingdom	Data Protection Act of 1998	Requires every organization processing personal data to register with the ICO (Information Commissioner's Office)
	Prime Minister, David Cameron, Plans Crackdown on Internet Pornography in 2014	Possessing violent pornography depicting rape scenes will become a crime
		Restrictions to online streaming video
		Internet giants will face tough new laws if they fail to blacklist key search terms
		Internet service providers will introduce a "default on" filter that will oblige homeowners to "opt in" to receive sexually graphic material
		Warning pages that pop up if users try to access illegal content
		The Child Exploitation and Online Protection Centre will be given greater powers to trace pedophiles who search using blacklisted phrases
		Internet industry has already agreed to use a database to proactively scan, block, and remove unacceptable images

Table 16.1 (continued)

Country	Law/regulation	Description
United States	Communications Decency Act (CDA) of 1996	Congress's first attempt to regulate children's access to sexually explicit material on the Internet
		Illegal to put "indecent" content on the Internet where kids can find it
		Supreme Court found the CDA unconstitutional in 1997 in Reno v. ACLU for "broad suppression of speech addressed to adults" (The term "indecent" was found to be too vague.)
	Child Online Protection Act (COPA) of 1998	Required commercial websites to verify proof of age before giving users access to sexually explicit material
		Challenged by the ACLU and other civil liberties organizations
		In 1999, a permanent injunction was ordered against the enforcement of COPA
		In 2003, COPA was found to be unconstitutional
	Children's Internet Protection Act (CIPA) of 2000	Required schools and libraries receiving federal technology funds to install pornography-blocking software on their computers
		The American Library Association filed suit alleging that the library portion of CIPA was unconstitutional
		In 2002, the U.S. District Court for the Eastern District of Pennsylvania agreed
		In 2003, the U.S. government appealed the district court's decision, and the Supreme Court overturned the district court's ruling
	Broadband Data Improvement Act of 2008	Requires appropriate online behavior be taught in schools

In addition, the International Society for Technology in Education (ISTE) developed National Educational Technology Standards (NETS) in 2008 which require cyberethics, cybersafety, and cybersecurity be taught in schools. The NETS were originally written for students, teachers, and administrators; however, they have recently been expanded to include coaches and computer science educators. No longer known as the NETS, the ISTE Standards focus on best practices in the teaching and learning of technology skills. Several countries have adopted the ISTE Standards because they:

- improve higher-order thinking skills, such as problem solving, critical thinking, and creativity;
- prepare students for their future in a competitive global job market;
- assist educators in designing student-centered, project-based, and online learning environments;
- guide systematic change in schools to create digital places of learning;

- and inspire digital age professional models for working, collaborating, and decision making. (ISTE 2012, P. 4)

In the United States, the American Library Association has developed standards for K-12 education which address the safe and ethical use of information technology. The organization's first set of standards was developed in 1998. The *Nine Information Literacy Standards for Student Learning* focus on information literacy, independent learning, and social responsibility. Standard 8 states, "The student who contributes positively to the learning community and to society is information literate and practices ethical behavior in regard to information and information technology" (AASL and AECT 1998, p. 36). In 2007, the American Library Association developed another set of standards to encompass a broader definition of information literacy. "Information literacy has progressed from the simple definition of using reference resources to find information. Multiple literacies, including digital, visual, textual, and technological, have now joined information literacy as crucial skills for this century" (AASL 2007, p. 3). These new *Standards for the Twenty-first-Century Learner* encourage students to use skills, resources, and tools to inquire, think critically, gain knowledge, draw conclusions, make informed decisions, apply knowledge to new situations, create new knowledge, share knowledge, and pursue personal growth. Three of the standards specifically address cybersafety and cyberethics:

- Standard 1.3.5- Use information technology responsibly.
- Standard 3.1.6- Use information and technology ethically and responsibly.
- Standard 4.3.4- Practice safe and ethical behaviors in personal electronic communication and interaction. (AASL 2007, p. 4, 6, 7).

Cybersafety Tips and Resources for Parents, Educators, and Children

Although laws, regulations, and standards have been written to protect children from online dangers, parents and educators must be proactive in ensuring that children practice cybersafety in the home and at school—especially since many young children are unaware that there's anything dangerous about the Internet. Dodge et al. (2011) interviewed 37 kindergarten, first, and second graders and found that only 16 of the children mentioned any "bad things" about the Internet, and only 20 of the children could name specific "bad things" when prompted. The 17 children who could identify "bad things" about the Internet mentioned the following:

- It breaks down sometimes.
- people who try to get your information
- junk mail
- blue screen
- when the Internet gets a cold or virus (p. 94)

None of the children mentioned anything about Internet predators, inappropriate content, commercials, or bullying.

Another study of young children's understanding of the risks associated with Internet use found that "while many children demonstrated proficiency in recognizing some of the potential dangers of the Internet, they did not spontaneously recall them or always respond in ways that would maintain their safety" (Ey and Cupit 2011, p. 61). Almost half of the 57 5–8-year-old children who were interviewed felt that it was safe to meet with people they only knew from the Internet because:

- They "knew" the person from their online interactions with him/her.
- They assumed they were interacting with another child.
- They were responding to an attractive birthday party or play date invitation.
- They were willing to take a risk because the person seemed trustworthy.

According to Ey and Cupit (2011), these responses raise serious concerns because "children's natural disposition to trust and the ease with which their focus can be diverted from safety to fun are characteristics paedophiles prey on" (p. 62).

Equally troubling responses were given to the question, "Who has taught you what you know about the Internet?" Of the 47 children who gave individual responses, the majority of the children ($n=21$) claimed to be self-taught. Only 13 of the children said that their parents taught them what they know about the Internet, and even less ($n=3$) said they learned about the Internet from their teachers. Other responses included siblings under 18 ($n=5$), other relatives ($n=4$), and other adults not related to them ($n=1$).

Today's children are teaching themselves about the Internet because adults are not sufficiently conversant with new technologies and/or are not providing necessary guidance or supervision. During their interviews of 37 kindergarten, first, and second graders, Dodge et al. (2011) found that 75 % of their participants use the Internet by themselves. For children to be safe online and learn the appropriate purposes and functions of the Internet, parents and educators must "actively participate" when children are using technology (Grey 2011, p. 79). There are many ways adults can actively participate in children's use of cybertechnologies and cybersafety education.

Tips for Parents

The following tips, provided by the San Diego County District Attorney (2010), provide comprehensive guidance for parents who want to take a proactive approach to protecting their children online:

1. Place your computer in a common area of the house.
2. Educate yourself about computers and the Internet.
3. Spend time with your children online.
4. Make reasonable rules and set time limits. Enforce them!
5. Educate yourself and your child about the dangers of the Internet.

6. Do not allow your child to go to private chat rooms, especially when you are not present.
7. Reinforce the guiding rule, "Don't talk to strangers."
8. Put accounts in your name and know your child's passwords.
9. Never allow your children to arrange a face-to-face meeting with someone they met online without your permission.
10. Do not let your child give out any personal information of any kind on the Internet.
11. Do not let your child download or upload pictures without your permission.
12. Utilize your Internet service provider's parental controls and commercial blocking and filtering software tools.
13. Be sensitive to changes in your child's behaviors that may indicate he/she is being victimized.
14. Be alert to a teenager or adult who is paying an unusual amount of attention to your child or giving him/her gifts.
15. Be aware of other computers your children could be using.
16. Be aware of your child using another person's screen name.
17. Develop a "contract" with your child about their Internet use.
18. Review the histories or logs of your computer to see where your children have been. (para. 9)

Tips for Educators

Like parents, "teachers need a thorough understanding of the risks and dangers of internet use and a familiarity with the relevant tools and policies" (Grey 2011, p. 79). Rob Nickel, former 14-year veteran of the Ontario Provincial Police, spent 7 years working undercover to catch and prosecute online child predators. He offers the following tips to teachers for cybersafety in the classroom:

1. Familiarize yourself with the dangers associated with online play and learning before entering the classroom.
2. Familiarize yourself with the applications your students are using on the Internet.
3. Make sure you know what applications, filters, and child protection software is installed on your school's computers.
4. Dedicate one class to a discussion of classroom policies and procedures for Internet use. Make students aware of activities they are allowed to engage in as well as those they are not.
5. Avoid letting students search and wander on the Internet. They could end up entering areas that are unsafe and may see things they should not be viewing. Select a few sites of interest and stay focused.
6. Watch for students who turn monitors off quickly, minimize screens when you walk by, laugh at something on the screen, group around someone else's computer, or look embarrassed.
7. Reward students who are acting responsibly in the class when on the Internet. Make them positive role models for the rest of the class.

8. Display positive messages around the classroom to reinforce the importance of Internet safety.
9. Instead of banning everything that students enjoy (chat rooms and email, for example) investigate ways in which you can use these technologies to enhance the teaching and learning experience. (para. 1–8)

Tips for Children

An excellent cybersafety policy to display in the early childhood classroom is the Childnet **SMART** Rules. Developed by Childnet International (2006) for Kid Smart, an award-winning safety program website for schools, these rules are simple and easy for young children to remember:

*S*afe	Keep safe by being careful not to give out personal information—such as your name, email, phone number, home address, or school name—to people who you don't trust online.
*M*eeting	Meeting someone you have only been in touch with online can be dangerous. Only do so with your parents' or carers' permission and even then only when they can be present.
*A*ccepting	Accepting emails, IM messages, or opening files, pictures or texts from people you don't know or trust can lead to problems—they may contain viruses or nasty messages!
*R*eliable	Someone online may be lying about who they are, and information you find on the internet may not be reliable.
*T*ell	Tell your parent, carer or a trusted adult if someone or something makes you feel uncomfortable or worried (para. 1–5).

In addition to Kid Smart, there are many other web resources that provide valuable information and training on cybersafety. Several of the websites that are designed for children deliver cybersafety curricula through virtual worlds and games. These sites are examples of ways in which adults can use children's online interests to, as Nickel (2004) recommends, "enhance the teaching and learning experience" (para. 8). Table 16.2 outlines some of the best web resources for cybersafety/cyberethics education.

Summary

"Over the last 5–6 years, there has been a substantial increase in internet usage by children under 9 years old" (Holloway et al. 2013, p. 4). Young children are using the Internet to watch videos, play games, search for information, do their homework, and socialize in virtual worlds. As evidenced by the chapters in this book, internet-capable technology has the potential to (1) support young children's visual and digital literacies, (2) promote creativity and arts-based learning in young children, (3) support culturally and linguistically diverse learners and young children with disabilities, (4) promote young children's problem solving and critical

Table 16.2 Web resources for cybersafety/cyberethics education

Stakeholder	Name/web address	Description
Parents	Cyber Smart: A Cybersafety Guide for Parents http://www.cybersmart.gov.au/parents.aspx	An overview of cyber issues, resources, and technology published by the Australian government.
	Family Online Safety Institute: Resources for Parents http://www.fosi.org/resources/internet-safety-resources-for-parents.html	Includes safety tips for parents, safety tips for kids, and a family online safety contract in English and Spanish.
	KidsHealth: Internet Safety for Parents http://kidshealth.org/parent/positive/family/net_safety.html	Information on internet safety laws, cyberbullying, protecting children from strangers online, computer-related repetitive stress injuries, and healthy habits for TV, video games, and the Internet.
	NetSmartz Workshop: Parents and Guardians http://www.netsmartz.org/Parents	Contains issues on blogging; cell phones; children as victims; cyberbullying; email, IM, and chat rooms; file sharing; gaming; identity theft; inappropriate content; internet safety; predators; revealing too much; sexting; social networking; and webcams. Also includes videos and presentations. Published by the National Center for Missing and Exploited Children.
	A Parent's Guide to Internet Safety http://www.fbi.gov/stats-services/publications/parent-guide	Includes warning signs of online risk, steps to take to report an online sexual predator, and actions parents can take to minimize online risk. Published by the U.S. Dept. of Justice's Federal Bureau of Investigation.
	Stay Safe Online: Parent Resources http://www.staysafeonline.org/data-privacy-day/parent-resources/	Provides information on child identity theft, online privacy, sexting, sextortion, social networking, and tracking kids online. Also provides links to guides and videos.
	Ten Simple Steps to Internet Safety http://www.commonsensemedia.org/blog/10-simple-steps-to-internet-safety	Instructs parents on how to (1) find the good stuff (and avoid the not-so-good); (2) explain how to recognize ads; (3) teach responsible online behavior; and (4) encourage digital citizenship.
Educators	Brainpop Educators http://www.brainpop.com/educators/community/bp-jr-topic/internet-safety/	Provides ideas for internet safety lessons, a downloadable internet safety poster, and a game for teaching internet safety skills.
	Common Sense on E-rate and CIPA: Toolkit for Teachers http://www.commonsensemedia.org/educators/erate-teachers	Includes a video tutorial, lesson plans for grades K-2, and a teacher verification document.
	Internet Safety for Schools and Teachers https://www.nspcc.org.uk/Inform/resourcesforprofessionals/onlinesafety/internet-safety-schools_wda94003.html	Includes resources and publications for schools and teachers to promote internet safety with students. Topics covered include: policies and guidance for schools, practice resources for teachers, and peer mentoring. Published by the National Society for the Prevention of Cruelty to Children.

16 Cybersafety in Early Childhood: What Parents and Educators Need to Know

Table 16.2 (continued)

Stakeholder	Name/web address	Description
	Kids.gov: Online Safety for Teachers https://kids.usa.gov/grown-ups/online-safety/index.shtml	Contains links to helpful resources, lesson plans, activities, and worksheets. Published by the U.S. General Services Administration.
	NetSmartz Workshop: Educators http://www.netsmartz.org/educators	Contains links to online safety education kits, teaching materials, presentations, and promotional items. Published by the National Center for Missing and Exploited Children.
	Stay Safe Online: Teach Online Safety Grades K-2 http://www.staysafeonline.org/teach-online-safety/grades-k-2	Provides basic tips for keeping students engaged and key concepts for students to understand and apply to their online experience. Also includes lesson plans, teaching materials, and posters.
	UK Safer Internet Centre: Teachers and Professionals http://www.saferinternet.org.uk/advice-and-resources/teachers-and-professionals	Provides advice and resources for educators, e-safety policies, and e-safety training sessions.
Children	CBBC Stay Safe http://www.bbc.co.uk/cbbc/topics/stay-safe	Characters from the Children's British Broadcasting Corporation present information about internet safety through games, videos, and songs.
	Disney Surf Swell Island: Adventures in Internet Safety http://home.disney.com.au/activities/surfswellisland/	Children visit different locations on Surf Swell Island and answer questions about internet safety to win tiki jewels that reveal secret words that lead them to the Treasure Palace.
	Faux Paw the Techno Cat http://kids.ikeepsafe.org/	Children may download and play one of four different games starring Faux Paw, an adventurous six-toed, Web-surfing cat. Sometimes Faux Paw runs into trouble while being on her computer and while playing video games. She learns that it is important to learn how to use the Internet safely and follow the rules.
	KidscomJr http://www.kidscomjr.com/games/safety/safety.html	Iggey and Rasper offer tips and a game for internet safety and good manners.
	KidSMART http://www.kidsmart.org.uk/	Presents important information for kids about mobiles, file sharing, social networking, chat, digital footprints, music games, competitions, and safe surfing. Provides recommendations for great sites on animals, film, health, the world, and sports. There are also links to sites created by young people.
	NetSmartzKids UYN: The Internet Safety Game http://www.netsmartzkids.org/adventuregames/theinternetsafetygame	Help Nettie and Webster learn to UYN (Use Your NetSmartz) when they're on the Internet. Children may choose to play the easy or hard version.
	Webonauts Internet Academy http://pbskids.org/webonauts/	Empowers kids to make responsible and respectful decisions in their online interactions. Taking on the role of a Webonaut, kids explore a series of missions that teach key issues of web safety and digital citizenship.

thinking skills, and (5) support infant and toddler language development. However, there are also drawbacks to allowing young children to use internet-capable technology. The Internet exposes children to inappropriate contact, inappropriate content, commercialism, and negative culture. These threats to the safety and well-being of children have prompted many countries to develop laws and regulatory practices that govern minors' access to certain material on the Internet. In the United States, many of these laws have been overturned or challenged in the courts because they infringe upon the First Amendment right to free speech. Consequently, "as soon as young children begin to engage with cybertechnologies, they should also begin cybersafety education" (Grey 2011, p. 77). According to Grey (2011), early childhood centers and elementary schools should use a multi-layered approach to cybersafety and work with parents to ensure that young children are protected from the dangers of the Internet. Grey's multi-layered approach includes tools (such as child-friendly search engines, firewalls, and filters), rules (including policies, procedures, and responsibilities), and education (including dialogue with young children on the benefits and risks of internet-capable technologies).

> Through gentle conversations, children will gradually understand that the virtual world is not the real world, and that virtual friends may not be real friends, but they will do so in a way that empowers them to feel control over their use of technology, rather than afraid to engage with it. (Grey 2011, p. 80)

The Internet provides wonderful learning opportunities that were not available to previous generations; however, young children's use of internet-capable technologies "creates a tension between the child's right to access the opportunities it creates and the child's right to be protected from harm" (Grey 2011, p. 77). With proper education and guidance from parents and teachers using the tips and resources presented in this chapter, young children can take advantage of the opportunities that new technologies provide while avoiding the dangers.

References

American Academy of Pediatrics. (2001). Media violence. *Pediatrics, 108*(5), 1222–1226.
American Association of School Librarians. (2007). Standards for the 21st-century learner. http://www.ala.org/aasl/sites/ala.org.aasl/files/content/guidelinesandstandards/learningstandards/AASL_LearningStandards.pdf. Accessed 7 April 2014.
American Association of School Librarians and Association for Educational Communications and Technology. (1998). *Information power: Building partnerships for learning.* Chicago: American Library Association.
Australian Institute of Family Studies. (2014). *The ACMA story.* http://www.acma.gov.au/Home/theACMA/About/The%20ACMA%20story.
Beresin, E. V. (2013). The impact of media violence on children and adolescents: Opportunities for clinical interventions. *American Academy of Child and Adolescent Psychiatry.* https://www.aacap.org/AACAP/Medical_Students_and_Residents/Mentorship_Matters/DevelopMentor/The_Impact_of_Media_Violence_on_Children_and_Adolescents_Opportunities_for_Clinical_Interventions.aspx. Accessed 7 April 2014.
Bronfenbrenner, U. (1979). *The ecology of human behavior: Experiments by nature and design.* Cambridge, MA: Harvard University Press.

Childnet International. (2006). Smart rules. *Kid Smart*. http://old.kidsmart.org.uk/yp/smart/. Accessed 7 April 2014.

Collins, S. (4 April 2013). Government speeds cyber bullying laws. *The New Zealand Herald*. http://www.nzherald.co.nz/nz/news/article.cfm?c_id=1&objectid=10875273. Accessed 7 April 2014.

Darlington, R. (2010). *Should the internet be regulated?* http://www.rogerdarlington.me.uk/regulation.html. Accessed 7 April 2014.

Dinning, B. (2013). Canada: Nova Scotia's cyber-safety act. *Mondaq*. http://www.mondaq.com/canada/x/271842/.../Nova+Scotias+CyberSafety+Act. Accessed 7 April 2014.

Dodge, A. M., Husain, N., & Duke, N. K. (2011). K-2 children's use and understanding of the Internet. *Language Arts, 89*(2), 86–98.

Ey, L., & Cupit, C. G. (2011). Exploring young children's understanding of risks associated with Internet usage and their concepts of management strategies. *Journal of Early Childhood Research, 9*(1), 53–65.

Goodbeans. (2014). *Panfu*. http://www.panfu.com.

Greenfield, P. M. (2004). Developmental considerations for determining appropriate Internet use guidelines for children and adolescents. *Applied Developmental Psychology, 25*, 751–762.

Grey, A. (2011). Cybersafety in early childhood education. *Australasian Journal of Early Childhood, 36*(2), 77–81.

Holloway, D., Green, L., & Livingstone, S. (2013). *Zero to eight: Young children and their internet use*. http://eprints.lse.ac.uk/52630/1/Zero_to_eight.pdf. Accessed 7 April 2014.

iKeepSafe. (2014). *Cyberbullying: How young does it start?* http://www.ikeepsafe.org/be-a-pro/relationships/cyberbullying-how-young-does-it-start/. Accessed 7 April 2014.

Information Commissioner's Office. (2014). *Data protection*. http://ico.org.uk/for_organisations/data_protection. Accessed 7 April 2014.

International Society for Technology in Education. (2012). Standards. *International society for technology in education*. http://www.iste.org/STANDARDS. Accessed 7 April 2014.

KidsHealth. (2014). *Cyberbullying*. http://kidshealth.org/parent/positive/talk/cyberbullying.html.

Kunkel, D. (2001). Children and television advertising. In D. G. Singer & J. L. Singer (Eds.), *Handbook of children and the media* (pp. 375–393). Thousand Oaks, CA: Sage.

Montgomery, K., & Pasnik, S. (1996). *Web of deception: Threats to children from online marketing*. Washington, DC: Center for Media Education.

National Academy of Sciences. (2003). Internet laws. *NetSafekids: A resource for parents*. http://www.nap.edu/netsafekids/pp_li_il.html. Accessed 7 April 2014.

National Center for Missing and Exploited Children. (2014). Inappropriate content for children. *NetSmartz workshop*. http://www.netsmartz.org/InappropriateContent#. Accessed 7 April 2014.

Nickel, R. (2004). Teachers. *Cyber safety*. http://www.cyber-safety.com/teachers.html. Accessed 7 April 2014.

North Carolina Department of Justice. (2014). *The grooming process*. http://www.ncdoj.com/Top-Issues/Internet-Safety/Protect-Kids-on-the-Internet/Online-Predators/The-Grooming-Process.aspx. Accessed 7 April 2014.

Owens, L. (2012). What to tell your kids about online piracy. *Internet safety for kids and families*. http://internetsafety.trendmicro.com/what-to-tell-your-kids-about-online-piracy. Accessed 7 April 2014.

Parents Protect. (2014). What is grooming? *Internet safety*. http://www.parentsprotect.co.uk/online_grooming.htm. Accessed 7 April 2014.

Pusey, P., & Sadera, W. A. (2011). Cyberethics, cybersafety, and cybersecurity: Preservice teacher knowledge, preparedness, and the need for teacher education to make a difference. *Journal of Digital Learning in Teacher Education, 28*(2), 83–88.

Rivers, I., & Noret, N. (2009). Ih8u: Findings from a five-year study of text and e-mail bullying. *British Educational Research Journal, 36*(4), 643–671.

San Diego County District Attorney. (2010). *Protecting children online: Facts for parents*. http://www.sdcda.org/preventing/protecting-children-online/facts-for-parents.html. Accessed 7 April 2014.

Schwartz, J. (25 December 2001). Trying to keep young internet users from a life of piracy. *The New York Times,* C1.
Sky, News. (2013). Internet porn: David Cameron plans crackdown. *Politics.* http://news.sky.com/story/1118734/internet-porn-david-cameron-plans-crackdown. Accessed 7 April 2014.
Vygotsky, L. (1978). *Mind in society: The development of higher mental processes.* Cambridge, MA: Harvard University Press.
Wooden, K. (2014). The 17 lures predators may use to exploit children. *Office of Radio and Television.* http://www.ortv.org/Charter/17_lures_predators_may_use.htm. Accessed 7 April 2014.

CPSIA information can be obtained at www.ICGtesting.com
Printed in the USA
LVOW10*1019091214

417977LV00011B/44/P